¡Exprésate!

Nancy Humbach

Sylvia Madrigal Velasco

Ana Beatriz Chiquito

Stuart Smith

John McMinn

HOLT, RINEHART AND WINSTON

A Harcourt Education Company

Orlando • **Austin** • New York • San Diego • Toronto • London

Holt Teacher Advisory Panel

Erick Ekker
Bob Miller Middle School
Henderson, NV

Dulce Goldenberg
Miami Senior High School
Miami, FL

Beckie Gurnish
Ellet High School
Akron, OH

Bill Heller
Perry High School
Perry, NY

MilyBett Llanos
Westwood High School
Austin, TX

Rosanna Perez
Communications Arts High
  School
San Antonio, TX

Jo Schuler
Central Bucks High School East
Doylestown, PA

Leticia Schweigert
Science Academy
Mercedes, TX

Claudia Sloan
Lake Park High School
Roselle, IL

Judy Smock
Gilbert High School
Gilbert, AZ

Catriona Stavropoulos
West Springfield High School
Springfield, VA

Nina Wilson
Burnet Middle School
Austin, TX

Janet Wohlers
Weston Middle School
Weston, MA

COVER PHOTOGRAPHY CREDITS

FRONT COVER (from top left to bottom right): ©Royalty Free/CORBIS; John Langford/HRW; ©Frans Lanting/Minden Pictures; ARGENPHOTO S.A./Luis Rosendo Productions/Image Bank Argentina; ©Creatas.

BACK COVER: Don Couch/HRW.

Acknowledgments appear on page R60, which is an extension of the copyright page.

HOLT and ¡EXPRÉSATE! are trademarks licensed to Holt, Rinehart and Winston, registered in the United States of America and/or other jurisdictions.

Printed in the United States of America

ISBN 0-03-074046-0

1 2 3 4 5 6 7   048   07 06 05 04

Authors

Nancy Humbach

Nancy Humbach is Associate Professor and Coordinator of Languages Education at Miami University, Oxford, Ohio. She has authored or co-authored over a dozen textbooks in Spanish. A former Fulbright-Hayes Scholar, she has lived and studied in Colombia and Mexico and has traveled and conducted research throughout the Spanish-speaking world. She is a recipient of many honors, including the Florence Steiner Award for Leadership in the Foreign Language Profession and the Nelson Brooks Award for the Teaching of Culture.

Sylvia Madrigal Velasco

Sylvia Madrigal Velasco was born in San Benito, Texas. The youngest of four siblings, she grew up in the Rio Grande Valley, between two cultures and languages. Her lifelong fascination with Spanish has led her to travel in many Spanish-speaking countries. She graduated from Yale University in 1979 and has worked for over 20 years as a textbook editor and author at various publishing companies. She has written bilingual materials, video scripts, workbooks, CD-ROMs, and readers.

Ana Beatriz Chiquito

Professor Ana Beatriz Chiquito is a native of Colombia. She teaches Spanish linguistics and Latin American culture at the University of Bergen, Norway, and conducts research and develops applications for language learning at the Center for Educational Computing Initiatives at the Massachusetts Institute of Technology. She has taught Spanish for more than thirty years and has authored numerous textbooks, CD-ROMs, videos, and on-line materials for college and high school students of Spanish.

Stuart Smith

Stuart Smith began her teaching career at the University of Texas at Austin from where she received her degrees. She has been a professor of foreign languages at Austin Community College, Austin, Texas, for over 20 years and has been writing textbook and teaching materials for almost as long. She has given presentations on language teaching methodology at ACTFL, SWCOLT, and TCCTA.

John McMinn

John McMinn is Professor of Spanish and French at Austin Community College, where he has taught since 1986. After completing his M.A. in Romance Linguistics at the University of Texas at Austin, he also taught Spanish and French at the secondary level and was a Senior Editor of World Languages at Holt, Rinehart and Winston. He is co-author of both Spanish and French textbooks at the college level.

Contributing Writers

Jeff Cole
Tucson, AZ
Mr. Cole developed activities for **Taller del escritor.**

Jodee Costello
Gunnison, CO
Ms. Costello wrote activites for **Vocabulario, Integración,** and **Comunidad.**

Jabier Elorrieta
The University of Texas at Austin
Mr. Elorrieta wrote **Letra y sonido.**

Karin Fajardo
Englewood, CO
Ms. Fajardo wrote vocabulary activities and material for **También se puede decir.**

Catherine Gavin
New York City, NY
Ms. Gavin wrote material for **Geocultura** and **Cultura.**

Pablo Muirhead
Shorewood, WI
Mr. Muirhead wrote suggestions for the story sequence art.

Gloria Munguía
Austin, TX
Ms. Munguía wrote activities for **Integración.**

Marci Reed
Austin, TX
Ms. Reed contributed to the selection of and wrote material for **Literatura y variedades.**

Mayanne Wright
Austin, TX
Ms. Wright contributed to the selection of and wrote material for **Leamos.**

Reviewers

These educators reviewed one or more chapters of the Student Edition.

Elizabeth Baird
Independence High School
Independence, OH

Paula Camardella Twomey
Ithaca High School
Ithaca, NY

Johnnie Eng
Alamo Heights High School
San Antonio, TX

Patricia Gander
Berkeley High School
Moncks Corner, SC

Laura Grable
Riverhead Central School District
Riverhead, NY

Mani Hernandez
Presentation High School
San Jose, CA

Yoscelina Hernandez
Montwood High School
El Paso, TX

Jorge Muñoz
St. Stephen's Episcopal School
Austin, TX

Jessica Shrader
Charlotte High School
Punta Gorda, FL

Sharlene Soto
D.C. Everest Jr. and Sr. High Schools
Wausau, WI

Nancy Walker de Llanas
George C. Marshall High School
Falls Church, VA

Field Test Participants

We thank the teachers and students who participated in the field test of *¡Exprésate! Levels 1–6.*

Tim Burel
West Middle School
Rockford, IL

Liliana Camarena
Gueillen Middle School
El Paso, TX

Mariluz Julio
Clover Junior High School
Clover, SC

Patrice Kahn
Noel Grisham Middle School
Round Rock, TX

Rebekeh Lindsey
Campbell Middle School
Daytona Beach, FL

Estela Morel
Corlears Middle School 56
New York, NY

Linda Schell
Landmark Middle School
Jacksonville, FL

Sarah Taylor
Richland Middle School
Richmond, VA

Rebecca Taylor-Norton
Beechwood Middle School
Cleveland, OH

Amanda York
George Washington Carver Academy
Waco, TX

Contenido en breve

Capítulo puente

México

Geocultura

Video/DVD

En video

Geocultura **GeoVisión**

Vocabulario 1 y 2 **ExpresaVisión**

Gramática 1 y 2 **GramaVisión**

Cultura **VideoCultura**

Video Novela **¿Quién será?**

Variedades

Visit Holt Online
go.hrw.com
KEYWORD: EXP1B CH6
Online Edition

Argentina

Geocultura

En video

Geocultura	**GeoVisión**
Vocabulario 1 y 2	**ExpresaVisión**
Gramática 1 y 2	**GramaVisión**
Cultura	**VideoCultura**
Video Novela	**¿Quién será?**
	Variedades

Visit Holt Online

go.hrw.com
KEYWORD: EXP1B CH7

Online Edition

Florida

Capítulo 8 Vamos de compras 130

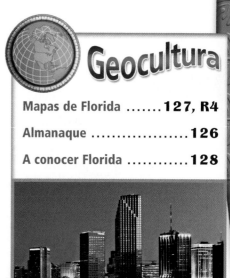

Video/DVD

En video

Geocultura	**GeoVisión**
Vocabulario 1 y 2	**ExpresaVisión**
Gramática 1 y 2	**GramaVisión**
Cultura	**VideoCultura**
Video Novela	**¿Quién será?**
	Variedades

Visit Holt Online

go.hrw.com
KEYWORD: EXP1B CH8
Online Edition

La República Dominicana

Capítulo 9 ¡Festejemos! 176

Geocultura

Video/DVD

En video

Geocultura **GeoVisión**

Vocabulario 1 y 2 **ExpresaVisión**

Gramática 1 y 2 **GramaVisión**

Cultura **VideoCultura**

Video Novela **¿Quién será?**

Variedades

Visit Holt Online

go.hrw.com
KEYWORD: EXP1B CH9
Online Edition

Perú

Capítulo 10 ¡A viajar! 222

Geocultura

Video/DVD

En video

Geocultura	GeoVisión
Vocabulario 1 y 2	ExpresaVisión
Gramática 1 y 2	GramaVisión
Cultura	VideoCultura
Video Novela	¿Quién será?
Variedades	

Visit Holt Online
go.hrw.com
KEYWORD: EXP1B CH10
Online Edition

xi

El español, ¿por qué?
Why Study Spanish?

Por lo mundial _Because it's worldwide_

Spanish is the fourth most commonly spoken language in the world. You can visit any one of 21 countries in the world that speak Spanish and feel at home. Even in the United States, knowing Spanish can open doors to you.

So whether you're in Europe, North, Central, or South America, or even Africa, as a Spanish speaker you won't have to rely on someone else to watch a television program or read a newspaper. You'll learn about things on your own. You'll truly be a citizen of the world.

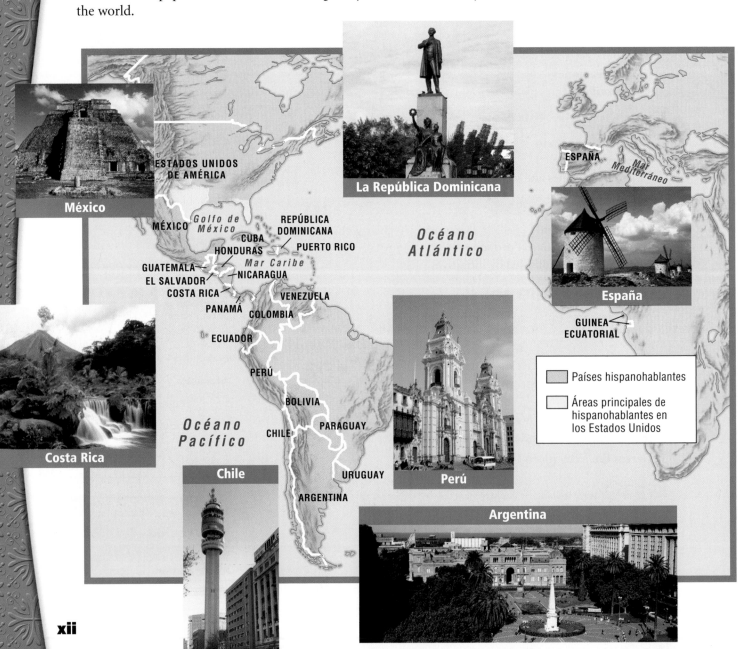

México

La República Dominicana

ESTADOS UNIDOS DE AMÉRICA

ESPAÑA

Mar Mediterráneo

España

Golfo de México

MÉXICO

REPÚBLICA DOMINICANA

CUBA

HONDURAS

PUERTO RICO

Mar Caribe

GUATEMALA

NICARAGUA

EL SALVADOR

COSTA RICA

PANAMÁ

VENEZUELA

COLOMBIA

ECUADOR

GUINEA ECUATORIAL

Océano Atlántico

PERÚ

BOLIVIA

Océano Pacífico

CHILE

PARAGUAY

Costa Rica

Chile

URUGUAY

ARGENTINA

Perú

Argentina

Países hispanohablantes

Áreas principales de hispanohablantes en los Estados Unidos

Por lo bello *Because it's beautiful*

You'll be amazed to discover how rich the Spanish-speaking world is in works of music, literature, science, religion, and art. The novels of Miguel de Cervantes or Isabel Allende, the paintings of Fernando Botero or Frida Kahlo, the poetry of Gabriela Mistral or Pablo Neruda: all these treasures and many more await you as you explore the Spanish-speaking world.

Ceramic tiles form this mural by Dominican artist Said Musa.

Traditional painted carts in Costa Rica are a part of El Festival de las Carretas.

The fountain of Cibeles, named after the goddess Cybele, is one of Madrid's best-known landmarks.

These young Costa Ricans are wearing traditional dance costumes.

Por lo práctico *Because it's practical*

You're living in the country with the fifth-largest Hispanic population in the world, more than 33 million people. And whether they're originally from Mexico, Puerto Rico, or Cuba—or from any other part of Latin America or Spain—almost nine out of ten are Spanish speakers.

Businesses, government agencies, educational institutions, and other employers will be looking for more bilingual employees every year. Give yourself an edge in the job market with Spanish!

Bilingual doctors, nurses, and others in the field of medicine provide care for Spanish-speaking patients.

Patricia Janiot is a popular anchor at the Spanish language news department of CNN En Español.

Miami is an international center and a multicultural hub for Latin American trade.

¡Porque puedes! _Because you can do it!_

Applying your learning skills to a new language will be challenging at first. But you have the tools you need to do the job. And you're lucky to be living at a time when there are almost no limits to your opportunities to practice Spanish. You can interact with Spanish speakers not just in your community but all over the world, via pen pal organizations, at the library, or through a multitude of resources and online networks.

Bicyclists stop at a spot overlooking the historic city of Toledo, Spain.

En fin, porque sí _Finally, just because..._

The best reason of all to study Spanish is because you want to! You know better than anyone what motivated you to enroll for Spanish class. It might be one of the reasons given here, such as getting a job, learning about world issues, or enjoying works of art. Or it might be something more personal, like wanting to communicate with Spanish-speaking friends and family, or travel. So pat yourself on the back and **¡Exprésate!**

En la clase de español
In Spanish Class

Here are some phrases you'll probably hear in your classroom, along with some responses.

Phrases:

Tengo una pregunta.
I have a question.

¿Cómo se dice…?
How do you say . . .?

¿Cómo se escribe…?
How do you spell . . .?

No entiendo. ¿Puede repetir?
I don't understand. Could you repeat that?

Más despacio, por favor.
More slowly, please.

¿Sabes qué significa (quiere decir)…?
Do you know what . . . means?

Gracias.
Thank you.

Perdón.
I'm sorry.

Responses:

¿Sí? Dime.
Yes? What is it?

Se dice…
You say . . .

Se escribe…
It's spelled . . .

Claro que sí.
Yes, of course.

No, no sé.
No, I don't know.

Sí, significa (quiere decir)…
Yes, it means . . .

De nada.
You're welcome.

Está bien.
It's okay.

Here are some things your teacher might ask you to do.

Levanten la mano.
Raise your hand.

Escuchen.
Listen.

¡Su atención, por favor!
Attention, please.

Silencio, por favor.
Silence, please.

Abran sus libros en la página…
Open your books to page . . .

Cierren los libros.
Close your books.

Estamos en la página…
We're on page . . .

Miren la pizarra (la transparencia).
Look at the board (transparency).

Saquen una hoja de papel.
Take out a sheet of paper.

Pasen la tarea (los papeles) al frente.
Pass the homework (the papers) to the front.

Levántense, por favor.
Stand up, please.

Siéntense, por favor.
Sit down, please.

Repitan después de mí.
Repeat after me.

Nombres comunes
Common Names

Here are some common names from Spanish-speaking countries.

Nombres de muchachas

Ana	Inés	Patricia
Bárbara	Irene	Pilar
Beatriz	Isabel	Rosalia
Cecilia	Josefina	Rosario
Cristina	Lourdes	Sonia
Dolores	María	Susana
Elena	Maribel	Tamara
Elisa	Marisol	Teresa
Emilia	Nuria	Vanesa
Fátima	Olga	Yolanda

Nombres de muchachos

Alfredo	Francisco	Óscar
Antonio	Gilberto	Pablo
Arturo	Héctor	Pedro
Bruno	Javier	Rafael
Carlos	Julio	Ramón
Daniel	Lorenzo	Roberto
Eduardo	Luis	Sergio
Enrique	Manuel	Tomás
Esteban	Marcos	Vicente
Fernando	Miguel	Víctor

Instrucciones
Directions

Throughout the book, many activities will have directions in Spanish. Here are some of the directions you'll see, along with their English translations.

Completa... con una palabra del cuadro.
Complete . . . with a word from the box.

Completa el párrafo con...
Complete the paragraph with . . .

Completa las oraciones con la forma correcta del verbo.
Complete the sentences with the correct form of the verb.

Con base en..., contesta cierto o falso. Corrige las oraciones falsas.
Based on . . ., respond with true or false. Correct the false sentences.

Con un(a) compañero(a), dramatiza...
With a classmate, act out . . .

Contesta las preguntas usando...
Answer the questions using . . .

Contesta (Completa) las siguientes preguntas (oraciones)...
Answer (Complete) the following questions (sentences) . . .

En parejas (grupos de tres), dramaticen...
In pairs (groups of three), act out . . .

Escoge el dibujo (la respuesta) que corresponde (mejor completa)...
Choose the drawing (the answer) that goes with (best completes) . . .

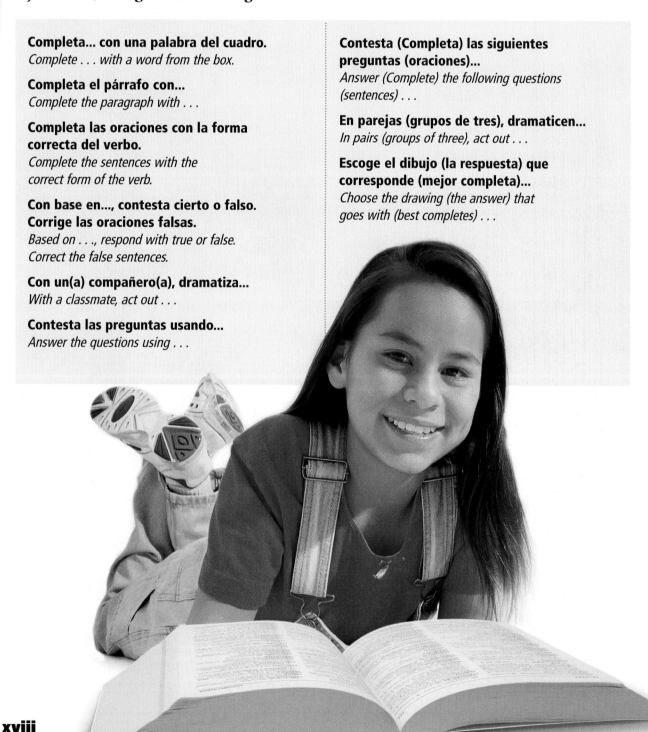

Escribe..., usando el vocabulario de la página...
Write . . ., using the vocabulary on page . . .

Escucha las conversaciones.
Decide qué conversación (diálogo)
corresponde a cada dibujo (foto).
*Listen to the conversations. Decide which conversation
(dialog) corresponds to each drawing (photo).*

Mira las fotos (los dibujos) y decide
(di, indica)...
*Look at the photos (drawings) and decide
(say, indicate) . . .*

Pon en orden...
Put . . . in order.

Pregúntale a tu compañero(a)...
Ask your partner . . .

Sigue el modelo.
Follow the model.

Túrnense para...
Take turns . . .

Usa el vocabulario de... para completar...
Use the vocabulary from . . . to complete . . .

Usa una palabra o expresión
de cada columna para escribir...
*Use one word or expression
from each column to write . . .*

Usa los dibujos para decir lo que pasa.
Use the drawings to say what is happening.

Sugerencias para aprender el español
Tips for learning Spanish

Listen

Listen carefully in class and ask questions if you don't understand. You won't be able to understand everything you hear at first, but don't feel frustrated. You are actually absorbing a lot even when you don't realize it.

Visualize

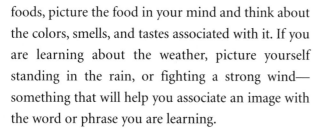

It may help you to visualize the words you are learning. Associate each new word, sentence, or phrase with a mental picture. For example, if you're learning words for foods, picture the food in your mind and think about the colors, smells, and tastes associated with it. If you are learning about the weather, picture yourself standing in the rain, or fighting a strong wind—something that will help you associate an image with the word or phrase you are learning.

Practice

Short, daily practice sessions are more effective than long, once-a-week sessions. Also, try to practice with a friend or a classmate. After all, language is about communication, and it takes two to communicate.

Speak

Practice speaking Spanish aloud every day. Don't be afraid to experiment. Your mistakes will help identify problems, and they will show you important differences in the way English and Spanish work as languages.

Explore

Increase your contact with Spanish outside class in every way you can. Maybe someone living near you speaks Spanish. It's easy to find Spanish-language programs on TV, on the radio, or at the video store, and many magazines and newspapers in Spanish are published or sold in the United States and are on the Internet. Don't be afraid to read, watch, or listen, even if you don't understand every word.

Connect

Making connections between what you learn in other subject areas and what you are learning in your Spanish class will increase your understanding of the new material, help you retain it longer, and enrich your learning experience.

Have fun!

Above all, remember to have fun! Learn as much as you can, because the more you know, the easier it will be for you to relax—and that will make your learning easier and more effective.

¡Buena suerte! (Good luck!)

Texas Essential Knowledge and Skills for Languages Other Than English

The activities in *¡Exprésate!* will help you develop the skills necessary to reach the novice progress checkpoint outlined in the Texas Essential Knowledge and Skills. Each activity in your book is referenced to the appropriate TEKS.

Levels I and II—Novice Progress Checkpoint

Knowledge and Skills

1. Communication The student communicates in a language other than English using the skills of listening, speaking, reading, and writing.

The student is expected to:

A. engage in oral and written exchanges of learned material to socialize and to provide and obtain information;

B. demonstrate understanding of simple, clearly spoken, and written language such as simple stories, high-frequency commands, and brief instructions when dealing with familiar topics; and

C. present information using familiar words, phrases, and sentences to listeners and readers.

2. Cultures The student gains knowledge and understanding of other cultures.

The student is expected to:

A. demonstrate an understanding of the practices (what people do) and how they are related to the perspectives (how people perceive things) of the cultures studied; and

B. demonstrate an understanding of the products (what people create) and how they are related to the perspectives (how people perceive things) of the cultures studied.

3. Connections The student uses the language to make connections with other subject areas and to acquire information.

The student is expected to:

A. use resources (that may include technology) in the language and cultures being studied to gain access to information; and

B. use the language to obtain, reinforce, or expand knowledge of other subject areas.

4. Comparisons The student develops insight into the nature of language and culture by comparing the student's own language and culture to another.

The student is expected to:

A. demonstrate an understanding of the nature of language through comparisons of the student's own language and the language studied;

B. demonstrate an understanding of the concept of culture through comparisons of the student's own culture and the cultures studied; and

C. demonstrate an understanding of the influence of one language and culture on another.

5. Communities The student participates in communities at home and around the world by using languages other than English.

The student is expected to:

A. use the language both within and beyond the school setting through activities such as participating in cultural events and using technology to communicate; and

B. show evidence of becoming a lifelong learner by using the language for personal enrichment and career development.

From Texas Education Agency   http://www.tea.state.tx.us/rules/tac/chapter114/ch114c.htmlg

Capítulo puente

Primera parte

Objetivos

In this section you will review how to

- ask and give names
- ask how someone feels and answer
- ask for and give personal information
- ask for and give descriptions
- talk about likes and dislikes
- use the verbs **ser, estar, gustar,** and **tener**

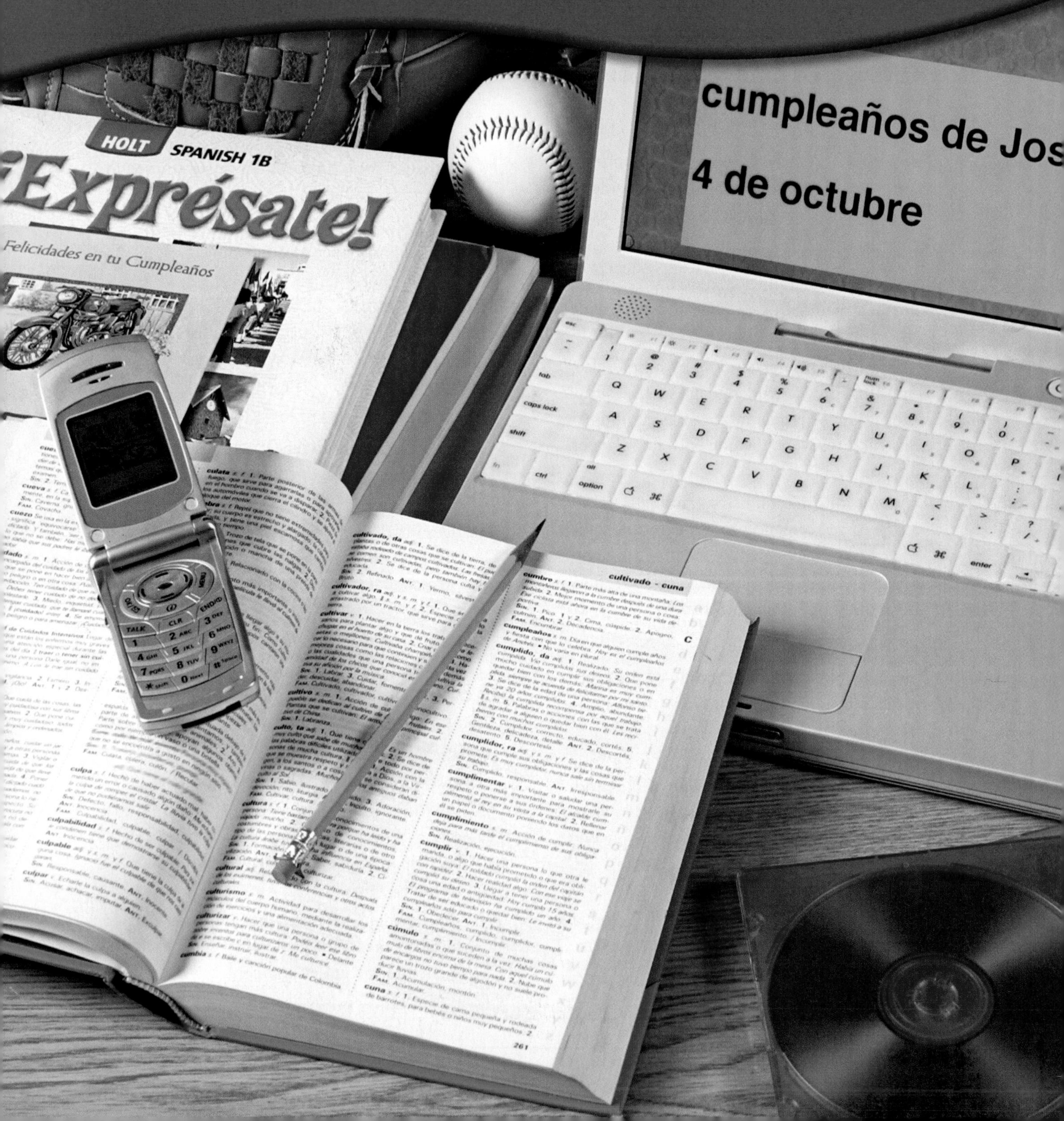

HOLT SPANISH 1B
¡Exprésate!
Felicidades en tu Cumpleaños
cumpleaños de Jos
4 de octubre
cultivado - cuna
261

Señora Ortiz: ¡Buenas tardes, Nico!
Nicolás: ¡Buenas tardes, señora Ortiz!

Entrenador: ¿Nicolás? Dime, ¿cómo es?
Profesora de arte: Es alto y rubio.
Entrenador: ¿Cuántos años tiene?
Profesora de arte: Tiene quince años.

Vocabulario
en acción **1**

ExpresaVisión

¿Cómo te llamas?

Me llamo José. ¿Y tú?

¿Cómo se llama usted?

Soy Alba García.

Teresa, éste es el señor Pidal. Él es mi profesor de español.

Encantada.

Igualmente.

Buenos días, Paco. ¿Qué tal?

Estoy bien, gracias. ¿Y usted?

Hola. ¿Cómo estás?

Más o menos. ¿Y tú?

¡Exprésate!

Interactive TUTOR

To ask for personal information	To respond
¿De dónde eres? *Where are you from?*	**Soy de Estados Unidos.** *I'm from the United States.*
¿Cuál es tu teléfono? *What is your telephone number?*	**Es tres-veintiséis-ochenta y nueve.** *It's three, twenty-six, eighty-nine.*
¿Cuál es el correo electrónico de Marisa? *What is Marisa's e-mail address?*	**Es eme punto a-ere-ce-e arroba ce-o-ele-e punto e-de-u** *It's m.arce@cole.edu*
¿Cuándo es tu cumpleaños? *When is your birthday?*	**Es el catorce de febrero.** *It's the fourteenth of February.*

Online
Vocabulario y gramática, pp. 1–5

Más vocabulario...

¿Quién es el muchacho?
Who is the boy?

(Él) es mi mejor amigo.
He is my best friend.

(Él) es estudiante.
He is a student.

¿Quién es la muchacha?
Who is the girl?

(Ella) es mi mejor amiga.
She is my best friend.

(Ella) es estudiante.
She is a student.

1 ¿Cómo se llama? ⬇1B

 Escuchemos As you listen, decide whether the people speaking are **a)** asking someone's name or **b)** giving a name.

2 Preguntas y más preguntas ⬇1B

Leamos Match each question to the correct response. There may be more than one correct answer.

1. ¿Qué tal Jorge?
2. ¿Quién es él?
3. ¿Cómo se llama usted?
4. ¿Cuál es tu correo electrónico?
5. ¿De dónde eres?
6. ¿Cuándo es tu cumpleaños?
7. ¿Cómo está usted?

a. Me llamo Manuel Solís Hidalgo.
b. Es guajiro@planeta.net
c. Muy bien, ¿y tú?
d. Soy de España.
e. Es el tres de enero.
f. Más o menos, ¿y usted?
g. Es Alberto Gutiérrez.

3 ¿Cuál es? ⬇1C

Escribamos Write an introduction or a short conversation for each of the following photos.

1.

2.

3.

4.

¡Exprésate!

To ask for descriptions	To respond
¿Cómo es Paco? *What is Paco like?*	**Paco es moreno. También es inteligente y un poco tímido.** *Paco has dark hair/a dark complexion. He is also intelligent and a little shy.*
¿Cómo eres? ¿Eres romántico(a)? *What are you like? Are you romantic?*	**Sí, soy bastante romántico(a).** *Yes, I am quite romantic.*
¿Cómo es la comida china? *What is Chinese food like?*	**Es muy deliciosa.** *It's very delicious.*

Interactive TUTOR

Online
Vocabulario y gramática, pp. 1–5

4 Mucho gusto ↴1B

Leamos Carla and Miguel are talking to a new student, Ana, on the first day of school. Complete the conversation using phrases from the word box.

TEKS Focus

1B Demonstrate understanding of simple, clearly spoken, and written language when dealing with familiar topics

Estoy	Igualmente	estás	Encantado	cuál
Regular	Son	Es	Cómo	Es de

MIGUEL ¡Hola, Carla! ¿Cómo ____1____ ?

CARLA ¡Hola Miguel! ____2____ bien. ¿Y tú?

MIGUEL ____3____ .

CARLA Miguel, ésta es Ana. ____4____ Perú.

MIGUEL ____5____ .

ANA ____6____ .

MIGUEL ¿____7____ son tus clases Ana?

ANA ____8____ buenas.

CARLA Ana, ¿____9____ es tu correo electrónico?

ANA ____10____ apaloma@mundo.net.

 # Comunicación

5 Encantado ↴1A

Hablemos Introduce the people in the pictures to a partner and tell where they are from and what they are like. Your partner should then respond to the introduction by introducing himself or herself, telling where he or she is from, and telling something about himself or herself. Then switch roles.

MODELO —Éste es mi amigo Juan. Él es de España. Es moreno y...

—Encantada, Juan. Me llamo Elaine. Soy de Nueva York. Soy seria y...

Juan
España

1. Arturo
Perú

2. Benito
Costa Rica

3. Timoteo
México

4. Sra. Galván
Chile

5. Sr. Cárdenas
Venezuela

GramaVisión

The verbs ser and estar

Interactive TUTOR

1 Use the irregular verb **ser** to identify or describe a person or thing. Also use the verb **ser** with **de** to tell where someone is from.

soy *I am*	**somos** *we are*
eres *you are*	**sois** *you are*
es *he is, she is, you are*	**son** *you are, they are*

Las películas **son** divertidas.
Movies are fun.

Juan **es de** Cuba.
Juan is from Cuba.

2 Use the irregular verb **estar** to say how you or someone else feels. You can also use the verb **estar** with **prepositions** to say where someone or something is in relation to another person or thing.

estoy *I am*	**estamos** *we are*
estás *you are*	**estáis** *you are*
está *he is, she is, you are*	**están** *you are, they are*

¿Cómo **está** usted?
How are you?

Estoy bien gracias.
I am fine, thank you.

¿Dónde **está** mi libro?
Where is my book?

Está encima de la mesa.
It's on top of the table.

Online

Vocabulario y gramática, pp. 1–5	Actividades, pp. 1–4

6 Juan y yo ✦1B

Leamos Complete each sentence with the correct form of either the verb **ser** or **estar.**

1. Juan y yo ===== en casa.
2. Él y yo ===== amigos.
3. Yo ===== de Chile.
4. Él ===== de Perú.
5. Juan va al parque hoy. ===== cerca de su casa.
6. No voy al parque con Juan porque yo no ===== bien.
7. Laura y Manolo ===== en la clase de inglés.
8. Mis padres ===== altos, pero yo ===== bajo.
9. ¿Cuál ===== esta clase? ¿Dónde ===== (yo)?
10. Tú ===== en la clase de biología.

7 **Somos así** 🔻1B, 1C

Escribamos Use the sentence starters below to write descriptions of yourself, your friends, your family, and your home. Also tell how you are feeling.

MODELO **Mi hermano es...**
Mi hermano es alto y divertido.

1. Yo estoy...
2. Mis amigos y yo somos...
3. Nuestra casa está...
4. Nuestro carro es...

5. Mis abuelos son...
6. Mis hermanos son...
7. Mi casa es...
8. Mi mejor amigo y yo somos...

8 **¿Cómo son?** 🔻1C

Escribamos/Hablemos Look at the pictures below and describe how each person feels and his or her characteristics.

MODELO **María es inteligente, seria y rubia.**
No está bien hoy.

María

1. **Ernesto** 2. **Pablo y Javier** 3. **Catarina y Miguel** 4. **Esmeralda**

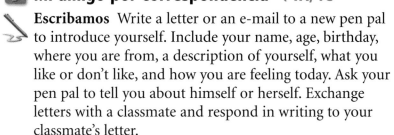

Comunicación

9 **Mi amigo por correspondencia** 🔻1A, 1C

Escribamos Write a letter or an e-mail to a new pen pal to introduce yourself. Include your name, age, birthday, where you are from, a description of yourself, what you like or don't like, and how you are feeling today. Ask your pen pal to tell you about himself or herself. Exchange letters with a classmate and respond in writing to your classmate's letter.

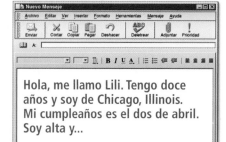

Hola, me llamo Lili. Tengo doce años y soy de Chicago, Illinois. Mi cumpleaños es el dos de abril. Soy alta y...

Gramática 1

Interactive TUTOR

The verbs gustar and tener

1 Use the verb **gustar** to say what people like. If the thing they like is singular, use **gusta**; if it is plural use **gustan**. Put one of these **pronouns** before **gustar** to say who likes something.

me gusta(n)	*I like*	**nos** gusta(n)	*we like*
te gusta(n)	*you* (**tú**) *like*	**os** gusta(n)	*you* (**vosotros**) *like*
le gusta(n)	*you* (**usted**) *like, he/she/ it likes*	**les** gusta(n)	*you* (**ustedes**) *like, they like*

2 Use the verb **tener** to tell what someone has. To conjugate the **yo** form drop the **-er** ending and add **-go** . The **-e** in the stem of **tener** changes to **-ie** in all forms except **yo, nosotros,** and **vosotros.**

yo ten**go**	nosotros(as) tenemos
tú t**ie**nes	vosotros(as) tenéis
Ud., él, ella t**ie**ne	Uds., ellos, ellas t**ie**nen

3 **Tener** is also used in these common expressions.

tener que + infinitive	*to have to do something*
tener ganas de + infinitive	*to feel like doing something*
tener prisa	*to be in a hurry*
tener (mucha) hambre	*to be (very) hungry*
tener (mucha) sed	*to be (very) thirsty*

Tengo prisa. Tengo que ir a un ensayo.
I'm in a hurry. I have to go to a rehearsal.

Online
Vocabulario y gramática, pp. 1–5 | Actividades, pp. 1–4

10 Vacaciones de verano ✈1B

Leamos Some friends are going to camp this summer. Complete their conversations with the pronouns **me, te, le, nos,** or **les.**

FELICIA ¡Hola! Me llamo Felicia y éste es Roberto. A nosotros ___1___ gusta nadar. ¿A ustedes ___2___ gusta nadar?

JUAN Sí, a mi hermana Raquel y a mí ___3___ gusta nadar y patinar. ¿A ustedes ___4___ gusta patinar?

FELICIA Bueno, a mí ___5___ gusta, pero a Roberto no ___6___ gusta.

ROBERTO Sí, es verdad, pero ___7___ gusta montar en bicicleta y ir a la playa. Raquel, ¿a ti ___8___ gusta ir a la playa?

RAQUEL Sí, a Juan y a mí ___9___ gusta ir a la playa.

11 El día de Lorenzo 🔻1B

Escuchemos Match each picture to the statements you hear about Lorenzo's busy day.

a.

b.

c.

d.

12 ¿Quién es? 🔻1B

Leamos Complete the sentences with the name(s) of the people that fit the descriptions below.

a. Juan y Beto

b. Laura

c. Pati y Tere

d. Memo

1. A ═══ le gusta comer helado.
2. A ═══ les gusta descansar y escuchar música.
3. A ═══ le gusta nadar.
4. A ═══ les gusta jugar videojuegos.

 Comunicación

13 ¿Quién es ella? 🔻1A

Hablemos In groups of four, role-play a situation where you know one person, but you don't know the other two. Take turns greeting everyone and introducing yourself and the person you know. Find out as much as you can about the other people.

MODELO —Hola. Me llamo... ¿Cómo te llamas?
—Me llamo... y éste es mi amigo...
—¿De dónde eres?
—Soy de...

TEKS Focus

1A Engage in oral and written exchanges of learned material to socialize and to provide and obtain information

Capítulo puente

Segunda parte

Objetivos

In this section you will review how to
- talk about what you and others like to do
- ask what a friend wants to do and answer for yourself
- use the verb **querer** with infinitives
- use **ir a** + an infinitive to talk about the future
- form and use regular **-ar** verbs
- place pronouns after prepositions

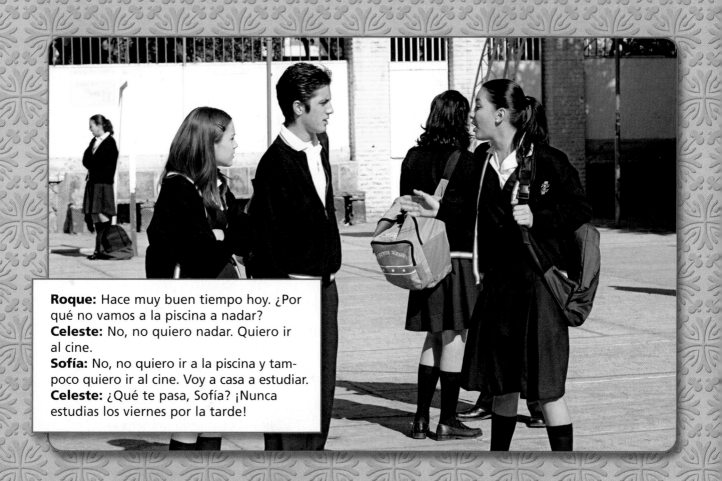

Roque: Hace muy buen tiempo hoy. ¿Por qué no vamos a la piscina a nadar?
Celeste: No, no quiero nadar. Quiero ir al cine.
Sofía: No, no quiero ir a la piscina y tampoco quiero ir al cine. Voy a casa a estudiar.
Celeste: ¿Qué te pasa, Sofía? ¡Nunca estudias los viernes por la tarde!

Mateo: ¿Qué tal si vamos al partido de béisbol?
Julia: Claro que sí.
Nicolás: No tengo ganas.
Mateo: ¿No tienes ganas? ¿Qué vas a hacer?

Vocabulario *en acción* **2**

Video/DVD

ExpresaVisión

A mis amigos y a mí nos gusta...

montar en bicicleta

correr

leer revistas y novelas

escuchar música

dibujar

hacer ejercicio

pasear

patinar

Más vocabulario...

alquilar videos	*to rent videos*	ir al cine	*to go to the movies*
cantar	*to sing*	nadar	*to swim*
comer	*to eat*	navegar por Internet	*to surf the Internet*
escribir cartas	*to write letters*	pasar el rato solo(a)	*to spend time alone*
hacer la tarea	*to do homework*	salir	*to go out*
ir al centro comercial	*to go to the mall*	ver televisión	*to watch television*

¿Qué te gusta hacer?

Visit Holt Online

go.hrw.com
KEYWORD: EXP1B PUENTE

Vocabulario 2 practice ⬍

A mí me gusta...

hablar por teléfono

bailar

descansar

Y me gusta jugar...

a juegos de mesa

al básquetbol

al béisbol

al fútbol

Más vocabulario...

¿Con quién?	
conmigo	with me
contigo	with you
con mi familia	with my family

Texas También se puede decir...

Spanish speakers in Mexico say **el baloncesto** instead of **el básquetbol,** and **andar en bicicleta** instead of **montar en bicicleta.** In Texas, **básquetbol** is often shortened to **básquet,** and **bicicleta** is shortened to **bici.**

¡Exprésate!

Interactive
TUTOR

To ask what someone likes or wants to do	To respond
¿Qué quieres hacer hoy? *What do you want to do today?*	**Ni idea.** *I have no idea.*
¿Quieres ir al cine conmigo? *Do you want to go to the movies with me?*	**Está bien./No, no quiero ir.** *All right./No, I don't want to go.*
¿A Lili le gusta ir al centro comercial? *Does Lili like to go to the mall?*	**Sí, porque le gusta ir de compras.** *Yes, because she likes to go shopping.*

Online
Vocabulario y gramática, pp. 6–10

14 Les gusta... 1B

Escuchemos Choose the most logical description based on the sentences you hear.

1. Es (extrovertida/tímida).
2. Es (muy activo/perezoso).
3. Es (trabajador/perezoso).
4. Son (atléticos/intelectuales).
5. Es (activa/seria).
6. Son (divertidas/serias).

15 ¿Qué les gusta? 1B

Leamos Match the sentences with the pictures.

1. A Tere le gusta hacer ejercicio.
2. A Nico le gusta cantar.
3. A Mila le gusta ver televisión.
4. A Beto y Toño les gusta jugar al básquetbol.
5. A José y Ana les gusta bailar.
6. A Paco y Lalo les gusta jugar a fútbol.

a.

b.

c.

d.

e.

f.

¡Exprésate!

To talk about your plans	
¿Qué haces los fines de semana?	**Cuando hace buen tiempo, voy al parque.**
What do you do on the weekends?	*When the weather is good, I go to the park.*
¿Qué vas a hacer el viernes próximo?	**Voy a ir a una fiesta.**
What are you going to do next Friday?	*I'm going to go to a party.*

Interactive TUTOR

Online
Vocabulario y gramática, pp. 6–10

16 ¿Qué tal si...? ↓1B

Leamos Lupe is calling her friend Tomás on her cell phone. Read the sentences of their conversation, and then put them in the most logical order.

<table>
<tr><th>Lupe</th><th>Tomás</th></tr>
<tr><td>—Estoy en el centro comercial. ¿Quieres ir al cine conmigo?</td><td>—¡Hola, Lupe! No hago nada importante. Dónde estás?</td></tr>
<tr><td>—Buena idea, Tomás. Nos vemos en diez minutos.</td><td>—Adiós. Hasta luego.</td></tr>
<tr><td>—¡Excelente! Y después de la película, ¿qué quieres hacer?</td><td>—¿Qué tal si vamos al parque? Hace buen tiempo hoy.</td></tr>
<tr><td>—Hola. ¿Tomás? Soy Lupe. ¿Qué haces?</td><td>—Sí, quiero ir. Voy a llegar en diez minutos.</td></tr>
</table>

17 ¿Quieres ir? ↓1C

Escribamos Write a sentence inviting a friend to do the activities pictured below. Then write what you think your friend will say in response.

MODELO —¿Quieres ir al parque conmigo?
—Sí, quiero ir al parque. Hace buen tiempo hoy.
(—No, no quiero ir. No me gusta el parque.)

   1.   2.   3.   4.   5.

Comunicación

18 Una invitación personal ↓1A

Hablemos Think of a place you'd like to go and something you'd like to do there. Invite two or three of your classmates to do the activity with you, and see how they respond. If they don't want to do the activity, be sure to ask them why.

MODELO —Jorge, ¿quieres ir al cine conmigo?
—No, no quiero ir al cine hoy.
—¿Por qué no?
—No me gusta ir al cine. Es aburrido.

> **TEKS Focus**
> **1B** Demonstrate understanding of simple, clearly spoken, and written language when dealing with familiar topics

GramaVisión

Gramática en acción 2

Objetivos

Using the verbs **querer**, **ir a** + infinitive, pronouns after prepositions, regular **-ar** verbs, and possessive adjectives

Interactive TUTOR

¡Te acuerdas?

The verb **querer** is a stem changing verb. The **e** in the stem changes to **ie** in all forms except **nosotros** and **vosotros**. Other **e** ⟶ **ie** stem changing verbs are **empezar** and **merendar**.

querer, ir a + infinitive, and pronouns

1 To say what you or others want or want to do, use a form of the verb **querer.** The form you use depends on the subject.

yo qu**ie**ro	nosotros queremos
tú qu**ie**res	vosotros queréis
Ud., él, ella qu**ie**re	Uds., ellos, ellas qu**ie**ren

2 To talk about what someone is or isn't going to do, use the present tense of **ir** with **a** followed by an **infinitive**.

¿**Vas a** estudiar? No, **voy a** descansar.
Are you going to study? *No, I'm going to rest.*

3 **Pronouns** have a different form when they come after prepositions such as **a** *(to)*, **de** *(of, from)*, **con** *(with)* and **en** *(in, on, at)*.

mí	nosotros(as)
ti	vosotros(as)
usted, él, ella	ustedes, ellos, ellas

4 With **gustar,** the phrase formed by **a** and a **pronoun** can be added to a sentence to clarify or emphasize the pronoun that's already there.

adds emphasis   *adds emphasis*   *clarifies*

¿**A ti** te gusta dibujar?   **A mi** no me gusta.   **A ella** le gusta.

Online

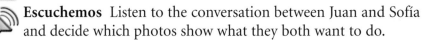

Vocabulario y gramática, pp. 6–10	Actividades, pp. 5–8

19 **Vamos al centro comercial** 🔽 1B

Escuchemos Listen to the conversation between Juan and Sofía and decide which photos show what they both want to do.

Gramática 2

20 ¿Cuál es la pregunta? ↓1B

Leamos Choose the question that best matches the answer given.

1. Juan no quiere ver televisión porque tiene mucha tarea.

 a. ¿Por qué Juan no quiere ver televisión?
 b. ¿Por qué a Juan no le gusta ver televisión?

2. Porque queremos alquilar un video.

 a. ¿Por qué no quiere ir al cine?
 b. ¿Por qué no quieren ir al cine?

3. No, a mí me gusta salir con amigos.

 a. Profesora, ¿a usted le gusta pasar el rato sola?
 b. Profesora, ¿a ella le gusta pasar el rato sola?

4. No, no quiero.

 a. ¿Quieren jugar a un videojuego?
 b. ¿Quieres jugar a un videojuego?

21 ¿Qué van a hacer? ↓1B, 1C

TEKS Focus

1C Present information using familiar words, phrases, and sentences

Escribamos Write five questions using a word or phrase from each column. Then write an answer to each of your questions.

MODELO —¿Vas a jugar al básquetbol?
—No, a mí no me gustan los deportes.

Tú	ir a	asistir a un concierto
Sr. González	querer	estudiar el español
Mi amiga		trabajar
Los estudiantes		visitar al abuelo
Ustedes		jugar en el parque
Ellas		ir a la escuela

 Comunicación

22 El fin de semana ↓1A

Hablemos Talk with a classmate about things you like to do or want to do this weekend. Take turns suggesting weekend activities based on what the other person says that he or she likes.

—A mí me gustan los deportes.
—¿Quieres jugar al básquetbol en el parque el sábado?
—Sí, quiero jugar al básquetbol contigo.

TUTOR

Regular -ar verbs and possessive adjectives

1 Every verb has a **stem** followed by some kind of **ending**. The stem tells the verb's meaning. An infinitive ending means the verb has no subject.

verb stem   *infinitive ending*

habl   **-ar**

2 To give the verb a subject you conjugate it. To conjugate a regular **-ar** verb in the present tense, drop the **-ar** ending of the infinitive and add these **endings**. Each ending goes with a particular subject.

yo cant**o**	nosotros(as) cant**amos**
tú cant**as**	vosotros(as) cant**áis**
Ud., él, ella cant**a**	Uds., ellos, ellas cant**an**

¿Te gusta **cantar**?   Sí, cant**o** todos los días.

3 **Possessive adjectives** show ownership or relationships between people. They are placed before the **noun**.

Owner			**Owner**				
yo	**mi** libro	nosotros(as)	**nuestro** libro	**nuestra** casa
	mis libros		**nuestros** libros	**nuestras** casas
tú	**tu** libro	vosotros(as)	**vuestro** libro	**vuestra** casa
	tus libros		**vuestros** libros	**vuestras** casas
usted ⎱ él/ella ⎰	**su** libro **sus** libros	ustedes ⎱ ellos/ellas ⎰	**su** libro **sus** libros	

4 **Possessive adjectives** agree with the **noun** that comes after them.

refers to   *agrees grammatically*

Martin vive con **nuestros abuelos.**

Online

Vocabulario y gramática, pp. 6–10	Actividades, pp. 5–8

Vocabulario y gramática, pp. 6–10 | Actividades, pp. 5–8

En inglés

In Spanish, verb conjugations in the present tense have six forms. The **subject pronouns (yo, tú, usted, él, ella, nosotros, vosotros, ustedes, ellos, ellas)** are often left out because the subject is understood from the ending of the verb.

In English, most verb conjugations in the present tense have only two forms. The **subject pronouns** are not left out.

    I sing   we sing
   you sing   you sing
he, she, it sings **they sing**

---

23 En mi familia ⬇ 1B

Leamos Choose the correct verbs to complete the conversation.

—Mariana, ¿cómo (paso/**pasas**) el fin de semana?

—Los sábados mis amigos y yo (pasan/**pasamos**) el rato juntos.

—¿Y es todo?

—No. A veces yo (**patino**/patinas) en el parque con José.

—Y tus padres, ¿cómo (**pasan**/pasamos) el fin de semana?

—Ellos (**montan**/montamos) en bicicleta.

—¿Y tu hermano Javier?

—Él siempre (practicas/**practica**) deportes. Es muy atlético.

24 El fin de semana de José ↴1C

Hablemos Based on the pictures, say what each person does on the weekend.

MODELO Estudio matemáticas.

Yo

1. Luisa   2. Mi papá   3. Nosotros   4. Mi hermano

5. Ellos   6. Gisela   7. Pati y Arturo   8. Mis amigos

25 La familia de Gregorio ↴1B

TEKS Focus

1B Demonstrate understanding of simple, clearly spoken, and written language when dealing with familiar topics

Leamos Gregorio is talking about his family with a friend. On a separate piece of paper, write the missing possessive adjectives.

—¿Cuántas personas hay en ____1____ familia?

—Somos seis en ____2____ familia: ____3____ padres, ____4____ dos hermanas, ____5____ hermano y yo.

—¿Dónde trabajan ____6____ padres?

—____7____ madre es médica. ____8____ trabajo es muy interesante. ____9____ padre trabaja con ____10____ padre, mi abuelo.

—Ustedes tienen una casa azul, ¿verdad?

—No, ____11____ casa no es azul, pero ____12____ carro es azul.

Comunicación

26 ¿Y qué haces tú? ↴1A

Hablemos/Escribamos Make a list of five things you do with your friends or family on the weekends. Ask a classmate if he or she does the same things. Then answer your classmate's questions.

MODELO —José y yo nadamos. ¿Nadas con tus amigos?
        —No, no nadamos. Vemos televisión.

Tercera parte

Objetivos

In this section you will review how to
- say what you have and need
- talk about classes and school supplies
- describe and talk about family relationships
- ask about other's responsibilities and talk about yours
- form **-er** and **-ir** verbs in the present tense
- form and use stem changing verbs
- form and use the verbs **hacer, poner,** and **tocar**

Nicolás: ¿Qué necesitas?
Mateo: A ver, necesito un lápiz... una goma... una regla... y papel.

Sofía: Ese niño travieso es mi hermano Quique. A Quique no le toca hacer los quehaceres. ¡Me parece injusto!

Vocabulario

en acción **3**

Vídeo/DVD

ExpresaVisión

Tengo muchas cosas, pero...

También necesito...

unas carpetas

unos bolígrafos

(todavía) necesito unos útiles escolares.

unos cuadernos

unos lápices
(un lápiz, *sing.*)

una regla

papel *(m.)*

una mochila

un diccionario

una computadora

zapatos *(m.)*

un reloj
(unos relojes, *pl.*)

ropa *(f.)*

Vocabulario 3

¿Qué clases tienes esta tarde?

Tengo historia...

CENTRO EDUCATIVO NUEVA ESPERANZA
400 mts Oeste del Beneficio La Meseta,
San Juan de Santa Bárbara Heredia,
Telfax (Primaria) 506.265.5393
Tel (Secundaria) 506.265.7934

Horas	Clases
8:00	*matemáticas*
8:50	*arte*
9:40	*biología*
10:30	*español*
11:20	*educación física*
12:10	*almuerzo*
13:00	*historia*
13:50	*inglés*

por la mañana

por la tarde

Más vocabulario...

las materias	*school subjects*
el alemán	*German*
el francés	*French*
las ciencias	*science*
la química	*chemistry*
el taller	*workshop*
la computación	*computer science*

Texas **También se puede decir...**

In Spain, a computer is called **un ordenador**, while in Colombia the word is **computador**.

In Latin America and Texas, many speakers say **una pluma, un lapicero,** or **un boli** instead of **un bolígrafo**. In Spain and Mexico **un lapicero** is a pencil case.

¡Exprésate!

To ask about school and classes	To respond
¿Necesitas algo para el colegio?	**Sí, necesito muchas cosas./No, no necesito nada.**
Do you need anything for school?	*Yes, I need a lot of things./No, I don't need anything.*
¿Qué clases tienes esta tarde después del almuerzo?	**Primero tengo español y después tengo computación.**
What clases do you have this afternoon after lunch?	*First I have Spanish and afterwards I have computer science.*
¿A qué hora tienes la clase de francés?	**Tengo francés a las dos y media.**
What time do you have French class?	*I have French at two-thirty.*

Interactive TUTOR

Online
Vocabulario y gramática, pp. 11–15

27 ¡No lo tengo! ⬤1B

Leamos Jorge says Lili has taken his dictionary without asking. Complete Lili's response using the words from the box.

Tengo en mi ___1___ unos ___2___, unas ___3___, y un ___4___. También tengo una ___5___, y mucho ___6___. ¡No tengo tu ___7___!

diccionario	papel	mochila	carpetas
lápices	calculadora	cuaderno	comida

28 ¿Qué clase tengo? ⬤1B

Leamos/Escribamos Ana can't remember her class schedule. Based on the schedule below, answer Ana's questions.

Día	lunes	martes	miércoles	jue
Horario				
8:45	historia	biología	historia	bio
9:40	matemáticas	computación	matemáticas	com
10:35	ed. física	arte	ed. física	arte
11:30	español	ciencias	español	cier
12:25	almuerzo	almuerzo	almuerzo	alm
12:55	química	inglés	química	ing
1:50	taller	francés	taller	frar

400 mts Oeste del Beneficio La Meseta, San Juan de Santa Barbara Heredia, Telfax 506.265.5393 Tel 506.265.7934

1. ¿Qué clase tengo después del almuerzo los lunes?
2. ¿Qué clase tengo los martes a las once y media?
3. ¿Qué clase tengo después de historia los miércoles?
4. ¿Qué clase tengo los martes a las dos menos diez?

¡Exprésate!

To ask about home and family	To respond
¿Cuántas personas hay en tu familia? *How many people are in your family?*	**En mi familia somos cuatro. Mi madre, mi padre, mi hermana y yo.** *In my family, there are four of us. My mother, my father, my sister, and I.*
¿Cómo son tus hermanos? *What are your brothers and sisters like?*	**Somos delgados y altos. Usamos lentes.** *We are thin and tall. We wear glasses.*
¿Dónde viven ustedes? *Where do you live?*	**Vivimos en un apartamento.** *We live in an apartment.*
¿Qué haces para ayudar en casa? *What do you do to help around the house?*	**A mí me toca cocinar la cena.** *I have to cook dinner.*

Interactive TUTOR

Online
Vocabulario y gramática, pp. 11–15

29 **¿Cierto o falso?** ↴ 1B

Escuchemos Mira el árbol genealógico *(family tree)* y escucha las oraciones. Indica si cada oración es **cierta** o **falsa.**

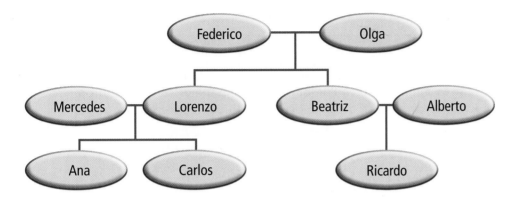

30 **Son hermanos** ↴ 1B

Leamos/Escribamos Answer the questions based on the family tree in Activity 29.

1. ¿Quién es la hermana de Lorenzo?
2. ¿Quién es la madre de Carlos?
3. ¿Cómo se llama el padre de Ricardo?
4. ¿Cómo se llama la abuela de Ana?
5. ¿Quién es la hermana de Carlos?
6. ¿Quién es el abuelo de Ricardo?
7. ¿Es Ana la hermana de Ricardo?
8. ¿Es Carlos el hermano de Ana?
9. ¿Son primos Carlos y Ricardo?

 Comunicación

31 **¿Y a quién le toca en tu casa?** ↴ 1A, 1C

Hablemos Ask three classmates the following questions. Who is most like you? Report your findings to the class.

1. ¿Cuántas personas hay en tu familia?
2. ¿Cuántos hermanos mayores tienes? ¿Cuántos menores? ¿Cómo son?
3. ¿Qué quehaceres casi siempre haces en casa?
4. ¿A quién le toca lavar los platos? ¿cortar el césped? ¿hacer las camas? ¿sacar la basura?

TEKS Focus

1A Engage in oral and written exchanges of learned material to socialize and to provide and obtain information

Vocabulario 3

Using -er and -ir verbs
and stem changing -ar,
-er, and -ir verbs

Gramática en acción 3

GramaVisión

Interactive
TUTOR

The present tense of -er and -ir verbs

1 To conjugate a regular **-er** or **-ir** verb in the present tense, drop the **-er** or **-ir** of the infinitive and add these **endings**.

	comer	**escribir**
yo	com**o**	escrib**o**
tú	com**es**	escrib**es**
Ud., él, ella	com**e**	escrib**e**
nosotros(as)	com**emos**	escrib**imos**
vosotros(as)	com**éis**	escrib**ís**
Uds., ellos, ellas	com**en**	escrib**en**

2 The following **-er** and **-ir** verbs have irregular **yo** forms.

hacer ⟶ yo ha**go**   poner ⟶ yo pon**go**

traer ⟶ yo trai**go**   saber ⟶ yo s**é**

ver ⟶ yo v**eo**   salir ⟶ yo sal**go**

Online

Vocabulario y gramática, pp. 11–15	Actividades, pp. 9–12

32 ## Conversaciones en la clase ⬇1B

Leamos Complete each sentence with the correct form of one of the verbs from the word box. In some sentences more than one verb is possible.

salir	escribir	tener	ver	poner	comer
hacer	saber	asistir	leer	abrir	traer

1. En nuestra clase, nosotros ▭▭▭ cartas a unos estudiantes en España. Los estudiantes en España también ▭▭▭ a nosotros.

2. —¿Tú ▭▭▭ con tus amigos este fin de semana?
   —No, no ▭▭▭. No hay tiempo. ¿Cuándo ▭▭▭ la tarea?

3. —¿▭▭▭ cuál es el número de teléfono de Paco?
   —No, no ▭▭▭.

4. —Profesor Álvarez, ▭▭▭ a los conciertos, ¿verdad?
   —No, no ▭▭▭ tiempo porque ▭▭▭ libros de ciencia ficción todos los días.

5. —¿Dónde ▭▭▭ todos tus útiles escolares?
   —▭▭▭ todos mis útiles escolares en mi mochila.

Gramática 3

33 **¿Con qué frecuencia...?** ⬇️**1B, 1C**

Hablemos/Escribamos Tell how often you do the following things:

MODELO Cocino todos los días.

cocinar

1. salir a patinar con amigos

2. hacer la tarea por Internet

3. comer con la familia

4. hacer ejercicio

5. correr con un(a) amigo(a)

6. escribir en el parque

7. beber algo después de clases

8. traer algo a un(a) amigo(a)

 Comunicación

34 **Entrevista** ⬇️**1A, 1C**

Hablemos/Escribamos Work in groups of four. Ask one member of your group how often he or she does the activities pictured above. Then tell the group what your partner said.

MODELO   JORGE   —¿Con qué frecuencia corres?

            SUSANA   —Corro todos los días.

35 **Hacemos cosas diferentes** ⬇️**1C**

Escribamos/Hablemos Write about things you always do, sometimes do, and never do. Then compare your activities with a partner's.

MODELO   —Yo siempre lavo los platos. A veces saco la basura.

> **TEKS Focus**
>
> **1C** Present information using familiar words, phrases, and sentences

Interactive TUTOR

Stem-changing verbs

1 Some verbs show a vowel stem-change from **e** to **ie** such as **empezar** *(to begin)*, **merendar** *(to have a snack)* and **querer** *(to want).* The **e** changes to **ie** in all but the **nosotros(as)** and **vosotros(as)** forms.

yo	emp**ie**zo	nosotros(as)	empezamos
tú	emp**ie**zas	vosotros(as)	empezáis
Ud., él, ella	emp**ie**za	Uds., ellos, ellas	emp**ie**zan

—¿A qué hora **empieza** la película? —**Empieza** a las siete.

2 **Dormir** *(to sleep)* is also a stem-changing verb. The **o** of the stem changes to **ue** in all forms except **nosotros(as)** and **vosotros(as).**

yo	d**ue**rmo	nosotros(as)	dormimos
tú	d**ue**rmes	vosotros(as)	dormís
Ud., él, ella	d**ue**rme	Uds., ellos, ellas	d**ue**rmen

El perro **duerme** poco. Ana y yo **dormimos** mucho.

3 Other verbs that follow this pattern are **almorzar** *(to have lunch),* **volver** *(to go or come back),* and **llover** *(to rain).*

Yo **almuerzo** poco. Tu perro **vuelve** a su casa. Hoy **llueve**.

4 To say what you have to do or whose turn it is to do something, use the verb **tocar** followed by an infinitive. **Tocar** may be used like **gustar.** The verb **parecer** means *to seem* and may also be used like **gustar** to ask for or give an opinion.

A mí siempre me **toca** sacar la basura. Me **parece** injusto.

Online

Vocabulario y gramática, pp. 11–15	Actividades, pp. 9–12

¿Te acuerdas?

In Spanish, regular verbs have **regular stems** and regular endings.

-ar	**habl**o	**habl**amos
	hablas	**habl**áis
	habla	**habl**an

-er	**com**o	**com**emos
	comes	**com**éis
	come	**com**en

-ir	**escrib**o	**escrib**imos
	escribes	**escrib**ís
	escribe	**escrib**en

36 **¡Qué lata!** ↓**1B**

 Escuchemos Based on the pictures below, decide whether the statements you hear are **cierto** or **falso.**

mi hermana

mi hermano

mi papá y mi hermano menor

mi mamá y yo

37 El sábado yo... ⚓1B

Leamos Use the correct forms of the verbs in parentheses to complete the conversation.

PACO —¿Qué haces los sábados Roberto?

ROBERTO —Siempre ===== (dormir) hasta las once.

PACO —Yo no. Siempre ===== (empezar) el día a las siete.

ROBERTO —Bueno, ¿===== (querer) jugar al fútbol el sábado?

PACO —No sé. Si no ===== (llover), ===== (jugar) al fútbol.

ROBERTO —Y si ===== (llover), ¿===== (querer) ir al cine?

PACO —Sí, está bien. ===== (querer) ver "El gato negro".

ROBERTO —Y después tú y yo ===== (volver) a mi casa. Mi familia ===== (merendar) a las cuatro.

38 ¿Cómo les parece? ⚓1B, 1C

Hablemos/Escribamos Everyone in the Ruíz family has something to do today. Write what José would say about their activities and how they feel about them.

MODELO **A mi papá le toca trabajar. Le parece bien.**

mi papá

1. mis hermanos

2. mi prima Zoraida

3. mis abuelos

4. mi tío, mi primo y yo

 Comunicación

39 ¿Qué quieres hacer este fin de semana? ⚓1A, 1C

Escribamos A classmate has written you a note asking if you want to do something on the weekend. Write back and say that the plans seem good, but you can't do anything until the afternoon because of your chores.

MODELO —¿Qué tal si vamos al parque para jugar al tenis?
—Me parece fenomenal si vamos por la tarde. Me toca limpiar la sala. ¿Qué te parece si jugamos a las cuatro?

TEKS Focus

1A Engage in oral and written exchanges of learned material to socialize and to provide and obtain information

El mundo hispanohablante

 Yasemin
Ciudad de México, México

—*¿Conoces la expresión, "Dime con quien andas y te diré quien eres"?*

—Sí, la conozco.

—*¿Cómo eres tú?*

—Yo soy bajita, inteligente, y amigable.

—*¿Qué cosas te gustan?*

—Me gusta el cine, el teatro, y las películas.

—*¿Cómo es tu mejor amigo?*

—Mi mejor amigo as alto, moreno, amigable, y muy inteligente.

—*¿Qué cosas le gustan a él?*

—Le gustan el teatro, las películas y los libros.

—*¿Cómo son ustedes?*

—Somos inteligentes y muy amigables.

—*¿Qué cosas les gustan a ustedes?*

—Nos gusta el cine, las películas y los libros.

—*¿La expresión se aplica en su caso?*

—Sí, sí se aplica porque siempre estamos juntos y porque somos muy inteligentes.

Roberto
Madrid, España

—*Dime, ¿adónde vas cuando hace buen tiempo?*

—Cuando hace buen tiempo, me gusta ir a la piscina o a bañarme con mis amigos a la playa.

—*¿Vas solo o vas con amigos?*

—Con mis amigos.

—*¿Qué te gusta hacer en ese lugar?*

—Jugar a la pelota y nadar.

—*¿Qué no te gusta hacer?*

—No me gusta nada estudiar.

—*¿Por qué no te gusta?*

—Porque es aburrido y prefiero patinar.

Para comprender 🌶1B

1. ¿Cómo es Yasemin?
2. ¿Cómo es el mejor amigo de Yasemin?
3. ¿Qué les gusta hacer a Yasemin y a su mejor amigo?
4. ¿Qué le gusta hacer a Roberto cuando hace buen tiempo?
5. ¿Qué hace él en la playa o en la piscina?
6. ¿A Roberto le gusta estudiar? ¿Por qué sí o por qué no?

Para pensar y hablar 🌶4B

What do you like to do when the weather is good? Are your outdoor activities similar to or different from Roberto's?

What characteristics or interests do you have in common with your friends? Are your friends very similar to you or very different?

¿Quién eres?

Contesta las siguientes preguntas.

Primera PARTE ↓1B

1. ¿Cómo te llamas?
2. ¿Cómo se llama tu profesor de español?
3. ¿De dónde eres?
4. ¿Cuál es tu correo electrónico?
5. ¿Cuándo es tu cumpleaños?
6. ¿Cuántos años tienes?
7. ¿Cómo eres?

Segunda PARTE ↓1B

8. ¿Qué te gusta hacer?
9. ¿Qué haces los fines de semana?
10. ¿Cuáles deportes te gustan?
11. ¿Te gusta más pasar el rato solo(a) o salir con amigos?
12. ¿Qué te gusta más el fútbol o el básquetbol?
13. ¿Qué vas a hacer el viernes próximo?
14. ¿Vas a ir al cine este fin de semana? ¿Con quién vas a ir?

Tercera PARTE ↓1B

15 ¿Qué necesitas para el colegio?

16 ¿Con qué frecuencia estudias matemáticas?

17 ¿A qué hora vas al colegio?

18 ¿A qué hora tienes la clase de inglés?

19 ¿Qué clase tienes después de español?

20 ¿Qué clases tienes esta tarde?

21 ¿Cuántas personas hay en tu familia?

22 ¿Cómo son tus hermanos?

23 ¿Dónde viven ustedes?

24 ¿Qué haces para ayudar en casa?

25 ¿Tienes ganas de ir al parque?

TEKS Focus

1A Engage in oral and written exchanges of learned material to socialize and to provide and obtain information

ENCUESTA ↓1A, 1C

Ask three classmates questions 3, 6, 9, 13, 20, and 24. Write their responses to your questions and turn them in to your teacher.

Video/DVD

GeoVisión

Geocultura México

▲ **El volcán Popocatépetl**
This active volcano, nicknamed **El Popo,** is in Mexico's central valley. At 5,465 meters, it is the second-highest peak in Mexico.

GOLFO DE CALIFORNIA

Baja California

► **México, D.F.**
Mexicans often refer to Mexico City as **el D.F. (Distrito Federal).** It is one of the largest cities in the world.

Almanaque

Población
103.400.165

Capital
La Ciudad de México

Gobierno
república federal

Idioma oficial
español

Moneda
peso mexicano

Código Internet
www.[ ].mx

◄ **Ballet Folklórico**
These dancers are wearing traditional costumes of Veracruz in southern Mexico.

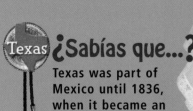 **Texas** **¿Sabías que...?**
Texas was part of Mexico until 1836, when it became an independent republic.

◄ La Barranca del Cobre Chihuahua's spectacular Copper Canyon, in the Sierra Madre mountains, resembles Arizona's Grand Canyon in scale.

▲ Agua Azul Agua Azul in Chiapas has turquoise-colored waterfalls and swimming holes.

▲ Tulúm These ruins are one of many sites left by the Maya people on the Yucatan Peninsula. The name **Tulúm** means *wall* in the Mayan language.

▼ Teotihuacán The ruins of this ancient city show what civilization in Mexico was like before the Aztecs came to power. Its Pyramid of the Sun is the third-largest pyramid in the world.

Map labels

Río Bravo del Norte
Río Conchos
Chihuahua
TEXAS
Barranca del Cobre
Sierra Madre Occidental
Sierra Madre Oriental
Monterrey
MÉXICO
San Luis Potosí
Guanajuato
Querétaro
Guadalajara
Río Lerma
OCÉANO PACÍFICO
CIUDAD DE MÉXICO
Valle Central
Morelia
Teotihuacán
Toluca
Morelos
Puebla
Popocatépetl
Ixtaccihuatl
Río Balsas
Sierra Madre del Sur
Oaxaca
GOLFO DE MÉXICO
Cancún
Mérida
Tulúm
PENÍNSULA DE YUCATÁN
BELICE
Agua Azul
Bonampak
Chiapas
GUATEMALA

↙ 3B

¿Qué tanto sabes?

What major volcano lies close to Mexico City?

A conocer México

El arte

► *Vendedora de Alcatraces* Diego Rivera (1886–1957) painted this picture, *Calla Lily Vendor*, in 1938. Rivera is also known for his many public murals.

◄ **Los antiguos murales mayas** These Mayan murals in Bonampak, Chiapas, are preserved in an ancient building.

► **La biblioteca de la Universidad Nacional Autónoma de México** The library at the National Autonomous University of Mexico is decorated with a giant mosaic showing the history of Mexico. Juan O'Gorman, a well-known Mexican architect, planned and built the library in the 1950s.

La arquitectura

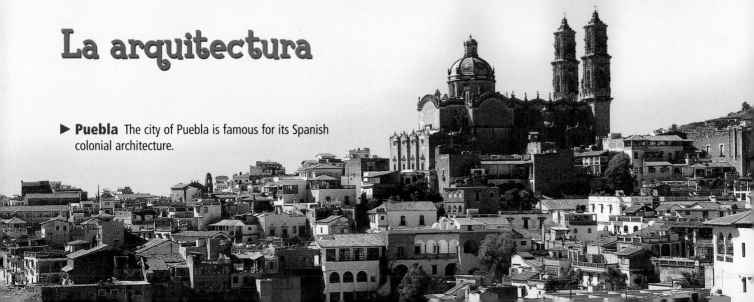

► **Puebla** The city of Puebla is famous for its Spanish colonial architecture.

Las celebraciones

Interactive
TUTOR

Visit Holt Online

go.hrw.com
KEYWORD: EXP1B CH6

Photo Tour

▶3B
¿Sabías que...?
About one-fourth of Mexico's population lives in or near Mexico City. Look at the **Almanaque** and calculate how many people that is.

▲ **El festival de La Guelaguetza** Every July, the city of Oaxaca hosts the **Festival de La Guelaguetza.** This celebration of dance and music dates to pre-Columbian times.

▶ **El festival del 16 de septiembre** September 16 is Independence Day, commemorating Mexico's independence from Spain. Mexicans all over the country celebrate with parades, parties, and fireworks.

La comida

▶ **Las empanadas de flor de calabaza** This **empanada,** or turnover, is made with pumpkin flowers.

▶ **Chiles en nogada** These green chiles stuffed with meat and nuts, with walnut sauce, are usually eaten in December.

▶ **El mole poblano** Mole is a sauce made from lots of ingredients, including chocolate, chiles, seeds, and nuts. It is often served over chicken or turkey.

6

¡A comer!

Objetivos

In Part 1 you will learn to:
- comment on food
- take someone's order
- make polite requests
- use the verbs **ser, estar, pedir, servir, preferir, poder,** and **probar**

In Part 2 you will learn to:
- talk about meals
- offer help and give instructions
- use direct objects and direct object pronouns
- form affirmative informal commands
- use affirmative informal commands with pronouns

¿Qué ves en la foto?

- **¿Dónde están los muchachos y qué hacen?**

- **¿Qué colores ves en la foto?**

- **¿Les gusta la comida o no?**

Texas

TEKS Look for the 👆 next to each activity to learn how it can help you achieve the goals of the **Texas Essential Knowledge and Skills,** found on page xxi.

El restaurante Las Lupitas en Coyoacán, Ciudad de México

Vocabulario
en acción 1

Video/DVD

ExpresaVisión

¿Qué vas a pedir?

un sándwich de atún

una ensalada

una ensalada de frutas

la salsa

unas papas fritas

un sándwich de jamón con queso

Más vocabulario...

Está...

riquísimo(a)	*very good (tasty)*
salado(a)	*salty*
picante	*spicy*
frío(a)	*cold*
(muy) caliente	*(very) hot*

Texas **También se puede decir...**

There are a variety of words in Spanish to say *lunch.* In Texas and the Southwest **el lonche** is common, while **la comida** is used in Spain, Mexico, and much of South America.

A *sandwich* is called **un emparedado** in many Spanish-speaking countries. It is also called **un bocadillo** in Spain, or **una torta** in Mexico and Colombia.

In Spain, **el jugo** is usually called **el zumo.**

Para tomar, puedes pedir...

 un jugo de naranja

 el agua

 un refresco

 la leche

En la mesa hay...

un plato hondo

un vaso

una servilleta

un plato

un cuchillo

un tenedor

una cuchara

¡Exprésate!

To comment on food

Interactive TUTOR

¿Qué tal si pruebas un sándwich de atún? Son muy buenos aquí.	**¡Ay no! Nunca pido atún. No me gusta.**
How about trying a tuna sandwich? They're very good here.	*Oh no! I never order tuna. I don't like it.*
Aquí preparan muy bien (mal) la salsa picante.	**(No) estoy de acuerdo.**
They make very good (bad) hot sauce here.	*I (don't) agree.*
¡Qué ricas están las papas!	**Sí, me encantan.**
The potatoes are really good (tasty)!	*Yes, I love them.*
¿Qué tal está la sopa de verduras?	**Está un poco salada.**
How's the vegetable soup?	*It's a little salty.*

Online
Vocabulario y gramática, pp. 17–19

▼2B, 4B

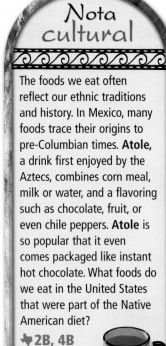

Nota cultural

The foods we eat often reflect our ethnic traditions and history. In Mexico, many foods trace their origins to pre-Columbian times. **Atole,** a drink first enjoyed by the Aztecs, combines corn meal, milk or water, and a flavoring such as chocolate, fruit, or even chile peppers. **Atole** is so popular that it even comes packaged like instant hot chocolate. What foods do we eat in the United States that were part of the Native American diet?

▼2B, 4B

TEKS Focus

4B Demonstrate understanding of the concept of culture through comparisons

---

1 **Una dieta balanceada** ▼1B

Leamos Choose the more healthful food for each item.

MODELO la pizza/la ensalada
la ensalada

1. las papas fritas/las verduras
2. el refresco/el agua
3. la sopa de verduras/el helado
4. la pizza/la ensalada de frutas
5. el jugo de naranja/el refresco
6. el helado/las frutas

7. el sándwich de jamón/ la ensalada
8. el sándwich de atún/la hamburguesa con queso
9. el refresco/la leche
10. las papas fritas/el sándwich de atún
11. la pizza/las verduras

2 **¿Qué tal está la comida?** ▼1B

Escuchemos Con base en cada comentario, indica si preparan bien o mal la comida.

1. la sopa
2. la hamburguesa
3. el sándwich de jamón
4. la ensalada

5. el sándwich de atún
6. las papas fritas
7. la sopa de verduras
8. el helado

3 **¿Cómo está la comida?** ▼1B

Leamos/Hablemos Read each question. Then look at the pictures and pretend you are the person answering the question.

MODELO —Soledad, ¿cómo están los refrescos?
—¡Están buenos!

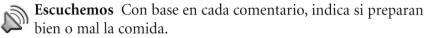

Soledad

1. Cristóbal, ¿cómo está el sándwich de queso?
2. Gloria, ¿cómo está la comida mexicana?
3. Mariano, ¿cómo está la sopa de papas?
4. Leticia, ¿cómo está el helado de chocolate?

Cristóbal

Gloria

Mariano

Leticia

4 **¿Qué necesito?** ↓1C

Escribamos Write a sentence for each photo that tells what you need to eat or to serve that food or drink.

MODELO **Para comer o servir la pizza necesito un plato y una servilleta.**

1.   2.   3.   4.   5.

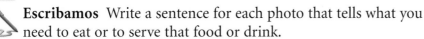

 Comunicación

5 **Comidas diferentes** ↓1C

Hablemos Work with two partners to come up with some unusual foods for a contest. Think up two foods for each category. Choose a spokesperson and present your creative food ideas to the class.

MODELO **comidas frías:**
helado de atún y...

> **TEKS Focus**
> **1C** Present information using familiar words, phrases, and sentences

| comidas frías | comidas calientes | comidas malas | comidas picantes |

6 **Comidas preferidas** ↓1A

Hablemos Take turns with your partner asking what he or she likes to eat and drink at various times of day. When you answer your partner, include the reason for your choices.

MODELO **después de clases** —**¿Qué te gusta comer/beber después de clases?**

—**Me gusta beber leche porque es buena.**

1. después de clases
2. cuando hace mucho calor
3. cuando hace frío
4. para el almuerzo los sábados

¡Exprésate!

To take someone's order	To request something
¿Qué desea usted?	**Quisiera un sándwich de queso.**
What would you (formal) like?	*I would like a cheese sandwich.*
¿Y para tomar?	**Para tomar, quiero jugo de tomate.**
And to drink?	*To drink, I want tomato juice.*
¿Desea algo de postre?	**Sí, ¿me trae un flan?**
Would you like something for dessert?	*Yes, could you bring me a flan?*
¿Algo más?	**¿Nos trae la cuenta, por favor?**
Anything else?	*Could you bring us the bill, please?*

Interactive TUTOR

Online
Vocabulario y gramática, pp. 17–19

TEKS Focus

1B Demonstrate understanding of simple, clearly spoken, and written language when dealing with familiar topics

7 ¡Camarero! 1B

Leamos Look at the drawings and match each one with what the people are probably saying to the waiter.

a. ¿Nos trae unas servilletas, por favor?

b. ¿Nos trae el menú, por favor?

c. ¿Me trae un plato limpio, por favor?

d. ¿Me trae un vaso de agua, por favor?

1.

2.

3.

4.

8 En el restaurante 🌵1C

Hablemos Ask a server politely for these items.

1.   2.   3.   4.   5.

9 ¿Cómo se dice? 🌵1C

Escribamos You are in a restaurant with a friend. Write how you would say the following in Spanish.

> **MODELO** **Ask your friend how the ham sandwich is.**
> **¿Qué tal está el sándwich de jamón?**

1. Suggest that your friend try the fruit salad.
2. Tell the server you would like a **flan.**
3. Say that the soup is a little spicy.
4. Say that the French fries are delicious.
5. Say that they make very good desserts here.
6. Ask the server to bring the bill.

Comunicación

10 ¿Qué desea usted? 🌵1A

Hablemos Imagine you are in a restaurant. You and your partner will play the roles of the server and the customer. Be sure to include the following information in your dialog.

> **MODELO** —¿Qué desea usted?
> —Quisiera...

1. what you want to eat
2. what you want to drink
3. what you think of the food
4. whether you want dessert
5. whether there's anything else you need

TEKS Focus

1A Engage in oral and written exchanges of learned material to socialize and to provide and obtain information

Video/DVD

Gramática *en acción* 1

GramaVisión

Interactive
TUTOR

Ser and estar

1 Both **ser** and **estar** mean *to be*, but they have different uses. Use **estar** to say where someone is or where something is located, and to ask and say how people are doing.

> La servilleta **está** en la mesa. **Estoy** bien, gracias.
> *The napkin is on the table.* *I'm fine, thanks.*

2 You have used **ser** to identify people and things; to say where they are from; to describe what someone or something is like; and to give the day, date, and time.

> Ricardo **es** mi amigo. **Es** de México. **Es** alto y simpático.
>
> **Es** lunes. **Es** el 2 de marzo. **Son** las cuatro en punto.

3 Both **ser** and **estar** can be used to describe foods and drinks. Use **ser** to describe what foods and drinks are normally like.

> —¿Cómo **es** el arroz con pollo? —**Es** riquísimo.
> *What is chicken and rice like?* *It's delicious.*

To say how something looks, tastes, or feels at a specific time, use **estar**.

> —¿Cómo **está** tu sopa? —**Está** fría.
> *How is your soup?* *It's cold.*

Online

Vocabulario y gramática, pp. 20–22	Actividades, pp. 15–18

Nota cultural

Corn is a food staple in many Spanish-speaking countries, but Mexico claims it as its own. The first varieties of corn were grown near the present-day capital, Mexico City, and can be seen in the National Museum of Anthropology. In Nahuatl, the language of the Aztecs, one word for corn was **elotl** *(eh'-lotl)*, which became **elote** in Mexican Spanish. What traditional dishes in the United States use corn as a staple ingredient? ↓2B, 4C

TEKS Focus
4C Demonstrate understanding of the influence of one language and culture on another

11 **¿Cómo son? ¿Cómo están?** ↓1B

Leamos Decide if these people are talking:

a) about the characteristics of a dish, or

b) about the flavor at a specific moment.

1. La sopa de verduras es buena para ti.
2. ¡Ay! ¡Qué caliente está la sopa!
3. Me gusta el flan de la tía Elena. Está rico.
4. No me gusta el atún. Es muy salado.
5. Preparan muy bien la salsa aquí. Está deliciosa, ¿verdad?
6. No nos gusta la salsa. Es muy picante.
7. ¿Quieres probar mi sándwich? Está rico.

Gramática 1

12 ¿Ser o estar? ⬇1B

Leamos/Escribamos Your new pen pal, Carla, has just written to you. Complete the letter with the correct form of the verb in parentheses. Then tell why **ser** or **estar** is used in each item.

> Hola. ¿Cómo ___1___ (eres/estás)? ___2___ (Soy/Estoy) Carla.
> ___3___ (Soy/Estoy) de Chicago. Y tú, ¿de dónde ___4___ (eres/estás)? Hoy ___5___ (es/está) lunes. ___6___ (Son/Están) las diez de la mañana y mis compañeros y yo ___7___ (somos/estamos) en la clase de español. La profesora ___8___ (es/está) la señora Gámez. La clase de español ___9___ (es/está) un poco difícil, pero me gusta.

13 ¿Cómo estás tú? ⬇1C

Escribamos Now write to Carla, answering her questions. Also, tell her about your day, using **ser** and **estar** correctly.

14 ¿Qué tal está...? ⬇1C

Hablemos Imagine you are in a restaurant. The server asks you how the food is. Answer, imagining the flavor of each dish.

MODELO —¿Qué tal la sopa de verduras?
—La sopa de verduras está muy rica.

1.

2.

3.

4.

5.

6.

Comunicación

15 ¿Te gustan? ⬇1A

Hablemos Choose five foods. Take turns with a partner asking each other if you like each of the foods.

MODELO —¿Te gustan los sándwiches de atún?
—Sí, me gustan mucho. Son deliciosos.

> **TEKS Focus** ⬎
> **1A** Engage in oral and written exchanges of learned material to socialize and to provide and obtain information

Interactive
TUTOR

Pedir and servir

1 In some **-ir** verbs with an **e** in the stem, this **e** changes to **i** in all the present-tense forms except those of **nosotros(as)** and **vosotros(as)**. Two such verbs are **pedir** *(to ask for, to order)* and **servir** *(to serve).*

yo **pi**do	nosotros(as) pedimos
tú **pi**des	vosotros(as) pedís
Ud., él, ella **pi**de	Uds., ellos, ellas **pi**den

—¿Qué vas a **pedir**?
What are you going to order?

—Siempre **pido** una ensalada.
I always order a salad.

yo **si**rvo	nosotros(as) servimos
tú **si**rves	vosotros(as) servís
Ud., él, ella **si**rve	Uds., ellos, ellas **si**rven

—¿Qué **sirven** en la cafetería?
What do they serve in the cafeteria?

—**Sirven** muchas comidas diferentes.
They serve many different foods.

Online

Vocabulario y gramática, pp. 20–22	Actividades, pp. 15–18

¿Te acuerdas?

Stem-changing verbs like **dormir** and **querer** do not change in the **nosotros(as)** and **vosotros(as)** forms.

d**ue**rmo	dormimos
d**ue**rmes	dormís
d**ue**rme	d**ue**rmen

qu**ie**ro	queremos
qu**ie**res	queréis
qu**ie**re	qu**ie**ren

16 **¿De quién habla?** 1B

 Escuchemos En cada oración, decide si la persona habla...
a. de ella misma *(herself)*
b. de otras personas y ella misma
c. de otras personas
d. de otra persona

17 **¿Qué pedimos?** 1B

Escribamos Write sentences that tell what these people might order in each situation.

MODELO **Para beber cuando hace mucho frío...**
(yo) Pido chocolate.

Para beber cuando hace mucho calor...

1. yo
2. mis amigos
3. mi familia y yo
4. mi mejor amigo(a)

Para almorzar cuando todos tenemos mucha hambre...

5. yo
6. mi mejor amigo(a)
7. mis padres
8. mis amigos y yo

18 ¿Qué servimos? ↓1C

Hablemos Carlos is telling a friend what these people serve at parties. What is he saying? Use the correct form of the verb **servir** in your answers.

MODELO nosotros

Siempre servimos helado.

1. yo

2. tú

3. tus amigos y tú

4. mi hermano y yo

5. mis amigos

6. mi madre

19 ¿Servir o pedir? ↓1B

Escribamos/Hablemos Completa las preguntas con la forma correcta de **pedir** o **servir**.

1. En un restaurante, ¿ ===== (pedir/tú) una ensalada o un sándwich?
2. ¿Qué refresco generalmente ===== (pedir) usted?
3. ¿Qué ===== (servir/ellos) en tu restaurante preferido?
4. ¿Qué ===== (servir/tú) en una fiesta?
5. ¿Qué ===== (pedir) tus padres en un restaurante mexicano?
6. ¿Quién ===== (servir) la cena *(dinner)* en tu casa?
7. ¿Qué tipo de sándwich ===== (pedir) tu amigo(a)?

TEKS Focus

1A Engage in oral and written exchanges of learned material to socialize and to provide and obtain information

Comunicación

20 Una entrevista ↓1A, 1B

Hablemos Use the questions in Activity 19 to interview your partner. Then let your partner ask you the questions.

TUTOR

Preferir, poder, and probar

1 The verb **preferir** has an **e → ie** stem change. It can be followed by a noun to say what someone *prefers* or by an **infinitive** to say what someone *would rather do* or *prefers to do*.

yo pref**ie**ro	nosotros(as) preferimos
tú pref**ie**res	vosotros(as) preferís
Ud., él, ella pref**ie**re	Uds., ellos, ellas pref**ie**ren

¿**Prefieres** jugo o leche en el almuerzo?

¿**Prefieres salir** o **ver** televisión?

2 The verbs **poder** and **probar** have an **o → ue** stem change. **Poder** is normally followed by an **infinitive** to say what someone *may, is able to,* or *can do.* **Probar** means *to try* something, as in *to taste.*

yo p**ue**do	nosotros(as) podemos
tú p**ue**des	vosotros(as) podéis
Ud., él, ella p**ue**de	Uds., ellos, ellas p**ue**den

¿Nos **puede traer** otra silla?   *Can you bring us another chair?*

yo pr**ue**bo	nosotros(as) probamos
tú pr**ue**bas	vosotros(as) probáis
Ud., él, ella pr**ue**ba	Uds., ellos, ellas pr**ue**ban

¿Qué tal si **pruebas** la sopa?   *How about trying the soup?*

Online

Vocabulario y gramática, pp. 20–22	Actividades, pp. 15–18

TEKS Focus

1B Demonstrate understanding of simple, clearly spoken, and written language when dealing with familiar topics

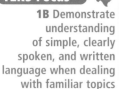

¿Te acuerdas?

Tener and **dormir** are also stem-changing verbs.

Ella t**ie**ne 16 años.
Tú d**ue**rmes mucho.

The **nosotros** and **vosotros** forms do not have stem changes.

T**e**néis un perro bonito.
D**o**rmimos más los sábados.

21 **Preferir, poder o probar** ⬇ **1B**

Escribamos Complete each sentence with the correct form of the verb in parentheses. Then write your own sentence using that same verb and the subject in parentheses.

MODELO Mi tío no ═══ (poder) comer el flan. (nosotros)
Mi tío no puede comer el flan.
No podemos comer las hamburguesas.

1. Analisa ═══ (preferir) el flan más que el helado. (mis amigos)
2. Yo siempre ═══ (probar) la sopa cuando ═══ (comer) en restaurantes. (mis amigos y yo)
3. Mi abuela no ═══ (poder) comer salsa picante. (mis padres)
4. Nosotros ═══ (preferir) almorzar en la cafetería. (usted)
5. Mis hermanas nunca ═══ (probar) los postres. No les gustan. (yo)

Gramática 1

22 ¿Qué prueban? ⬇1C

Escribamos/Hablemos Based on what these people like, say what dish they always try when they go to a new restaurant.

MODELO A Lucinda le gustan los postres. Ella...
Ella siempre prueba el flan.

1. A Andrés le gusta el atún. Él...
2. A ustedes les gusta el postre. Ustedes...
3. A Linda y a Jorge les gusta el jamón. Ellos...
4. A Elsa y a mí nos gustan las frutas. Nosotras...
5. Lucinda, a ti te gustan las verduras. Tú...
6. A mí me gustan el queso y la salsa de tomate. Yo...

23 Rompecabezas ⬇1B, 1C

Escribamos Usa una palabra o expresión de cada columna para escribir seis oraciones.

MODELO Prefiero tomar jugo.

1	**2**	**3**
yo	preferir	la cuenta
mi mejor amigo(a)	servir	tomar jugo o leche
tú	pedir	una sopa de...
mis compañeros	querer	comida italiana
el (la) profesor(a)	probar	una ensalada de...
mis amigos y yo		algo de postre

Probando platos en un restaurante, Ciudad de México

Comunicación

24 ¿Qué prefieres hacer? ⬇1A

Escribamos/Hablemos Write what you like to do at each of the indicated times. Then ask three classmates what they like to do. Try to find someone who likes the same things that you like.

MODELO —¿Qué prefieres hacer los viernes por la noche?
—Prefiero... ¿Y tú?

1. los jueves por la noche
2. los sábados por la tarde
3. los sábados por la mañana
4. los domingos por la mañana
5. los domingos por la noche
6. los martes por la tarde
7. los miércoles por la noche
8. los lunes por la mañana

Cultura

VideoCultura

 Comparaciones

Platos típicos mexicanos

¿Cuál es tu plato preferido y cómo es? ✦ 2B, 4B

«A buena hambre no hay mal pan» dice el refrán, y ¿qué mejor pan que un plato que nos encanta? Todos tenemos un plato preferido que no sólo es delicioso sino que muchas veces nos hace recordar a nuestra familia, nuestro país de origen y nuestras costumbres. En Estados Unidos, ¿qué platos son regionales o nacionales? ¿Son éstos algunos de tus platos preferidos? ¿Qué crees que son algunos platos preferidos de jóvenes en otros países?

Angélica
Ciudad de México, México

Angélica describes her favorite dish and how it is made. Are any of your favorite dishes similar to the ones Angélica describes?

Dime, ¿cuáles son dos o tres platos típicos de México?

Bueno, está el mole, el pozole y los chiles en nogada.

¿Cuál es tu plato favorito?

Los chiles en nogada.

Dime cómo es.

Son muy ricos porque además de ser picantes, también son dulces.

¿Qué llevan?

Bueno, tiene el chile poblano, la carne molida, pasitas, acitrón,

crema, nueces y un poquito de granada.

¿Es un plato típico de la región donde vives?

Claro, en el Distrito Federal se consume mucho.

Muchas gracias, Angélica.

No hay de qué, al contrario.

Estados Unidos

MÉXICO   Golfo de México

Ciudad de México ★

Océano Pacífico

TEKS Focus

4B Demonstrate understanding of the concept of culture through comparisons

Paula
Santo Domingo, República Dominicana

Paula describes typical Dominican dishes. Are any typical dishes from where you live similar to Dominican dishes?

Dime, ¿cuáles son unos platos típicos en la República Dominicana?

El plato más típico de la República Dominicana es el arroz con habichuela y carne, que puede ser de res o pollo.

¿Cuál es tu plato favorito?

El moro de guandules con pescado.

¿Me puedes decir cómo es?

El moro de guandules es una mezcla de guandules con arroz y un poco de salsa para el color. Y el pescado se hace con el limón y sal y ajo.

¿Es un plato típico de tu región?

Sí, es muy típico.

Muchas gracias, Paula.

Gracias a ti.

REPÚBLICA DOMINICANA
Océano Atlántico
★ Santo Domingo

Cultura

Para comprender ↓1B

1. ¿Qué plato se come mucho en el Distrito Federal?
2. ¿Cómo es el plato preferido de Paula?
3. ¿Cuáles son tres platos típicos de México?
4. ¿Cómo son los chiles en nogada?
5. ¿Qué se come con el arroz con habichuelas?
6. ¿Cuál es el plato más típico de la República Dominicana?

Para pensar y hablar ↓4B

Angélica and Paula tell us about their favorite dishes, both of which are typical of their countries. How are their favorite dishes different? Do they seem simple to make or do they seem rather complicated? Are there foods unique to where you live? What are they?

Cuaderno para hispanohablantes, pp. 45–52

Texas

Comunidad ↓2B, 5B

All around Texas there are plenty of opportunities to eat Mexican and Tex-Mex food, but especially so in the open-air markets along the border. There you can ask for an **horchata mexicana,** a sweet drink made with rice, water, cinnamon, and sugar. Also all over Texas, many Mexicans and Mexican Americans make **tamales**—a traditional dish prepared with corn, a meat or bean filling, wrapped in corn husks, and then steamed. The preparation is quite a holiday event! Research some traditional foods from your city or area of Texas to find out if these foods are associated with a holiday or a celebration.

Vendedor de frutas, Ciudad Juárez

Vocabulario
en acción 2

ExpresaVisión

El desayuno en casa

los cereales

el durazno

el chocolate

la naranja

la manzana

el café con leche

el pan dulce

el pan tostado

el tocino

los huevos

Texas | **También se puede decir...**

In Central and South America, as well as in Spain, **un melocotón** is used instead of **un durazno**.

In some parts of Texas, Mexico, and Central America, speakers refer to an egg as **un blanquillo**.

Vocabulario 2

¿Qué hay de cena?

el pollo

la carne

el maíz

las zanahorias

el bróculi

las espinacas

el pastel

Texas **También se puede decir...**

For many Spanish speakers, *corn on the cob* is **la mazorca.** In Texas, Mexico, and Central America, it is **el elote.** In Andean countries, such as Bolivia and Ecuador, it is called **el choclo.**

¡Exprésate!

To talk about meals

Interactive TUTOR

¿Qué desayunas?	**Siempre desayuno cereales con leche.**
What do you have for breakfast?	*I always have cereal with milk for breakfast.*
¿Qué quieres hoy de almuerzo?	**¿Qué tal si almorzamos ensalada de pollo?**
What do you want for lunch today?	*How about we have chicken salad for lunch?*
¿Qué hay de cena? Tengo mucha hambre.	**Vamos a cenar pescado, arroz y espinacas.**
What is there for dinner? I'm very hungry.	*We're going to have fish, rice, and spinach for dinner.*

Online
Vocabulario y gramática,
pp. 23–25

▶ **Vocabulario adicional — Comida, p.R7**

TEKS Focus

2A Demonstrate understanding of practices (what people do) and how they relate to perspectives (how people perceive things) of the cultures studied

⚜Restaurante don José⚜

～ PLATOS DEL DÍA ～
Ensalada de atún
Arroz con pollo
Tacos de pollo
Sopa de pescado
Tacos de verduras

～ BEBIDAS ～
Refrescos
Jugos
(de manzana, de naranja, de zanahoria)

～ POSTRES ～
Pastel de chocolate
Helado de mango

25 Tengo mucha hambre ↓1B

Leamos Completa las oraciones con las palabras más lógicas.

1. ¿Qué hay de ═══ ? Tengo mucha hambre.
   a. tomar   b. cena   c. pastel
2. Hoy vamos a almorzar ═══.
   a. cereales   b. pan dulce   c. pollo
3. No me gustan los postres. Voy a comer ═══.
   a. flan   b. pastel   c. un durazno
4. Ricardo siempre desayuna cereales con ═══.
   a. leche   b. zanahorias   c. arroz
5. Me encantan las verduras. Siempre como muchas ═══.
   a. naranjas   b. espinacas   c. manzanas
6. No me gusta el ═══. Es muy salado.
   a. tocino   b. pastel   c. durazno

26 ¿Desayuno o cena? ↓1B

Hablemos Which of these foods do you eat for breakfast and which ones do you eat for dinner?

MODELO los huevos
         Como los huevos para el desayuno.

1. el tocino   6. el pan tostado
2. el pescado   7. el maíz
3. las espinacas   8. el brócoli
4. las zanahorias   9. el café con leche
5. el arroz con pollo 10. los cereales con leche

27 En el restaurante ↓1B

Leamos/Escribamos Suggest something for each of the following people from the menu at **Restaurante don José.**

MODELO **A Alicia le gustan los postres.**
         Alicia, ¿qué tal si pruebas el pastel?

1. Juana quiere probar comida mexicana.
2. De postre, Julio prefiere comer algo muy frío.
3. De tomar, Elena y su amigo quieren un jugo.
4. A Manolo y a mí nos gusta el pollo.
5. Carmen nunca pide carne.
6. A Julio le gusta el pescado.
7. Tere siempre pide algo con chocolate para el postre.
8. Pablo y María quieren cenar pero no pueden comer la carne.
9. Eduardo tiene mucha hambre. Quiere una cena grande.

28 Tienen hambre ⬇1C

✏ **Escribamos** Write two sentences about each drawing. Identify what meal the people are eating, at what time they eat, and what they like to eat.

8:00

13:00

19:00

29 Y yo como... ⬇1C

✏ **Escribamos** Write a paragraph comparing and contrasting what you eat and what time you eat with the meal times of the people pictured in Activity 28.

  Comunicación

30 ¿Qué comes tú? ⬇1A

👥 **Hablemos** Work with a partner. Take turns asking and answering the following questions.

1. ¿Qué desayunas?
2. ¿Dónde almuerzas?
3. ¿A qué hora cenas?
4. ¿Qué vas a cenar esta noche?
5. ¿Te gustan las comidas picantes?
6. ¿Cuál es tu jugo preferido?

31 ¿Qué van a pedir? ⬇1A, 1C

👥 **Hablemos/Escribamos** Imagine that you are going on an all-day fieldtrip. A local restaurant is going to cater breakfast, lunch, and dinner for the trip. With a group of classmates, make a menu that shows what the restaurant will offer for each meal. Then ask two members of your group what they are going to order. (**¿Qué vas a pedir?**) Be prepared to role-play a scene where you order meals, pretend to eat the meal, and comment on the food.

> **TEKS Focus**
> **1C** Present information using familiar words, phrases, and sentences

¡Exprésate!

To offer help	To give instructions	
¿Necesitas ayuda? *Do you need help?*	**Sí, saca el pollo y ponlo en el horno (el microondas).** *Yes, get out the chicken and put it in the oven (the microwave).*	**Interactive TUTOR**
¿Puedo ayudar? *Can I help?*	**Saca el flan del refrigerador.** *Take the flan out of the refrigerator.* **¿Por qué no preparas los sándwiches?** *Why don't you make the sandwiches?*	
¿Pongo la mesa? *Shall I set the table?*	**Sí, ponla, por favor.** *Yes, set it, please.*	**Online** Vocabulario y gramática, pp. 23–25

32 ¿En qué puedo ayudar? ⬇1B

Escuchemos Mira las fotos y escucha la conversación entre Patricia y su madre. Decide qué parte del diálogo corresponde a cada foto.

33 La cena ⬇1B

Leamos Marlena and her mother are talking about how she can help with the dinner preparations. For each of Marlena's questions, choose her mother's probable response.

MARLENA

1. ¿Necesitas ayuda, mamá?
2. ¿Saco las frutas del refrigerador?
3. ¿Necesitas un plato hondo?
4. ¿Pongo el pollo en el horno?
5. ¿Pongo la mesa en la cocina?
6. ¿Necesito poner cuchillos?
7. ¿Puedo ayudar con el postre?

LA MADRE

a. Sí, ponlo en el horno.
b. Sí, ¿por qué no preparas el flan?
c. Sí, hija, necesito ayuda.
d. Sí, pon los cuchillos.
e. No, ponla en el comedor, por favor.
f. Sí, me trae un plato hondo.
g. Sí, saca las frutas, por favor.

34 Mucha ayuda ♦1B

Leamos Read the questions and match them with a picture.

1. ¿Necesitas ayuda con tus hermanos?
2. ¿Por qué no sacas más leche del refrigerador?
3. Hijo, ¿me traes el libro, por favor?
4. ¿Puedo ayudar con la tarea?

35 ¿Cómo te ayudo? ♦1B

Escribamos Write this conversation between Rita and José who are preparing a special breakfast for their mother's birthday.

tocino	refrigerador	duraznos	saca
ponla	pongo	ayudar	preparas

JOSÉ   ¿Puedo ═══ con el desayuno?

RITA   Sí, ¿por qué no ═══ el pan tostado?

JOSÉ   Bueno. ¿Saco el jugo de naranja del ═══, también?

RITA   Sí, ═══ el jugo, y ponlo en la mesa.

JOSÉ   ¿Preparas huevos y ═══, también?

RITA   No, mamá prefiere cereales con ═══.

JOSÉ   ¿═══ la mesa en la cocina?

RITA   No, ═══ en el patio, porque hace buen tiempo.

Comunicación

36 Sí, por favor ♦1A, 1C

Escribamos/Hablemos With a partner, write a dialog between a child and parent getting ready to serve a meal. Then take turns with another pair of classmates role-playing your dialogs. You can say . . .

¿Cómo puedo ayudar?   ¿Por qué no me ayudas con...?

¿Pongo...?   Pon..., por favor.

¿Saco... del refrigerador?   Sí, saca... del refrigerador.

TEKS Focus

1A Engage in oral and written exchanges of learned material to socialize and to provide and obtain information

Gramática en acción 2

GramaVisión

Interactive TUTOR

Direct objects and direct object pronouns

1 Verbs can be followed by **direct objects**, the person or thing receiving the action of the verb.

Rafaela pone **la mesa**.   Siempre pido **la sopa**.

2 A **direct object** can be a noun or a pronoun. Use **direct object pronouns** to avoid repeating nouns that have already been mentioned. These pronouns must agree with the nouns they stand for.

	Masculine	**Feminine**
SINGULAR	**lo** *him, it*	**la** *her, it*
PLURAL	**los** *them*	**las** *them*

—¿Quién va a pedir **el flan**?   —Yo **lo** voy a pedir.

3 **Direct object pronouns** go before the conjugated verb. If there is an infinitive in the sentence, the pronouns go before the conjugated verb or are attached to the end of the infinitive.

—¿Quién prepara **los sándwiches**?   —Yo **los** preparo.

—¿Quién va a preparar **la cena**?   —Mi padre **la** va a preparar.

        —Mi padre va a preparar**la**.

Online

| Vocabulario y gramática, pp. 26–28 | Actividades, pp. 19–22 |

¿Te acuerdas?

Pronouns take the place of nouns. They have different forms depending on how they're being used in the sentence.

Ana es mi amiga. **Ella** es muy simpática. **La** llamo por teléfono todos los días.

37 **¿Qué comes?** ⬇1B

Leamos/Escribamos Answer the questions, using the correct direct object pronoun.

1. —¿Desayunas huevos por la mañana?
   —Sí, ===== desayuno todos los días.

2. —¿Pides tocino con los huevos?
   —No, nunca ===== pido.

3. —¿Tomas leche en el desayuno?
   —No, nunca ===== tomo.

4. —¿Comes naranjas por la mañana?
   —Sí, siempre ===== como.

38 **¿A quién le tocan los quehaceres?** ↓1B, 1C

Escribamos Who does the following chores at your house. Use the correct direct object pronoun in your answers.

MODELO ¿Quién prepara la cena?
Yo la preparo. (Mi hermano la prepara.)

1. ¿Quién limpia la casa?
2. ¿Quién pone la mesa?
3. ¿Quién corta el césped?
4. ¿Quién hace las camas?
5. ¿Quién sirve el desayuno?
6. ¿Quién arregla los cuartos?
7. ¿Quién saca la basura?
8. ¿Quién pasa la aspiradora?

Visit Holt Online

go.hrw.com
KEYWORD: EXP1B CH6
Gramática 2 practice

Gramática 2

39 **¿Qué van a traer?** ↓1B

Escribamos Write a sentence telling who is going to bring the following foods and drinks to the Spanish Club party.

MODELO flan
Yo lo voy a traer. (Yo voy a traerlo.)

1. La profesora
2. Miguel
3. Tomás y Raquel
4. Elsa y yo
5. Tú

 Comunicación

40 **¿Cuándo lo hacemos?** ↓1A, 1C

Hablemos/Escribamos Make a chart like the one pictured. Then in small groups, take turns asking and answering each other about how frequently you do the following things. Use direct object pronouns in your answers.

MODELO preparar tu almuerzo
—¿Cón qué frecuencia preparas tu almuerzo?
—Lo preparo a veces.

TEKS Focus
1C Present information using familiar words, phrases, and sentences

1. preparar el desayuno
2. beber refrescos
3. comer pizza
4. comprar el almuerzo en la cafetería
5. poner la mesa
6. almorzar hamburguesas y papas fritas

todos los días	a veces	nunca

Affirmative informal commands

1 To tell someone you address as **tú** to do something, use an **affirmative informal command**.

2 To form the affirmative informal command of regular or stem-changing verb, just drop the final **s** off the end of the **tú** form of the verb.

(tú) hablas→	**habla**	you speak→	speak
(tú) comes→	**come**	you eat→	eat
(tú) pides→	**pide**	you ask (for)→	ask (for)

Pide un sándwich de pollo.   *Order a chicken sandwich.*

3 Some verbs have irregular affirmative informal command forms.

tener→ **ten** *(have)*   ir→ **ve** *(go)*   hacer→ **haz** *(do, make)*
venir→ **ven** *(come)*   ser→ **sé** *(be)*   salir→ **sal** *(go out, leave)*
poner→ **pon** *(put)*

4 Here are some verbs you might use to ask someone to help you in the kitchen. They all have regular command forms. Note that **calentar** is an **e → ie** stem-changing verb.

abrir *to open*   calentar (ie) *to heat up*   mezclar *to mix*
añadir *to add*   cortar *to cut*   sacar *to take out*

Corta las zanahorias, por favor.   *Cut the carrots, please.*
Calienta el chocolate.   *Heat the chocolate.*

Online
| Vocabulario y gramática, pp. 26–28 | Actividades, pp. 19–22 |

La ensalada de frutas ⬇1B

Leamos/Escribamos Graciela is helping her brother prepare a fruit salad. Complete each sentence with the correct informal command. Then reorder the sentences logically.

1. (Servir) ===== la ensalada fría.
2. (Lavar) ===== las frutas.
3. (Probar) ===== la ensalada para ver qué tal está.
4. (Añadir) ===== un poco de azúcar *(sugar)* a la mezcla de frutas y jugo de naranja.
5. (Cortar) ===== las frutas en trozos *(pieces)* con el cuchillo.
6. (Poner) ===== los trozos en un plato hondo.
7. (Tener) ===== cuidado con el cuchillo.
8. (Mezclar) ===== las frutas con un poco de jugo de naranja.

Nota cultural

In Mexico many people buy snacks like cucumbers or roasted corn with chile powder, mango, pineapple, or watermelon from street vendors. For their afternoon snack, Argentines, Uruguayans, Chileans, and Colombians meet in tearooms to drink tea or coffee and eat sandwiches or pastries. Spaniards have a **merienda** around 6:00 P.M., a small snack such as **chocolate** and **churros** or **pan.** Compare your snacks to those in Spanish-speaking countries. Do you have a snack with your friends or family at a particular time? What do you eat? ⬇**2A, 4B**

TEKS Focus

2A Demonstrate understanding of practices (what people do) and how they relate to perspectives (how people perceive things) of the cultures studied

42 ¡Sé buena estudiante! ↓1B

Escribamos Your friend wants to improve her grades. Tell her what she needs to do.

> **MODELO** estudiar mucho
> **Estudia mucho.**

1. hacer la tarea
2. ir a clase todos los días
3. salir temprano para el colegio
4. escuchar bien en clase
5. trabajar en clase
6. venir conmigo a la biblioteca
7. ser trabajadora
8. tener los útiles contigo

Comunicación

43 Necesito ayuda ↓1C

Hablemos Your parents need help with the chores. With a partner, take turns saying what needs to be done. Use **tú** commands.

> **MODELO** **Lava los platos.**

TEKS Focus

1C Present information using familiar words, phrases, and sentences

1.

2.

3.

4.

5.

6.

44 Te toca a ti ↓1C

Hablemos Imagine that you and your partner are doing each other's chores. Take turns giving each other instructions, using **tú** commands.

> **MODELO** —Lava el carro.
> —Saca la basura.

Gramática 2

Affirmative informal commands with pronouns

Interactive TUTOR

1 You know that the **direct object pronoun** goes immediately before the conjugated verb. It can also be attached to the end of an infinitive.

—¿Siempre preparas **la cena**?

—No, no **la** preparo siempre, pero hoy sí voy a preparar**la**.

2 When you use a pronoun with an affirmative informal command, attach it to the end of the verb. Then add an accent to the stressed vowel of the verb, unless the verb is only one syllable long.

—¿Preparo **la carne**? — Sí, prepára**la**.

—¿Pongo **los vasos** en la mesa? — Sí, pon**los** allí.

> **Online**
>
> | Vocabulario y gramática, pp. 26–28 | Actividades, pp. 19–22 |

Texas

Nota cultural

Barbecue (from the Taíno word *barbacuá*) is one of the most traditional foods of Texas. One way of preparing barbecue is to grill it outdoors over a fire made with chunks of mesquite or other aromatic wood. Mexican Americans normally serve **barbacoa** with jalapeños, salsa, beans, and tortillas. What other traditional foods are popular in Texas? ↓**2B, 4C**

TEKS Focus ↓

2B Demonstrate understanding of products (what people create) and how they relate to perspectives (how people perceive things) of the cultures studied

---

45 ¿De qué hablas? ↓**1B**

Leamos Identify the direct object pronoun in each sentence. Then decide which item it refers to.

1. Ponlo en el refrigerador.
   a. el queso b. la leche c. el libro
2. Sácala del horno.
   a. la basura b. el tocino c. la pizza
3. Ábrelo otra vez.
   a. el durazno b. el refrigerador c. la aspiradora
4. Córtalas con el cuchillo.
   a. las zanahorias b. las servilletas c. la manzana
5. Sírvela en el plato hondo.
   a. los cereales b. la sopa c. los refrescos
6. Mézclalo con el bróculi.
   a. el queso b. el flan c. los huevos
7. Mézclalos en el plato hondo.
   a. los huevos b. las naranjas c. los tenedores

46 Ponlas aquí. ↓**1B**

Hablemos A friend is helping you move. Tell him where to put these things.

MODELO **el refrigerador**
Ponlo en la cocina.

1. la cama
2. la televisión
3. la comida
4. los vasos
5. el microondas
6. los libros
7. los videojuegos
8. las sillas
9. la mesa

47 **¿Qué hago?** 1B

 Escuchemos Escucha las preguntas de Nuria y escoge la respuesta más lógica para cada una.

a. Caliéntalo en el horno.

b. Sácalos del refrigerador y ponlos en la mesa.

c. No, todavía no. Ponla con las otras bebidas.

d. Sí, ponlas a calentar en el microondas.

e. Córtalas y mézclalas en un plato hondo.

48 **El amigo desesperado** 1B

Escribamos Your friend wants to prepare supper for his parents, but he doesn't know how to cook! Answer his questions, using **tú** commands and direct object pronouns.

1. ¿Caliento la sopa antes de preparar el pollo o después?

2. ¿Pongo las servilletas al lado de o encima de los platos?

3. ¿Saco el flan del refrigerador antes de comer o después?

4. ¿Mezclo el café con leche o con agua?

5. ¿Preparo el pollo con zanahorias o con espinacas?

6. ¿Sirvo el helado con la comida o con el postre?

7. ¿Pruebo la ensalada antes de añadir el atún o después?

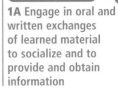

TEKS Focus
1A Engage in oral and written exchanges of learned material to socialize and to provide and obtain information

Comunicación

49 **¡Arregla la casa!** 1A

Hablemos With a partner, take turns playing the roles of señor Gonzaga and his daughter. She asks what she should do in each picture, and he answers, using **tú** commands.

MODELO —Papá, ¿qué hago primero?
　　　　　—¡Lava los platos!

 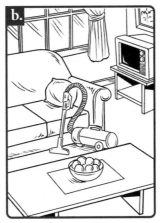 

Conexiones culturales

Bienvenido al nuevo mundo de comida Some believe that the New World's most important gift to Europe was not gold, silver, or jewels, but food. In the 1400's, Europeans were used to a bland diet with little variety. After the Spaniards brought back fruits and vegetables from the Americas, the eating habits of Europeans changed forever. The Spaniards, in turn, brought the first cattle, sheep, pigs, and chickens to the Americas.

NUEVO MUNDO

blueberries
chili peppers
cacao
corn
cranberries
pecans
pinto beans
potatoes
pumpkins
squash
string beans
sunflowers
tomatoes
turkeys

VIEJO MUNDO

apples
chickens
cattle
grapes
lemons
lettuce
limes
mangoes
oranges
pigs
sheep
wheat

Conexiones Culturales

1 El día de acción de gracias ↓2B

Below are some foods you might find at a typical Thanksgiving meal. Based on the maps and information on page 70, which of these foods in boldface come from the "Old World" and which from the Americas?

roast **turkey**   **pecan** pie   **cranberry** sauce

orange ambrosia   **apple** pie   string **beans**   **ham**

bread   **pumpkin** pie   **corn**   mashed **potatoes**

Conexión Economía doméstica

TEKS Focus

3B Use the language to obtain, reinforce, or expand knowledge of other subject areas

Tostadas El origen del maíz The cultivation of corn was developed by the Maya in what is now Mexico. Corn tortillas, made from ground corn flour, were central to the daily diet of the Maya.

2 ¿De dónde son? ↓1B, 3B

¿Cuáles de los ingredientes para las tostadas son originalmente de Europa y cuáles son de las Américas?

Tostadas

24 tostadas
1/2 kg de frijoles refritos
1 kg de queso
8 chiles

2 kg de pollo cocido
2 cabezas de lechuga
4 tomates

Procedimiento. Pon los frijoles, el queso, los chiles y el pollo encima de las tostadas. Entonces, pon las tostadas en el horno a 400° F por tres minutos. Ponles la lechuga y los tomates.

3 ¿Cuánto necesito? ↓2A, 3B

Convert the kilogram measurements for refried beans, cheese, and chicken to pounds using the conversion formula. For example, if a recipe called for 3 kilograms (kg) of flour, then you would multiply 2.2 x 3 to find out you need 6.6 lbs. of flour.

Conversions
1 kilogram (kg) =
2.2 pounds (lbs.)

¿Quién será?

Episodio 6

⬇1B, 3A

E S T R A T E G I A

Recognizing a make-believe situation In order to understand this episode, it
is helpful to recognize that certain parts are make-believe. With the help of her little brother, a
little imagination, and the cooperation of her parents, Sofía turns an ordinary event into a more
interesting experience. As you read the **Novela** or watch the video, figure out which parts are
make-believe and then see what problem Sofía's make-believe situation creates for her.

En México

*Sofía va a casa a preparar la cena.
Marcos la mira para ver adónde va.*

Quique Sofía, ¡es tarde! Mamá y papá están
por llegar.
Sofía Ya sé, Quique.
Quique ¿Y la cena?
Sofía No te preocupes, Quique. No es tu problema.
Yo la voy a preparar.

Novela en video

3

Quique ¿En qué puedo ayudar? ¿Pongo la mesa?

Sofía Sí, ponla.

Quique ¿Y los menús?

Sofía Ponlos en el comedor.

4

Sofía Señor y señora Corona. Bienvenidos al *Restaurante Sofía*. Veo aquí que tienen reservación para dos personas a las ocho en punto.

Sr. Corona Sí, señorita.

5

Sra. Corona Señorita, ¿nos puede traer los menús, por favor?

Quique Aquí están los menús, señora, señor.

Sr. Corona ¿Cómo están los tamales oaxaqueños hoy?

Sofía Riquísimos, señor, pero, malas noticias, no quedan tamales oaxaqueños.

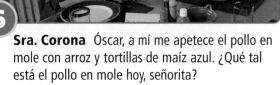

6

Sra. Corona Óscar, a mí me apetece el pollo en mole con arroz y tortillas de maíz azul. ¿Qué tal está el pollo en mole hoy, señorita?

Sofía No lo recomiendo, señora. Está un poco salado.

A **CONTESTA**

Check your understanding of the **Novela** by answering these questions.

1. Why is Sofía hurrying home after ballet class?

2. Why did Quique make menus?

3. What special occasion is being celebrated?

4. What foods do her parents ask about?

7

Sr. Corona Y ¿el bistec, señorita? Aquí dice que viene con puré de papa y unas zanahorias.

Sofía Sí, señor, excelente decisión, el bistec es delicioso, pero… lo siento mucho. No sirvo bistecs los viernes.

8

Un poco más tarde.

9

Sra. Corona Pues, dígame, señorita, ¿cuál es la especialidad de la casa?

Sofía La especialidad de la casa son ¡LAS FLAUTAS! Y si no le importa, señor, aquí tiene la cuenta. ¿Me la puede pagar ahora?

En España

La profesora decide adónde va Marcos ahora.

10

Estados Unidos

MÉXICO   Golfo de México

Ciudad de México ★

Océano Pacífico

Chile

Buenos Aires ★ **ARGENTINA**

Océano Atlántico

B CONTESTA

1. What is the house specialty?
2. Where is Marcos in this episode?
3. Where is he going next?
4. Why do you think he is going there?

Actividades

1 El menú de Quique

Match the food from the menu with the best description.

1. El pollo en mole
2. las flautas
3. el bistec con papas
4. los tamales oaxaqueños

a. not available on Fridays
b. it's a little salty
c. they are all gone
d. the house specialty

2 ¿Quién lo diría?

According to the **Novela**, who would most likely say each of the following things?

1. Pon los menús en el comedor.
2. Me gusta el pollo en mole.
3. ¡Bienvenidos a mi restaurante!
4. Aquí tienen ustedes los menús, señores.
5. Ahora vas a Argentina.

3 ¿Comprendes la Novela?

Check your understanding of the events in the story by answering these questions.

1. What is the make-believe situation in this episode?
2. What role does Quique play in the make-believe situation?
3. What excuses does Sofía offer for the foods they order? Why?
4. Why does she finally offer them **las flautas**? Do you think she made them herself? Why or why not?

> **Próximo episodio**
> *Marcos leaves to go to another country. How many more countries does he have to visit?*
> PÁGINAS 114–117 ▶

Leamos y escribamos

TEKS Focus

3A Use resources in the language and cultures being studied to gain access to information

ESTRATEGIA

para leer The *genre* of a reading tells you what kind of writing to expect. Some examples of different genres are legend, short story, novel, poem, essay, and play. Knowing the genre of a text will help you predict what it's about.

A Antes de leer ↓ 3A, 3B

The following is a version of a legend about Quetzalcoatl, a god of the Aztec, Maya, and other cultures in Mexico and Central America. Before reading it, write a list of the characteristics you would expect to find in a legend.

La montaña del alimento[1]

Es una época muy difícil en la tierra[2]. Los hombres están desesperados porque no hay alimento y todos tienen mucha hambre. Van a hablar con Quetzalcóatl, la serpiente emplumada[3] y le explican que no tienen nada que comer.

Quetzalcóatl, dios compasivo[4], noble y generoso, decide ayudar a los hombres. Va a la montaña del alimento. Allí ve a un grupo de hormigas[5] gigantes que cuidan una fabulosa cantidad de maíz, la comida de los dioses. Quetzalcóatl les pide a las hormigas unos granos de maíz.

—¿Por qué quieres tú el maíz? —preguntan ellas.

—Mi gente tiene hambre —explica Quetzalcóatl.

—¿Son dioses tu gente? —dice una de las hormigas.

—No —responde Quetzalcóatl. —Son simplemente gente con hambre que vive sobre la tierra.

—Este maíz es sólo para los dioses —dicen las hormigas.

—Busca[6] comida en otra parte.

Quetzalcóatl se va, pero no se da por vencido[7]. Vuelve a la montaña en la forma de una inmensa e imponente hormiga. Las hormigas le permiten entrar y el dios ve con admiración que hay granos de maíz de muchos colores. Les dice que nunca ha visto[8] granos rojos, amarillos, azules o morados y las hormigas, orgullosas[9] de su maíz, le dan un grano de cada color.

El dios vuelve rápidamente a la tierra y les enseña a todos a cultivar el maíz. Después de un tiempo hay mucho alimento y la gente de la tierra no vuelve a tener hambre nunca más.

1 food　**2** earth　**3** the feathered serpent　**4** compassionate god　**5** ants
6 Look for　**7** doesn't give up　**8** he has never seen　**9** proud

B Comprensión ↴3B

Answer the following questions in complete sentences.

1. ¿Qué problema tienen los hombres de la tierra?
2. ¿Quién va a ayudar a los hombres? ¿Por qué?
3. ¿Qué les dice Quetzalcóatl a las hormigas y qué responden ellas?
4. ¿Qué pasa cuando Quetzalcóatl vuelve a la montaña?
5. ¿Qué hace el dios al regresar a la tierra?

C Después de leer ↴4B

Legends often reflect the values and beliefs of a culture. What values are reflected in this legend? Explain your choices. What are some similarities between this legend and other legends or stories you have read?

TEKS Focus

5A Use the language both within and beyond the school setting by participating in cultural events and using technology to communicate

Taller del escritor

SALSA (para 4 personas)
4 tomates grandes
1 cebolla mediana
2 cucharadas de cilantro fresco
1 cucharada de vinagre
1 latita de chiles verdes

Corta el tomate, la cebolla y el cilantro. Añade sal al gusto. Mezcla todos los ingredientes. Sirve con tostadas.

ESTRATEGIA

para escribir Arranging your writing in the order in which events happen helps you write more clearly. When you give written instructions such as recipes, the ordering of elements is important.

¿Cómo lo preparas? ↴1C, 5A

Imagine you are invited to a Spanish club potluck lunch where you are asked to exchange your favorite recipe from a Spanish-speaking country with other guests. Write a simple recipe for a dish with clear instructions on how to prepare it.

1 Antes de escribir

- List the foods you need to prepare your dish.
- Arrange them in the order you will need them.
- Write a command telling what needs to be done with each ingredient.

2 Escribir y revisar

After listing your ingredients, use command forms and adjectives to describe in detail the different steps in the preparation.
Para hacer una ensalada de frutas muy rica, usa muchas frutas diferentes.

Exchange your recipe with a classmate to see if it sounds appetizing to him or her. Your classmate may suggest an addition to your dish. Check for spelling and punctuation as well as for logical order.

3 Publicar

You may want to illustrate your recipe and display it on a poster board in class or post it on a school-sponsored web site. Consider trying a few in class or at home.

Online
Cuaderno para hispanohablantes, pp. 45–52

Leamos y escribamos

Repaso capítulo 6

interactive
TUTOR

1 Write a dialog between two friends and a server in a restaurant. In the dialog, include comments on the food and polite requests for the items in the photos below. ↴1C

2 Completa el párrafo con las formas correctas de los verbos del cuadro. ↴1B

poder	estar	pedir
ser	preferir	servir

Mis amigos y yo no ___1___ almorzar en casa porque siempre ___2___ en el colegio, pero los fines de semana ___3___ cenar en el Restaurante Don Carlos. La comida ___4___ muy deliciosa allí. Yo siempre ___5___ una ensalada y me gusta también la sopa porque siempre ___6___ caliente. Mis amigos ___7___ el pescado porque les encanta. También ___8___ unos sándwiches riquísimos en el restaurante.

3 Answer the questions about what you eat. ↴1C

1. ¿Qué desayunas?
2. ¿Qué vas a almorzar hoy? ¿Te gusta la comida de la cafetería?
3. ¿Qué quieres cenar esta noche?
4. ¿Qué te gusta pedir cuando vas a un restaurante?
5. ¿Qué prefieres, la carne o el pescado?
6. ¿Qué sirven ustedes de cena en casa los fines de semana?

4 Tell your friends what to do to help you get ready for a party. Use **tú** commands and direct object pronouns. ↴**1B**

1. ¿La sala? (limpiar)
2. ¿Las frutas? (poner)
3. ¿Los sándwiches? (hacer)
4. ¿Los refrescos? (sacar)
5. ¿La carne? (calentar)
6. ¿El cuarto? (arreglar)
7. ¿Las zanahorias? (cortar)
8. ¿El café? (servir)

5 Contesta las siguientes preguntas en español. ↴**2A, 2B**

1. What are some foods that reflect Mexico's indigenous heritage?
2. In most Spanish-speaking countries, when is the big meal of the day?
3. What are some popular snack foods in Mexico? In other Spanish-speaking countries?
4. Name three foods that are native to the Americas, and three that are native to Europe.

6 Veronica, Antonio y Carlos están en un restaurante. Escucha mientras hablan de lo que van a comer. Luego contesta las preguntas. ↴**1B**

1. ¿Quién tiene sed?
2. ¿Quién pide un refresco?
3. ¿Qué prefiere Carlos?
4. ¿Cómo es la sopa?
5. ¿Van a pedir unos sándwiches?

7 Usa los dibujos para decir *(to tell)* qué pasa. ↴**1C**

Visit Holt Online

go.hrw.com
KEYWORD: EXP1B CH6

Chapter Self-test

Repaso

4 Gramática 2
- direct objects and direct object pronouns
- affirmative informal commands with pronouns
pp. 60–65

5 Cultura
- **Comparaciones** pp. 52–53
- **Notas culturales** pp. 42, 46, 56, 62
- **Conexiones culturales** pp. 70–71

TEKS Focus

2B Demonstrate understanding of products (what people create) and how they relate to perspectives (how people perceive things) of the cultures studied

Gramática 1
- uses of **ser** and **estar**
  pp. 46–47
- **pedir** and **servir**
  pp. 48–49
- **preferir, poder** and
  probar
  pp. 50–51

Repaso de Gramática 1

Uses of ser	Uses of estar
• to say where people are from	• to talk about location
• to tell the day, date, and time	• to say how people are doing
• to identify people and things by what they're normally like	• to say how something looks, feels, tastes at a given time

pedir e ⟶ i	
pido	pedimos
pides	pedís
pide	piden

servir e ⟶ i	
sirvo	servimos
sirves	servís
sirve	sirven

The verbs **poder** and **probar** are **o ⟶ ue** stem-changing verbs.

The verb **preferir** is an **e ⟶ ie** stem-changing verb. See page 50.

Gramática 2
- direct objects and direct
  object pronouns
  pp. 60–61
- affirmative informal
  commands
  pp. 62–63
- affirmative informal
  commands with pronouns
  pp. 64–65

Repaso de Gramática 2

Direct object pronouns		
	Masculine	**Feminine**
SINGULAR	lo	la
PLURAL	los	las

Affirmative informal commands			
Regular	**Irregular**		
habl**a**	ten	ve	haz
com**e**	ven	sé	sal
pid**e**	pon		

Attach direct object pronouns to affirmative commands.

TEKS Focus

1B Demonstrate
understanding
of simple, clearly
spoken, and written
language when dealing
with familiar topics

Letra y sonido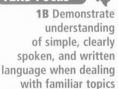

La letra d
- At the beginning of a phrase, or after **n** or **l**, the
  letter **d** is similar to the English *d* in *Daniel:* **d**eli-
  cioso an**d**ar, hon**d**o, un **d**ía, el **d**eporte.
- After other consonants and especially after a
  vowel, it is much like English *th* in *then:* na**d**ar,
  me**d**ia, cua**d**erno, ma**d**re, uste**d**, aburri**d**o, tar**d**e,
  ver**d**e, la**d**o, a **d**ormir.

Trabalenguas
Me han dicho
que has dicho un dicho,
un dicho que he dicho yo,
ese dicho que te han dicho
que yo he dicho, no lo he dicho;
y si yo lo hubiera dicho,
estaría muy bien dicho.

Dictado ↓1B, 1C
Escribe las oraciones de la grabación.

Repaso de Vocabulario 1

Commenting on food

el **agua** *(f.)*	*water*
el **atún**	*tuna*
(muy) caliente	*(very) hot*
encantar	*to really like, to love*
la **ensalada (de frutas)**	*fruit salad*
(No) estoy de acuerdo.	*I (don't) agree.*
el **flan**	*flan, custard*
frío(a)	*cold*
el **jamón**	*ham*
el **jugo de...**	*. . . juice*
la **leche**	*milk*
las **papas**	*potatoes*
las **papas fritas**	*French fries*
Para tomar puedes pedir...	*You can order . . . to drink.*
pedir(i)	*to order*
picante	*spicy*
preparar	*to prepare, to make*
probar(ue)	*to try, to taste*
el **queso**	*cheese*
¿Qué tal está(n)...?	*How is (are) the . . .?*
el **refresco**	*soft drink*
riquísimo(a)	*delicious*

la **salsa**	*sauce, gravy*
(un poco) salado(a)	*(a little) salty*
el **sándwich de...**	*. . . sandwich*
servir(i)	*to serve*
la **sopa (de verduras)**	*(vegetable) soup*
el **tomate**	*tomato*

Making polite requests

la **cuchara**	*spoon*
el **cuchillo**	*knife*
la **cuenta**	*bill*
desear	*to want, to wish for, to desire*
el **plato**	*dish, plate*
el **plato hondo**	*bowl*
poder	*to be able to, can*
el **postre**	*dessert*
querer	*to want*
Quisiera...	*I would like . . .*
la **servilleta**	*napkin*
el **tenedor**	*fork*
tomar	*to drink, to take*
traer	*to bring*
el **vaso**	*glass*

Repaso de Vocabulario 2

Talking about meals

almorzar(ue)	*to eat lunch*
el **arroz**	*rice*
el **bróculi**	*broccoli*
el **café (con leche)**	*coffee (with milk)*
la **carne**	*meat*
la **cena**	*dinner*
cenar	*to eat dinner*
los **cereales**	*cereal*
el **chocolate**	*chocolate*
el **desayuno**	*breakfast*
desayunar	*to eat breakfast*
el **durazno**	*peach*
las **espinacas**	*spinach*
el **huevo**	*egg*
la **manzana**	*apple*
el **maíz**	*corn*
la **naranja**	*orange*
el **pan**	*bread*

el **pan dulce**	*pastries*
el **pan tostado**	*toast*
el **pastel**	*cake*
el **pescado**	*fish*
el **pollo**	*chicken*
el **tocino**	*bacon*
la **zanahoria**	*carrot*

Offering help

la **ayuda**	*help*
ayudar	*to help*
¿Puedo...?	*Can I . . .?*
el **refrigerador**	*refrigerator*

Useful verbs for cooking

añadir	*to add*
calentar	*to heat up*
cortar	*to cut*
mezclar	*to mix*

Integración
capítulos 1-6

1 Escucha los comentarios sobre la comida y escoge la foto correspondiente. ⬇1B

A

B

C

D

2 Mrs. Ramírez is going to fix supper. Read the recipes and answer the questions that follow. Write your answers in Spanish. ⬇1B, 1C

ENSALADA MIXTA

1 lechuga grande
4 tomates
1 taza de arroz cocido
100 g atún de lata
1/2 zanahoria rallada
1/2 cebolla picada

Se limpian las verduras y se cortan en trozos. Se mezcla todo junto y se sirve con aceite, vinagre, sal y pimienta.
Raciones 6–8
Tiempo–15 minutos

TORTILLA ESPAÑOLA

4 huevos
4 papas medianas
1/2 cebolla
sal y aceite de oliva

Corta las papas y la cebolla en pedacitos. Fríe con aceite en una sartén. Bate los huevos y mézclalos con las papas. Agrega la sal. Tapa con otra sartén y fríe al gusto. Dale la vuelta con la sartén superior y cocina el otro lado.
Raciones 6–8
Tiempo–30 minutos

1. What vegetable do the two recipes have in common?
2. Name three vegetables Mrs. Ramírez needs to fix supper.
3. What is the first step in the recipe for the **tortilla española**?
4. Name two extra ingredients in the **ensalada mixta** that are not listed in the ingredients at the top of the recipe.
5. How many people can Mrs. Ramírez feed with these recipes?
6. How much time should she plan on to cook supper?

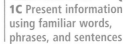
3 Discuss this painting by Mexican muralist Diego Rivera with a partner. The Spanish sentence prompts will guide your conversation. After you have completed the sentences, write a short paragraph in Spanish together describing the painting in your own words. ↴**1A, 1C**

1. Las mujeres son... (*description*)
2. Ellas traen...
3. Los hombres son... (*description*)
4. Ellos tienen...
5. El señor español quiere comprar...

TEKS Focus
1C Present information using familiar words, phrases, and sentences

The Market of Cuernavaca in the Age of the Spanish Conquest,
Diego Rivera (1886–1957)

4 Situación

Imagine you are interviewing a Mexican exchange student about typical daily meals in Mexico. With a partner, take turns playing the roles of the exchange student and interviewer. Your conversation should cover the following topics. ↴**1A**

▶ What is the student's favorite food and beverage?

▶ Which foods and drinks does she or he typically have for each meal?

▶ At what time are meals served?

▶ Is there a favorite dish the family eats for dinner?

▶ Does the student usually eat dessert? If so, what does he or she prefer?

Integración

Video/DVD

GeoVisión

Geocultura Argentina

▲ **Buenos Aires** The capital of Argentina is located at the mouth of the **Río de la Plata** estuary on the Atlantic coast.

▶ **San Carlos de Bariloche**
The town of San Carlos de Bariloche on **Lago Nahuel Huapí** is in the Andes Mountains. This area is known as "the Switzerland of the Andes."

▶ **La Pampa** The Pampa region is the land of **gauchos** and the center of livestock raising in Argentina. The flat, fertile land is similar to the Great Plains of North America.

Almanaque

Población
37.812.817

Capital
Buenos Aires

Gobierno
república

Idioma oficial
español

Moneda
peso argentino

Código Internet
www.[ ].ar

OCÉANO
PACÍFICO

◀ **Trajes folklóricos**
These young Argentines sport traditional dress.

Texas **¿Sabías que...?**
The romanticized image of the Texas cowboy, an independent rider herding livestock on the lone prairie, is much like the image of the Argentine **gaucho**.

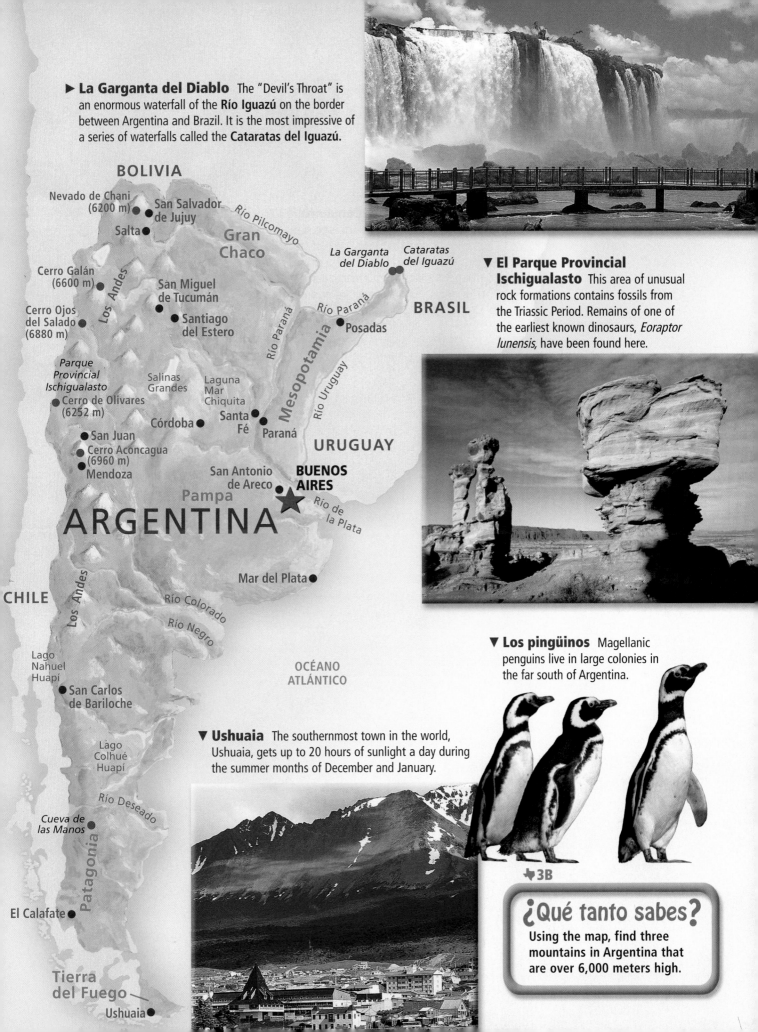

► **La Garganta del Diablo** The "Devil's Throat" is an enormous waterfall of the **Río Iguazú** on the border between Argentina and Brazil. It is the most impressive of a series of waterfalls called the **Cataratas del Iguazú**.

BOLIVIA

Nevado de Chani
(6200 m)

San Salvador
de Jujuy

Salta

Río Pilcomayo

Gran
Chaco

Cerro Galán
(6600 m)

Los Andes

San Miguel
de Tucumán

Cerro Ojos
del Salado
(6880 m)

Santiago
del Estero

La Garganta
del Diablo

Cataratas
del Iguazú

Río Paraná

Posadas

BRASIL

Río Paraná

Parque
Provincial
Ischigualasto

Salinas
Grandes

Laguna
Mar
Chiquita

Mesopotamia

Río Uruguay

▼ **El Parque Provincial Ischigualasto** This area of unusual rock formations contains fossils from the Triassic Period. Remains of one of the earliest known dinosaurs, *Eoraptor lunensis,* have been found here.

Cerro de Olivares
(6252 m)

Córdoba

Santa
Fé

Paraná

URUGUAY

San Juan

Cerro Aconcagua
(6960 m)

Mendoza

San Antonio
de Areco

**BUENOS
AIRES**

Pampa

ARGENTINA

Río de
la Plata

CHILE

Mar del Plata

Los Andes

Río Colorado

Río Negro

OCÉANO
ATLÁNTICO

Lago
Nahuel
Huapí

San Carlos
de Bariloche

Lago
Colhué
Huapí

Río Deseado

Cueva de
las Manos

Patagonia

El Calafate

▼ **Ushuaia** The southernmost town in the world, Ushuaia, gets up to 20 hours of sunlight a day during the summer months of December and January.

▼ **Los pingüinos** Magellanic penguins live in large colonies in the far south of Argentina.

Tierra
del Fuego

Ushuaia

↓ 3B

¿Qué tanto sabes?

Using the map, find three mountains in Argentina that are over 6,000 meters high.

A conocer Argentina

La arquitectura

◄ **Iglesia y Convento de San Francisco de Salta** The Church of St. Francis is in Salta, a city in northwest Argentina. The 53-meter-high tower, one of the highest in South America, was designed by Spanish and Italian architects.

▲ **La Boca, Buenos Aires** This neighborhood was originally home to Italian immigrants who used parts of abandoned ships to build their houses. **La Boca** is famous for the tango music that echoes in its streets.

El arte

▼ **La Cueva de las Manos** The Cave of the Hands in Patagonia is decorated with outlines of hands painted over 10,000 years ago.

▲ *Vuel Villa* **(1936)** This painting is by Xul Solar (1887–1963), an Argentine artist of German heritage. He had great influence on the development of modern art in Argentina.

Las celebraciones

◆ 2A, 2B

¿Sabías que...?

Between 1857 and 1939, 3.5 million people immigrated to Argentina from many countries. How do you see the cultures of immigrants reflected in the cities, architecture, festivals, and customs of Argentina?

◄ **La Fiesta de la Semana de la Tradición** This major festival held in **San Antonio de Areco** is dedicated to **gauchos** and their traditions.

► **El Festival de Tango** The tango originated in immigrant neighborhoods of Buenos Aires in the 1880s. The music is a combination of African rhythms, European folk music, and popular **gaucho** songs.

La comida

► **Las picadas** A **picada** is a restaurant that serves a huge variety of appetizers prepared with cheese, meat, seafood, and nuts.

◄ **El mate** Between four o'clock and six o'clock in the afternoon, Argentines young and old drink **mate**, a tea made from leaves of the **yerba** plant. **Mate** is served in a hollowed-out gourd (**calabacita**) with a metal straw (**bombilla**).

▼ **Calabacitas de mate con bombilla**

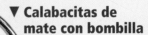

Capítulo 7

Cuerpo sano, mente sana

Objetivos

In Part 1 you will learn to:
- talk about your daily routine
- talk about staying fit and healthy
- form verbs with reflexive pronouns
- use infinitives with conjugated verbs and prepositions
- use stem-changing verbs (review)

In Part 2 you will learn to:
- talk about how you feel
- give advice
- use the verbs **estar, sentirse,** and **tener**
- form negative informal commands
- use direct object and reflexive pronouns with informal commands

¿Qué ves en la foto?

- **¿Qué les gusta hacer a los muchachos en la foto?**

- **¿Dónde están los muchachos?**

- **¿Adónde van a ir?**

TEKS Look for the 🔻 next to each activity to learn how it can help you achieve the goals of the **Texas Essential Knowledge and Skills,** found on page xxi.

La cordillera de los Andes entre Argentina y Chile

Vocabulario

en acción 1

ExpresaVisión

Por la mañana, tengo que...

despertarme a las seis,

levantarme

y vestirme.

peinarme.

maquillarme.

afeitarme.

lavarme los dientes.

la nariz

la cara

los dientes

el peine

la boca

la toalla

el maquillaje

la navaja

la pasta de dientes

el jabón

el cepillo de dientes

▶ **Vocabulario adicional** — **Partes del cuerpo,** p. R10

Por la tarde, después de clases, voy a...

estirarme antes de hacer ejercicio.

el brazo

la pierna

la pantorrilla

entrenarme. Me gusta levantar pesas.

los hombros

el pecho

la espalda

Por la noche, necesito...

quitarme la ropa,

bañarme y ponerme el piyama

y acostarme temprano.

¡Exprésate!

To talk about your daily routine

Interactive TUTOR

¿Estás listo? ¿Qué te falta hacer?	**¡Ay, no! Acabo de levantarme. Tengo que lavarme la cara antes de desayunar.**
Are you ready? What do you still have to do?	*Oh, no! I just got up. I have to wash my face before I eat breakfast.*
¿Qué tienes que hacer para prepararte?	**Tengo que secarme el pelo, pero no encuentro la secadora de pelo.**
What do you have to do to get ready?	*I have to dry my hair, but I can't find the hair dryer.*

Online
Vocabulario y gramática, pp. 29–31

▶ **Vocabulario adicional** — Partes del cuerpo, p. R14

Vocabulario 1

Dos muchachas se entrenan en Buenos Aires

1 **¿Qué te falta hacer?** 1B

Leamos Completa las oraciones con la palabra más apropiada entre paréntesis.

1. Quiero lavarme (las manos/la pantorrilla) antes de cenar.
2. Me gusta (acostarme/entrenarme) temprano por la mañana.
3. Tengo que estirarme (la boca/los brazos) antes de levantar pesas.
4. Necesito lavarme (los dientes/la nariz) después de comer.
5. ¿Dónde está (la navaja/la secadora)? Tengo que secarme el pelo.

2 **¿Qué vas a hacer primero?** 1B

Hablemos ¿En qué orden vas a hacer las siguientes cosas?

MODELO vestirme/bañarme
            Primero voy a bañarme y luego voy a vestirme.

1. bañarme/levantarme
2. secarme el pelo/bañarme
3. lavarme la cara/maquillarme
4. lavarme el pelo/peinarme
5. ponerme la ropa/bañarme
6. acostarme/ponerme el piyama
7. quitarme la ropa/ponerme el piyama
8. vestirme/salir para el colegio

3 **La familia López** 1B

Leamos The López family is getting ready for the day. Match each sentence with one of the pictures below.

1. Primero voy a lavarme los dientes y luego voy a lavarme las manos.
2. Primero voy a leer y luego voy a afeitarme la cara.
3. Voy a levantarme primero. Luego voy a bañarme y vestirme.
4. Voy a maquillarme y peinarme.

a. el señor López

b. Ernesto

c. la señora López

d. Adela

4 ¿Estás listo? ⬦1B

Escribamos Write the question **¿Qué tienes que hacer?** and an answer for each item. Say what you have to do and what you need to do it.

MODELO ¿Qué tienes que hacer?
Tengo que afeitarme, pero primero tengo que encontrar la navaja.

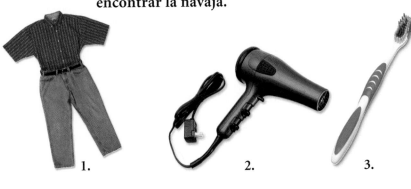

1.   2.   3.   4.

5.   6.   7.   8.

   Comunicación

5 Mi rutina ⬦1A

Hablemos Work with a partner. Write eight sentences each about your daily routine, using **necesito** or **me gusta** with the following verbs. Then read your sentences aloud, asking each other questions about your routines. Include phrases such as **¿a qué hora?, a veces, por la mañana, por la noche,** and days of the week.

MODELO —Me gusta entrenarme por la mañana.
—¿A qué hora?

despertarme	bañarme	estirarme	lavarme los dientes
levantarme	vestirme	entrenarme	acostarme

TEKS Focus

1A Engage in oral and written exchanges of learned material to socialize and to provide and obtain information

¡Exprésate!

To talk about staying fit and healthy

Interactive TUTOR

¿Cómo te mantienes en forma?	**Corro y levanto pesas. Entreno las piernas y los brazos.**
How do you stay in shape?	*I run and lift weights. I work out my legs and my arms.*
¿Qué haces para relajarte?	**Me entreno. También duermo la siesta o escucho música.**
What do you do to relax?	*I work out. I also take a nap or listen to music.*

Online
Vocabulario y gramática, pp. 29–31

TEKS Focus

2A Demonstrate understanding of practices (what people do) and how they relate to perspectives (how people perceive things) of the cultures studied

Nota cultural

Argentina boasts some of the finest ski resorts in the world. Argentina's city of Bariloche is well known for its July ski season. Each August, Bariloche celebrates the National Snow Party, a week of winter celebrations. Why do you think the ski season is in July and August in Argentina? ⬦2A

6 El sábado ⬦1B

Escuchemos Escucha la conversación entre Juan y Laura sobre los planes de ella para el sábado. Luego completa las oraciones con las palabras correctas.

1. Voy a levantarme (temprano/tarde) este sábado.
2. (Corro/Levanto pesas/No me entreno) los sábados.
3. (Casi siempre/A veces/Nunca) almuerzo en casa los sábados.
4. Voy a bañarme (por la mañana/por la tarde) este sábado.
5. Quiero (relajarme/salir con mis amigos) este sábado por la tarde.
6. (Siempre/A veces/Nunca) duermo la siesta por la tarde los sábados.
7. Para relajarme, prefiero (leer/escuchar música/ir de compras).

7 Una rutina sana ⬦1B

Leamos A student in Argentina has written telling how he stays in shape. Complete his letter with the best choice of words.

Nuevo Mensaje

Archivo Editar Ver Insertar Formato Herramientas Mensaje Ayuda

Enviar Cortar Copiar Pegar Deshacer Deletrear Adjuntar Prioridad

B *I* U A

¡Hola, amigo!
Para mantenerme en ___1___, me entreno mucho. Por la mañana ___2___ pesas. Siempre ___3___ las piernas y los brazos. Durante la semana por la tarde ___4___ en el parque.
Los domingos ___5___ la siesta por la tarde. Para relajarme normalmente ___6___ música. ¿Qué haces tú para relajarte? Y, ¿cómo te ___7___ en forma?
Hasta luego,
Javier Almería Perón

8 Y tú, ¿qué haces? ↓1B, 1C

Escribamos Write an answer to Javier's letter in Activity 7 and tell him about your own ways of staying fit and healthy. Use his letter as a model.

 Comunicación

9 Y a ti, ¿qué te gusta? ↓1A

Hablemos Take turns with a partner pretending you are the person in the following photos. Ask each other how you stay in shape, answer with the activity, and tell what parts of the body you work out.

MODELO —¿Cómo te mantienes en forma?
—Hago ejercicio. Entreno las piernas y el estómago.

1.

2.

3.

4.

5.

6.

10 ¿Cómo te mantienes en forma? ↓1A, 1C

Escribamos/Hablemos First write the following questions and your answers on a piece of paper. Then ask the questions to two or three classmates, and jot down their answers. Are their answers similar to yours or different? Be prepared to report your survey to the class.

1. ¿Cómo te mantienes en forma?
2. ¿Te gusta hacer ejercicio?
3. ¿Qué haces para relajarte?
4. ¿Prefieres entrenarte o relajarte?

TEKS Focus
1C Present information using familiar words, phrases, and sentences

Vocabulario 1

 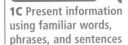

Gramática en acción 1

GramaVisión

Interactive TUTOR

Verbs with reflexive pronouns

1 If the subject and object of a verb are the same, a **reflexive pronoun** can be used. The reflexive pronoun shows that the subject acts upon itself. When you conjugate a verb like **lavarse,** include the reflexive pronoun that agrees with the subject.

yo **me** lavo	nosotros(as) **nos** lavamos
tú **te** lavas	vosotros(as) **os** laváis
Ud., él, ella **se** lava	Uds., ellos(as) **se** lavan

2 **Reflexive pronouns** can go before a conjugated verb or can be joined to the end of an **infinitive**. After reflexive verbs, use **el, la, los** or **las** with parts of the body or clothing.

(Yo) **Me** voy a **lavar** la cara.
I'm going to wash my face.

(Yo) Voy a **lavarme** la cara.
I'm going to wash my face.

3 Verbs such as **acostar (ue)** can be used with **reflexive pronouns** that refer to the subject or with direct objects that are different from the subject.

different from the subject
Juan **acuesta** a los niños.
Juan puts the children to bed.

refers to the subject
Juan **se acuesta.**
Juan goes to bed.

4 These are some other verbs with **reflexive pronouns**.

afeitar**se**	levantar**se**	preparar**se**
bañar**se**	mantener**se** (ie)	quitar**se**
despertar**se** (ie)	maquillar**se**	relajar**se**
entrenar**se**	peinar**se**	secar**se**
estirar**se**	poner**se**	vestir**se** (i)

Online
| Vocabulario y gramática, pp. 32–34 | Actividades, pp. 27–30 |

11 **¿Qué hace Manuel?** 1B

Escuchemos Escucha lo que dice Manuel. ¿Va al colegio o se acuesta?

Nota cultural

Keeping in shape is easy for surfers along the 500 miles of Texas coastline. Good surfing spots include South Padre Island, Corpus Christi, Matagorda, Port Aransas, and Galveston. Surfers check weather reports, Internet bulletins, and live video from Web cameras because the surf changes quickly along the Texas coast. Why do you think hurricanes in the Gulf of Mexico attract surfers to Texas? **2A**

12 Por la mañana ↘1B

Leamos María is talking about her typical day. Read the paragraph and decide if the reflexive pronoun is needed with each verb.

Mis padres ___1___ (levantan/se levantan) a las seis todos los días. Mientras mi padre ___2___ (prepara/se prepara) para ir al trabajo, mi madre va a la cocina, ___3___ (lava/se lava) las manos y ___4___ (prepara/se prepara) el desayuno para la familia. Mi hermano menor y yo ___5___ (levantamos/nos levantamos) a las siete. Mientras mamá y yo ___6___ (vestimos/nos vestimos), papá ___7___ (viste/se viste) a mi hermano. Después del desayuno, mamá ___8___ (lava/se lava) los platos rápidamente mientras mi hermano y yo ___9___ (lavamos/nos lavamos) los dientes antes de salir de la casa.

TEKS Focus

1B Demonstrate understanding of simple, clearly spoken, and written language when dealing with familiar topics

13 ¿Qué y cuándo? ↘1C

Escribamos Mira las fotos. Escribe una oración para cada foto.

el señor Vargas por la mañana

MODELO El señor Vargas se afeita por la mañana.

1. Laura
   7:00 A.M.

2. ellas
   por la tarde

3. nosotros
   los fines de semana

4. tú
   por la noche

 Comunicación

14 Cuéntame de ti ↘1A

Hablemos Work in small groups. Use these phrases to ask each other what you do on Saturdays. Answer, adding details of your routine.

MODELO —Berta, ¿qué haces los sábados?
—Me levanto tarde y veo televisión.

relajarse	entrenarse en el gimnasio
levantarse temprano	ponerse ropa vieja
maquillarse/afeitarse	salir con los amigos

Gramática 1

Interactive TUTOR

El gimnasio Megatlón,
Buenos Aires

Online
Vocabulario y gramática, pp. 32–34 | Actividades, pp. 27–30

Using infinitives

1 A **reflexive pronoun** can go at the end of an **infinitive** or before a conjugated verb. The meaning does not change.

Yo no quiero **estirarme** hoy.   =   Yo **me** quiero **estirar** hoy.
I don't want to stretch today.

2 To say what someone just did, use the present tense of **acabar de** followed by an **infinitive.**

Acabo de **lavar** el carro.   Los niños acaban de **acostarse.**
I just washed the car.   *The children just went to bed.*

3 Use the preposition **para** before an **infinitive** to explain your purpose for doing something. Prepositions and prepositional phrases such as **a**, **para**, **antes de**, and **después de** are followed by verbs in the **infinitive.**

Tengo que levantarme temprano **para presentar** un examen.
I have to get up early (in order) to take an exam.

En inglés

In English, you can say **in order to** or just **to** to explain your purpose for doing something.

I need to call John (**in order**) **to** *see* how he's doing.

In Spanish, you can use **para** followed by an infinitive to explain your purpose for doing something. If you're talking about going somewhere to do something, use **a** followed by an infinitive.

Necesito llamar a Juan **para** saber cómo está.

Necesito ir al gimnasio **a** levantar pesas.

15 **¿Qué sigue?** ↓1B, 1C

Escribamos Choose the correct form of the verb in parentheses to complete each sentence.

1. (**se levanta, se levantan, me levanto, levantarse, levantarme**)
   a. Mis padres ===== a las seis de la mañana.
   b. Mi padre ===== primero.
   c. (Yo) ===== temprano todos los días también, pero prefiero ===== a las nueve o diez.

2. (**se viste, me visto, vestirse, vestirme**)
   a. Mi madre desayuna antes de =====.
   b. (Yo) prefiero desayunar después de =====.
   c. (Yo) siempre ===== en el baño.

3. (**me lavo, nos lavamos, lavarme, lavarnos**)
   a. Después de desayunar voy al baño a ===== los dientes.
   b. (Yo) siempre ===== los dientes por la mañana.
   c. En el colegio no nos gusta ===== los dientes.

4. (**se acuesta, me acuesto, nos acostamos, acostarse, acostarme**)
   a. Nosotros ===== tarde en mi familia.
   b. (Yo) ===== primero, a las once.
   c. Mi padre no ===== hasta la medianoche porque prefiere leer un poco antes de =====.

16 Antes de acostarte ↲1B, 1C

Hablemos Tell when you are going to do the following things.

MODELO **bañarme**

Me voy a bañar esta noche antes de acostarme.

1. levantarme
2. acostarme
3. ponerme el piyama
4. relajarme
5. entrenarme
6. vestirme

17 ¿Cuál es la situación? ↲1C

Escribamos/Hablemos Look at the photos. Indicate what these people have just done or what they are going to do.

MODELO **Yo acabo de afeitarme.**

 yo

1. ella   2. él   3. tú   4. Juan

   Comunicación

18 ¿Cómo es tu rutina? ↲1A, 1C

Escribamos/Hablemos Prepare five questions to ask a classmate, using words from each group. Then answer your classmate's questions. Be prepared to report what your partner says to the class.

MODELO —Luis, ¿vas a levantarte temprano mañana?
—No, mañana es sábado. Voy a levantarme tarde.
—Luis va a levantarse tarde mañana.

ir a	acostarse	todos los días
necesitar	despertarse	temprano
tener que	entrenarse	tarde
querer	estirarse	por la mañana
poder	levantarse	por la noche
	mantenerse en forma	por la tarde
	peinarse	mañana
	ponerse	el sábado
	relajarse	antes de desayunar
	vestirse	después de estudiar

TEKS Focus

1A Engage in oral and written exchanges of learned material to socialize and to provide and obtain information

Gramática 1

Argentina

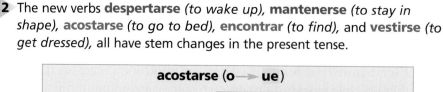

Repaso   Stem-changing verbs

Interactive TUTOR

1 In the present tense, some verbs have one of three types of stem changes: (**e ➞ ie**), (**o/u ➞ ue**), or (**e ➞ i**) in all but the **nosotros** and **vosotros** forms.

2 The new verbs **despertarse** (to wake up), **mantenerse** (to stay in shape), **acostarse** (to go to bed), **encontrar** (to find), and **vestirse** (to get dressed), all have stem changes in the present tense.

acostarse (o ➞ ue)	
yo me ac**ue**sto	nosotros (as) nos acostamos
tú te ac**ue**stas	vosotros (as) os acostáis
Ud., él, ella se ac**ue**sta	Uds., ellos, ellas se ac**ue**stan

Mi hermana y yo **nos acostamos** a las diez.

vestirse (e ➞ ie)	
yo me v**i**sto	nosotros (as) nos vestimos
tú te v**i**stes	vosotros (as) os vestís
Ud., él, ella se v**i**ste	Uds., ellos, ellas, se v**i**sten

Mi abuela **se viste** de ropa elegante.

Online

Vocabulario y gramática, pp. 32–34	Actividades, pp. 27–30

¿Te acuerdas?

Here are some **stem-changing verbs** you have seen so far.

querer (e ➞ ie)

poder (o ➞ ue)

jugar (u ➞ ue)

pedir (e ➞ i)

TEKS Focus

1B Demonstrate understanding of simple, clearly spoken, and written language when dealing with familiar topics

19 **Nuestra rutina** ✦1B

Escuchemos Decide si estas oraciones son **ciertas** o **falsas.**

1. El papá de Camila se acuesta antes que su mamá.
2. Su hermano se acuesta después de jugar al ajedrez por Internet.
3. Su mamá sirve huevos, tocino y pan tostado para el desayuno.
4. Por la mañana, Camila y su hermano se levantan tarde.
5. Después de desayunar, Camila se viste y se maquilla.

20 **La rutina familiar** ✦1B

Leamos/Escribamos Completa las oraciones con las formas correctas de los verbos lógicos entre paréntesis.

Por la tarde mi hermana ___1___ (servir/jugar) videojuegos pero yo ___2___ (probar/empezar) mi tarea a las tres. Nosotras ___3___ (servir/almorzar) la cena todos los días. Mis padres ___4___ (acostar/preferir) cenar temprano. Mi padre siempre ___5___ (querer/servir) leer un libro después de cenar pero mi madre ___6___ (dormir/preferir) escuchar música. Yo siempre ___7___ (levantarse/acostarse) antes de las diez de la noche.

21 ¿Cuándo lo hacen? ↓1B

Escribamos Write sentences telling when everyone does the following activities.

> **MODELO** Luis/acostarse ▦▦▦
> **Luis se acuesta temprano.**

1. mis amigos y yo/acostarse ▦▦▦
2. los sábados/Carlitos/vestirse ▦▦▦
3. mi amigo/no/encontrar/su tarea ▦▦▦
4. ¿tú/encontrar/secadora de pelo ▦▦▦?
5. mis padres/ siempre/acostarse ▦▦▦
6. mis amigos y yo/vestirse/rápido ▦▦▦

22 ¿Qué pasa en casa? ↓1B, 1C

Escribamos Write two short paragraphs. Use the verbs given to describe what is happening in each drawing.

1.

2.

jugar	llover
poder	querer

probar	servir
preferir	vestirse

 Comunicación

23 Tu rutina diaria ↓1A

Hablemos Use these phrases to interview a classmate about a typical school day.

despertarse temprano/tarde	vestirse en menos de veinte minutos
dormir mucho/poco	dormir la siesta
jugar un deporte	encontrar tu mochila/libro de español
volver a casa	empezar la tarea

Cultura

Comparaciones
Interactive TUTOR

Parque Palermo, Argentina

¿Cómo te mantienes en forma? ↓ 2A, 4B

La necesidad de mantenerse en forma es universal. En Argentina los jóvenes prefieren mantenerse en forma practicando el esquí, el patinaje en hielo y el hockey, también el ciclismo, la natación, el windsurf, el tae-kwondo, el alpinismo y, desde luego, el fútbol. Muchos jóvenes se mantienen en forma con la práctica del fútbol todos los fines de semana. ¿Qué diferencia hay entre lo que hacen estos jóvenes y lo que haces tú para mantenerte en forma?

Miguel
Buenos Aires, Argentina

Miguel talks about what he does to stay in shape. What kinds of exercise do you do?

¿Crees que estás en forma ahora?

Eh, sí creo que estoy en forma, me mantengo, trato siempre de salir a correr, cosas por el estilo, cosas de mantenerme siempre en forma.

¿Cómo te mantienes en forma?

Practico gimnasia acrobática desde hace nueve años. Este, salgo a correr, distintos tipos de deportes... me gusta un poquitito de todo, muy variado.

Para ti, ¿qué es lo difícil de mantenerte en forma?

Lo difícil de mantenerse en forma, yo creo que es mantener una cons-tancia en un entrenamiento, fijarse objetivos y a partir de ahí, bueno, a ver qué pasa.

¿Qué haces para relajarte?

Me gusta leer. Me gusta escuchar música, especialmente leer porque como quien dice, este, en un cuerpo sano, mente sana.

Chile

Buenos Aires

ARGENTINA

Océano Atlántico

Ivania
San José, Costa Rica

Ivania talks about how exercise and diet help her stay in shape. How do diet and exercise affect the way you feel?

¿Crees que estás en forma en este momento?

Sí, sí creo que estoy en forma.

¿Cómo te mantienes en forma?

Yo para mantenerme en forma camino, corro o voy al gimnasio.

Para ti, ¿qué es lo difícil de mantenerte en forma?

Para mí, lo difícil de mantenerme

es poder evitar comer chocolate, picaditas o helados.

¿Qué haces para relajarte?

Yo para relajarme hago muchas cosas, leo poemas, hablo con mis amigos, salgo a pasear.

Para comprender 1B, 2A

1. ¿Qué hace Miguel para mantenerse en forma? ¿Qué deportes le gustan a Miguel?
2. ¿Por qué es difícil para Miguel mantenerse en forma?
3. ¿Cómo se mantiene en forma Ivania? ¿Qué le gusta comer a Ivania?
4. ¿Qué hacen Miguel e Ivania para relajarse? ¿Qué cosa hacen los dos? En tu opinión, ¿es cierto lo que dice Miguel, "en un cuerpo sano, mente sana"? ¿Por qué?

Para pensar y hablar 2A, 4B

Very often exercise involves going to the gym. But, simple things like walking or riding a bike to places can be enough exercise. Both Miguel and Ivania live in cities in their home countries where places are often within walking distance. Are places easy to walk to in your community, or are they spread out so you have to ride there in a car or bus? How can the way a city is built make it easy or hard for a person to get exercise?

Cuaderno para hispanohablantes, pp. 53–60

Comunidad

Popular Sports in Texas 4B, 5A

Soccer is popular in all of Latin America and in many areas of Texas. Most Texas cities have soccer leagues for all ages. There are programs patterned after Latin American programs to develop soccer players as young as six years old up through adult professional players. In Dallas you can attend a professional game and watch the Dallas Burn players. If there is a league in your area, you might be able to interview a trainer or coach in Spanish because many of them are from Mexico or other parts of Latin America. If you get to meet Claudio Reyna or Carlos Llamosa, members of the U.S. national soccer team, you can greet them in Spanish! What other sports are popular in both Latin America and your city or area of Texas?

The Dallas Burn

Objetivos
Talking about how you
feel, giving advice

Vocabulario
en acción 2

Video/DVD

ExpresaVisión

LOS MUSCULOS

EL ESQUELETO HUMANO

¿Qué te pasa?

Me duele. . .

la cabeza

el oído

la garganta

el estómago

el pie

¿Cómo se sienten?

Está cansada.

Está aburrido.

Para cuidarte la salud debes...

hacer yoga

caminar

Está nerviosa.

Está triste.

Más vocabulario...

bajar de peso	to lose weight
buscar un pasatiempo	to find a hobby
dejar de fumar	to stop smoking
estar contento (a)	to be happy
subir de peso	to gain weight

seguir una
dieta sana

¡Exprésate!

To ask how someone feels	To respond
Te veo mal. *You don't look well.*	**Es que estoy enferma. Tengo catarro.** *I'm sick. I have a cold.*
¿Qué te pasa? ¿Te duele algo? *What's wrong with you? Does something hurt?*	**Me siento (un poco) cansado y me duelen los pies (las manos).** *I feel (a little) tired and my feet (hands) hurt.*
¿Qué tiene Rosita? *What's the matter with Rosita?*	**Le duele la garganta.** *Her throat hurts.*

Interactive TUTOR

Online
Vocabulario y gramática,
pp. 35–37

▶ **Vocabulario adicional** — En el consultorio, p. R8

Vocabulario 2

24 **Debes cuidarte mejor** ↙ **1B**

Leamos Lee lo que varios amigos te dicen sobre sus problemas. Escoge la mejor respuesta para cada situación.

1. Me duelen mucho los ojos.
2. Siempre estoy aburrido.
3. Me siento muy cansada.
4. Nunca como frutas ni verduras.
5. Siempre me duele la garganta.
6. Quiero bajar de peso.

7. Tengo catarro.
8. Me duelen los pies.

a. Debes dejar de fumar.
b. Necesitas seguir una dieta sana.
c. ¡Usa tus lentes!
d. ¿Qué tal si buscas un pasatiempo?
e. Debes comer menos y hacer ejercicio.
f. No debes correr sin *(without)* zapatos.
g. Debes dormir lo suficiente.
h. Toma jugo de naranja y descansa.

25 **¿Estás bien?** ↙ **1B**

Leamos A teacher has noticed that you look unwell. After class you have a conversation. Refer to **Exprésate** on page 101 to complete your part of the conversation.

LA PROFESORA	TÚ
Te veo mal.	Es que estoy ___1___ .
¿Qué te pasa?	Tengo ___2___ y me siento un poco ___3___ .
¿Te duele algo?	Sí, me duele ___4___ .
Debes llamar a tu mamá por teléfono.	No puedo, ella está ___5___ también.
Y, ¿qué tiene ella?	Le duele ___6___ .

26 **¿Qué te duele?** ↙ **1B, 1C**

Hablemos Explain what part(s) of the body hurt(s) if you can't do the following activities.

MODELO correr

No puedo correr. Me duelen las piernas y los pies.

1. hablar
2. levantar pesas
3. comer
4. escribir
5. oír *(to hear)*

6. estudiar
7. bailar
8. leer
9. jugar al tenis
10. patinar

27 ¿Cómo estamos? 1B

 Escribamos On a separate paper, write the five sentence starters and complete each one with a logical ending from the second column.

1. Yo estoy triste porque...
2. Juan está enfermo y...
3. Maricarmen está nerviosa porque...
4. Los niños están aburridos porque...
5. La Sra. Romero está cansada porque...

a. ella no duerme bien.
b. no tienen nada que hacer.
c. mi perro está enfermo.
d. tiene que presentar un examen.
e. le duele el estómago.

TEKS Focus

1B Demonstrate understanding of simple, clearly spoken, and written language when dealing with familiar topics

 Comunicación

28 ¿Cómo se siente? 1A

 **Hablemos** Look at the drawings. With a partner, take turns asking what is wrong with each person and answering with what hurts.

MODELO —¿Qué tiene Rosa?
—Le duele...

Rosa

Midori

Conchita

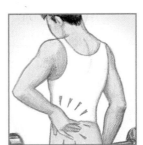

Jeff

Linda

Donna

Benito

Now take turns with your partner playing the roles of the people above. Ask each other what's wrong, and answer as if you were the person in the drawing.

MODELO —Jeff, te veo mal. ¿Qué tienes?
—Es que me duele...

Vocabulario 2

Nota cultural

Mate is a popular South American drink made from an herb called **yerba mate**. The dried herb is placed in a gourd or metal cup, also called a **mate,** and hot water is slowly poured from a kettle called a **pava. Mate** is sipped through a metal straw called a **bombilla** that filters out the loose tea. When the cup of **mate** is finished, more water is added to the leaves. What kinds of herbal teas or other drinks are popular where you live? Is coffee more popular than tea in your community? ↓**2A, 4B**

TEKS Focus

2A Demonstrate understanding of practices (what people do) and how they relate to perspectives (how people perceive things) of the cultures studied

¡Exprésate!

Interactive
TUTOR

To give advice

¿Sabes qué? Comes muy mal. No debes comer tanto dulce ni grasa.

You know what? You eat very badly. You shouldn't eat so many sweets nor so much fat.

Para cuidarte mejor, debes dormir lo suficiente.
¿Por qué no te acuestas más temprano?

To take better care of yourself, you should get enough sleep. Why don't you go to bed earlier?

No debes ver demasiada televisión.

You shouldn't watch too much television.

Online
Vocabulario y gramática, pp. 35–37

29 ¿Qué te pasa? ↓1B

 Escuchemos Escucha las conversaciones. Escoge el consejo *(advice)* apropiado.

a. Debes usar lentes.

b. Necesitas dormir lo suficiente.

c. ¿Qué tal si caminas o montas en bicicleta?

d. Tienes que relajarte. Debes hacer yoga.

e. Hombre, ¡debes seguir una dieta sana!

f. ¡Deja de fumar!

g. Debes estirarte antes de hacer ejercicios.

30 La vida de Consuelo ↓1B, 1C

Leamos/Escribamos Read these notes that Consuelo has made about her health and eating habits. For each comment, write some advice on what she should or should not do to improve her health.

> Como mucho chocolate y hamburguesas.
>
> Estoy a veces cansada.
>
> Me duelen los ojos por la noche.
>
> Estoy aburrida por la mañana.
>
> No hago ejercicio.

31 ¿Sano o no? 1B

Leamos Read the paragraphs about Leo and Juan, and then decide whether the statements that follow are **cierto** or **falso.** If a statement is **falso,** change it to make it read **cierto.**

LEO

Leo es un hombre de 50 años. Se levanta por la mañana a las 6:00 y corre por una hora. Come frutas, verduras y toma leche. No come carne. Por la tarde levanta pesas. Se acuesta a las 22:00 de la noche.

JUAN

Juan tiene 35 años. No hace ejercicio nunca. Come mucha pizza y toma refrescos todos los días. Ve la televisión por la noche. Fuma mucho y siempre está cansado. Se acuesta a la 1:00 de la mañana.

---

1. Juan no debe comer tanta grasa.
2. Leo no duerme lo suficiente.
3. Juan debe dejar de fumar.
4. Leo come muy mal.
5. Juan no cuida la salud.
6. Leo levanta pesas por la mañana.

  Comunicación

32 ¿Cómo te sientes? 1A

Hablemos Talk about these drawings with a partner. What's wrong with these people? What should they do or not do to feel better?

1. Selena   2. Víctor   3. Anastasio

33 Un cuestionario 1A

Escribamos/Hablemos Write a questionnaire in Spanish to find out how your classmates are doing today. Ask how each person is feeling, if anything hurts, what kind of mood he or she is in, and why. Also ask what each person usually eats for breakfast. Then, offer advice about how he or she might feel better.

TEKS Focus

1A Engage in oral and written exchanges of learned material to socialize and to provide and obtain information

---

Estar, sentirse, and tener

Interactive TUTOR

1 You have used **ser** to tell what people and things are normally like. Use **estar** with adjectives describing mental or physical states or conditions.

Mi amigo **es** joven.	**Está** muy cansado.
My friend is young.	*He's very tired.*

2 Like **estar**, **sentirse** *(to feel)* can be used with adverbs **bien/mal** or with adjectives to describe mental or physical states The verb **sentirse** is an **e → ie** stem-changing verb.

yo me s**ie**nto	nosotros(as) nos sentimos
tú te s**ie**ntes	vosotros(as) os sentís
usted, él, ella se s**ie**nte	ustedes, ellos(as) se s**ie**nten

Nos sentimos cansados.	No **se sienten** bien.
We feel tired.	*They don't feel well.*

3 The following **tener expressions** with a **noun** describe a mental or physical state.

tener frío *to be cold*	**tener miedo** *to be afraid*
tener calor *to be hot*	**tener sueño** *to be sleepy*

Online

Vocabulario y gramática, pp. 38–40	Actividades, pp. 32–35

34 ¿Cómo están? **1B**

Escuchemos Escucha las oraciones y decide qué dibujo corresponde a cada oración. Algunos dibujos se usan más de una vez.

a.   b.   c.   d.   e.

35 **En el colegio** ↓1B

Leamos/Escribamos Rita is talking about her school. First, complete the sentences with the correct form of **estar, sentirse,** or **tener.** Then rewrite each sentence, changing it to reflect your own situation.

> **MODELO** **A veces Luis está aburrido en la clase de matemáticas.**
> **Casi nunca estoy aburrido(a) en mis clases.**

1. Muchos estudiantes ═══ miedo de los exámenes de inglés.
2. Joaquín y Mateo ═══ nerviosos cuando presentan un examen.
3. Muchos estudiantes ═══ calor cuando practican deportes.
4. Nos gusta mucho el arte y ═══ contentos en la clase de arte.
5. Mi amiga Matilde siempre ═══ hambre antes del almuerzo.
6. A veces nosotros ═══ sueño después de almorzar.
7. Mis profesores no ═══ enfermos casi nunca.

36 **¿Quién es?** ↓1B

Escribamos Use **estar, sentirse,** or **tener** and the adjective for each number to write sentences describing how these people are feeling.

Leti

Marta

Ricardo

Vicente

1. sueño   3. sed   5. miedo   7. calor
2. enfermo(a)   4. nervioso(a) 6. mal   8. cansado

 Comunicación

37 **Un catarro** ↓1A

Hablemos With a classmate, act out the following situation. You have a cold and are describing how you feel. A friend gives you advice about how you should take care of yourself. Use at least five of the following words in your role-play.

enfermo(a)	frío	calor	sed
cansado(a)	mal	sueño	me duele(n)

Gramática 2

Negative informal commands

Interactive TUTOR

¿Te acuerdas?

These verbs have irregular **affirmative informal command forms**.

hacer	haz
ir	ve
poner	pon
salir	sal
ser	sé
tener	ten
venir	ven

1 An **affirmative command** tells someone what to do. The **informal affirmative command** form of most verbs is the present tense **tú** form without the final **-s**.

> **Come** bien y **duerme** lo suficiente.
> *Eat right and get enough sleep.*

2 A **negative command** tells someone not to do something. To form the **negative informal command** of most **-ar** verbs, drop the final **o** of the **yo** form and add **-es**.

> (yo) fum**o** → no fum**es**
> (yo) trabaj**o** → no trabaj**es**

> **No trabajes** tanto.   *Don't work so much.*

3 To form the **negative informal command** of most **-er** and **-ir** verbs, drop the final **o** of the **yo** form and add **-as**.

> (yo) veng**o** → no veng**as**
> (yo) com**o** → no com**as**
> (yo) duerm**o** → no duerm**as**

> **No duermas** hasta tarde.   *Don't sleep late.*

> **No pongas** las frutas en la sopa.   *Don't put . . .*

4 These verbs have irregular forms of the **negative informal command**.

> dar → **no des**
> ir → **no vayas**
> ser → **no seas**

Online

| Vocabulario y gramática, pp. 38–40 | Actividades, pp. 32–35 |

---

38 Consejos ↴1B

Leamos/Hablemos ¿Qué le dicen los padres a su hijo?

1. (Come/No comas) verduras.
2. (Compra/No compres) muchos dulces.
3. (Sal/No salgas) tarde para el colegio.
4. (Haz/No hagas) tu tarea.
5. (Pon/No pongas) los pies en la mesa.
6. (Vuelve/No vuelvas) tarde a casa.
7. (Ve/No vayas) al colegio.
8. (Sé/No seas) bueno.
9. (Arregla/No arregles) tu cuarto.

"¡No corras Lalo!"

39 **¿Qué deben hacer?** 💬1B

Escribamos Using commands, tell a friend if he or she should or should not do the things in parentheses.

> **MODELO** **Si siempre estás enfermo... (fumar/dormir lo suficiente/comer dulces)**
> **No fumes. Duerme lo suficiente. No comas dulces.**

1. Si quieres cuidarte la salud... (comer verduras/hacer ejercicio/pasar el día delante de la televisión)

2. Si te duelen los pies... (correr/descansar/ir a bailar)

3. Si siempre estás aburrido... (dormir tanto/salir con los amigos/buscar un pasatiempo)

4. Si no entiendes algo en la clase de matemáticas... (estudiar más/hacer la tarea/ver tanta televisión)

5. Si siempre estás cansado... (volver tarde a casa/dormir más/salir con los amigos todas las noches)

40 **Para salir bien** 💬1B

Escribamos Imagine a younger friend of yours is going to attend your school next year. Give the friend some advice about what he or she should do or not do in order to have a good year.

> **MODELO** **comer en clase**
> **No comas en clase nunca.**

1. correr en clase
2. participar en un deporte o club
3. interrumpir a los profesores
4. ser tímido
5. estudiar todos los días

Un colegio en Argentina

 Comunicación

41 **Nuestros problemas** 💬1A, 1C

Escribamos/Hablemos On a separate sheet of paper, write a real or imaginary problem. Hand all the "problems" to the teacher, who will write some of them on the board. In pairs, prepare some solutions to the problems. Be prepared to role-play your conversation about problems and solutions for the class.

> **MODELO** —Siempre tengo sueño en mi primera clase.
> —¡Duerme más en casa!

Interactive TUTOR

Object and reflexive pronouns with commands

1 **Direct object pronouns** and **reflexive pronouns** are attached to the end of **affirmative commands**. A written accent mark goes over the stressed vowel of the verb, unless the verb is only one syllable long.

> **Levánta**te y **pon**te los zapatos.
> *Get up and put your shoes on.*

2 **Direct object pronouns** and **reflexive pronouns** go in between **no** and the verb in the **negative command form**.

> Este libro es pésimo. **No lo** leas.
> *That book is awful. Don't read it.*
>
> **No te** levantes muy tarde.
> *Don't get up too late.*

Online

| Vocabulario y gramática, pp. 38–40 | Actividades, pp. 32–35 |

Vocabulario y gramática, pp. 38–40 | Actividades, pp. 32–35

¿Te acuerdas?

Words ending in a **vowel**, **-n,** or **-s** are normally stressed on the next-to-last syllable. If another syllable is stressed, there must be a written accent on its vowel.

es**tá**	**es**ta
te**lé**fonos	**len**tes
jóvenes	**jo**ven

42 **Más consejos** 🔽1B

Leamos/Hablemos Escoge el consejo apropiado.

1. ¿Tienes sueño?
   a. ¡Acuéstate!
   b. ¡No te acuestes!
2. ¿Te duelen los pies?
   a. ¡No me quites los zapatos!
   b. ¡Quítate los zapatos!
3. Vamos a comer.
   a. ¡Lávate las manos!
   b. ¡No te laves las manos!
4. Necesitas dormir más.
   a. ¡Levántate!
   b. ¡No te levantes!
5. ¿Tienes frío?
   a. ¡Vístete!
   b. ¡No te entrenes!
6. ¿Estás nervioso?
   a. ¡Relájate!
   b. ¡No te estires!
7. ¿Tienes catarro?
   a. ¡No me cuides!
   b. ¡Cuídate!
8. Los libros son muy aburridos.
   a. ¡No los leas!
   b. ¡Léelos!
9. ¿Los pies?
   a. Ponlos en la mesa.
   b. ¡No los pongas en la mesa!
10. ¿Llegar al colegio por la mañana?
    a. Sal temprano.
    b. No salgas temprano, sal tarde.
11. ¿Está fría la sopa?
    a. ¡No la calientes!
    b. ¡Caliéntala!

43 El hombre prehistórico ⬇1B

Leamos/Escribamos A caveman has arrived in your classroom through a time warp. He does the following things. Use informal commands to explain to him how these things are done.

MODELO Se baña en la cocina.
¡No te bañes en la cocina! ¡Báñate en el baño!

1. Se pone el piyama para salir.
2. Se lava los dientes con una toalla.
3. Se levanta a las once de la noche.
4. Se baña con la pasta de dientes.
5. Se viste en el patio.
6. Se acuesta en la mesa.
7. Se peina con el jabón.
8. Se afeita con un cuchillo.

44 ¿Qué hago con esto? ⬇1B

Escribamos/Hablemos Follow the **modelo** to tell the caveman what he should or should not do with the following items.

MODELO poner los platos (en el piso/en la mesa)
¡No los pongas en el piso! ¡Ponlos en la mesa!

1. lavar la ropa (en la casa/en el carro)
2. usar los lentes (para cortar/para leer)
3. limpiar las ventanas (con jugo/con agua y jabón)
4. pasar la aspiradora (en la sala/en el césped)
5. poner la computadora (en el escritorio/en el microondas)
6. el arroz con pollo (comer con los pies/con un tenedor)

TEKS Focus

1A Engage in oral and written exchanges of learned material to socialize and to provide and obtain information

Comunicación

45 La madre cansada ⬇1A

Hablemos Con un(a) compañero(a), dramatiza las tres conversaciones entre la madre y el hijo en los dibujos.

Conexiones culturales

Conexión Idiomas

El béisbol Baseball is very popular in Latin America, especially in the Caribbean. Many players from Caribbean countries have gone on to play in the major leagues in the United States. Because baseball originated in the U.S., many of the Spanish words for the sport come from the English words. Words borrowed directly from one language to another are called loanwords.

TEKS Focus

4C Demonstrate understanding of the influence of one language and culture on another

1 El lenguaje del béisbol ↓1B, 4C

Work with a group to identify which of the baseball terms below are borrowed from English. Decide which English word each comes from.

el pelotero/la pelotera
el jardinero/la jardinera
el lanzador/la lanzadora
bases robadas

batear
el hit
la pelota
el jonrón

el récord
pichear
el cuadrangular
ranqueado

2 Palabras del español ↓1B, 4C

English has also borrowed words from Spanish. Below are some Spanish loanwords found in English. What does each word mean? Use a dictionary if you're not sure.

patio
rodeo
salsa

adobe
lasso
arroyo

tornado
poncho
mosquito

Conexión Ciencias sociales

Los peloteros latinoamericanos Approximately one out of every six players in the major leagues in the United States is from Latin America.

Juan Antonio (Sánchez) Marichal, dominicano
Lanzador, Los Gigantes de San Francisco
Electo al Salón de Fama en 1983

Atanasio 'Tony' Pérez Regal, cubano
Primera base, Los Rojos de Cincinnati
Electo al Salón de Fama en 2000

3 El clima y el béisbol ↓3A

Read the photo captions to find out where these three players are from. Look at the maps on pages R5–R6 to find their countries. Where are these countries in relation to the equator? In relation to the U.S.? Based on what you know about weather and seasons, would the climate in the Caribbean be good for playing baseball?

4 Las temporadas ↓2A

Many Latin American baseball teams play in the Caribbean Series every February. This event ends the winter baseball season for those countries. How does this compare with the baseball season in the U.S.?

Roberto Clemente Walker,
puertorriqueño
Jardinero derecho, Los Piratas
de Pittsburgh
Electo al Salón de Fama en 1973

Conexiones Culturales

¿Quién será?

Episodio 7

⬇1B, 3A

Understanding a character's motives To understand a character, you must first understand motives—why he or she is doing something or acting a certain way. To understand someone's motives, you must watch behavior. Nicolás has to get ready to go to his grandmother's birthday lunch. Can you tell from his actions whether he really wants to go? When he tells his grandmother he is sick, what is his motive? As you read the **Novela** or watch the video, notice what he does and decide what his motive is.

En Puerto Rico

La mamá de Nicolás quiere hablar con él. Él tiene que alistarse para el almuerzo de cumpleaños de su abuela.

Océano Atlántico   San Juan ★
PUERTO RICO
Mar Caribe

1

Sra. Ortega ¿Nicolás? ¿Hijo?

2

Sra. Ortega ¿Nicolás, estás listo? Hijo, ya sabes que hoy es el cumpleaños de tu abuela y tenemos que ir a almorzar con ella.

Bañate con
SuperSuave, el jabón
que te hace sentir
¡súper suave!

3 **Sra. Ortega** ¡Nicolás, por favor!
¡Levántate, hijo! Tienes que bañarte. Aquí
está el jabón.

Lávate el
pelo con el champú
Estrella y ¡brilla como
una estrella!

4 **Sra. Ortega** ¡Nicolás, por favor!
¡También tienes que lavarte el pelo!
Aquí está el champú.

Lávate los
dientes con la pasta
de dientes Sonrisa.

5 **Sra. Ortega** Nicolás, ¿no me oyes? Abre
esta puerta, ¡ahora mismo! Sé que necesitas pasta de dientes... aquí está.

Nicolás,
levántate, báñate,
lávate el pelo y los
dientes y ¡alístate!

6

Novela en video

A CONTESTA

What's happening in the **Novela**? Answer these questions to make sure you
understand.

1. Why does Mrs. Ortega want Nicolás to get cleaned up? What is Nicolás
doing in his room while she's talking to him?

2. What happens on the TV when Sra. Ortega holds up the soap? the shampoo?

ciento quince **115**

7

Abuela Nicolás, te veo cansado.
Nicolás Sí, abuela, me siento un poco
cansado. Tengo frío y me duele la cabeza.

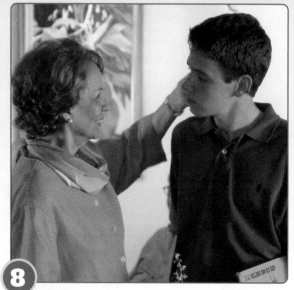

8

Abuela Anda, vete, acuéstate un rato. Te
despertamos cuando esté listo el almuerzo.
Nicolás Gracias, abuela.

9

Nicolás se acuesta pero no descansa.

B CONTESTA

1. What happens to Nicolás
at his grandmother's
house?

2. How does Nicolás say he
feels?

Actividades

1 ¿Cierto o falso?

Tell whether each statement is **cierto** or **falso**. If it is **falso,** correct it.

1. La pasta de dientes se llama 'Estrella.'
2. Hoy es el cumpleaños de Nicolás.
3. Nicolás está cansado y tiene catarro.
4. En la cama, Nicolás descansa.

2 ¿Cómo se dice?

Find and write down the words and phrases in the **Novela** that . . .

1. Sra. Ortega uses to tell Nicolás to get up.
2. his grandmother uses to tell Nicolás that he looks tired.
3. Sra. Ortega uses to tell Nicolás to take a bath and wash his hair.
4. his grandmother uses to tell Nicolás to lie down.

3 ¿Comprendes la Novela?

Check your understanding of the events in the story by answering these questions.

1. How can you tell from Nicolás's actions whether he wants to go to the birthday lunch?
2. What event in the story is Nicolás's fantasy?
3. Does he really not feel well at his grandmother's? How do you know?
4. What is Nicolás's motive for his actions throughout the episode?

> **Próximo episodio**
> *Marcos has to go to Miami next. Can you predict what he might be doing there?*
> PÁGINAS 160–163 ▶

Leamos y escribamos

TEKS Focus

3A Use resources in the language and cultures being studied to gain access to information

ESTRATEGIA

para leer Background knowledge is the information you already know about something. Before you read something, take a moment to recall what you already know about a topic. This will make it easier to guess the meaning of unknown words or phrases.

A Antes de leer ⬇1B, 3A

Think about what you already know about health and diet. Now read the following article and try to infer the meanings of the words marked with a red asterisk by using context clues.

¡En buena salud!

Cecilia Mendoza, famosa entrenadora* y nutricionista argentina, contesta algunas preguntas sobre la salud y la dieta.

¿Qué es mejor para mantenerse en forma: levantar pesas o hacer aeróbicos?

Las dos actividades son buenas. Puedes hacer aeróbicos cuatro veces* por semana y levantar pesas dos veces por semana. Y recuerda[1], siempre debes estirarte después de hacer ejercicio.

¿Por cuánto tiempo se debe hacer una actividad aeróbica?

La intensidad de una actividad determina su duración. Si la actividad requiere más energía, no hay que hacerla por mucho tiempo.

¿Qué dieta recomiendas para bajar de peso?

Lo más importante es comer comida sana y prestar atención[2] a la cantidad* de comida que comes. Si reduces el tamaño* de las porciones y sigues las recomendaciones de la pirámide alimenticia, vas a bajar de peso.

Sufro[3] mucho de estrés durante el año escolar. ¿Qué puedo hacer?

Para reducir[4] el estrés, haz lo siguiente: duerme lo suficiente, haz ejercicio todos los días, come una dieta sana, no tomes bebidas con cafeína[5], maneja* bien tu tiempo, toma las cosas con calma y siempre respira[6] profundamente*.

1 remember   2 pay attention
3 I suffer   4 reduce
5 caffeinated beverages   6 breathe

Pirámide alimenticia

grasas, dulces
muy poco

leche, yogur, queso
2–3 porciones

carne, pollo, pescado
huevos, nueces, frijoles
2–3 porciones

verduras
3–5 porciones

frutas
2–4 porciones

pan, arroz, cereales, tallarines
6–11 porciones

B Comprensión ♦ 1B

¿Son **ciertas** o **falsas** las siguientes oraciones? Corrige las oraciones falsas.

1. Cecilia Mendoza sólo *(only)* habla del ejercicio.
2. Para mantenerse en forma es necesario levantar pesas todos los días.
3. La intensidad de un ejercicio determina la cantidad de tiempo que debes hacerlo.
4. Para bajar de peso sólo es necesario seguir una dieta sana.
5. Para reducir el estrés es importante tener una vida sana.

C Después de leer ♦ 1B

Which of Cecilia's recommendations do you already follow? How difficult would it be for you to follow all of her recommendations? Which ones would be the most difficult to follow? Why?

Clínica Fierro

¿Te duele...?
- _____
- _____

¿Estás...?
- _____
- _____

Interactive TUTOR

Taller del escritor

ESTRATEGIA

para escribir Graphic organizers can help you organize your thoughts visually and are especially helpful in designing posters and charts. Consider bulleted charts or cluster bubbles as you plan your poster.

El doctor te aconseja... ♦ 1C

Imagine you are a doctor who believes that people should take a more active role in avoiding or curing their illnesses. Design a poster for the patients' waiting room listing common symptoms followed by your suggestions on how to avoid or cure the problem.

1 Antes de escribir

List the symptoms in question form: **¿Te duele la garganta? ¿Estás cansado(a)?** Then write one suggestion to solve each problem or illness.

2 Escribir y revisar

- Use a graphic organizer to plan where you'll write the symptoms and suggested solutions on a poster.
- Write down the symptoms.
- Write out suggestions telling patients what to do. Use expressions for giving advice as well as affirmative and negative commands.
- Read your poster of symptoms and advice to a classmate.
- Check for proper use of vocabulary, spelling, and punctuation.
- Revise your poster if needed.

3 Publicar

Illustrate your poster and show it to the class. Share one piece of advice from it.

Cuaderno para hispanohablantes, pp. 53–60

Leamos y escribamos

Repaso capítulo 7

1 Todos se preparan para salir. ¿Qué tiene que hacer cada persona para prepararse? ↘1B

Miguelito

el señor Blanco

Elena

2 Completa el párrafo con las formas correctas de los verbos en paréntesis. ↘1B

Por la mañana, mi madre ___1___ (dormir) hasta las seis. Luego, ella ___2___ (levantarse) y ___3___ (vestirse) antes de desayunar. Yo me levanto muy temprano para ___4___ (entrenarse) antes de ir. Después de la escuela, mis hermanos y yo ___5___ (poder) ver un poco de televisión antes de empezar la tarea. A veces mi hermana Maribel ___6___ (jugar) videojuegos. Por la noche, (yo) ___7___ (bañarse) y luego escucho música para ___8___ (relajarse) un poco antes de acostarme.

3 Prepara una lista de consejos para un(a) amigo(a) usando las palabras de los cuadros. ↘1B

MODELO **No debes comer tanto dulce si no quieres subir de peso.**

1	**2**	**3**
Debes No debes	comer tanto dulce acostarte tarde comer verduras hacer yoga buscar un pasatiempo entrenarte cuidarte	si estás aburrido(a) si siempre tienes catarro si no quieres subir de peso si siempre tienes sueño para mantenerte en forma para seguir una dieta sana para relajarte

4 Your friend has problems. Write informal commands using the verbs in parentheses to give advice to your friend. ↴1B

1. No tengo nada que hacer después de clases. Estoy aburrido.
   (ser perezoso/buscar un pasatiempo)
2. Siempre me siento muy cansado en clase.
   (acostarse más temprano/dormir en clase)
3. Me duele el estómago después de comer en un restaurante.
   (comer comida sana/pedir muchos postres)
4. Me duelen los ojos y la cabeza.
   (ver tanta televisión/comprar lentes)

5 Contesta las preguntas. ↴2A, 4A

1. What sport is practiced in July in Bariloche?
2. Name some foods that are popular in Argentina.
3. What is **mate**? How is it prepared?
4. Name two loanwords in Spanish that are borrowed from English. Then name two words that English has borrowed from Spanish.

 6 Escucha la conversación entre Roberto y Laura. Luego di si las oraciones que siguen (*that follow*) son **ciertas** o **falsas**. ↴1B

7 Mira los dibujos y con un(a) compañero(a), dramaticen la conversación. ↴1C

4 Gramática 2
- **estar, sentirse,** and **tener**
- negative informal commands
- object and reflexive pronouns with commands
  pp. 106–111

5 Cultura
- **Comparaciones**
  pp. 98–99
- **Notas culturales**
  pp. 90, 102, 104
- **Conexiones culturales**
  pp. 112–113

TEKS Focus
4A Demonstrate understanding of the nature of language through comparisons

Repaso de Gramática 1

Some verbs are used with **reflexive pronouns** if the subject and object of the verb are the same. For a list of such verbs, see page 92.

lavarse			
me	lavo	**nos**	lavamos
te	lavas	**os**	laváis
se	lava	**se**	lavan

Use the **infinitive** of a verb after **acabar de, para, antes de, después de.**

> **Acabo de** bañarme. Necesito una toalla **para** secarme.

For the forms of acostarse (**o** → **ue**), encontrar (**o** → **ue**), and vestirse (**e** → **i**), see page 96.

Repaso de Gramática 2

To describe mental or physical states or conditions use:

> **estar** bien/mal/*adjective*
> **tener** frío/calor/miedo/sueño
> **sentirse** bien/mal/*adjective*

An **object** or **reflexive pronoun** goes just before the verb in **negative commands** and is attached to the end of an **affirmative command.**

fumar → **no fumes**	dar → **no des**
dormir → **no duermas**	ser → **no seas**
levantarse → **no te levantes (levánta te)**	ir → **no vayas**
leer → **no lo leas**	

Letra y sonido (g) (gu)

La letra g

- The letters **g** and **gu** sound like the "hard" *g* in *game* at the beginning of a phrase starting with **ga, gue, gui, go, gu, gr, gl** or when these follow an **n:**

  gato, **g**uerra, **g**uitarra, ten**g**o, un **g**usto, ¡**G**rita!

- The letters **g** and **gu** sound much softer than the *g* in *game* when **ga, gue, gui, go, gu, gr, gl** follow a vowel or a consonant other than **n:**

  mi **g**ato, á**g**uila, al**g**o, mucho **g**usto, ne**g**ro

Trabalenguas

Tres tigres tragaban trigo en un trigal, y el más grande se puso a entigretar.

Contigo entró un tren con trigo un tren con trigo contigo entró.

Dictado ◆1B

Escribe las oraciones de la grabación.

Repaso de Vocabulario 1

Talking about your daily routine

acabar de	to just (have done something)
acostarse (ue)	to go to bed
afeitarse	to shave
antes de	before
bañarse	to bathe
la boca	mouth
el brazo	arm
la cara	face
el cepillo de dientes	toothbrush
despertarse (ie)	to wake up
los dientes	teeth
encontrar (ue)	to find
entrenarse	to work out
la espalda	back
estar listo(a)	to be ready
estirarse	to stretch
los hombros	shoulders
el jabón	soap
lavarse	to wash
levantarse	to get up
levantar pesas	to lift weights
maquillarse	to put on makeup
el maquillaje	makeup
la nariz	nose
la navaja	razor
la pantorrilla	calf
la pasta de dientes	toothpaste
el pecho	chest
peinarse	to comb your hair
el peine	comb
la pierna	leg
el piyama	pajamas
ponerse	to put on
prepararse	to get ready
¿Qué te falta hacer?	What do you still have to do?
quitarse	to take off
la secadora de pelo	hair dryer
secarse	to dry
la toalla	towel
vestirse (i)	to get dressed

Talking about staying fit and healthy

mantenerse (ie) en forma	to stay in shape
¿Qué haces para relajarte?	What do you do to relax?

Repaso de Vocabulario 2

To talk about how you feel

bajar de peso	to lose weight
buscar un pasatiempo	to look for a hobby
la cabeza	head
caminar	to walk
el cuello	neck
los dedos	fingers
dejar de fumar	to stop smoking
doler (ue)	to hurt
Es que...	It's because/just that . . .
estar aburrido(a)	to be bored
estar cansado(a)	to be tired
estar contento(a)	to be happy
estar enfermo(a)	to be sick
estar nervioso(a)	to be nervous
estar triste	to be sad
el estómago	stomach
la garganta	throat
hacer yoga	to do yoga
Le duele(n)...	His (Her) . . . hurt(s).
Me duele(n)...	My . . . hurt(s).
las manos	hands
el oído	(inner) ear
los pies	feet
¿Qué te pasa?	What's wrong with you?
¿Qué tiene...?	What's the matter with . . . ?
seguir (i) una dieta sana	to eat a balanced diet
sentirse (ie)	to feel
subir de peso	to gain weight
¿Te duele algo?	Is something hurting you?
tener catarro	to have a cold
Te veo mal.	You don't look well.

To give advice

No debes...	You shouldn't . . .
demasiado(a)	too much
dormir lo suficiente	to get enough sleep
tanto dulce	so many sweets
tanta grasa	so much fat
ni	neither
Para cuidarte la salud debes...	To take care of your health, you should . . .
Para cuidarte mejor...	To take better care of yourself . . .
tanto(a)	so much, so many

For expressions with tener . . . . *see page 106.*

Integración
capítulos 1-7

1 Escucha la descripción de una mañana típica en casa de los
Muñoz. Escoge la foto correspondiente. ✦1B

A

B

C

D

TEKS Focus

1C Present information using familiar words, phrases, and sentences

2 Read this letter to an advice columnist from a teen magazine.
Then answer the questions in Spanish. ✦1B, 1C

> ## *Querida* Dameesperanza...
>
> **Querida Dameesperanza:**
> *Tengo muchas clases difíciles y soy muy trabajadora. Mis amigos prefieren salir y no estudiar. Quiero salir con ellos, pero no puedo porque tengo mucha tarea. ¿Qué debo hacer?*
>
> — *Frustrada*
>
> *Querida Frustrada:*
> **Sí, debes estudiar, pero necesitas relajarte también. Puedes estudiar dos o tres horas cada noche. Entonces, los viernes y sábados puedes ir con tus amigos a un partido o al cine. ¡No necesitas pasar todas las noches en la biblioteca!**

1. How does Frustrada describe herself?
2. How does she describe her friends?
3. What does Frustrada want to do?
4. Why can't she do what she wants to?
5. What does the advice columnist tell Frustrada to do on weekdays?
6. Where does the columnist suggest Frustrada go on weekends?

3 This painting shows a family traveling through the vast grasslands of Argentina in the 1860s. Imagine what their living conditions and health concerns might have been during this trip. Write five descriptive sentences about the people in the painting. Use the adjectives below and tell who might be feeling this way and why. 🦅1C

- cansado(a)
- aburrido(a)
- triste(a)
- nervioso(a)
- contento(a)

by Prilidiano Pueyrredón, 1823-70, Argentinian; The Art Archive / Museo Nacional de Bellas Artes Buenos Aires / Dagli Orti

Viajeros con carrata en las pampas
por Prilidiano Pueyrredón (1823–1870)

4

Situación

You're helping at your school's annual health fair by conducting a survey in Spanish. Write five or six questions to ask a classmate. Find out the following information.

▶ How does the student stay in shape?

▶ What does the student do to relax?

▶ Which foods does the student typically eat?

▶ At what times does he or she go to bed and get up?

▶ How is the student feeling right now?

After your partner answers your questions, suggest one thing that he or she could do to improve his or her health. 🦅1A

Integración

Video/DVD

GeoVisión

Geocultura
Florida

▲ **Cítricos** Florida is one of the world's largest exporters of citrus fruit. Spanish explorers first brought oranges to Florida in the 1500s.

Panama City

Río Apalachicola

▼ **Miami** Many people from Spanish-speaking cultures live in the Miami area. Miami is on the Atlantic coast of Florida, only 322 kilometers (200 miles) northeast of Havana, Cuba.

Almanaque

Población
15.982.378

Capital
Tallahassee

Moneda
dólar estadounidense

Economía
manufactura, turismo, productos de frutas cítricas, pesca comercial, electrónica, comercio con Latinoamérica

Texas **¿Sabías que...?**
The traditions of Spanish-speaking people in Florida and Texas have a great influence on the culture and daily lives of all people in those states. In Florida the influence is mainly Cuban, while in Texas the influence is mainly Mexican.

◄ **Florida** For its abundance of colorful flowers, the Spanish explorer **Juan Ponce de León** named this peninsula **Pascua Florida**, meaning *Flowery Easter*.

▶ **Parque Nacional de los Everglades** Everglades National Park is the only place in the world where crocodiles and alligators live alongside each other in the wild.

GEORGIA

★ **TALLAHASSEE**

Jacksonville

Río Saint Johns

St. Augustine

Río Suwannee

FLORIDA

OCÉANO ATLÁNTICO

GOLFO DE MÉXICO

Orlando

Cape Canaveral

Tampa

BAHÍA DE TAMPA

Lago Okeechobee

▲ **Cape Canaveral** The Kennedy Space Center exists in harmony with the Merritt Island National Wildlife Refuge. The refuge is home to 15 threatened or endangered species, including bald eagles and manatees.

Fort Lauderdale

Miami

Parque de los Everglades

BAHÍA BISCAYNE

La Habana, Cuba (145km)

CAYOS DE FLORIDA

ESTRECHO DE FLORIDA

▼ **Los Cayos de Florida** The Florida Keys are a chain of islands connected by 42 bridges, including the famous Bahia Honda Bridge.

▲ **La Pequeña Habana** Little Havana is a neighborhood in Miami where many Cuban Americans live and do business.

🍀3B

¿Qué tanto sabes?

How is Florida's economy a reflection of its geographic location?

A conocer Florida

La comida

▲ **Comida floribeña** "Floribbean" cuisine combines the flavors of traditional Caribbean dishes with foods native to Florida. Floribbean dishes often include seafood, tropical fruits, and zesty herbs and spices.

▲ **Las croquetas y las empanadas** Croquettes and **empanadas** are Cuban foods that are popular in Miami. **Flan** is a common dessert at restaurants in Little Havana.

El arte

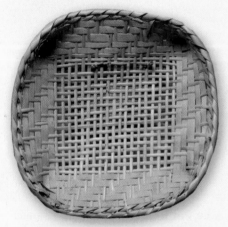

▲ **Los seminoles** The Seminole people weave traditional baskets out of dried grasses from the Everglades wetlands.

▲ *Calle Ocho* This painting shows the heart of Miami's Cuban culture: a scene from the famous 8th Street, or **Calle Ocho**. The artist, Mildrey Guillot, was born in Havana, Cuba, and moved to Miami in 1962.

La arquitectura

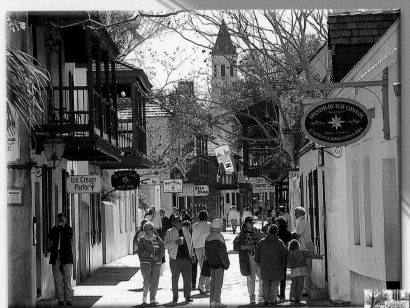

Interactive
TUTOR

Visit Holt Online
go.hrw.com
KEYWORD: EXP1B CH8
Photo Tour

◆2A, 2B
¿Sabías que...?
During the 1960s, more than 260,000 Cuban refugees arrived in the United States. How does Cuban culture affect the arts, food, and festivals of Miami?

◀ **St. Augustine** The colonial architecture reflects St. Augustine's Spanish roots.

Las celebraciones

▲ **El Carnaval de Miami** The Carnival of Miami in Little Havana includes the **Festival de la Calle Ocho**, a celebration of Miami's Hispanic culture.

▲ **El Festival de Jazz Latino** The Latin Jazz Festival is part of the Carnival of Miami. Latin jazz is a combination of American jazz with Afro-Cuban rhythms and percussion instruments.

Vamos de compras

Objetivos

In Part 1 you will learn to:
- ask for and give an opinion
- offer and ask for help in a store
- use **costar** and numbers to one million
- use demonstrative adjectives and make comparisons
- form the verb **quedar**

In Part 2 you will learn to:
- say where you went and what you did
- talk on the phone
- form the preterite of **-ar** verbs
- use the verb **ir** in the preterite
- use **-ar** verbs with reflexive pronouns in the preterite

¿Qué ves en la foto?

- **En la foto, ¿qué tiempo hace?**
- **¿Qué van a hacer los amigos?**
- **¿A ti te gusta ir de compras?**

Texas

TEKS Look for the ✦ next to each activity to learn how it can help you achieve the goals of the **Texas Essential Knowledge and Skills,** found on page xxi.

De compras en Miami, Florida

Vocabulario en acción 1

Video/DVD

ExpresaVisión

En la tienda de ropa

¿Qué le parece esta camisa?

Muy bien. También me gustaría comprar un saco.

el cliente (la cliente)

el dependiente (la dependiente)

un suéter

una chaqueta

un saco

un abrigo

un par de pantalones vaqueros

Más vocabulario...

Es...	It's . . .
de algodón	made of cotton
de lana	made of wool
de seda	made of silk
para hombres	for men
para mujeres	for women
para niños	for children

▶ **Vocabulario adicional** — Ropa, p. R10

Texas También se puede decir...

In Spain, you might hear **pantalones tejanos** as well as **vaqueros**. A sweater is called **un jersey** and tennis shoes are **zapatillas de tenis**.

Bluejeans are also known as **pantalones de mezclilla** and T-shirts are **playeras** in Mexico and Texas. Many Spanish speakers have borrowed the term **bluejeans** directly from English.

¿Qué ropa llevas hoy?

Visit Holt Online

go.hrw.com
KEYWORD: EXP1B CH8

Vocabulario 1 practice

Voy al gimnasio. Llevo...

un sombrero

una camiseta

unos pantalones cortos

unos zapatos de tenis

Voy a salir con amigos. Llevo...

un vestido

unas sandalias

Voy a clase. Llevo...

una blusa

una falda

unas botas

Voy a salir al teatro. Llevo...

una camisa

unos pantalones

unos calcetines

unos zapatos

¿Qué color te gusta más?

rojo   azul   verde   amarillo   morado   blanco   negro   anaranjado   gris   café

¡Exprésate!

To ask for an opinion	To give your opinion
¿Qué te parece el traje de baño anaranjado? *What do you think of the orange bathing suit?*	**Me parece feo y cuesta mucho. ¡Es un robo!** *It's ugly and costs a lot. It's a rip-off!*
¿Cómo me queda la camiseta? *How does the T-shirt fit me?*	**Te queda muy bien. Y está a la (última) moda.** *It looks good on you. And it's in (the latest) style.*
¿Y el/la...? ¡Cuesta ochenta dólares! *What about this . . .? It costs $80.00!*	**¡Qué caro(a)! Además, está pasado(a) de moda.** *How expensive! Besides, it's out of style.*
La bolsa es una ganga, ¿verdad? *The purse is a bargaín, isn't it?*	**Tienes razón. Es muy barata.** *You're right. It's very inexpensive.*

Interactive TUTOR

Online
Vocabulario y gramática, pp. 41–43

▶ **Vocabulario adicional** — Ropa, p. R10

Vocabulario 1

1 **¿Les gustan?** 🔽1B

Escuchemos Basándote en los comentarios, decide si a las personas les gusta o no les gusta la ropa de que hablan.

1. la camisa
2. la blusa
3. el saco
4. el vestido
5. las botas

6. la chaqueta
7. el sombrero
8. el traje de baño
9. los pantalones vaqueros
10. el abrigo

2 **La ropa nueva** 🔽1B

Leamos Alicia is helping her sister Mónica shop for new clothes. Choose Alicia's best response for each of Mónica's comments.

MÓNICA	**ALICIA**
1. ¿Cómo me queda la camisa?	a. Sí, está a la última moda.
2. ¿Qué te parece la blusa roja?	b. ¡Qué barato! ¡Es una ganga!
3. El abrigo cuesta doce dólares.	c. Es fea. No me gusta la roja.
4. ¿Está a la moda el saco de algodón?	d. Te queda muy bien.

3 **¿Qué te parecen?** 🔽1B

Leamos Complete Mónica's and Alicia's conversation, based on the clothing pictured below.

MÓNICA

—¿Qué te ___1___ la chaqueta negra?

—Los ___3___ verdes son una ganga, ¿no?

—¿___6___ me quedan los vaqueros?

—¿Y el ___9___ amarillo? ¿Te gusta?

—¿La ___12___ roja es cara no?

ALICIA

—Es muy ___2___ . Solo cuesta $25.

—¡___4___ ! Además, están pasados ___5___ .

—Te quedan muy ___7___ . Están a la ___8___ , también.

—Me parece ___10___ y cuesta mucho. ¡Es un ___11___ !

—Sí, tienes ___13___ . Es cara.

4 **¿Qué ropa llevan?** 1C

Escribamos For each member of the Morelos family, write a list of his or her clothing. Include colors, possible fabrics, and adjectives of your choice.

> **MODELO** El señor Morelos tiene una camisa blanca de algodón y unos pantalones vaqueros.

   Comunicación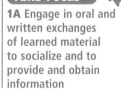

5 **La familia Morelos** 1A, 1C

Hablemos In groups of five, play the roles of the members of the Morelos family from Activity 4. Introduce yourself to the class. Tell your name, family relationship, and age. Tell one thing you like to do. Then describe what you are wearing.

> **MODELO** Me llamo Antonio Morelos. Soy el padre. Tengo... años. Me gusta... Hoy de ropa llevo...

TEKS Focus

1A Engage in oral and written exchanges of learned material to socialize and to provide and obtain information

6 **En la tienda de ropa** 1A

Hablemos With a partner, play the roles of a clerk in a clothing store and a student shopping for clothes. Follow the format below.

EL/LA DEPENDIENTE	EL/LA CLIENTE
Greet the shopper and ask if you can help him or her.	Say you would like to buy a cotton shirt.
Ask what he or she thinks of the blue shirt and say it costs $50.	Say it is ugly and expensive.
Ask what he or she thinks of the red shirt and say it costs $15.	Say it is the latest style and is a bargain.

With your partner, repeat the conversation and change the clothing items, cost, and shopper's reaction.

To offer and ask for help in a store	
¿En qué le puedo servir? *How can I help you?*	**Busco una camisa de seda.** *I'm looking for a silk shirt.* **Estoy mirando, nomás.** *I'm just looking.*
¿Qué número/talla usa? *What shoe/clothing size do you wear?*	**Uso el/la 8.** *I wear a size 8 in shoes/clothes.*
¿Cómo le queda la camisa? *How does the shirt fit you?*	**Me queda bien/mal. Necesito una talla más grande/pequeña.** *It fits well/poorly. I need a bigger/smaller size.*
¿A qué hora cierra la tienda? *What time does the store close?*	**Cierra a las siete.** *It closes at 7:00.*

Interactive **TUTOR**

Online
Vocabulario y gramática,
pp. 41–43

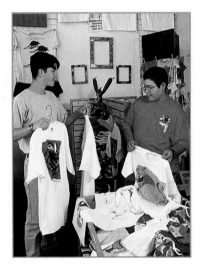

7 La camiseta perfecta ◆1B

Leamos Read the conversation between **el dependiente** and Raúl. Answer the questions that follow.

DEPENDIENTE	Buenos días. ¿En qué le puedo servir?
RAÚL	Me gustaría comprar una camiseta.
DEPENDIENTE	¿Le gustan las camisetas de algodón?
RAÚL	Sí, busco una camiseta blanca.
DEPENDIENTE	¿Qué talla usa?
RAÚL	Me queda bien la talla grande. ¿Cuánto cuestan las camisetas?
DEPENDIENTE	Las camisetas blancas cuestan siete dólares.
RAÚL	¡Qué baratas! ¡Son una ganga!
DEPENDIENTE	¿Busca más ropa?
RAÚL	No gracias. ¿A qué hora cierra la tienda?
DEPENDIENTE	Cierra a las nueve de la noche.

1. ¿Qué quiere comprar Raúl?
2. ¿Qué talla usa?
3. ¿Cuánto cuestan las camisetas blancas?
4. ¿Es cara la camiseta?
5. ¿Quiere comprar algo más?
6. ¿A qué hora cierra la tienda?

8 **¿Qué dices?** ↓1B, 1C

Escribamos Write this list of questions and statements. Then write a response to each using the clues given.

1. ¿En qué le puedo servir? *(I'm just looking.)*
2. ¿Vas a comprar un vestido? *(No, I'm looking for a skirt.)*
3. ¿Qué talla usa? *(I wear a size 7.)*
4. ¿Cómo le queda el abrigo? *(It fits poorly, I need a bigger one.)*
5. Busco unos zapatos. *(What size do you wear?)*
6. ¿A qué hora cierra la tienda? *(It closes at 8:30 P.M.)*

Comunicación

9 **¡Qué ropa tan rara!** ↓1A

 Hablemos With a partner, describe what Marieta, Carlos, and Juan are wearing. What is the weather like? Tell what clothing each person needs to be wearing.

MODELO Marieta lleva... Hace frío y nieva.
Ella necesita llevar...

1. Marieta   2. Carlos   3. Juan

10 **Hablando de ropa** ↓1A

 Hablemos Take turns with a partner asking and answering the following questions.

1. ¿Qué te parece la ropa de... *(famous person)*?
2. ¿Prefieres las camisas de seda o de algodón?
3. ¿Qué ropa está a la última moda?
4. ¿Qué ropa está pasada de moda?
5. ¿Cómo te queda la ropa de talla "extra-grande"?
6. ¿A qué hora cierra la tienda donde te gusta comprar ropa?

Vocabulario 1

GramaVisión

Costar, numbers to one million

Interactive
TUTOR

1 Use the verb **costar (o → ue)** to talk about what something costs. **Costar** is usually only used in the third person.

> La blusa **cuesta** treinta dólares. Las botas **cuestan** setenta dólares.

2 To tell what something costs, you may need to use larger numbers.

100	cien	600	seiscientos(as)
101	ciento uno(a)	700	setecientos(as)
102	ciento dos	800	ochocientos(as)
200	doscientos(as)	900	novecientos(as)
300	trescientos(as)	1.000	mil
400	cuatrocientos(as)	2.000	dos mil
500	quinientos(as)	1.000.000	un millón (de)

3 Use **uno** when counting. **Uno** at the end of a number changes to **un** before a masculine noun and **una** before a feminine noun: **veintiún dólares, veintiuna faldas.**

> Tengo **ciento un** dólares.   Tengo **veintiuna** bolsas.

4 **Cien(to)** is used with both masculine and feminine nouns, but 200, 300, and so on agree with the noun they modify. **Mil** does not change.

cien dólares   **ciento** tres dólares   **doscientos** seis dólares   **mil** dólares

cien sillas   **ciento** dos sillas   **doscientas** cuatro sillas   **mil** sillas

5 **Un millón** changes to **millones** in the plural. Use **de** after **millon(es)** when it is followed by a noun.

> 3.520.312 = tres **millones** quinientos veinte mil trescientos doce

> **un millón de** dólares   **dos millones de** personas

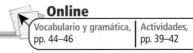

Online

Vocabulario y gramática, pp. 44–46	Actividades, pp. 39–42

TEKS Focus

1B Demonstrate understanding of simple, clearly spoken, and written language when dealing with familiar topics

Un supermercado en Miami

11 **¡Qué caro!** ⬇1B

Escuchemos Escribe los números que corresponden a los precios.

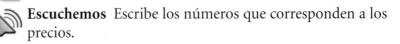

Gramática 1

12 **Tenemos que pagar** ✦1C

Escribamos Write out each number in words.

MODELO $354

trescientos cincuenta y cuatro dólares

1. $2.168
3. $1.550
5. $11.721
2. $1.319.672
4. $213.434
6. $1.946

13 **El inventario** ✦1C

Escribamos/Hablemos You have to write a clothing inventory list in the warehouse where you work. Use the list below to write sentences that tell how many of each type of clothing item are in stock.

MODELO botas 22.336
Tenemos veintidós mil, trescientos treinta y seis pares de botas.

zapatos	367.555	blusas	3.689
faldas	19.324	sombreros	475
pantalones	150.743	bolsas	2.079
camisas	4.597	camisetas	78.521

Nota cultural

Shopping in small-town flea markets in Texas is a unique experience. You can find almost anything for sale, including crafts, antiques, food, clothing, and plants. In larger cities, the markets are in huge warehouse buildings, and shoppers enjoy snacks and the music of Tejano bands. Canton, Texas, located about 60 miles east of Dallas, has the world's largest flea market. Why do you think flea markets are so popular? ✦2A

Comunicación

14 **¡Vamos de compras!** ✦1A

Hablemos With a partner, create a conversation between a clerk and a shopper as they talk about each item pictured below.

MODELO —Quiero comprar el suéter de muchos colores. ¿Cuánto cuesta?
—Cuesta doscientos nueve dólares.
—¡Es un robo! No voy a comprarlo.

$209

$18

$39

$472

$63

$289

$5

Demonstrative adjectives and comparisons

1 **Demonstrative adjectives** point out things. Use forms of **este** for things close to you. Use forms of **ese** for things farther away.

		Masculine	Feminine
this	SINGULAR	**este**	**esta**
these	PLURAL	**estos**	**estas**
that	SINGULAR	**ese**	**esa**
those	PLURAL	**esos**	**esas**

Me gusta **este** vestido, pero me gusta más **esa** falda.

2 Use these expressions with adjectives to compare things. The adjective agrees in gender and number with the object described.

más + *adjective* + **que**	*more . . . than*
tan + *adjective* + **como**	*as . . . as*
menos + *adjective* + **que**	*less . . . than*

Esta camiset**a** es **más bonita que** esa camiseta.

Esta camiset**a** es **tan bonita como** esa camiseta

Esta camiset**a** es **menos bonita que** esa camiseta.

3 These adjectives have irregular comparative forms.

bueno(a)	*good*	malo(a)	*bad*
mejor(es)	*better*	**peor(es)**	*worse*
joven	*young*	viejo(a)	*old*
menor(es)	*younger*	**mayor(es)**	*older*

Este disco compacto es **malo,** pero ese disco es **peor.**

4 Use **más que, menos que,** and **tanto como** to say if someone does something *more than, less than,* or *as much as* someone else.

Efraín compra **tanto como** Isabel.

Mis padres salen **menos que** mis abuelos.

Online

Vocabulario y gramática, pp. 44–46	Actividades, pp. 39–42

Nota cultural

In Florida it is common to see men wearing **guayaberas,** embroidered short-sleeved cotton or linen shirts. These shirts originated in Cuba over 200 years ago. Ramón Puig, a Cuban immigrant in Miami, is famous for his guayabera shirts and has custom-made them for celebrities. What fashions were developed in the United States and imported to other countries? ✦4C

TEKS Focus

4C Demonstrate understanding of the influence of one language and culture on another

---

15 **¿De qué habla?** ✦1B

Escuchemos Escucha mientras estas personas dicen qué cosa prefieren. Escribe lo que prefieren en otro papel. Si les gustan las dos cosas igualmente, escribe **las dos.**

16 Amigos ▾1B

Leamos Read the descriptions of Bartolomé and Nidia. Then, complete the comparisons with **más ... que, menos ... que,** or **tan ... como** and the correct form of the adjective in parentheses.

Bartolomé tiene 12 años. Es alto, guapo y muy simpático. Es bastante serio y estudia mucho. Es muy buen estudiante. Le gusta pasar el rato solo y leer libros y revistas. No le gustan los deportes. Nidia tiene 13 años. Es baja, guapa y muy simpática. No le gusta estudiar y no es muy buena estudiante. Le gusta practicar deportes y salir con amigos.

MODELO Bartolomé es ═══ (serio) ═══ Nidia.
Bartolomé es más serio que Nidia.

1. Bartolomé es ═══ (alto) ═══ Nidia.
2. Nidia es ═══ (guapo) ═══ Bartolomé.
3. Bartolomé es ═══ (simpático) ═══ Nidia.
4. Nidia es ═══ (atlético) ═══ Bartolomé.
5. Bartolomé es ═══ (extrovertido) ═══ Nidia.

17 Comparaciones ▾1B, 1C

Escribamos/Hablemos Now compare yourself to the two people in Activity 16. ♻ **¿Se te olvidó?** Adjective agreement, p. 56

MODELO **Soy menor que Bartolomé. Él es más serio que yo, pero yo soy...**

 Comunicación

18 Prefiero... ▾1A

Hablemos Talk with a partner about these things you see in a store. Decide which item from each pair you prefer and say why.

MODELO —¿Prefieres estos zapatos negros o esos zapatos blancos?
—Prefiero los zapatos blancos. Son mejores. Son menos caros y más bonitos y me gusta más el color.

Interactive
TUTOR

Quedar

1 Use the verb **quedar** to say how something *fits* or *looks* on someone. **Quedar** works like **parecer** and **gustar.** Use **queda** when talking about one thing. Use **quedan** when talking about more than one thing.

(a mí) me queda(n)	(a nosotros/as) nos queda(n)
(a ti) te queda(n)	(a vosotros/as) os queda(n)
(a Ud., a él, a ella) le queda(n)	(a Uds., a ellos, a ellas) les queda(n)

one thing
Esa blusa te **queda** bien. *That blouse looks good on you.*

more than one thing
Estas botas me **quedan** grandes. *These boots are too big for me.*

2 Adjectives like **grande** and **pequeño(a)**, as well as adverbs like **bien** and **mal**, can follow **quedar.** All adjectives must agree, but the adverbs don't change form.

agrees
Esta falda me queda **pequeña**. Me queda **mal**.
This skirt is too small for me. It fits me badly.

agrees
Estas botas me quedan **grandes**. No me quedan **bien**.
These boots are too big for me. They don't fit me well.

Online
| Vocabulario y gramática, pp. 44–46 | Actividades, pp. 39–42 |

¡Te acuerdas?

The verb **parecer** *(to seem)* can be used like **gustar.**

Esa falda me **parece** fea.

¿Cómo te **parecen** estos pantalones?

TEKS Focus

1B Demonstrate understanding of simple, clearly spoken, and written language when dealing with familiar topics

19 **Comentarios** 🔽**1B**

Leamos Graciela and Leonora are shopping. Read Graciela's comments and choose Leonora's probable response.

1. Me gustan esos zapatos. ¿Vas a comprarlos?
   a. No, me quedan grandes.   **b.** Sí, te quedan muy bien.

2. Esa blusa es una ganga, ¿no te parece?
   a. Me parece muy cara.   **b.** Le queda pequeña.

3. Prefiero los pantalones vaqueros a los pantalones cortos.
   a. Les gustan los pantalones vaqueros.
   b. Te quedan mejor que los pantalones cortos.

4. ¿Están estos pantalones a la última moda?
   a. Te quedan pequeñas.   **b.** Me parecen pasados de moda.

5. Me encantan estas sandalias rojas. Son número 6.
   a. Te quedan pequeñas. Usas el número 7, ¿no?
   b. Les parecen bonitas.

6. Necesito un regalo para Joaquín. Voy a comprarle un libro.
   a. Le queda bien.   **b.** Me parece aburrido.

20 **¿Cómo le queda?** ⬇1B

Escuchemos Escucha mientras varias personas hablan de ropa en una tienda. Para cada comentario, indica si el artículo de ropa **a**) le queda bien o **b**) le queda mal a la persona.

21 **¿Es bonita la ropa?** ⬇1B

Leamos/Escribamos Complete the conversation between Daniela and her mother. Use the correct form of **quedar** or **parecer** and the appropriate pronoun.

> **MODELO** **A mí me queda grande esta falda. Además, me parece fea.**

—Mamá, me gusta ese vestido. A ti, ___1___ muy bien.

—Gracias, pero necesito otra talla. ___2___ pequeño. ¿Qué ___3___ esta blusa? Es bonita, ¿no?

—Uy, ___4___ fea. Además, cuesta una fortuna.

—Daniela, ¿qué ___5___ estas botas? Debo comprarlas para Raquel?

—Pero mamá, mira esas botas negras. No cuestan mucho y son muy bonitas. De verdad, ___6___ feas las botas amarillas. No me gusta ese color.

—Bueno, a nosotras no ___7___ bien nuestros zapatos viejos. ¿Quieres comprar unos nuevos?

—¡Ay sí! Por ejemplo, estos zapatos negros ___8___ muy bonitos.

Comunicación

22 **¿Qué te parece?** ⬇1A

Hablemos In pairs, give your opinion of the clothes that Luisa and Tomás are wearing. Do you like them? Are the clothes pretty? Ugly? Expensive? How do the clothes fit them? Take turns making comments.

> **MODELO** **El sombrero de Luisa no me gusta. Es feo y caro. Le queda grande.**
> **Me gusta la camiseta de Tomás. Es muy bonita pero también es un poco cara.**

Cultura

Video/DVD

VideoCultura

Comparaciones
 Interactive **TUTOR**

De compras en la Pequeña Habana

¿Qué te gusta comprar cuando vas de compras? ↓4B

Sin duda, vas de compras y tienes un lugar donde te encanta ir. ¿Qué diferencias hay entre un centro comercial, un almacén y un mercado al aire libre? En los países de habla hispana, la gente puede ir a grandes almacenes para comprar de todo. También es posible ir a tiendas pequeñas donde venden sólo un tipo de producto. De todos modos, parece que los jóvenes hispanohablantes van de compras con frecuencia. Estas personas nos dicen qué les gusta comprar y adónde van cuando tienen ganas de comprar algo nuevo. ¿Compras las mismas cosas?

Dayana
Miami, Florida

Dayana goes shopping first, then meets with a friend. How does this compare to your shopping habits?

¿Qué compras cuando vas de compras?

Cuando voy de compras, me gusta comprar CDs, zapatos, blusas, pantalones. Cosas así.

¿Adónde fuiste de compras la última vez?

La última vez que fui de compras fui a un centro comercial.

¿Qué clase de tienda es?

El centro comercial es... hay varias tiendas. Hay tiendas de discos, tiendas de películas, tiendas de zapatos, de todo tipo de ropa, vestidos. Cosas así.

¿Qué compraste?

Cuando fui de compras, compré unos discos, una película, unos aretes. Compré unos zapatos, unos pantalones y un vestido.

¿Qué más hiciste allí?

Fui a almorzar y me compré un helado. Después me encontré con una de mis amigas y charlamos.

Cultura

Miriam
Madrid, España

Miriam goes to a movie after shopping. What do you like to do after shopping?

¿Qué compras cuando vas de compras?

Pues, me gustar comprar pantalones ajustados, pantalones anchos, camisetas de colores y deportivas.

¿Adónde fuiste la última vez?

A «Tres Aguas», un centro comercial.

¿Qué clase de tienda es?

Pues, es de aire libre… muchas tiendas y mucho ocio.

¿Qué compraste?

Compré unos pantalones, una camiseta y unas deportivas.

¿Qué más hiciste allí?

Pues, después me fui con mis amigas al cine y a tomar una hamburguesa.

Para comprender ↓1B

1. ¿Qué compró Dayana la última vez que fue de compras?
2. ¿Qué compró Miriam la última vez que fue de compras?
3. ¿A quién le gusta comprar zapatos?
4. ¿Cómo es el centro comercial «Tres Aguas»?
5. ¿Quién fue a comer algo después de ir de compras?

Para pensar y hablar ↓4B

Dayana and Miriam both enjoy shopping for clothes, among other things. When you go shopping, what do you like to buy? For both girls, a shopping trip means spending time with friends. With whom do you normally go shopping? Where do you go? What do you like or not like about shopping?

Cuaderno para hispanohablantes, pp. 61–68

Texas

Comunidad

¿Dónde vas de compras? ↓5B

A lot of commercial traffic crosses the border between El Paso, Texas, and Ciudad Juárez, in Chihuahua, Mexico. Texans like to buy authentic Mexican goods in the stores of Ciudad Juárez, where they are less expensive than in Texas. The food is delicious in Ciudad Juárez, too! Many citizens of Ciudad Juárez travel to El Paso to shop in their favorite stores. Plan a trip with your class to visit a store and practice speaking Spanish with the employees. You can ask them where they are from and how many years they've been in your town.

Colorful ceramic masks from Mexico

Vocabulario
en acción 2

Video/DVD
ExpresaVisión

> Me gusta ir de compras...

a la joyería

un anillo

unos aretes

una pulsera

a la librería

unas tarjetas

unas revistas de tiras cómicas

unos DVDs (m)

al almacén

a la tienda de música

unos audífonos

un disco compacto (en blanco)

▶ **Vocabulario adicional** — De compras, p. R7

Cuando voy de compras, me gusta...

mirar las vitrinas

ir a la plaza de comida

ir a la zapatería

ir a la juguetería

unos juguetes

Más vocabulario...

ahorrar	*to save*
el dinero	*money*
gastar	*to spend*
vender	*to sell*
(de todo)	*(everything)*

Vocabulario 2

¡Exprésate!

To ask where someone went and what someone did	To respond
¿Adónde fuiste anoche/ayer/anteayer? *Where did you go last night/yesterday/the day before yesterday?*	**Fui a la heladería a tomar un batido.** *I went to the ice cream shop to have a milkshake.*
¿Qué hiciste el fin de semana pasado? *What did you do last weekend?*	**Fui al centro comercial y compré unos zapatos. Pagué una fortuna.** *I went to the mall and bought some shoes. I paid a fortune.*

Interactive
TUTOR

Online
Vocabulario y gramática,
pp. 47–49

23 ¿Dónde están? ↘1B

 Escuchemos Listen to the conversations and decide where each takes place.

24 ¿Adónde fuiste? ↘1B

Leamos Complete Ricardo's story about his trip to the mall with the best words from the box.

batido	pulsera	discos	librería	juguetería	vitrinas

Primero fui a la ___1___ a comprar un diccionario para mi clase de español. También compré unos ___2___ compactos. Luego fui a la joyería a comprarle una ___3___ a mi mamá. Pagué una fortuna por un videojuego en la ___4___. Me gusta mirar las ___5___ en el almacén pero no compré nada allí. Finalmente fui a la heladería a tomar un ___6___ de chocolate.

25 Fui de compras ↘1B

Hablemos/Escribamos Di adónde fuiste y qué compraste (*you bought*).

MODELO **Fui a la tienda de música esta semana. Compré unos discos compactos.**

1.

2.

3.

4.

5.

6.

7.

8.

26 **Yolanda en el centro comercial** ↓1B

Leamos/Escribamos Yolanda wrote in her journal about a shopping trip she took yesterday, but she seems to be confused! Rewrite her summary and replace each underlined word with one that makes more sense.

> <u>Hoy</u> fui al centro comercial. Fui a la <u>heladería</u> a comprar un DVD. Compré un juguete en la <u>tienda de ropa</u> y pagué una fortuna por <u>unas revistas</u> en la zapatería. En la plaza de comidas compré <u>pantalones vaqueros</u>. Luego fui a la <u>tienda de música</u> a comprar un anillo para mi hermana. También fui a la <u>librería</u> a comprar una camisa, unos zapatos y un sombrero. Al final fui a la <u>zapatería</u> a comprar una tarjeta para el cumpleaños de mi padre. ¡Me gusta <u>ahorrar</u> dinero!

 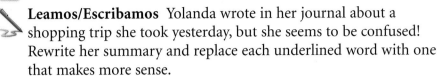

Comunicación

27 **¿Adónde fuiste?** ↓1A

Hablemos With a partner, take turns asking each other if you went to the following places last weekend. When answering, mention something that you bought there.

MODELO —¿Fuiste a la zapatería el fin de semana pasado?
—Sí, fui a la zapatería y compré...

1. la zapatería
2. la tienda de música
3. el almacén
4. la joyería
5. la juguetería
6. la librería
7. la plaza de comidas
8. la heladería
9. la tienda de ropa

TEKS Focus

1A Engage in oral and written exchanges of learned material to socialize and to provide and obtain information

28 **Una encuesta** ↓1A, 1C

Hablemos Working in groups of three or four, make a chart of the last three stores where you've bought something, and what you purchased. Be prepared to compare your findings with those of other groups.

MODELO —¿Adónde fuiste de compras?
—Fui a 'Libromundo' y compré un libro.

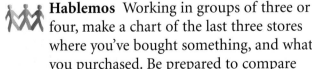

	Ricky	Monika	Luis
1	Libromundo: un libro		
2			
3			

¡Exprésate!

To talk on the phone

Aló/Bueno/Diga.	**Hola. ¿Está Andrés?**
Hello.	*Hi. Is Andrés there?*
¿De parte de quién?	**Habla Felipe.**
Who's calling?	*Felipe speaking.*
Espera un momento, ya te lo (la) paso.	**Gracias, señor(a) León.**
Wait a moment. I'll get him (her).	*Thanks, Mr.(Mrs.) León.*
Lo siento, no está. ¿Quieres dejarle un recado?	**Sí, por favor, que me llame después.**
I'm sorry. He's (She's) not here. Would you like to leave a message?	*Yes, please ask him to call me later.*
	No, gracias. Llamo más tarde.
	No, thanks, I'll call back later.

Interactive TUTOR

Online
Vocabulario y gramática, pp. 47–49

29 La llamada ↓1B

Leamos Marta is calling her friend Elena at home. Elena's mother answers the phone. Reorder the sentences logically to create their conversation.

—Hola, señora Beltrán. ¿Está Elena?

—Espera, Marta, ya te la paso.

—Habla Marta.

—Bueno.

—Gracias, señora. Hasta luego.

—¿De parte de quién?

Hola. ¿Está Felipe?

TEKS Focus

1B Demonstrate understanding of simple, clearly spoken, and written language when dealing with familiar topics

30 ¡Diga! ↓1B

Leamos Choose a phrase from column B that is an appropriate telephone response to the phrase in column A.

MODELO —¿Está Amalia, por favor?
—Un momento, por favor.

A	B
1. ¿De parte de quién, por favor?	a. ¿Puedo dejar un recado?
2. El señor Chávez no está.	b. Un momento, por favor.
3. ¿Está Omar, por favor?	c. Bien, gracias, ¿y usted?
4. ¿Aló?	d. Gustavo Muñoz.
5. Bueno, señora, llamo más tarde.	e. Adiós.
6. ¿Cómo está?	f. ¿Está la doctora Pérez?

Gramática 2

36 Roberto y sus amigos 1B, 1C

Escribamos/Hablemos Look at each photo and write what the people did yesterday. Then write if you also did the same activity.

Tomás

MODELO **Tomás cortó el césped ayer. Yo también corté el césped.**

1. Sara/anteayer

2. ellos/el sábado pasado

3. tus amigas/ayer

4. Pablo y Mila/anoche

5. Carmela/
el martes pasado

6. Luis/ayer por la tarde

 Comunicación

37 Ayer por la noche 1A

Hablemos In small groups, ask who did the following things last night.

MODELO —**¿Estudiaste anoche?**
—**Sí, estudié mucho. (No, no estudié.)**

cantar	hablar por teléfono	pasear
dibujar	comprar ropa	mirar televisión
escuchar música	montar en bicicleta	pasar el rato solo(a)
estudiar	nadar	alquilar un video

Preterite of ir

Interactive
TUTOR

1 To say where someone went at a certain time in the past, use **ir** *(to go)* in the **preterite**. Its preterite forms are irregular.

yo	**fui**	nosotros(as)	**fuimos**
tú	**fuiste**	vosotros(as)	**fuisteis**
Ud., él, ella	**fue**	Uds., ellos, ellas	**fueron**

2 Remember to use **adónde** to ask where someone went.

—¿**Adónde fuiste** ayer?   *Where did you go yesterday?*
—**Fui** al cine.   *I went to the movies.*

3 Use **a** + **infinitive** after **ir** to say why someone went somewhere.

Fuimos a la librería **a comprar** libros.
We went to the bookstore to buy books.

Online
Vocabulario y gramática, pp. 50–52 | Actividades, pp. 43–46

En el Festival de la Calle Ocho, Miami

38 De tienda en tienda ⬇1B

Leamos Choose the correct word in parentheses to complete the paragraph.

Ayer ___1___ (fui/fuimos) con mi familia al centro comercial. Mi hermana Delia ___2___ (fuiste/fue) al almacén a comprar pantalones. Mis padres ___3___ (fuimos/fueron) a la librería y mi hermano ___4___ (fue/fuiste) a la juguetería. Por fin todos ___5___ (fuimos/fuiste) a la heladería a tomar un batido.

39 ¿Fuiste al festival este año? ⬇1B, 1C

Escribamos Combine a word or phrase from each section to make six sentences. Tell where these people went and what they did.

MODELO **Fui al cine a ver una pelicula.**

yo	ir	al cine	a comprar
tú		al parque	a leer
mi mejor amigo(a)		al estadio	a comer
mi familia y yo		al almacén	a ver
mis padres		al restaurante	a jugar
mi profesora		a la biblioteca	a estudiar
mi hermano		a la librería	
		al colegio	

---

40 **Contesta personalmente** ↓1B, 1C

TEKS Focus
1B Demonstrate understanding of simple, clearly spoken, and written language when dealing with familiar topics

Escribamos Escribe la respuesta a cada pregunta. Contesta las preguntas según tu propia vida.

1. ¿Fuiste al colegio ayer?
2. ¿Fue al colegio ayer tu mejor amigo(a)?
3. ¿Fueron tus amigos y tú al centro comercial la semana pasada?
4. ¿Adónde fuiste anteayer?
5. ¿Adónde fueron tus amigos y tú el sábado pasado?
6. ¿Adónde fue tu familia el fin de semana pasado?

41 **¿Adónde fueron? ¿Qué compraron?** ↓1B, 1C

Escribamos/Hablemos María is saying where everyone went shopping and what they bought. Based on the photos, write what she says.

MODELO Carlos y Carmen fueron a la juguetería. Compraron videojuegos.

Carlos y Carmen

1. nosotros 2. papá 3. mis amigas 4. Yo 5. Gabi y Rebeca

Comunicación

42 **Tiendas y compras** ↓1A

Hablemos On a scrap of paper write down three stores you went to and what you bought there. Do not let your partner see what you write! Your partner will ask you questions and try to guess where you went and what you bought. Take turns guessing and answering.

Tiendas	Cosas que compré
Muy de Moda	falda
Ropa y Más	sandalias
Joyería Sánchez	pulsera

MODELO —¿Compraste un disco compacto?
—No, compré unos audífonos.
—¿Fuiste a la tienda de música?
—Sí, fui a la tienda de música.

Interactive
TUTOR

Repaso Preterite of -ar verbs with reflexive pronouns

1 Use the **preterite** to talk about what happened at a particular point in the past and to narrate a sequence of events in the past. Use the correct form of the **reflexive pronoun** when necessary.

levantarse

yo **me** levanté	nosotros(as) **nos** levantamos
tú **te** levantaste	vosotros(as) **os** levantasteis
Ud., él, ella **se** levantó	Uds., ellos, ellas **se** levantaron

Me levanté y **me** bañé.   *I got up and took a bath.*

2 Stem-changing **-ar** verbs in the present tense don't have a stem-change in the **preterite**.

Ayer **me** desperté a las seis y **me** acosté a las diez.

Yesterday I woke up at six and I went to bed at ten.

Online

Vocabulario y gramática, pp. 50–52	Actividades, pp. 43–46

43 **¡Qué día más ocupado!** ✈1B

Escuchemos Escucha lo que hicieron Enrique y Lupita ayer. Según *(according to)* lo que oyes, pon los dibujos en orden cronológico *(chronological order).*

a.

b.

c.

d.

e.

f.

g.

h.

44 La familia de Luis ✏️1B

Leamos/Escribamos Luis and his family usually do ⟨...⟩ne things, but this week they did things differently. Comp⟨...⟩ each sentence with the correct forms of the verb in parenth⟨...⟩ in the present or preterite tense.

MODELO Patricia <u>se baña</u> por la mañana pero esta se⟨...⟩na <u>se bañó</u> por la noche.

1. Cada día papá ═══ antes del desayuno, pero ayer no ═══. (afeitarse)

2. Siempre ═══ a las 8:00, pero el miércoles yo ═══ a la⟨...⟩is para estudiar. (despertarse)

3. Ana y yo ═══ a las 3:30, pero ayer ═══ a las 5:00. (reg⟨...⟩ar)

4. Papá y mamá ═══ la cena juntos, pero mamá trabajó ta⟨...⟩así que solamente la ═══ juntos el jueves y el viernes. (prep⟨...⟩)

5. Patricia, tú ═══ temprano por lo general, pero anoche ═══ después de la medianoche. (acostarse)

45 En mi familia ✏️1C

TEKS Focus

1C Present information using familiar words, phrases, and sentences

Hablemos Based on Activity 44, tell what you and your family usually do, and what you did differently this week. Replace nar⟨...⟩ in Activity 44 with names from your family, and use different verbs if you like.

MODELO **Generalmente me levanto a las 7:00, pero hoy me levanté a las 8:00.**

Comunicación

46 ¿Qué pasó? ✏️1C

Hablemos Con un(a) compañero(a), mira los dibujos y di adónde fueron Felipe y Cristina y qué hicieron.

Conexiones culturales

Conexión Historia

1 Las figuras históricas ⬇2B

Many Latin American countries have pictures of important historical figures on their coins and paper bills, just as we have a picture of Abraham Lincoln on the five-dollar U.S. bill. Match the following people in Latin American history to the currencies that were named for them or that carry their pictures.

1. **Lempira,** the chief of the Lenca people, who fought heroically against the Spanish conquerors.

2. **Sor Juana Inés de la Cruz** (Juana de Asbaje), a nun who was a devoted scholar and poet in seventeenth-century Mexico.

3. **Francisco Hernández de Córdoba,** a Spanish explorer who founded the colonial cities of Granada and León.

A **córdoba:** Nicaragua

B **peso:** México

C **lempira:** Honduras

2 ¡Te toca a ti! ⬇1C

Pretend your state is actually a country. Work with a partner to create money for your "country." Include drawings of famous people and symbols that are important in your state. Draw examples of both sides of a coin or the paper money. Use the Spanish words for numbers to write the value of your coin or paper money. Present the money you designed to the class.

Can your classmates identify your symbols and colors and explain what they mean?

Conexión Matemáticas

Conexiones Culturales

3 De compras ➴3A

In Spain and most Spanish-speaking countries, you can shop in neighborhood shops that specialize in one type of food or item. Large stores are common in big cities. Smaller shops and open markets are still popular, however, and they're within walking distance from most homes. Imagine you have 5.75€ (euros) to spend on fruit at the local fruit stand (la frutería).

1. Decide which kinds of fruit to buy.

2. Calculate how much change you will get back.

3. Where would you go to buy fruit in your hometown?

Mercado San Miguel, Madrid, España

las fresas
1.30€/kg.

las naranjas
2.00€/kg.

las manzanas
2.30€/kg.

el melón
3.00€/kg.

¿Quién será?

Episodio 8

🕊 1B, 3A

ESTRATEGIA

Recognizing different points of view When the same story is told from different points of view, it is important to keep track of who is telling what. This is because the same events can be interpreted in a completely different way by everyone who experienced them. The truth probably lies somewhere between the different versions. As you read the **Novela** or watch the video, keep track of whose view is being expressed, Sofía's or Celeste's. What do you think really happened?

En México

Celeste habla con Sofía. Celeste quiere ir de compras a buscar ropa y zapatos para la fiesta del sábado.

Celeste Hola, Sofía, Necesito comprar una falda, una blusa y unos zapatos para la fiesta del sábado.

Sofía Está bien.

Celeste Perfecto. ¿Por qué no nos encontramos en Kulte a las diez y media?

1

La versión de Sofía

Fui con Celeste a Kulte, una tienda de ropa.

No me hizo caso. Compró una falda horrible. Luego, se probó una blusa morada.

2

Celeste ¿Qué te parece esta falda azul? ¿Me queda bien?

Sofía No te queda nada bien. Te debes probar otra.

Celeste Ah, qué bueno que estás de acuerdo. Es muy bonita. Me gusta muchísimo.

Celeste ¿Te gusta esta blusa morada? ¿Me queda bien?

Sofía No, Celeste; de veras que no. ¡Está pasada de moda! Y necesitas otra talla.

Celeste ¡Me queda perfecta! Y está a la última moda, ¿no crees?

3

Traté de convencerla. Pero nada. Gastó su dinero en una blusa fea. Luego fuimos a la sección de zapatos.

Celeste ¿Qué piensas de estos zapatos? ¿Van bien con la blusa y la falda?

Sofía ¿Sabes qué? ¡Estás más loca que un zapato!

Celeste ¡Perfecto! Me voy a llevar estos zapatos. Ahora estoy lista para la fiesta del sábado. ¡Voy a estar a la última moda con mi nueva falda, blusa y zapatos!

4

A CONTESTA

What is happening in the **Novela**? Check your understanding by answering the questions.

1. Why does Celeste call Sofía?

2. What does Sofía say about the skirt? the blouse? the shoes?

3. In Sofía's version, what does Celeste say about the things she bought?

Novela en video

La versión de Celeste

Fui con Sofía a Kulte. No me gustó mucho la falda azul pero le gustó tanto a Sofía que la compré.

Celeste ¿Qué té parece esta falda azul? ¿Me queda bien?

Sofía ¡Te queda muy bien! ¡Muy bonita! Definitivamente debes comprarla.

Celeste ¿Estás segura? No sé.

Sofia ¡Te prometo! ¡Te ves increíble!

5

Luego me probé una blusa morada. Gasté mi dinero en una blusa que no me queda bien.

Celeste ¿Te gusta esta blusa morada? ¿Me queda bien?

Sofía ¡Claro que sí! ¡Está a la última moda! Y es una ganga. ¡Mira el precio!

Celeste Pues, sí, tienes razón. Es muy barata. Pero...

Sofía ¿Pero qué? Hazme caso. Debes comprarla.

6

Luego fuimos a la sección de zapatos.

Celeste ¿Qué piensas de estos zapatos? ¿Van bien con la blusa y la falda?

Sofía ¡Mujer! ¡Estos zapatos son más bonitos que todos los zapatos en todo el mundo!

Celeste ¿De veras? Bueno, si te gustan a ti, los voy a comprar.

7

Celeste Sofía, tengo que regresar a Kulte Tengo que devolver la falda, la blusa y los zapatos. ¿Vas conmigo?

Sofía Sí, pero ¿por qué vas a devolver todo?

Celeste Mamá dice que me veo horrible en esa falda y esa blusa y que los zapatos son más horribles que la ropa. No sé por qué me dejaste comprarlos.

8

B **CONTESTA**

1. In Celeste's version, what does Sofía say about the skirt? the blouse? the shoes?

2. According to Celeste, why does she end up buying the clothes and shoes?

3. What does Celeste's mother make her do?

Actividades

1 ¿Cómo lo diría?

Look through the story to find and write down Spanish words, phrases, and sentences that you could use to say the following.

1. It fits me well.
2. It's the latest style!
3. You should try on something else.
4. What do you think of this skirt?
5. It's a bargain!

2 ¡Opiniones!

The two girls don't seem to agree on Sofía's comments about the clothing that Celeste tried on. Look through the story to see how each girl remembers what Sofía said about each thing.

1. What advice does Sofía remember giving about . . .
   la falda?
   la blusa?
   los zapatos?
2. What advice from Sofía does Celeste remember hearing about . . .
   la falda?
   la blusa?
   los zapatos?

3 ¿Comprendes la Novela?

Check your understanding of the events in the story by answering these questions.

1. Based on what you found in Activity 2, what could have led to two such different interpretations of the same events?
2. How would you respond to Celeste's statement, **No sé por qué me dejaste comprarlos?**

> **Próximo episodio**
> *Marcos is going to another country. Where is he going? What do you think?*
> PÁGINAS 206–209 ▶

ciento sesenta y tres **163**

Leamos y escribamos

ESTRATEGIA

para leer Visualizing what you read in a story helps you better understand it. As you read, create pictures in your mind of each scene or event. This will help you connect what you know to what you are reading and help you summarize the main events of the story.

A Antes de leer ↘1B, 3B

Read the first paragraph of the story. Draw the picture that it brings to mind. What does this image tell you about the man and his servant? As you read the rest of the story, continue drawing pictures of how you imagine the events of each scene.

Una moneda¹ de ¡Ay!

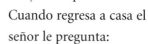

En un pueblo, como muchos otros pueblos, vive un gran señor con muchos sirvientes. Pedro, el sirviente más nuevo, es un muchacho que al señor le parece un poco tonto. Para burlarse de él², lo llama, le da dos monedas y le dice:

—Pedro, vete al mercado y cómprame una moneda de uvas y otra de ¡Ay!

El pobre Pedro va al mercado y compra las uvas, pero cada vez que pregunta por la moneda de ¡Ay!, todos los vendedores se ríen de él³.

Finalmente Pedro se da cuenta⁴ que el señor quiere burlarse de él. Entonces decide poner las uvas en una bolsa⁵ y sobre las uvas pone un manojo de espinos⁶.

Cuando regresa a casa el señor le pregunta:

—¿Fuiste al mercado?

—Sí, señor.

—¿Y lo traes todo?

—Sí, señor. Todo está en la bolsa.

El señor parece sorprendido⁷. Rápidamente mete la mano⁸ en la bolsa y al tocar los espinos, exclama:

—¡Ay!

—Y debajo están las uvas— le dice Pedro.

1 coin **2** to make fun of him **3** the vendors laugh at him **4** he realizes
5 a bag **6** handful of thorns **7** seems surprized **8** puts his hand in

B Comprensión ✏1B

Contesta las siguientes preguntas con oraciones completas.

1. ¿Quién es Pedro?
2. ¿Qué debe comprar Pedro en el mercado?
3. ¿Por qué se ríen los vendedores de Pedro?
4. ¿Qué hay en la bolsa que Pedro le da al señor?
5. ¿Cómo reacciona el señor cuando Pedro le dice que trae todo?
6. ¿Qué hace el señor cuando mete la mano en la bolsa?

C Después de leer ✏1B, 3B

Summarize the story using the drawings you made while reading it. Explain how you visualized each scene. What did each scene reveal about the characters? Did you find the ending of the story humorous? Why?

> **TEKS Focus**
>
> **3B** Use the language to obtain, reinforce, or expand knowledge of other subject areas

Taller del escritor

Ropa	Lo que (no) me gusta	Lo que (no) le gusta a mi amigo(a)

ESTRATEGIA

para escribir When you write about differing opinions, choose terms that show sharp, clear contrasts. Using charts can help you visualize and contrast differing points of view.

A mí me parece perfecto... ✏1C

Imagine you are shopping for clothes with a friend. However, you can't agree about anything today! If you think something looks good and fits well, your friend says it looks awful. Write five things you're shopping for that you and your friend have different opinions about.

1 Antes de escribir

Make a chart. In one column, list at least five pieces of clothing. In the next column write what you like or don't like about each item. In the third column, write the differing opinions your friend has.

2 Escribir y revisar

Using your chart, write about your shopping trip. Include your and your friend's opinions about the clothes: how they fit, if they look good, or if they are in style. Include details to back up each opinion.

Read your draft at least two times, comparing it with your chart. Are the contrasting opinions clear? Check spelling and punctuation.

3 Publicar

Share your paragraph with the class. Ask your classmates to respond by giving their opinions or preferences regarding the clothing.

Online
Cuaderno para hispanohablantes, pp. 61–68

Leamos y escribamos

Repaso capítulo 8

Interactive TUTOR

1 Tell what each item is, and what size and color you want or need. ✈1C

1.   2.   3.

4.   5.   6.

2 You are at the mall with a friend. Compare what you see at the stores with similar things you have at home. Begin with **¿Qué te parece(n)...?** and the correct form of **este(a).** Tell how much each thing costs. ✈1B

1. mesa de plástico, $125/tu mesa
2. sofá de seda, $1.199/tu sofá
3. cama grande, $1.831/tu cama
4. cuatro plantas de seda, $45/tus plantas
5. refrigerador negro, ultra moderno, $2.057/tu refrigerador
6. teléfono azul y verde, $62/tu teléfono

3 Escoge la respuesta apropiada para cada oración. ✈1B

1. ¿Adónde fuiste el lunes por la noche?
2. Hola. ¿Está Andrés?
3. Compré aretes y un anillo.
4. Lo siento, no está. ¿Quieres dejarle un recado?
5. ¿Qué hiciste en la tienda de música?

a. Espera un momento. Ya te lo paso.
b. ¿Fuiste a una joyería o a un almacén?
c. Fui a la biblioteca a estudiar.
d. Escuché muchos discos compactos.
e. Sí, por favor, que me llame después.

4 Complete Carolina's description of her day, using the preterite of the verbs in parentheses. ↓ **1B**

Hoy ___1___ (despertarse, yo) temprano para ir de compras con mi familia. ___2___ (ir, nosotros) al centro comercial nuevo. Le ___3___ (comprar, yo) una pulsera a mi abuela. Ignacio ___4___ (mirar) las vitrinas, nomás. Mamá y papá ___5___ (gastar) mucho dinero en DVDs. Por la tarde, mis padres ___6___ (tomar) un batido y Federico ___7___ (ir) al cine. Nosotros ___8___ (regresar) a casa a las seis. Todos ___9___ (acostarse) tarde.

5 Contesta las siguientes preguntas. ↓ **2A, 2B**

1. How do you refer to clothing and shoe sizes in Spanish-speaking countries?

2. What are **guayaberas** and where did they originate?

3. Where would you likely see customers bargaining with vendors? Where wouldn't you?

4. Who were Lempira, Sor Juana Inés de la Cruz, and Francisco Hernández de Cordoba? How were they honored?

6 Escucha y escribe qué cosas te comprarías *(would buy)* y en qué tienda. ↓ **1B**

7 Describe lo que ves en los dibujos. En oraciones completas, di qué dicen Felipe y Cristina, y qué compraron. ↓ **1C**

Visit Holt Online

go.hrw.com
KEYWORD: EXP1B CH8
Chapter Self-test

Repaso

4 Gramática 2
• preterite of **-ar** verbs
• preterite of **ir**
• preterite of **-ar** verbs with reflexive pronouns
pp. 152–157

5 Cultura
• **Comparaciones** pp. 144–145
• **Notas culturales** pp. 134, 140, 148, 152
• **Conexiones culturales** pp. 158–159

TEKS Focus

2A Demonstrate understanding of practices (what people do) and how they relate to perspectives (how people perceive things) of the cultures studied

Florida

ciento sesenta y siete **167**

Repaso de Gramática 1

100	cien	600	seiscientos(as)
101	ciento uno(un)	700	setecientos(as)
102	ciento dos	800	ochocientos(as)
200	doscientos(as)	900	novecientos(as)
300	trescientos(as)	1.000	mil
400	cuatrocientos(as)	2.000	dos mil
500	quinientos(as)	1.000.000	un millón (de+*noun*)

singular subject   *plural subject*

La bolsa cuest**a** cien dólares. Las botas cuest**an** ciento veintiún dólares.

este/ese saco	**más**+*adj.*+**que**	**mejor(es)/mayor(es) que**
estos/esos sacos	**tan**+*adj.*+**como**	
esta/esa blusa	**menos**+*adj.*+**que**	**peor(es)/menor(es) que**
estas/esas blusas		

The verb **quedar** is used to say how something fits and is conjugated like **gustar**: **me/te/le/nos/os/les queda(n)**+*adjective/adverb*.

Repaso de Gramática 2

The verb comprar has regular **preterite** forms; the verb ir is irregular.

compr**é**	compr**amos**	fui	fuimos
compr**aste**	compr**asteis**	fuiste	fuisteis
compr**ó**	compr**aron**	fue	fueron

The **preterite** is used to say what happened at a specific point in the past and to narrate a sequence of events. Verbs with reflexive pronouns in the **preterite** have the same preterite endings as other verbs.

Ayer **fui** al cine con mis amigos, **regresé** tarde a casa y **me** acosté.

Letra y sonido

El acento ortográfico

- Words ending in a vowel, **-n,** or **-s** are usually stressed in the next-to-last syllable. Exceptions have an accent mark over the stressed vowel:
  ni<u>ño</u>, <u>jo</u>ven, <u>com</u>pras, se<u>má</u>foro, alma<u>cén</u>, <u>jó</u>venes
- Words ending in a consonant other than **-n,** or **-s** are usuallly stressed in the last syllable. Exceptions have an accent mark over the stressed vowel:
  pa<u>pel</u>, ciu<u>dad</u>, repe<u>tir</u>, <u>án</u>gel, <u>lá</u>piz, <u>Héc</u>tor

Trabalenguas
El célebre cerebelo del cerebro celebrará con celeridad una celebérrima celebración.

Dictado ♦1B
Escribe las oraciones de la grabación.

Repaso de Vocabulario 1

Asking for and giving opinions

además	besides
barato(a)	inexpensive
caro(a)	expensive
costar (ue)	to cost
a la (última) moda	in (the latest) style
Es un robo.	It's a rip-off.
ese(a)	that
este(a)	this
feo(a)	ugly
la ganga	bargain
pasado(a) de moda	out of style
pequeño(a)	small
quedar bien/mal	to fit well/badly
tener razón	to be right
Colors . . . . See page 133.	

Asking for and offering help in a store

el abrigo	(over)coat
la blusa	blouse
la bolsa	purse
las botas	boots
los calcetines	socks
la camisa	shirt
la camiseta	T-shirt
cerrar (ie)	to close
la chaqueta	jacket
el/la cliente	client, customer
de algodón/lana/seda	(made of) cotton/wool/silk
el/la dependiente	salesclerk
¿En qué le puedo servir?	How can I help you?
Estoy mirando, nomás.	I'm just looking.
la falda	skirt
llevar	to wear
Me gustaría...	I would like . . .
el número	(shoe) size
los pantalones (cortos/vaqueros)	pants (shorts/jeans)
un par de...	a pair of . . .
para hombres/mujeres/niños	for men/women/children
el saco	jacket
las sandalias	sandals
el sombrero	hat
el suéter	sweater
la talla	(clothing) size
la tienda de ropa	clothing store
el traje de baño	swimsuit
usar	to use, to wear
el vestido	dress
los zapatos (de tenis)	(tennis) shoes
Numbers to one million . . . . See page 138.	
Demonstrative adjectives and comparisons . . . . See page 140.	

Repaso de Vocabulario 2

Saying where you went and what you did

ahorrar	to save money
el almacén	department store
el anillo	ring
anoche	last night
anteayer	day before yesterday
los aretes	earrings
los audífonos	headphones
ayer	yesterday
comprar	to buy
el dinero	money
el disco compacto (en blanco)	(blank) CD
el DVD	DVD
gastar	to spend
la heladería	ice cream shop
la joyería	jewelry store
la juguetería	toy store
los juguetes	toys
la librería	bookstore
mirar las vitrinas	to window shop
pagar (una fortuna)	to pay (a fortune)
la plaza de comida	food court in a mall
la pulsera	bracelet
la revista de tiras cómicas	comic book
la tarjeta (de cumpleaños)	greeting card (birthday card)
la tienda de...	. . . store
tomar un batido	to have a milkshake
vender (de todo)	to sell (everything)
la zapatería	shoe store
Talking on the phone . . . . See page 150.	

Integración

capítulos 1-8

 1 Escucha el anuncio y escoge la respuesta más apropiada. ↓1B

1. Los audífonos son ▬▬▬.
   - **a.** de la más alta calidad
   - **b.** muy caros

2. Esta tienda vende ▬▬▬.
   - **a.** pocos videos
   - **b.** muchos videos

3. Casa Electrónica tiene ▬▬▬.
   - **a.** muchas cosas caras
   - **b.** pocas cosas caras

4. Casa Electrónica nunca ▬▬▬.
   - **a.** tiene descuentos
   - **b.** cierra

5. Según el anuncio, vas a ▬▬▬.
   - **a.** ahorrar dinero
   - **b.** pagar mucho

2 Con base en el anuncio, haz comparaciones entre las siguientes cosas, usando **más que, menos que** y **tan ... como**. ↓1B, 3A

1. sandalias para mujeres/sandalias para hombres
2. blusas de seda/blusas de algodón
3. sombreros para hombres/sombreros para mujeres
4. pulseras/anillos y aretes
5. camisas para mujeres/camisas para hombres

3 The woman in this painting has come to **el mercado** *(the market)* to buy **mangos, papayas, plátanos,** and **cocos,** all common tropical fruits. Write a conversation between the woman and the shopkeeper in Spanish.

- The people greet each other.
- The shopkeeper asks how he can help.
- The woman asks prices of various items.
- The shopkeeper answers with the prices, then compares two of the items.
- The woman decides what to buy.
- They say goodbye to each other.

After you have written your conversation, take turns acting it out with a partner. ↓**1A, 1C**

> **TEKS Focus** ▶
>
> **1A** Engage in oral and written exchanges of learned material to socialize and to provide and obtain information

Mercado caribeño **por Dr. Dominica Alcantara**

Dr. Dominica Alcantara © 2003

Integración

4

Situación

In small groups, create a department store in your classroom. Each group sets up a different department: clothing, accessories, school supplies, furniture, personal items (such as soap and shampoo), or food. Make signs for your department that show

▶ the items for sale

▶ their prices

▶ any special sales

After all the store departments are set up, play the roles of shoppers and clerks who buy and sell the merchandise. ↓**1A, 1C**

Video/DVD

GeoVisión

► **Concurso anual en Cabarete**
A windsurfing competition takes place every June near the town of Cabarete.

Geocultura
La República Dominicana

HI

HAITÍ

▼ **Santo Domingo** The capital of the Dominican Republic, Santo Domingo, is located on the southern coast of the country at the mouth of the Ozama River.

Almanaque

Población
8.581.477

Capital
Santo Domingo

Gobierno
democracia representativa

Idioma oficial
español

Moneda
peso dominicano

Código Internet
www.[ ].do

▼ **Hermanos dominicanos** In the Dominican Republic, it is common to see siblings of different ages spend time together.

Texas

¿Sabías que...?
Baseball star Sammy Sosa was born in **San Pedro de Macorís,** Dominican Republic. His career in Major League Baseball began with the Texas Rangers in 1989.

◄ **El Parque Nacional de los Haitises** This park is in the province of **Samaná**. You can see low hills called **mogotes** in the waters of the **Bahía de Samaná**.

► **El Pico Duarte** The **Pico Duarte** was named for Juan Pablo Duarte, a 19th-century revolutionary.

Río Yaque del Norte

PANIOLA

Puerto Plata
Sosúa
Cabarete
Cordillera Septentrional
Santiago
La Vega
Río Yuna
Samaná
BAHÍA DE SAMANÁ
OCÉANO ATLÁNTICO
Pico Duarte (3087 m.)
Jarabacoa
Cordillera Central
Río Ozama
Parque Nacional de los Haitises
Río Chavón
SANTO DOMINGO
San Pedro de Macorís
Higüey
La Romana
Sierra de Neíba
Río Yaque del Sur
Río Ocoa
Altos de Chavón
ISLA SAONA
Lago Enriquillo

REPÚBLICA DOMINICANA

MAR CARIBE

ISLA BEATA

▲ **Altos de Chavón** This artists' village in the province of **La Romana** sits on the bluffs above the **Río Chavón**.

▼ **El Lago Enriquillo** The largest saltwater lake in the Caribbean is in the Dominican Republic near the border with Haiti. It lies 40 meters below sea level.

▲ **Las iguanas y los cocodrilos** American crocodiles and various species of iguanas live in Lake Enriquillo.

⬇3B

¿Qué tanto sabes?
What national park sits along the **Bahía de Samaná**?

ciento setenta y tres **173**

A conocer la República Dominicana

La arquitectura

▲ **Casas de madera** Colorful wooden houses with sheet metal roofs are common in the Dominican Republic.

► **La Basílica de Higüey** This church has some of the most interesting modern architecture in the Dominican Republic. The concrete structure features a 75-meter-tall arch.

El arte

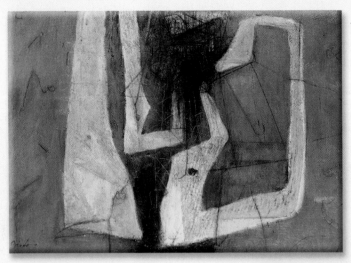

◄ *El Once*
This painting is by the Dominican artist **Ramón Oviedo** (1927–). Oviedo is considered one of the most important modern painters in Latin America.

▼ **Mural cerámico** The Dominican artist Said Musa (1956–) is known for his many colorful murals. Musa created this public mural in Santo Domingo out of ceramic tile.

Las celebraciones

Interactive TUTOR

Visit Holt Online
go.hrw.com
KEYWORD: EXP1B CH9
Photo Tour

▶ **El Carnaval de Santo Domingo** In Santo Domingo, **Carnaval** is celebrated every February with parades and fantastic costumes.

▼ **El Festival del Merengue** **Merengue** is the national music and dance of the Dominican Republic.

2B
¿Sabías que...?
The Dominican Republic is smaller than West Virginia, yet this island nation has an enormous variety of ecosystems and wildlife. In what ways can you see that nature is enjoyed and protected in the Dominican Republic?

La comida

▲ **El sancocho** A hearty meat and vegetable stew, **sancocho** is made on special occasions in the Dominican Republic.

◀ **Puesto de yaniqueque** **Yaniqueque** stands are common on beaches of the Dominican Republic. Similar to johnnycakes, **yaniqueques** are round, flat pieces of fried dough.

9

¡Festejemos!

Objetivos

In Part 1 you will learn to:
- ask about plans
- ask about past holidays
- use the preterite of **-er** and **-ir** verbs
- use the preterite of **-ar** verbs (review)
- say what you plan to do using **pensar** with infinitives

In Part 2 you will learn to:
- ask about preparing for a party
- greet and introduce others
- say goodbye
- use direct object pronouns
- use **conocer** and personal **a**
- form and use the present progressive tense

¿Qué ves en la foto?

- **En la foto, ¿qué llevan los muchachos?**

- **¿Hace buen tiempo o mal tiempo?**

- **¿Qué hacen los hombres *(men)* detrás de los muchachos?**

Texas

TEKS Look for the ✦ next to each activity to learn how it can help you achieve the goals of the **Texas Essential Knowledge and Skills,** found on page xxiii.

El Malecón, Santo Domingo

Vocabulario
en acción 1

Video/DVD

ExpresaVisión

Los días festivos

el Día de la Independencia

el Día de la Madre

la Semana Santa

el Día de los Enamorados

el Día del Padre

el Hanukah

la Navidad

la Nochevieja

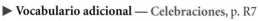

el Día de Acción de Gracias

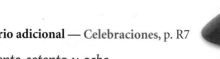

▶ **Vocabulario adicional** — Celebraciones, p. R7

Vocabulario 1

recibir regalos

ver fuegos artificiales

abrir regalos

¿Cómo lo festejaron?

reunirse con (toda) la familia

mandar tarjetas

Más vocabulario...

el Año Nuevo	New Year's Day
celebrar	to celebrate
decorar la casa	to decorate the house
invitar	to invite
ir...	
a misa	to mass
a la sinagoga	to the synagogue
al templo	to the temple

¡Exprésate!

Interactive TUTOR

To ask about plans	To respond
¿Qué vas a hacer el Día de la Independencia?	**Pienso hacer una fiesta o tener un picnic.**
What are you going to do on Independence Day?	*I plan to throw a party or have a picnic.*
¿Qué planes tienen para la Nochebuena?	**Pensamos pasarla con mis abuelos, como siempre.**
What plans do you have for Christmas Eve?	*We plan to spend it with my grandparents, as always.*

Online
Vocabulario y gramática, pp. 53–55

Un desfile, Santo Domingo

1 Días festivos ⬇1B

Leamos/Hablemos Lee las siguientes oraciones y decide qué día festivo le corresponde a cada una.

1. Papá Noel trae muchos regalos.
2. Decoramos con los colores azul, blanco y rojo.
3. Muchas personas salen para una cena romántica.
4. Compramos algo especial para nuestras madres.
5. Muchas personas van a la sinagoga.
6. La gente va a misa a la medianoche.
7. Nos reunimos con la familia en noviembre para una comida especial.
8. Hacemos algo para nuestros papás.
9. La gente sale a ver fuegos artificiales.

2 ¿Qué hago? ⬇1B

Leamos Jorge le escribe un correo electrónico a Lili sobre sus planes para la próxima semana. Lee su correo electrónico y las oraciones a continuación. Di si cada oración es cierta o falsa.

1. Jorge tiene todo listo para el cumpleaños de su papá y el Día de la Madre.
2. El papá de Jorge dice que no quiere nada para su cumpleaños.
3. Van a celebrar el cumpleaños del papá de Jorge el viernes.
4. Jorge piensa comprarle flores a su mamá para el Día de la Madre.
5. Jorge le compró un disco compacto a su mamá en abril.

3 Celebraciones ↴1B, 1C

Escribamos Con base en las fotos, describe cómo estas personas van a pasar los días festivos. Escribe por lo menos dos oraciones para cada foto.

MODELO La familia celebra el Día de la Madre. Los hijos preparan comida especial para la madre.

la familia

1. mis padres

2. mi familia y yo

3. mis hermanas

4. mis amigos

Comunicación

4 ¿Qué planes tienes para...? ↴1A, 1C

TEKS Focus
1C Present information using familiar words, phrases, and sentences

Hablemos Work with a group of classmates to plan a party. Decide who you will invite, what kind of food you will have, and what music you will listen to. Also agree on a date, time, and place for the party. As you are talking about your plans, give your opinion using **me parece** or (**no**) **estoy de acuerdo.** Be prepared to present your plans to the class.

MODELO —¿Qué tal si invitamos a todos nuestros compañeros de clase?

—No estoy de acuerdo. Me parece mejor invitar a doce personas, no más.

—Está bien, pero tenemos que invitar a...

5 La invitación ↴1A, 1C

Escribamos With a partner, write an invitation to a party. The invitation should say what is being celebrated, the date, time, and place of the party as well as anything your guests should bring. Exchange invitations with another pair of classmates and write a response. Say whether you can go to the party and what you will bring. If you can't go to the party, say why.

¡Exprésate!

To ask about past holidays	To respond
¿Dónde pasaron la Navidad el año pasado? *Where did you spend Christmas last year?*	**La pasamos en casa de mis tíos.** *We spent it at my aunt and uncle's house.*
¿Qué tal estuvo? *How was it?*	**Estuvo a todo dar. Nos reunimos a comer.** *It was great. We got together to eat.*

Interactive
TUTOR

Online
Vocabulario y gramática,
pp. 53–55

6 ¿Qué celebraron? 1B

Leamos Escoge la actividad que le corresponde a cada día festivo.

1. Mis hermanos cocinaron una cena especial para mamá. Ella descansó todo el día.

2. Los amigos mandaron muchas tarjetas, dulces y flores.

3. Nos reunimos con la familia para una cena especial.

4. Toda la familia le compró regalos para papá. Él descansó todo el día.

5. Fuimos a una fiesta y no nos acostamos hasta la una o las dos de la mañana.

6. La familia Rodríguez cenó en el parque para ver fuegos artificiales.

7. Compramos regalos para todos y toda la familia fue a misa.

a. el Día de la Independencia

b. el Día del Padre

c. el Día de Acción de Gracias

d. la Navidad

e. el Día de la Madre

f. el Día de los Enamorados

g. la Nochevieja

7 Entre amigos 1B

Leamos Pon en orden las oraciones de la siguiente conversación entre Lourdes y Manuel.

— ¿Qué tal estuvo?

— ¿Qué planes tienes para el Año Nuevo?

— Hola, Lourdes, ¿cómo estás? ¿Cómo pasaron la Navidad?

— Pues, la pasamos con mi familia en casa de los abuelos.

— ¡Hola, Manuel!

— No sé, pero creo que lo voy a pasar con mis primos.

— Estuvo bien. Nos reunimos a decorar la casa, comer y abrir regalos.

8 ¿Pasado o futuro? ↓1B

 Escuchemos Escucha la conversación entre Luis y Rosa. Indica si cada cosa ya *(already)* ocurrió el Día de Acción de Gracias o va a ocurrir el día de la Navidad.

	ya ocurrió	va a ocurrir
1. ir a casa de los abuelos		
2. almorzar en un restaurante		
3. ir al cine		
4. pasar la noche en casa		
5. decorar la casa		
6. ir a misa		
7. abrir regalos y comer		
8. dormir en casa de los abuelos		

9 Mi día festivo preferido ↓1B, 1C

 Escribamos Write a short paragraph about your favorite holiday. Explain how you celebrate the holiday and who celebrates the holiday with you. Also explain why it is your favorite holiday.

MODELO **Mi día festivo preferido es el Día de Acción de Gracias. Es mi día favorito porque toda la familia va a la casa de mi abuela y...**

Nota cultural

On February 27th, Independence Day, Dominicans celebrate **Carnaval**. In Santo Domingo, children and adults gather to watch a parade along **El malecón**, one of the main streets. The parade includes floats, marching bands, dancers, and **diablos cojuelos**. These figures wear brightly-colored, horned masks and costumes covered with toys, mirrors, and shiny objects. What celebrations in the United States or in other countries are similar to the Dominican **Carnaval**?

↓2A, 4B

 # Comunicación

10 ¿Cómo lo van a pasar? ↓1A

Hablemos Ask a classmate which holiday is his or her favorite, how he or she celebrates that day, and what plans he or she has for this year's celebration. Also ask your classmate why that holiday is his or her favorite. Then your classmate should ask you the same questions.

MODELO —¿Cuál es tu día festivo preferido?

—Es la Nochevieja.

—¿Cómo celebran la Nochevieja tú y tu familia?

—Primero salimos con nuestros tíos y primos y luego...

—¿Por qué es la Nochevieja tu día festivo favorito?

—Es mi día festivo favorito porque...

> **TEKS Focus**
> **1A** Engage in oral and written exchanges of learned material to socialize and to provide and obtain information

Gramática en acción 1

Objetivos
Using the preterite of **-ar**, **-er**, and **-ir** verbs; **pensar** with **que** and **pensar** with infinitives

Preterite of -er and -ir verbs

Interactive TUTOR

1 The **preterite** is used to talk about what happened at a specific point in the past. To form the **preterite** of **-er** and **-ir** verbs, add these endings to the verb's stem.

volver	escribir
yo volv**í**	yo escrib**í**
tú volv**iste**	tú escrib**iste**
Ud., él, ella volv**ió**	Ud., él, ella escrib**ió**
nosotros(as) volv**imos**	nosotros(as) escrib**imos**
vosotros(as) volv**isteis**	vosotros(as) escrib**isteis**
Uds., ellos, ellas volv**ieron**	Uds., ellos, ellas escrib**ieron**

—¿**Recibieron** la tarjeta?   —Sí, la **recibimos** ayer. Gracias.

2 Regular **-er** and **-ir** verbs have the same endings in the **preterite**. Stem-changing **-er** verbs don't have a stem change in the **preterite**.

—¿Por qué no fuiste a la fiesta?   —Porque me **dolió** la garganta.

3 The verb **ver** has regular **preterite** endings but without written accents.

yo v**i**	nosotros(as) v**imos**
tú v**iste**	vosotros(as) v**isteis**
Ud., él, ella v**io**	Uds., ellos, ellas v**ieron**

Online

Vocabulario y gramática, pp. 56–58	Actividades, pp. 51–54

¿Te acuerdas?

To form the preterite of a regular **-ar** verb, add these endings to the verb's stem.

merend**é**	merend**amos**
merend**aste**	merend**asteis**
merend**ó**	merend**aron**

No **-ar** verbs have stem changes in the preterite.

11 **La Navidad de Pablo** 🔊1B

Leamos Escoge el verbo correcto entre paréntesis.

Pablo y sus padres ____1____ (salimos/salieron) muy temprano para la casa de sus abuelos el día de Navidad, donde ____2____ (se reunieron/me reuní) con toda la familia. Pablo ____3____ (vimos/vio) a unos tíos que viven lejos. Primero todos ____4____ (comí/comieron) y Pablo ____5____ (bebiste/bebió) tres vasos de limonada. Después de la comida ellos ____6____ (abrimos/ abrieron) los regalos y a las cuatro ____7____ (fuimos/fueron) a misa.

12 Ahora, ¿qué dice Pablo? ↓1B, 1C

Escribamos Vuelve a escribir el párrafo de la Actividad 11 desde el punto de vista (*point of view*) de Pablo. ¿Qué dice él?

13 El Año Nuevo ↓1B, 1C

Escribamos/Hablemos Mira las fotos. Según (*according to*) Marco, ¿quiénes hicieron estas cosas para celebrar el Año Nuevo?

MODELO comer en un restaurante
Mis padres comieron en un restaurante.

mi hermano y yo

mis abuelos

mis padres

1. beber muchos refrescos
2. salir a un restaurante
3. beber café
4. comer pastel de chocolate
5. asistir a una fiesta
6. comer pizza
7. ver televisión
8. reunirse con la familia

 Comunicación

14 La semana pasada ↓1A

Hablemos Pregúntale a un(a) compañero(a) si hizo las cosas de la Actividad 13 la semana pasada.

MODELO —¿Saliste a un restaurante?
—Sí, salí a un restaurante la semana pasada.

15 ¿Qué hiciste? ↓1A

Hablemos Use the phrases in the word box to write four questions for a classmate about how he or she celebrated several holidays last year. Take turns answering each other's questions.

escribir tarjetas	reunirse con la familia	recibir regalos
ver fuegos artificiales	salir a comer	asistir a una fiesta

TEKS Focus
1A Engage in oral and written exchanges of learned material to socialize and to provide and obtain information

La República Dominicana

ciento ochenta y cinco **185**

Interactive
TUTOR

Repaso The preterite

1 Compare the preterite forms of regular **-ar**, **-er**, and **-ir** verbs and the irregular verb **ir**.

	invitar	comer	salir	ir
yo	invit**é**	com**í**	sal**í**	fui
tú	invit**aste**	com**iste**	sal**iste**	fuiste
usted, él, ella	invit**ó**	com**ió**	sal**ió**	fue
nosotros(as)	invit**amos**	com**imos**	sal**imos**	fuimos
vosotros(as)	invit**asteis**	com**isteis**	sal**isteis**	fuisteis
ustedes, ellos, ellas	invit**aron**	com**ieron**	sal**ieron**	fueron

—¿**Saliste** con tus amigos?
Did you go out with your friends?

—Sí, **fuimos** a una fiesta.
Yes, we went to a party.

—¿A quiénes **invitaron** a la fiesta?
Who did they invite to the party?

—A todos. **Comimos** y **bailamos** mucho.
Everyone. We ate and danced a lot.

Online
| Vocabulario y gramática, pp. 56–58 | Actividades, pp. 51–54 |

¡Te acuerdas?

Stem-changing **-ar** and **-er** verbs have no stem changes in the preterite.

El regalo c**o**stó veinte dólares.

No v**o**lvimos hasta *(until)* las once.

16 ¿Cuándo? ↯1B

 Escuchemos Escucha las oraciones y decide si la joven habla de **a)** lo que su familia siempre hace o de **b)** lo que hizo.

17 ¿Qué tal estuvo? ↯1B, 1C

 Escribamos Indica qué hicieron las siguientes personas en varias fiestas. Luego di qué tal estuvo cada fiesta—a todo dar o aburrida.

MODELO **nosotros (no salir hasta muy tarde)**
No salimos hasta muy tarde.
La fiesta estuvo a todo dar.

1. su tía (cantar ópera)
2. yo (bailar toda la noche)
3. nosotros (comer muy bien)
4. sólo *(only)* cuatro personas (ir a la fiesta)
5. Laura y José (jugar al ajedrez)
6. muchas personas interesantes (hablar conmigo)
7. nosotros (pasar una noche fenomenal)
8. todos (salir temprano de la fiesta)
9. yo (ver a muchos de mis amigos)
10. mis primos (escribir tarjetas de Navidad)

18 Padres especiales ↓1C

Escribamos ¿Cómo festejó cada familia el Día del Padre y el Día de la Madre?

MODELO Pasaron el Día de la Madre con la abuela.

el Día de la Madre

el Día del Padre

19 El calendario de Arturo ↓1B, 1C

Leamos/Escribamos Use the information from the calendar to write at least seven sentences about what Arturo did for each holiday. Then compare his activities with yours.

MODELO El 4 de julio Arturo fue a la playa.
No fui a la playa, pero sí comí en el parque.

14 de febrero	4 de julio	25 de diciembre	31 de diciembre
mandar tarjetas	ir a la playa	abrir regalos	ir a una fiesta
abrir regalos	ver fuegos artificiales	reunirse con la familia	bailar
comer chocolate	comer en el parque	ir a la iglesia	reunirse con amigos

 Comunicación

20 ¿Y tú? ↓1A

Hablemos Pregúntale a tu compañero(a) cómo celebró los días festivos de la Actividad 19.

MODELO —¿Recibiste muchas tarjetas para el Día de los Enamorados?
—Recibí muchas tarjetas y unos regalos también.

Pensar que and pensar with infinitives

1 The **e → ie** stem-changing verb **pensar** means *to think*. When it's followed by **que,** it means *to think that . . .*

yo **pie**nso	nosotros(as) pensamos
tu **pie**nsas	vosotros(as) pensáis
Ud., él, ella **pie**nsa	Uds., ellos(as) **pie**nsan

Pienso que los invitados van a hablar y bailar toda la noche.
I think that the guests are going to talk and dance all night.

2 **Pensar** can also be followed by an **infinitive** to say what *someone plans* to do or *intends* to do.

—¿Qué **piensan hacer** para celebrar el Año Nuevo?
What do you plan to do to celebrate New Year's Eve?

—**Pensamos ir** a esquiar.
We plan to go skiing.

Online
Vocabulario y gramática, pp. 56–58	Actividades, pp. 51–54

TEKS Focus

4B Demonstrate understanding of the concept of culture through comparisons

Nota cultural

Celebrations call for special foods. In the Dominican Republic, a food served during the Christmas season is **pasteles en hoja**. This dish is prepared by boiling and mashing green plantains. The mashed plantains are then spread onto plantain leaves. Next, the leaves are stuffed with ground beef or chicken. Finally, the stuffed leaves are folded, tied with string, and placed in a pot of boiling water. Which other cultures have dishes similar to this? Is there a similar dish in your culture? ↯**2B, 4B**

21 **Este año pienso...** ↯**1B**

Leamos/Escribamos Completa cada resolución de Año Nuevo *(New Year's resolution)* de manera lógica. Usa el verbo **pensar** y las siguientes palabras en tus respuestas.

relajarse más	seguir una dieta más sana
gastar menos en regalos	tomar una clase de francés
volver a la universidad	hacer más ejercicio
ir a la casa de los abuelos	pasar más tiempo en casa

MODELO Voy a comer más verduras.
   Pienso seguir una dieta más sana.

1. Mi madre va a estudiar mucho.
2. Mi hermano y yo vamos a mantenernos en mejor forma.
3. Mi padre va a tomar menos café y no va a trabajar hasta tarde.
4. Vamos a reunirnos con todos mis tíos para la Navidad.
5. Mi madre va a estudiar francés.
6. Mis padres van a ahorrar dinero este año.
7. No voy a salir con mis amigos todos los sábados.
8. Mi hermana mayor no va a trabajar tanto.
9. Voy a pasar más tiempo con mis abuelos.

22 El Día de la Independencia ➥1C

Escribamos/Hablemos Mira los dibujos e indica cómo todos piensan pasar el 4 de julio. Luego usa **pienso que** para dar tu opinión sobre los planes.

MODELO Pienso ir a la playa con mis amigos.
Pienso que va a ser muy divertido.
Pienso que me voy a divertir mucho.

yo

1. mis amigos y yo

2. unos amigos

3. mis padres

4. mi hermana

5. por la noche, mis padres y yo

6. mis abuelos

 # Comunicación

23 ¡Ven a mi fiesta! ➥1A

Hablemos With a classmate, talk about a party you are planning to have. You should talk about the reason for the party, where it will be, the guests, music, and food. You and your classmate can use phrases from the word box to ask questions and to respond.

Pienso que...	(No) estoy de acuerdo.	Prefiero...
fenomenal	pésimo(a)	divertido(a)
(No) me gusta(n).	¡Buena idea!	delicioso(a)

Cultura

Comparaciones

Interactive
TUTOR

🔻 2A, 4B

Carnaval en la República Dominicana

¿Qué días festivos se celebran en tu país?

En los países hispanohablantes, los días festivos y los festivales son muy importantes. A veces los festivales son religiosos, y a veces son de sabor nacional o regional. De todos modos, toda la comunidad participa, y es común cerrar los colegios, tiendas y otros negocios para celebrar. Estas personas hablan de los días festivos en su país y de la manera en que se celebran. ¿Son días festivos que celebras también? ¿Los celebras igual que ellos? Si son festivales que no celebras, ¿te acuerdas de otros que sí celebras?

☀ Waldemar
Santo Domingo, la República Dominicana

Waldemar talks about his favorite holiday, **Semana Santa.** What is your favorite holiday and how do you celebrate it?

¿Me puedes decir cuáles son dos o tres días festivos que se celebran en República Dominicana, y en qué fechas son?

Celebramos la Semana Santa, que es la segunda semana de abril. Celebramos el Día de la Madre, catorce de mayo. Y también celebramos las Navidades.

¿Cuál es tu día festivo favorito?

Me gusta mucho la Semana Santa.

¿Qué significa para ti la Semana Santa?

Es una semana muy espiritual.

¿Cómo pasaste la Semana Santa el año pasado?

Muy común. Como todo el mundo, fuimos a la iglesia mucho. Pasé mucho tiempo con mi familia.

REPÚBLICA DOMINICANA

Océano Atlántico

★ Santo Domingo

Diana
El Paso, Texas

Diana shares a special meal with her family at Christmas. How do your holiday celebrations compare with hers?

¿Me puedes decir dos o tres días festivos que se celebran aquí en El Paso?

Claro, aquí en El Paso festejamos el Día de la Independencia de Estados Unidos, que es el cuatro de julio. También festejamos la Navidad, que es el veinticinco de diciembre, y el Día de Gracias, que es el último jueves de noviembre.

¿Qué día festivo es tu favorito?

Mi día festivo favorito es la Navidad.

¿Cómo pasaste la Navidad el año pasado?

Toda mi familia nos sentamos en la casa de los abuelos, y comimos pavo.

Cultura

Para comprender 1B

1. ¿Cuáles son tres días festivos que se celebran en la República Dominicana?
2. ¿Dónde pasó Diana la Navidad el año pasado?
3. ¿En qué día se celebra el Día de Acción de Gracias en Estados Unidos?
4. ¿Adónde fue Waldemar y su familia durante la Semana Santa?

Para pensar y hablar 2A

Waldemar and Diana say that their favorite holidays are **Semana Santa** and **la Navidad.** Why do you think they chose those holidays as their favorites? How is the way in which Waldemar and Diana spent their favorite holidays alike? What are your favorite holidays? Why are those days important to you?

Cuaderno para hispanohablantes, pp. 69–76

Comunidad 4B, 5A

What Mexican holidays do you celebrate?

Two Mexican holidays celebrated in Texas are **Cinco de Mayo** and **El 16 de Septiembre,** Mexican Independence Day. There are also festivals that celebrate the Mexican roots of many Texans. For example, in Brownsville, Texas and Matamoros, Tamaulipas, people celebrate **Charro Days** every year. Mexic-Arte, a museum in Austin, presents eighty programs about Mexican holidays a year. What Mexican holidays does your community celebrate? To find out how people in your community take part in such festivities, interview in Spanish someone who helps organize them. Try to attend a festival. How are the Texan and Mexican cultures represented?

Charro Days in Brownsville, Texas

Vocabulario *en acción* 2

Video/DVD

ExpresaVisión

mandar invitaciones

Ahora estamos haciendo preparativos para la fiesta sorpresa

colgar (ue) decoraciones, decorar

Entremeses

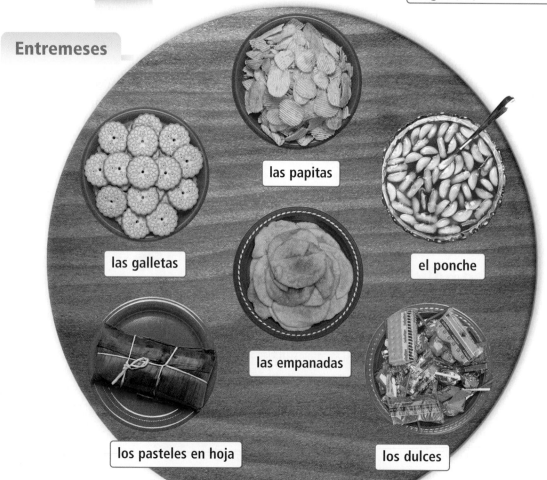

las papitas

las galletas

el ponche

las empanadas

los pasteles en hoja

los dulces

▶ Vocabulario adicional — Regalos, p. R10

Los invitados van a...

enseñar fotos

charlar

contar (ue) chistes

Más vocabulario...

Las fiestas

el aniversario	*anniversary*
la boda	*wedding*
el cumpleaños	*birthday*
el día de tu santo	*your saint's day*
la fiesta sorpresa	*surprise party*
la graduación	*graduation*
la quinceañera	*girl's fifteenth birthday*

 También se puede decir...

In the Dominican Republic, finger foods are called **bocadillos** or **picaderas,** but they may also be called **tapas** in Spain, **botanas** in Mexico, **pasapalos** in Venezuela, **bocas** in Costa Rica and El Salvador, or **apetitos** in Texas.

¡Exprésate!

To ask about preparing for a party	To respond
¿Está todo listo para la fiesta? ¿Ya terminaste con los preparativos? *Is everything ready for the party? Did you already finish the preparations?*	**Sí. Anoche compré las flores y preparé el ponche.** *Yes. Last night I bought the flowers and made the punch.*
¿Qué están haciendo los jóvenes ahora? *What are the young people doing now?*	**Están colgando la piñata.** *They are hanging the piñata.*

Interactive **TUTOR**

Online
Vocabulario y gramática, pp. 59–61

24 **¡Vamos a festejar!** ↓1B

Leamos/Hablemos Completa las oraciones con la(s) palabra(s) apropiada(s).

decoraciones ✓	ponche ✓	está listo	invitados	fiesta sorpresa ✓
empanadas ✓	piñata	chistes	cumpleaños ✓	pasteles en hoja

1. Hoy es el ===== de mi primo Paco.
2. Esta noche hay una =====. Va a ser muy divertida.
3. Todo ===== para la fiesta.
4. Anteayer mi mamá, mis hermanos y yo preparamos los =====.
5. Esta mañana limpiamos la casa y luego colgamos las =====.
6. Ahora mi papá está colgando la ===== en el patio.
7. En unas horas, los ===== van a llegar a nuestra casa.
8. En la fiesta, vamos a beber ===== y comer muchas =====.
9. Voy a contar muchos ===== también.

25 **¿Cuál palabra?** ↓1B

Leamos Read each list of words and phrases for holidays and holiday activities and decide which word or phrase does not belong with the others.

1. preparar el ponche/ir a la iglesia/colgar la piñata
2. ir a misa/contar chistes/celebrar el día de tu santo
3. mandar tarjetas y flores/celebrar El Día de los Enamorados/enseñar fotos
4. ir a la quinceañera/pasar el rato solo(a)/mandar invitaciones
5. mandar tarjetas/ir a la iglesia/asistir a la boda
6. celebrar la graduación/comprar regalos/ver los fuegos artificiales

26 **¡Ya las compré!** ↓1B, 1C

Leamos/Escribamos Miguel is worried about the preparations for the party. Answer his questions by telling him that the preparations have already been done.

MODELO —¿Compró las galletas Carlos?

—Sí, Carlos ya las compró.

1. ¿Mandaste las invitaciones?
2. ¿Colgaron las decoraciones Lili y Ana?
3. ¿Compraron el pastel tú y Sara?
4. ¿Colgó la piñata María?
5. ¿Prepararon los tamales tus tíos?
6. ¿Terminaste con los preparativos?

27 **La fiesta de Mila** ⬇1B, 1C

Escribamos/Hablemos Contesta las siguientes preguntas con base en el dibujo.

1. ¿Qué ocasión especial festejaron?
2. ¿Qué preparativos hicieron *(did they make)* antes de la fiesta?
3. ¿Qué tal estuvo la fiesta?
4. ¿Qué pasó en la fiesta?

  Comunicación

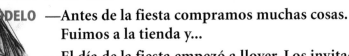

28 **Historia de una fiesta** ⬇1B, 1C

Escribamos/Hablemos With two classmates, write a story about the preparations for a party, the party itself, and what happened after the party. Each member of the group should write one section of the story. Compare each part of the story carefully so that it makes sense when you read the three parts together. Be prepared to present your narrative to the class.

TEKS Focus

1B Demonstrate understanding of simple, clearly spoken, and written language when dealing with familiar topics

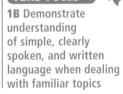

MODELO —**Antes de la fiesta compramos muchas cosas. Fuimos a la tienda y...**

—**El día de la fiesta empezó a llover. Los invitados llegaron tarde y...**

—**Después de la fiesta limpiamos la casa. Empezamos en la cocina y...**

La República Dominicana

ciento noventa y cinco **195**

¡Exprésate!

To greet, introduce others, and say goodbye

¡Qué gusto verte!	**¡Tanto tiempo sin verte!**
It's great to see you!	*Long time, no see!*
¿Qué hay de nuevo?	**Lo de siempre.**
What's new?	*Same as usual.*
Te presento a mis padres.	**Tanto gusto. ¡Feliz aniversario!**
I'd like you to meet my parents.	*So nice to meet you. Happy anniversary!*
Chao, te llamo más tarde.	**Vale. Que te vaya bien.**
Bye, I'll call you later.	*Okay. Hope things go well for you.*
	Cuídate.
	Take care.

Online
Vocabulario y gramática,
pp. 59–61

29 Saludos, despedidas y presentaciones ↓1B

Escuchemos Indica si cada expresión es **a)** un saludo *(a greeting)*, **b)** una despedida *(a farewell)*, o **c)** una presentación *(an introduction)*.

30 ¡Qué gusto verte! ↓1B

Leamos Escoge la mejor respuesta a cada oración.

1. Voy a llegar tarde. No puedo hablar ahora.
2. Hasta luego.
3. Te presento a mi hermano.
4. Hoy es nuestro aniversario.
5. ¿Qué hay de nuevo?
6. Después de dos años, volví de África.

a. Lo de siempre.
b. ¡Feliz aniversario!
c. Chao, te llamo más tarde.
d. Que te vaya bien.
e. ¡Tanto tiempo sin verte!
f. Tanto gusto.

31 ¿Qué dices? ↓1B

Leamos/Hablemos Decide qué expresiones de **¡Exprésate!** puedes usar en estas situaciones.

1. Ves a un amigo después de tres años.
2. Acabas de presentar a dos amigos.
3. Estás con tus padres y ves a un amigo que no los conoce.
4. Vas a hablar por teléfono con un amigo más tarde.
5. Un amigo va a la República Dominicana por dos años.
6. Estás muy contento(a) de ver a un amigo.
7. Un amigo quiere saber qué hiciste ayer pero no hiciste nada nuevo.
8. Tu hermana va a subir a la montaña Everest y después pasar un año en China.

32 **Te presento a...** ↓1B

Leamos Lili and José haven't seen each other for a while. Complete the conversation with appropriate phrases from **¡Exprésate!**

JOSE   Hola Lili. ¡Tanto ___1___ !

LILI   ¡Qué gusto verte! ¿Qué hay ___2___ ?

JOSE   ___3___ .

LILI   José, ___4___ a mi mamá.

JOSE   ___5___ .

SRA. LÓPEZ   Igualmente.

LILI   José, ¿quieres venir a una fiesta mañana?

JOSE   Lo siento. No puedo ir. Mañana voy a Florida.

LILI   Vale. ___6___ .

 Comunicación

33 **¿Qué dicen?** ↓1C

 Escribamos/Hablemos Work with a partner. Choose two photos and write conversations based on each photo. Be prepared to role-play each conversation for the class.

TEKS Focus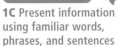

1C Present information using familiar words, phrases, and sentences

1.

2.

3.

4.

34 **Una reunion** ↓1A, 1C

Escribamos/Hablemos In groups of three role-play the following situation. Three years from now you meet a middle school friend at a party. You have come to the party with a new friend from high school. Introduce your new friend. Talk with both friends about the party and about what you are doing now in high school. Be prepared to present your role-play to the class.

GramaVisión

Direct object pronouns

Interactive TUTOR

1 Direct objects are people or things that receive the action of a verb. To avoid repetition, the **direct object pronouns** can take their place.

Subject	Direct Object		Subject	Direct Object	
yo	**me**	me	nosotros(as)	**nos**	us
tú	**te**	you	vosotros(as)	**os**	you
usted (m.)	**lo**	you	ustedes (m.)	**los**	you
usted (f.)	**la**	you	ustedes (f.)	**las**	you
él	**lo**	him	ellos	**los**	them
ella	**la**	her	ellas	**las**	them

la stands for Paula

—¿Invitaste a **Paula?**   —Sí, **la** invité. Ella viene.
Did you invite Paula?   *Yes, I invited her. She's coming.*

2 When answering a question, remember to change the **direct object pronoun**, if necessary.

object me changes to te

—¿**Me** vas a llamar?   —Sí, **te** llamo más tarde.
Are you going to call me?   *Yes, I'll call you later.*

Online

Vocabulario y gramática, pp. 62–64	Actividades, pp. 56–59

¿Te acuerdas?
The **direct object pronouns lo** *(it)*, **la** *(it)*, **los** *(them)* and **las** *(them)* can stand for things as well as people.

—¿Ya compraste **las flores?**

—Sí, ya **las** compré.

35 **Invitaciones** ↓1B, 1C

Escribamos Indica a qué celebración invitaste a las siguientes personas. Sigue el modelo.

MODELO **La invité a la quinceañera.**

Ana

1. a mis abuelos   2. a mi profesora   3. a mis amigas   4. a mi primo

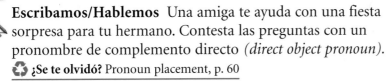

36 Una fiesta sorpresa ↴1B, 1C

Escribamos/Hablemos Una amiga te ayuda con una fiesta sorpresa para tu hermano. Contesta las preguntas con un pronombre de complemento directo *(direct object pronoun)*. ♻ **¿Se te olvidó?** Pronoun placement, p. 60

> **MODELO** Vas a llevar a *tu hermano* a la fiesta, ¿verdad? (sí)
> Sí, voy a llevarlo. (Sí, lo voy a llevar.)

1. ¿*Me* vas a llamar antes de la fiesta, ¿verdad? (sí)
2. Él no debe ver *a los invitados* antes de entrar, ¿verdad? (no)
3. ¿Debo poner *los regalos* en la mesa del patio? (sí)
4. ¿Invitaste *a los estudiantes de su clase?* (sí)
5. ¿Él no vio *las decoraciones?* (no)
6. ¿Tus padres *te* ayudaron a preparar todo? (sí)
7. ¿Tu hermano menor *nos* va a interrumpir durante los preparativos? (no)
8. ¿*Me* necesitas para algo más? (no)

37 ¡No nos fastidies! ↴1B, 1C

Escribamos/Hablemos Usando un pronombre de complemento directo con el imperativo, dile a cada persona qué debe o no debe hacer. ♻ **¿Se te olvidó?** Object pronouns and commands, p. 110

> **MODELO** Hablas con tus amigos y tu hermano los interrumpe.
> ¡No nos interrumpas!
> Un amigo nunca te invita a salir.
> ¡Invítame a salir!

1. Un amigo que habla español nunca te ayuda a estudiar.
2. Hablas de algo secreto con un amigo y tu hermano los escucha.
3. El hermano menor de un amigo es antipático y tu amigo siempre lo trae cuando ustedes salen.
4. Tu mejor amigo no te llama.
5. Quieres comprar un regalo de cumpleaños para tu hermana y tu amigo la invita a ir de compras con ustedes.

 Comunicación

38 Planes para una fiesta ↴1A

Hablemos In pairs, talk about plans for a party. When will you have the party? Say who is going to help you with the preparations. What are you going to serve? What are you going to need and where are you going to put everything?

> **MODELO** —¿Cuándo quieres hacer tu fiesta de cumpleaños?
> —Quiero hacerla en dos semanas.

Gramática 2

Nota cultural

In most Spanish-speaking countries, including the Dominican Republic, dancing is an important part of any party. All kinds of music are played, food is served, and parties often do not end until the early morning hours. Spanish-speaking and Latin American countries have given us some of the most popular dances, including **merengue, salsa, samba, cha-cha-chá, tango, rumba,** and **cumbia.** Are these dances popular where you live? ↴2A, 4C

TEKS Focus

1A Engage in oral and written exchanges of learned material to socialize and to provide and obtain information

Conocer and personal a

Interactive
TUTOR

1 The verb **conocer** is used to say you know people or meet them, or that you are familiar with a place or a thing. It is irregular in the **yo** form.

yo cono**zco**	nosotros(as) conocemos
tú conoces	vosotros(as) conocéis
Ud., él, ella conoce	Uds., ellos, ellas conocen

—Aquí viene mi prima Claudia. ¿Quieres conocerla?
—Ya la **conozco**.

2 When a name or noun referring to a person is the **direct object** of **conocer** or other verbs, the word **a** comes before it. This **a** has no translation.

—¿**Conoces a mi hermano**?
—Sí, **conozco a toda tu familia**.

The preposition **a** combines with the definite article **el** to form the contraction **al**.

▶ **Online**

Vocabulario y gramática, pp. 62–64	Actividades, pp. 56–59

Vocabulario y gramática, pp. 62–64 · Actividades, pp. 56–59

Nota cultural

Texas is rich in cultural heritages, including Mexican, German, Polish, Scottish, and Czech. Ethnic celebrations are popular throughout the state, and include El Cinco de Mayo, Wurstfest in New Braunfels, and the Czech festival in Praha, all celebrated with traditional food, music, and dancing. The University of Texas Institute of Texan Cultures in San Antonio annually hosts the Texas Folklife Festival. Is there a popular festival in your area? ↓**2A, 4B**

39 **¿Conoces estas obras?** ↓**1B, 2B**

✎ **Escribamos** Indica si conoces o no las obras *(works)* de estos hispanos famosos. Usa un pronombre de complemento directo.

MODELO Sí, la conozco.
(No, no la conozco.)

la música de
Andrés Segovia

1. las películas de
Antonio Banderas

2. los libros de
Isabel Allende

3. las canciones de
Shakira

4. las obras de
Pablo Picasso

40 Presentaciones ⬇1B

Leamos Completa la siguiente conversación con las formas correctas de **conocer**, los pronombres de complemento directo o la palabra **a**.

SONIA Mario y Daniel, ¡qué gusto verlos! ¿ __1__ a mi hermano Carlos?

DANIEL No, no lo __2__.

SONIA Carlos, te presento __3__ mis amigos Mario y Daniel. Mario y Daniel, les presento __4__ mi hermano Carlos.

CARLOS Mario, ¿no eres el primo de Alberto Martínez?

MARIO Sí, soy su primo. ¿ __5__ conoces?

CARLOS Sí, lo __6__ muy bien. Está en mi clase de historia y a veces jugamos al tenis después de clases.

Un supermercado en la República Dominicana

41 ¿Se conocen? ⬇1B

Leamos/Escribamos Lee cada oración. Indica si estas personas conocen a las personas o las cosas entre paréntesis. Repite la respuesta usando un pronombre de complemento directo.

MODELO **Mis padres siempre invitan a mi mejor amigo a nuestra casa. (mi mejor amigo)**
Mis padres conocen bien a mi mejor amigo.
Mis padres lo conocen bien.

1. Juan habla con Sara todos los días. (Sara)
2. Mi tía sabe dónde están las tiendas, los restaurantes, el colegio, el correo y el cine. (la ciudad)
3. Mis abuelos quieren venir a mi colegio pero no saben dónde está. (el pueblo)
4. Mi mejor amigo viene a mi casa los fines de semana. (mi casa)
5. Mi madre quiere hablar con mi profesor de español pero no sabe cómo se llama. (mi profesor de español)
6. Lola está en mi clase de inglés. Es muy simpática. (Lola)

Comunicación

42 Un encuentro ⬇1A

Hablemos Imagine that you are at a party. In groups of four, take turns introducing two of your classmates to another person. You can use Activity 40 as model for your conversation.

Gramática 2

Interactive TUTOR

Present progressive

1 To say what is happening right now, use the present progressive. To form the present progressive, combine a conjugated form of **estar** with the present participle. Form the present participle by replacing **-ar** with **-ando** and **-er** or **-ir** with **-iendo**.

cantar → cant**ando**

Rosa **está** cant**ando**. *Rosa is singing.*

comer → com**iendo**

Estamos com**iendo**. *We are eating.*

2 When the stem of an **-er** or **-ir** verb ends in a vowel, form the present participle by changing **i** to **y**.

leer → le**y**endo

¿**Estás** le**y**endo? *Are you reading?*

3 The participles of stem-changing **-ir** verbs like **pedir, venir, dormir,** and **servir** change o → **u** and e → **i**. There are no stem changes for **-ar** and **-er** verbs.

dormir → d**u**rmiendo   servir → s**i**rviendo

4 The verb **ir** is not usually used in the present progressive. Use the simple present tense instead.

—¿**Vas** a la fiesta?   *Are you going to the party?*

—No, **voy** a la biblioteca.   *No, I'm going to the library.*

5 **Direct object** and **reflexive pronouns** can go before the conjugated form of **estar** or can be attached to the end of the present participle. When you attach the direct object or reflexive pronoun to the end of the present participle, place an accent mark on the stressed vowel.

¿La tarea? **La** estoy haciendo. (Estoy haciéndo**la**)

¿Mis hijos? **Se** están bañando. (Están bañándo**se**.)

Online

| Vocabulario y gramática, pp. 62–64 | Actividades, pp. 56–59 |

Online
Vocabulario y gramática, pp. 62–64 | Actividades, pp. 56–59

En inglés

In English, the present progressive can mean that something is happening right now, is happening regularly, or is going to happen in the future.

Everyone *is celebrating* in the living room.

We *are spending* a lot of time together.

Tomorrow I *am leaving* for La Paz.

In Spanish, the present progressive can mean that something is happening right now or is happening regularly. However, it is not used for what is going to happen in the future. Instead, the simple present is used.

Todos **están celebrando** en la sala.

Estamos pasando mucho tiempo juntos.

Mañana **salgo** para La Paz.

---

43 **¿Qué están haciendo?** ◆1B

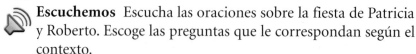

Escuchemos Escucha las oraciones sobre la fiesta de Patricia y Roberto. Escoge las preguntas que le correspondan según el contexto.

a. ¿Qué están haciendo ustedes?

b. ¿Qué están haciendo los invitados?

c. ¿Qué está haciendo tu madre?

44 **¿Dónde están?** 🔻1B, 1C

 Escribamos/Hablemos Indica qué están haciendo las siguientes personas según el contexto. Menciona varias posibilidades.

> **MODELO** **Consuelo está en su cuarto.**
> **Está durmiendo. Está estudiando.**

1. Lupe está en la clase.
2. Juan y Carlos están en el parque.
3. Laura y José están en una fiesta de cumpleaños.
4. Mi hermana y yo estamos en la cocina.
5. Estás en una tienda.
6. Tu primo y tú están en un restaurante.

   Comunicación

45 **Pantomimas** 🔻1B, 1C

 Hablemos Each student should present one of the following actions without speaking. The class tries to guess what he or she is doing.

hablar por teléfono	abrir un regalo	escribir una tarjeta
lavarse los dientes	secarse el pelo	maquillarse
peinarse	servir comida	acostarse

46 **Una fiesta** 🔻1C

Hablemos With a classmate, describe the party. Use the first picture to talk about what happened before the party, the second to talk about what is happening, and the third to say what the people are planning to do after the party.

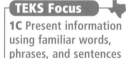

Conexiones culturales

Conexión Matemáticas

1 El día del árbol ↓2A, 4B

In Venezuela people celebrate a holiday each spring called **el Día del Árbol.** It's a day when students and companies help beautify their community by planting trees such as **la acacia,** a kind of flowering tree, or **la palma,** palm tree. At some schools students plant fruit trees and flowers in a school garden.

1. What kind of tree would you prefer to plant and why? How do trees help the environment?

2. If you plant a four-foot-tall palm tree this year that grows nine inches a year, how tall will it be when you're 18? when you are 50?

3. Is there a similar holiday where you live? Explain.

TEKS Focus
4B Demonstrate understanding of the concept of culture through comparisons

Conexión Literatura

2 La invitación ⬇1B

Look at the following poem. See if you can guess what the poem is about before you begin reading. Make sure to use reading strategies such as thinking about the topic, looking for cognates, and looking for words you've already learned.

Sube a mi tronco

El árbol gigantesco te invita

El que bebe agua cristalina y canta aire azul

¡Ven! Sube a mis hombros, juega en mis brazos

¡Ven! Conoce el mundo desde un océano lejano

Descansa con la música verde de mis hojas

Baila conmigo el flamenco de mis flores

Y come la fruta rica del bosque

¡VEN!

SUBE

¡VEN!

SUBE

¡VEN!

1. What do you think the poem is about? What is the tree inviting someone to do?

2. Write your own poem about your favorite park or your favorite holiday celebration. Play with the shape as shown in the poem above, and make your letters illustrate what you're describing.

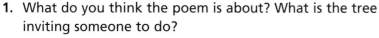

La República Dominicana

doscientos cinco **205**

Conexiones Culturales

¿Quién será?
Episodio 9

⤷ 1B, 3A

ESTRATEGIA

Predicting When you plan an event, many things can go wrong. Before you read the **Novela** or watch the video, write a list of things that need to be done before a party. Write them in a logical sequence, then think about one or two things on your list that could go wrong. Compare your list with things mentioned in this episode. Based on the photos, predict what you think might go wrong in this episode. Read the **Novela** or watch the video to see how close your prediction was.

En Puerto Rico

Océano Atlántico San Juan
★
PUERTO RICO
Mar Caribe

Nicolás hace los preparativos para la fiesta de cumpleaños de Mateo.
Quiere la ayuda de su hermana Irene.

1

Nicolás ¿Qué estás haciendo Irene?
Irene Estoy decorando la terraza.
Nicolás No, lo estás haciendo mal. Si quieres ayudar, anda a la cocina. Abre la lata de atún y prepara el dip. ¿De acuerdo?
Irene Bien, Nicolás.

2

Mamá Irene, hija, ¿ya sacaste la basura?
Irene No, mamá, todavía no.
Mamá Sácala por favor.
Irene Está bien, mamá.

3

Mamá Oye Irene, me parece que Picasso tiene hambre. ¿Quieres ponerle comida?
Irene Bien mamá.

4

Julia Bueno Nicolás, ¿cómo va? ¿Tú conoces a Mari?
Nicolás Claro que la conozco. ¿Qué tal, Mari? Permiso un momento. Voy a traer la comida.

5

Nicolás Bueno, por fin llegaste Mateo, el invitado de honor. Feliz cumpleaños. Este año pienso hacerte una fiesta muy buena.

Mateo Mejor que la del año pasado.

Nicolás ¿Qué pasó el año pasado?

6

Mateo Julia mandó las invitaciones a todos pero en la invitación no escribió en la casa de Nicolás. Escribió en la casa de Julia.

Nicolás Julia, Mateo y yo nos reunimos aquí, pero todos los invitados se reunieron en la casa de Julia.

7

Mamá Nicolás, ¿cómo va todo?

Nicolás Muy bien, mamá. Todos están en la sala. Están charlando. Acabo de poner la comida.

Mamá Muy bien. Tu hermana y yo vamos a la casa de los abuelos por un rato. Te llamo más tarde, ¿eh?

Nicolás Gracias mamá.

COMIDA DE GATO

8

Nicolás ¿Qué cosa? No puede ser. Y ya lo están comiendo.

A CONTESTA

1. What special occasion are the young people about to celebrate?
2. What does Nicolás want Irene to do?
3. What is the cat's name in the story?
4. What does Mamá ask Irene to do?
5. Where do Mamá and Irene go?

9

Mateo Nicolás, ¿Qué estás haciendo?

Nicolás Nada. ¿Por qué me lo preguntas?

10

Nicolás ¡¿Le puiste comida de gato al dip?!

Irene ¿Qué va? No, saqué una lata de atún del gabinete.

Nicolás Pensé que le pusiste comida de gato.

En España

La profesora considera los candidatos.

11

Profesora Nueve candidatos. Sólo falta uno y luego puedo tomar mi decisión final.

B CONTESTA

1. What did Irene put in the dip?

2. What is **La profesora** looking forward to?

Actividades

1 ¿Quién lo dijo?
Look at the story to help you remember who said each.

1. ¿Ya sacaste la basura?
2. Acabo de poner la comida.
3. ¡Ay! ¿Qué cosa? ¡No puede ser!
4. Estoy decorando la terraza.
5. Nicolás, ¿qué estás haciendo?

2 ¡Qué lío!
Mira la **Novela** para poner las oraciones en el orden correcto.

1. Julia y Mari llegaron a la fiesta.
2. Irene sacó la basura.
3. Nicolás pensó que los amigos comieron comida de gato.
4. Irene y Mamá salieron para la casa de los abuelos.

3 ¿Comprendes la Novela?
Check your understanding of the events in the story by answering these questions.

1. What went wrong at Mateo's party last year?
2. Why is Nicolás so upset? What does he think happened?
3. Who straightens out the misunderstanding? What does she tell Nicolás?
4. Why does Nicolás look uneasy when Mateo asks him what he is doing?
5. What did you predict would happen?
6. Are the two things that went wrong realistic? Has anything like this ever happened to you?

> **Próximo episodio**
> *The Professor is finally going to reveal what the ten candidates are for. Can you predict what will happen in the final episode?*
> PÁGINAS 252–255 ▶

Leamos y escribamos

TEKS Focus

3A Use resources in the language and cultures being studied to gain access to information

A Antes de leer ➤ 3A

 Use the strategy to determine the meaning of the title of this song and the words in boldface. What clues helped you to determine the meanings?

Las mañanitas

Estas son las mañanitas
que **cantaba** el Rey David;
a las muchachas bonitas
se las cantamos aquí.

Despierta mi bien despierta,
mira que ya **amaneció**.
Ya los pajaritos cantan,
la luna ya se metió[1].

Qué linda está la mañana
en que vengo a saludarte,
venimos todos con gusto
y placer[2] a **felicitarte**.

Canción de cumpleaños

Celebro tu cumpleaños
tan pronto veo **asomar** el sol
y en este día glorioso
pido tu dicha[3] al Señor,
porque lo he considerado[4]
como el regalo mejor.

Toma mi abrazo[5] que yo te doy,
y mucha felicidad.

1 already set **2** pleasure **3** happiness
4 I have regarded it **5** hug

B Comprensión ↓1B

Contesta las siguientes preguntas con oraciones completas.

1. ¿Qué se celebra con estas dos canciones?
2. ¿Qué hace en este momento la persona a quién se le dedican *Las mañanitas?*
3. ¿Cómo se describe el día de la celebración en las dos canciones?
4. ¿Por qué vienen las personas a cantar la serenata?
5. En la segunda canción, ¿qué se considera el "regalo mejor"?

C Después de leer ↓2A, 4B

Can you think of other occasions that might be celebrated with a serenade? How do the songs compare to others you have heard to celebrate birthdays?

Taller del escritor

Mensaje Instantáneo

Archivo Editar Ver Herramientas Ayuda

Agregar nombre   Advertir   Bloquear   Imprimir

A:

¿Cómo va la fiesta?

Enviar

ESTRATEGIA

para escribir Descriptions with interesting details can improve your writing. After choosing a topic, brainstorm adjectives and adverbs that will liven up the description or narrative.

¡Juy, qué desastre! ↓1A, 1C

Last year you and your brothers planned a surprise party for your parents' anniversary. It went so well that you decided to do it again, but things aren't going as well this year. No one made the punch, so the guests are thirsty, and the dog is eating from people's plates. Your older brother couldn't come, but he's sent you an instant message asking for a report. Write back, comparing this party to last year's.

1 Antes de escribir

What were the highlights of last year's party? Which disasters from this year's party will you mention? Brainstorm and organize some descriptive details about each party using a cluster diagram.

2 Escribir y revisar

Use your cluster diagram to compare and contrast this year's party with last year's. Use details from the diagram to organize the comparison. You may want to ask your brother for advice. Read your draft twice, comparing it with your diagrams. Check spelling, punctuation, and verb usage. Have you used past-tense verbs to describe last year's party and the present progressive to talk about what's going on now? Then exchange papers with a classmate for a peer edit.

3 Publicar

Read the description of the party to the class. Have the other students give you advice about how to save the party.

Online
Cuaderno para hispanohablantes, pp. 69–76

Leamos y escribamos

Repaso capítulo 1

1 Mira las fotos y decide qué día festivo representa cada foto. Luego di cómo se celebra el día y qué planes tienes. ↓**1B**

1.   2.   3.

4.   5.   6.

2 Completa las oraciones con el verbo correcto en el pretérito. ↓**1B**

—Hola, Vero. ¿Cómo estás? ¿Qué hiciste ayer?

—Bueno, como sabes, ayer fue el Día de la Madre. Por la mañana, yo ___1___ (preparar/colgar) el desayuno para mi mamá. José y Beto ___2___ (empezar/limpiar) y ___3___ (decorar/comer) la sala. Por la tarde, nosotros ___4___ (volver/ir) al parque para tener un picnic. Y tú, ¿cómo ___5___ (pasar/mandar) el día?

—Yo ___6___ (ir/invitar) a la iglesia con mi familia. Cuando (nosotros) ___7___ (volver/merendar) a casa, mi mamá ___8___ (pensar/abrir) sus regalos.

3 Completa las oraciones con las palabras apropiadas. ↓**1B**

1. Hoy es la ═══ de Pablo y Carla. Es en la iglesia San Juan.
2. Hay más de cien ═══ porque ═══ muchas invitaciones.
3. Después de la ceremonia hay una ═══.
4. Vamos a comer pastel y beber mucho ═══.
5. En un año, ellos van a festejar su primer ═══.
6. Ellos nos van a enseñar ═══ de la ceremonia.

4 Completa la siguiente conversación. ↓1B

—¿Conoces __1__ Juan Antonio Machado?

—No, no lo __2__ . ¿Quién es?

—Es mi primo. Muchas veces él __3__ ayuda con mi tarea de historia. __4__ puede ayudar a ti también si quieres.

—Buena idea, gracias.

—¿Qué __5__ estudiando ustedes ahora en historia?

—__6__ (Estar) estudiando la Guerra Civil.

—No te preocupes. Juan __7__ va a ayudar (a nosotros).

5 Answer the following questions. ↓2A, 2B

1. Name some celebrations in the Spanish-speaking world.
2. What are **pasteles en hoja**? When are they eaten?
3. What is a **quinceañera**? Is there a similar event in the United States?
4. How is **el Día del Árbol** celebrated in Venezuela?

6 Escucha mientras *(while)* Rita habla de una fiesta. Luego contesta las preguntas. ↓1B, 1C

7 Mira los dibujos. Escribe por lo menos seis oraciones describiendo lo que le pasa a Paco. ↓1B, 1C

4 **Gramática 2**
• direct object pronouns
• **conocer** and personal **a**
• present progressive
pp. 198–203

5 **Cultura**
• **Comparaciones**
pp. 190–191
• **Notas culturales**
pp. 183, 188, 194, 199
• **Conexiones culturales**
pp. 204–205

TEKS Focus
1C Present information using familiar words, phrases, and sentences

Gramática 1

- preterite of **-ar, -er,** and **-ir** verbs
  pp. 184–187
- **pensar que** and **pensar** with infinitives
  pp. 188–189

Repaso de gramática 1

invitar		comer		salir	
invit**é**	invit**amos**	com**í**	com**imos**	sal**í**	sal**imos**
invit**aste**	invit**ásteis**	com**iste**	com**ísteis**	sal**iste**	sal**ísteis**
invit**ó**	invit**aron**	com**ió**	com**ieron**	sal**ió**	sal**ieron**

The verb **ver** has regular **-er** endings but without written accents.

The verb pensar followed by **que** means *to think*. When it's followed by an **infinitive,** it means *to plan* or *to intend.*

Pienso que debes comprar un regalo.
Pienso comprar un regalo.

Gramática 2

- direct object pronouns
  pp. 198–199
- **conocer** and personal **a**
  pp. 200–201
- present progressive
  pp. 202–203

Repaso de gramática 2

me	me	nos	us
te	you (familiar)	**os**	you (familiar)
lo	him, you (formal)	**los**	them, you (formal)
la	her, you (formal)	**las**	them, you (formal)

When the direct object of a verb like conocer *(to meet, to know, to be familiar with)* is a person, use the personal **a**.

No **conozco a** Juan.

The present progressive tense is formed by using a form of the verb **estar** and a **present participle** ending in either **-ando** for **-ar** verbs or **-iendo** for **-er** and **-ir** verbs.

Estamos celebrando el cumpleaños de mi hermano.

Raquel **está escribiendo** una carta.

Letra y sonido   a e i o u

Vocales fuertes (a, e, o) y débiles (i, u)

- When **a, e,** or **o** are together, or when **i** or **u** is next to another vowel and has an accent, they are considered separate syllables:
  Raf**ae**l, d**ía**, t**ea**tro, tr**ae**r, p**aí**s, vid**eo**, t**ío**, m**aíz**
- When an unaccented **i** or **u** is next to a vowel, they form one syllable. When they come before the other vowel, the **i** sounds like the English *y* in *yes* and the **u** sounds like the English *w* in *well*:
  p**ia**no, sal**ió**, c**ui**dad, n**ue**vo, b**ai**lar, **au**to, s**ei**s

Trabalenguas

Cómo quieres que te quiera
Si el que quiero que me quiera
No me quiere como quiero que me quiera.

Dictado ◆1B

Escribe las oraciones de la grabación.

Repaso de Vocabulario 1

To talk about plans

el Año Nuevo	New Year's Day
como siempre	as always
celebrar	to celebrate
decorar la casa	to decorate the house
el Día de Acción de Gracias	Thanksgiving Day
el Día de los Enamorados	Valentine's Day
el Día de la Independencia	Independence Day
el Día de la Madre	Mother's Day
el Día del Padre	Father's Day
hacer una fiesta	to have a party
Hanukah	Hanukkah
invitar	to invite
la Navidad	Christmas
la Nochebuena	Christmas Eve
la Nochevieja	New Year's Eve
Pensamos...	We plan to . . .
¿Qué planes tienen para...?	What plans do you have for . . .?

la Semana Santa	Holy Week
tener un picnic	to have a picnic

To talk about past holidays

abrir regalos	to open gifts
el año pasado	last year
los días festivos	holidays
Estuvo a todo dar.	It was great.
festejar	to celebrate
La pasamos en casa de...	We spent it at . . .'s house.
mandar tarjetas	to send cards
la misa	mass
pasar	to spend
¿Qué tal estuvo?	How was it?
recibir regalos	to receive gifts
reunirse con (toda) la familia	to get together with the (whole) family
la sinagoga	synagogue
el templo	temple
ver fuegos artificiales	to see fireworks

Repaso de Vocabulario 2

To ask about preparing for a party

ahora	now
el aniversario	anniversary
anoche	last night
la boda	wedding
charlar	to talk, chat
colgar (ue)	to hang (up)
contar (ue) chistes	to tell jokes
el cumpleaños	birthday
las decoraciones	decorations
el día de tu santo	your saint's day
los dulces	candy, sweets
las empanadas	turnover-like pastries
enseñar fotos	to show photos
los entremeses	appetizers
la fiesta sorpresa	surprise party
¿Está todo listo para la fiesta?	Is everything ready for the party?
las galletas	cookies
la graduación	graduation
las invitaciones	invitations
los invitados	guests
los jóvenes	young people
mandar	to send

las papitas	potato chips
los pasteles en hoja	Dominican tamales
la piñata	piñata
el ponche	punch
los preparativos	preparations
¿Qué están haciendo?	What are they doing?
la quinceañera	girl's fifteenth birthday
los tamales	tamales
terminar	to finish
ya	already

To greet, introduce others, and say goodbye

Chao, te llamo más tarde.	Bye, I'll call you later.
conocer	to know, to meet, to be familiar with
Cuídate.	Take care.
Lo de siempre.	Same as usual.
¡Feliz aniversario!	Happy anniversary!
¡Qué gusto verte!	It's great to see you!
¿Qué hay de nuevo?	What's new?
Tanto gusto.	So nice to meet you.
¡Tanto tiempo sin verte!	Long time, no see!
Te presento a...	I'd like you to meet . . .
Vale. Que te vaya bien.	Okay. Hope things go well for you.

Integración
capítulos 1-9

 1 Escucha las descripciones y escoge la foto correspondiente. **1B**

A	B	C	D

2 Lee el anuncio y luego contesta las preguntas con **a) cierta** o **b) falsa**. ⬇**1B, 3A**

¿VAS A FESTEJAR? ¡Servicio en 24 horas!

"Llámanos para organizar tus bodas, quinceañeras y cumpleaños."

Bizcochos

Tostones

Arroz con pollo

Dulces de leche

Especializados en comida dominicana

¡Siempre a tiempo!
Piensa en Fiesta Lala para tus celebraciones. Más de 25 años de experiencia. –Sra. Lala Quiñones

Fiesta Lala
Avenida Cruz 300
teléfono: (632) 290-0623
servicio todos los días

1. La especialidad de Fiesta Lala es comida mexicana.
2. Fiesta Lala puede ayudar con tus celebraciones de lunes a domingo.
3. La señora Quiñones tiene poca experiencia.
4. Fiesta Lala puede servirte en un día.
5. Fiesta Lala sólo ayuda con las fiestas de cumpleaños.

3 Imagine you're at the party in this painting. First, write a story about two of the people you see. Include sentences and descriptions that tell

- the names of the people
- which holiday they're celebrating
- what they're doing now
- what each did earlier to prepare for the party

Then, with a partner role-play a conversation two people in the painting might have. ⬇1A, 1C

TEKS Focus

1C Present information using familiar words, phrases, and sentences

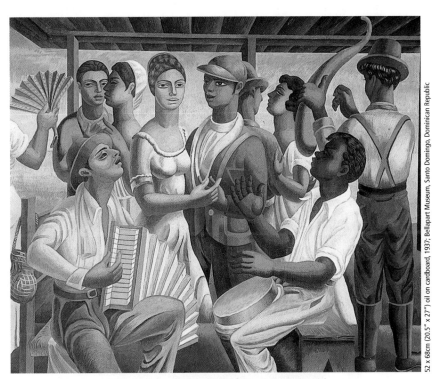

52 x 68cm (20.5" x 27") oil on cardboard, 1937; Bellapart Museum, Santo Domingo, Dominican Republic

Merengue por Jaime Colson (1901–1975)

4

Situación

You have just arrived at a birthday party for a Spanish-speaking friend. You have lots of questions about the party. Take turns with a partner playing the roles of the guest and the friend celebrating his or her birthday. ⬇1A

▶ Say "Happy Birthday" to your friend.

▶ Ask who did the decorating.

▶ Find out who prepared the food.

▶ Ask if there is a **piñata**.

▶ Find out what everyone is going to do at this party.

Integración

217

Video/DVD
GeoVisión

Geocultura
Perú

▲ **El río Amazonas** The Amazon River begins as a small mountain stream in the Andes of southern **Perú**. It then flows across the Peruvian rain forest and Brazil into the Atlantic Ocean.

Cerro Viejo (3934 m)

Chiclayo ●
Cajamar●

▼ **Lima** The capital lies on the coast in one of the driest regions of **Perú**. Here you can see Miraflores, the commercial district of Lima.

Almanaque

Población
27.949.639

Capital
Lima

Gobierno
república constitucional

Idiomas
español, quechua, aymara

Moneda
nuevo sol

Código Internet
www.[ ].pe

▼ **Jóvenes peruanos** These dancers are from the northern coast of **Perú**.

¿Sabías que...?
Texas is only one-third the size of **Perú** in area, but the population density of Texas is twice that of **Perú**.

COLOMBIA

ECUADOR

Río Tigre

Río Napo

Río Amazonas

Iquitos

Río Marañón

◄ Los Andes The Andes Mountains make up a large part of **Perú**. Some of the highest peaks are more than 6,000 meters high.

Cordillera Oriental

Río Ucayali

BRASIL

Pucallpa

► Pisac In the Andean town of Pisac, life is very different than in Lima. This outdoor market reflects Incan traditions carried on by the Quechua people.

Trujillo

Los Andes

PERÚ

Nevado Huascarán (6768 m)

Cordillera Occidental

Río Urubamba

Parque Nacional del Manu

LIMA

Huancayo

Cordillera Oriental

Machu Picchu

Pisac

Cuzco

Nevado Coropuna (6613 m)

BOLIVIA

Líneas de Nazca

Cordillera Occidental

Nazca

▼ El Parque Nacional del Manu This park is in the rain forest of southeastern **Perú**. Manu is the most wildlife-dense rain forest in the world. Much of its wildlife is endangered, including predators like this jaguar.

Puno

Lago Titicaca

Altiplano Andino

OCÉANO PACÍFICO

Arequipa

Volcán Misti (5822 m)

CHILE

◄ El lago Titicaca At an altitude of 3,810 meters, Lake Titicaca is the highest lake in the world that can support shipping. Boats called **balsas de totora** are made of reeds that grow on the lakeshore.

¿Qué tanto sabes?

What are the three major languages of **Perú**? ↓ **3A, 3B**

doscientos diecinueve **219**

A conocer Perú

La arquitectura

▲ **Cuzco** The Spanish-built **Iglesia de Santo Domingo** sits on a massive Incan stone foundation. In the city of Cuzco, Spanish and Incan architecture are often found in the same building.

▲ **Machu Picchu** Located on a mountaintop near Cuzco, this city was abandoned by the Incas about 500 years ago. It was rediscovered in 1911 and is one of the most important archaeological sites in **Perú**.

El arte

▲ **Los tejidos** Quechua people in the Andes region are famous for weaving and knitting colorful, intricate fabrics that are used for clothing. The finest material is made from alpaca wool.

▼ **Las famosas líneas de Nazca** The famous Nazca Lines are found in the desert near the southern coast of **Perú**. The lines form giant birds, people, and geometric designs that can only be seen clearly from the air.

Las celebraciones

Visit Holt Online
go.hrw.com
KEYWORD: EXP1B CH10
Photo Tour

▶ **El Concurso Nacional de Marinera** A dance contest and festival is held every January in the coastal city of Trujillo. The festival celebrates **la marinera,** the national dance of **Perú.**

♥ **2B**
¿Sabías que...?
The walls of Incan buildings are made of heavy stones fitted together without mortar. The stones are so well cut that you cannot even fit a credit card into the seams. Why do you think many of these walls are still standing today?

▶ **El Concurso Nacional del Caballo Peruano de Paso** This horse show and competition centers on the Peruvian Paso, known as one of the finest horse breeds in the world.

La comida

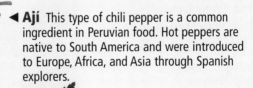

◀ **Ají** This type of chili pepper is a common ingredient in Peruvian food. Hot peppers are native to South America and were introduced to Europe, Africa, and Asia through Spanish explorers.

◀ **El ceviche** Ceviche is made of raw fish cured with lemon juice, onion, and **ají. Cevicherías,** restaurants that serve ceviche, are popular in **Perú.**

10

¡A viajar!

Objetivos

In Part 1 you will learn to:
- ask for and give information
- remind and reassure someone
- speak about the past in the preterite (review)
- form the preterite of verbs ending in **-car, -gar,** and **-zar**
- use **hacer** in the preterite

In Part 2 you will learn to:
- talk about a trip
- express hopes and wishes
- use the informal commands of verbs with spelling changes and irregular forms
- correctly place direct object pronouns (review)
- use verbs followed by infinitives (review)

¿Qué ves en la foto?

- **¿Qué tiempo hace en la foto?**

- **¿Qué hacen los muchachos?**

- **¿Adónde van ahora?**

TEKS Look for the ⬟ next to each activity to learn how it can help you achieve the goals of the **Texas Essential Knowledge and Skills,** found on page xxi.

Ruinas incaicas, Cuzco

Vocabulario *en acción* 1

Video/DVD

ExpresaVisión

En el aeropuerto

la agente

el mostrador

facturar el equipaje

hacer cola

el pasajero

el control de seguridad

la puerta

la sala de espera

el avión

esperar

¿Dónde puedo **recoger las maletas?**

Allí, en **el reclamo de equipaje.**

Bienvenidos al Aeropuerto

el reclamo de equipaje

las maletas

ADUANA / CUSTOMS

la aduana

▶ **Vocabulario adicional** — Vacaciones, p. R15

Vocabulario 1

Voy a **abordar el avión** ahora. Tengo todo. No quiero **perder** nada.

la bolsa

la billetera

el boleto de avión

la tarjeta de embarque

el carnet de identidad

el pasaporte

Más vocabulario...

abordar (un avión)	to board (a plane)
comenzar (ie) un viaje	to begin a trip
encontrarse (ue) con (alguien)	to meet up with (someone)
esperar	to wait
hacer un viaje	to take a trip
irse	to leave
perder (ie) el vuelo	to miss the flight
sentarse (ie)	to sit down
los servicios	restrooms

Texas **También se puede decir...**

Some Latin American speakers say **la valija** instead of **la maleta.**

In Latin America you will hear **chequear el equipaje** instead of **facturar el equipaje.** In Texas, you may hear **checar el equipaje.**

El boleto is sometimes called **el billete, el ticket, la boleta, el tiquete,** or **el pasaje.**

¡Exprésate!

Interactive TUTOR

To ask for information	To give information
¿Me puede decir dónde está la oficina de cambio? *Can you tell me where the money exchange is?*	**Está a la vuelta.** *It's around the corner.*
¿Sabe usted a qué hora sale/llega el vuelo 954? *Do you know at what time Flight 954 leaves/arrives?*	**Lo puede ver allí en esa pantalla.** *You can see it there on that monitor.* **Sí, sale/llega a las cuatro en punto.** *Yes, it leaves/arrives at four on the dot.*
¿Dónde se puede conseguir un mapa? *Where can I get a map?*	**Lo siento, no sé.** *I'm sorry, I don't know.*

Online
Vocabulario y gramática, pp. 65–67

▶ **Vocabulario adicional** — Vacaciones, p. R15

1 ¿Dónde están? 1B

Escuchemos Mira las fotos y escucha las conversaciones. Decide qué foto corresponde a cada conversación.

a.

b.

c.

d.

Nota cultural

The Uros Islands on Lake Titicaca are man-made and constructed of *totora*, a reed-like grass that grows on the lake's bed. Though walking on the surface is like walking on a water bed, there are reed houses, schools, churches, and even a post office. The Uros people also make reed boats to travel to the mainland. What do you think life is like on these islands? ⬇2A, 2B

TEKS Focus

2A Demonstrate understanding of practices (what people do) and how they relate to perspectives (how people perceive things) of the cultures studied

2 Definiciones 1B

Leamos/Escribamos Completa las oraciones.

reclamo	embarque	seguridad	vuelo	salida
cola	cambio	avión	aeropuerto	billetera

1. Un ═══ es donde llegan y salen los aviones.
2. Una ═══ es una línea de personas que esperan.
3. Necesitas una tarjeta de ═══ para abordar un ═══.
4. En la pantalla está el número del ═══ y la hora de la ═══.
5. El agente abre el equipaje en el control de ═══.
6. Puedes conseguir soles peruanos en la oficina de ═══.
7. Puedes recoger tus maletas en el ═══ de equipaje.
8. Una ═══ es algo pequeño donde puedes poner tu dinero.

3 Conversaciones 1B

Leamos/Escribamos Completa las conversaciones con base en las fotos de la Actividad 1.

1. —¿Sabe usted dónde están ═══?
   —Sí, cómo no. Están ═══.
2. —¿Me puede decir a qué hora llega ═══ 179?
   —Lo siento, ═══. Pero lo puede ver allí en esa ═══.
3. —¿Dóndé puedo ═══ el equipaje?
   —Tiene que ir a ese ═══ y hacer ═══.
4. —¿Sabe usted dónde ═══ la aduana?
   —Lo ═══, no sé.

4 **¿Sabes viajar?** ↓1B

Leamos Complete these travel sentences by matching words in the first column with an appropriate ending in the second column.

1. Para abordar un avión...
2. En la pantalla...
3. Necesitas un boleto...
4. Los pasajeros...
5. Se puede recoger las maletas...

a. se puede ver las salidas y llegadas.
b. hacen cola en el mostrador para hablar con el agente.
c. en el reclamo de equipaje.
d. necesitas una tarjeta de embarque.
e. para hacer un viaje en avión.

 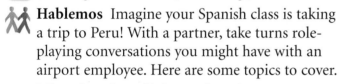 **Comunicación**

5 **Un viaje de curso** *(class trip)* ↓1A

 Hablemos Imagine your Spanish class is taking a trip to Peru! With a partner, take turns role-playing conversations you might have with an airport employee. Here are some topics to cover.

- What time does flight 316 leave?
- Where do I check my bags?
- Where can I get a boarding pass?
- Where are the restrooms?
- Where can I get a map?
- Where can I pick up my bags?
- Where is the money exchange?

6 **Consejos del profesor** ↓1A

Escribamos/Hablemos Your teacher is telling you what you need to do to get ready for the class trip. Work in groups of three to complete the instructions by turning the cues below into informal commands. Then take turns telling each other what to do.

MODELO **cambiar/dinero**   **Cambia el dinero en el aeropuerto.**

1. comprar/un pasaporte y un boleto
2. traer/el carnet de identidad
3. hacer cola/el mostrador
4. facturar/el equipaje con el agente
5. esperar/la sala de espera
6. abordar /con la tarjeta de embarque
7. no perder/el vuelo

TEKS Focus

1A Engage in oral and written exchanges of learned material to socialize and to provide and obtain information

 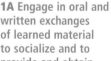

¡Exprésate!

Interactive TUTOR

To remind and reassure	
¿Ya sacaste el dinero?	**Sí, ya lo saqué.**
Did you already get the money?	*Yes, I already got it.*
	No, todavía no. Debo pasar por el cajero automático.
	No, not yet. I need to go by the automatic teller machine.
¿Ya hiciste la maleta?	**No, todavía tengo que hacerla.**
Did you already pack your suitcase?	*No, I still have to pack it.*
¡Ay, dejé la cámara en casa!	**No te preocupes. Puedes comprar una cámara desechable en cualquier tienda.**
Oh, I left the camera at home!	*Don't worry. You can buy a disposable camera at any store.*

Online
Vocabulario y gramática,
pp. 65–67

Una familia de Sevilla, España

7 El viaje de Gabriela ↓1B

Leamos Gabriela has been visiting her grandparents in Lima, and is now saying goodbye to return to her school in the U.S. Complete their conversation using the best choice of words.

preocupes	hiciste	tengo	dejé
sale	sacaste	cajero	pasaporte

ABUELO   ¿Encontraste tu ___1___ ?

GABRIELA   Sí, abuelo, lo ___2___ en mi bolsa.

ABUELO   ¿Y ya ___3___ el dinero que necesitas?

GABRIELA   No, todavía no. Debo pasar por el ___4___ automático.

ABUELA   ¿___5___ bien las maletas?

GABRIELA   Sí, tengo todo mi equipaje.

ABUELA   ¿Tienes tu cámara?

GABRIELA   No te ___6___ , abuelita, no la ___7___ en casa. La tengo en mi maleta.

ABUELO   Bueno. El vuelo ___8___ a las dos. Tenemos que salir para el aeropuerto.

TEKS Focus

1C Present information using familiar words, phrases, and sentences

8 ¿Qué más? ↓1C

Escribamos On a separate piece of paper, make two columns. In the first column, write the things that Gabriela has already done. In the other, list the tasks she still has to do before the airplane takes off.

9 **Una lista** ✈1B

 Leamos/Escribamos Leticia has checked off the things she has already done to get ready for her trip to Peru. Read her list and write sentences that tell what she already did and what she still has to do.

Cosas por hacer:

sacar la tarjeta de embarque

√ encontrar el pasaporte

√ sacar dinero

√ comprar el boleto

facturar el equipaje

comprar revistas para el viaje

 Comunicación

10 **¿Ya lo hiciste?** ✈1A

 Hablemos With a partner play the roles of Leticia and her parent. The parent will ask Leticia if she has done the things on the list in Activity 9, and Leticia will answer.

> **MODELO** **Madre o Padre** —¿Ya sacaste el dinero?
> **Leticia** —Sí, pasé por el cajero automático ayer.

11 **¿Me puede decir...?** ✈1A

Hablemos With a partner, take turns playing the roles of an airport information clerk and Spanish-speaking passengers in the following situations. Remember to be polite!

> **MODELO** PASAJERA —¿Me puede decir dónde puedo comprar un mapa?
> TÚ —Sí, señora. Lo puede comprar en la tienda a la vuelta.

1. A man has arrived from Chile and asks where the money exchange is. Give him directions.

2. A woman is looking for flight 394 to Mexico City. Point out the monitor to her.

3. Another traveler left his glasses at home and needs help reading the monitor. Help him find the flight number, when it leaves, and the gate it leaves from.

4. A woman from Venezuela is looking for the baggage claim and customs. Tell her where she should get in line.

Objetivos

Review of the preterite; preterite of **-car, -gar, -zar** verbs; preterite of **hacer**

Gramática
en acción

Repaso The preterite

Interactive
TUTOR

1 Use the preterite to talk about what happened at a specific point in the past and to narrate a sequence of events in the past.

> **Me levanté** temprano, **comí** el desayuno y **fui** al aeropuerto.

2 You know how to form the preterite of all regular verbs. Remember that **-ar** and **-er** verbs do not have stem changes in the preterite.

	esperar	perder	abrir
yo	esper**é**	perd**í**	abr**í**
tú	esper**aste**	perd**iste**	abr**iste**
Ud., él, ella	esper**ó**	perd**ió**	abr**ió**
nosotros(as)	esper**amos**	perd**imos**	abr**imos**
vosotros(as)	esper**asteis**	perd**isteis**	abr**isteis**
Uds., ellos, ellas	esper**aron**	perd**ieron**	abr**ieron**

Esperamos una hora. *We waited an hour.*
Perdí mi boleto. *I lost my ticket.*

Online
| Vocabulario y gramática, pp. 68–70 | Actividades, pp. 63–66 |

¿Te acuerdas?

To say where someone *went,* use **ir** *(to go)* in the preterite.

fui	fuimos
fuiste	fuisteis
fue	fueron

12 **¡Qué viaje más difícil!** ⬇1B

Escuchemos Jesse acaba de regresar de un viaje difícil. Escucha lo que dice y completa las oraciones con la respuesta correcta.

1. A las 8:00, Jesse ══════.
   a. llegó al aeropuerto en taxi   **b.** salió de la casa
2. Jesse regresó a casa porque ══════.
   a. dejó el boleto allí   **b.** olvidó sus lentes
3. Al llegar al aeropuerto, Jesse ══════.
   a. compró un libro   **b.** se encontró con sus amigos
4. En el control de seguridad, los agentes ══════.
   a. facturaron el equipaje   **b.** abrieron las maletas
5. Juan regresó al mostrador porque ══════.
   a. recogió el equipaje   **b.** perdió la tarjeta de embarque
6. Al fin, Carlos y Jesse ══════.
   a. abordaron el avión   **b.** perdieron el vuelo

13 ¿Qué pasó? ↓1C

Escribamos/Hablemos Imagina que eres Daniela. Indica qué pasó el día en que ella y su familia fueron de viaje.

MODELO (yo) **Me levanté temprano.**

yo

1. nosotros

2. mi padre

3. mis padres

4. el agente

5. los agentes

6. yo

 Comunicación

14 Un buen viaje ↓1A

Hablemos In groups of three, act out the following situation. An exchange student calls his parents after he arrives in Lima, Peru. The parents ask questions about the trip and the student answers. Take turns playing the different roles, and use the verbs listed below.

MODELO —¿Esperaste mucho tiempo antes de abordar?
—No, no esperé mucho.

dejar	abordar	esperar	abrir
recoger	ir al mostrador	perder	encontrarse

TEKS Focus

1A Engage in oral and written exchanges of learned material to socialize and to provide and obtain information

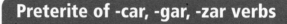

Preterite of -car, -gar, -zar verbs

Interactive TUTOR

1 Verbs ending in **-car**, **-gar**, and **-zar** have a spelling change in the **yo** form in the preterite.

In **-car** verbs, the **c** changes to **qu**.	In **-gar** verbs, the **g** changes to **gu**.	In **-zar** verbs, the **z** changes to **c**.
sa**qu**é	lle**gu**é	comen**c**é
sa**c**aste	lle**g**aste	comen**z**aste
sa**c**ó	lle**g**ó	comen**z**ó
sa**c**amos	lle**g**amos	comen**z**amos
sa**c**asteis	lle**g**asteis	comen**z**asteis
sa**c**aron	lle**g**aron	comen**z**aron

Comencé a las 8:00. **Llegué** al aeropuerto y **saqué** dinero.
I started at 8:00. I arrived at the airport and got money.

Online

| Vocabulario y gramática, pp. 68–70 | Actividades, pp. 63–66 |

---

15 Cuando viajo... ✈1B

 Escuchemos Indica si Carmen habla de **a**) lo que siempre hace cuando viaja o de **b**) lo que hizo *(did)* la última vez que viajó.

16 La tarjeta postal ✈1B

Leamos/Escribamos Completa la tarjeta postal que recibió Lili con la forma correcta del pretérito de los verbos.

encontrar	comenzar	buscar	llegar	almorzar
comprar	pagar	facturar	sacar	ir

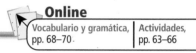

Hola Liliana,

Ya sabes que __1__ el día a las 7:00 y que __2__ al aeropuerto en taxi. Cuando __3__, fui directamente al mostrador donde __4__ el boleto y __5__ el equipaje. Después, __6__ un mapa en la librería y __7__ dinero del cajero automático. __8__ un sándwich y __9__ una tienda para comprarte un regalo, pero no __10__ nada. Voy a buscarte algo en Cuzco.

Con cariño,
Tía Juana

17 ¿Quién? ↴1C

Escribamos/Hablemos Escribe oraciones y di quién hizo las siguientes cosas.

MODELO llegar al aeropuerto
Olivia llegó al aeropuerto a las siete.

Olivia

TEKS Focus
1C Present information using familiar words, phrases, and sentences

| llegar al aeropuerto | levantarse | sacar dinero |
| pagar el boleto | buscar los servicios | almorzar en un restaurante |

1. Ana

2. Felipe

3. Maricela y yo

4. yo

5. Ricardo y Elena

6. yo

 Comunicación

18 La fiesta de despedida ↴1A

Hablemos Last night there was a going away party for a friend who is moving, but you couldn't go. Ask a classmate what happened at the party, using the verbs given below.

| colgar decoraciones | comenzar la fiesta | llegar | jugar juegos de mesa |
| tocar instrumentos | contar chistes | bailar | preparar la comida |

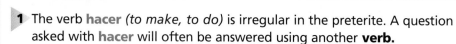

Preterite of hacer

1 The verb **hacer** *(to make, to do)* is irregular in the preterite. A question asked with **hacer** will often be answered using another **verb.**

yo **hice**	nosotros(as) **hicimos**
tú **hiciste**	vosotros(as) **hicisteis**
Ud., él, ella **hizo**	Uds., ellos, ellas **hicieron**

—¿Qué **hiciste** ayer?   *What did you do yesterday?*
—**Fui** a la oficina de correo.   *I went to the post office.*

2 In weather expressions, use **hizo** to specify how long conditions lasted or how many times a weather event occurred. Use **nevó** and **llovió** to say *it snowed* and *it rained.*

—¿Qué tiempo **hizo** ayer?   —**Hizo** mal tiempo. **Llovió** todo
                              el día.

El año pasado nunca **hizo** viento.

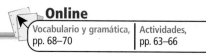

Online

Vocabulario y gramática, pp. 68–70	Actividades, pp. 63–66

Nota cultural

The Incas called *quinoa* the Mother Grain. Every year the emperor planted the first seeds and on solstice, priests made quinoa offerings to Inti, the Sun. The Incan armies, which frequently marched for days at a time, ate war balls, a mix of quinoa and fat. Quinoa is still eaten in Peru and is imported to the United States for its high nutritional value. How do you think quinoa is used in recipes?

↓2B

TEKS Focus

2B Demonstrate understanding of products (what people create) and how they relate to perspectives (how people perceive things) of the cultures studied

---

19 **Antes de comenzar el viaje** ↓1B

Leamos Lee lo que dice Pablo e indica si **a)** habla de sí mismo *(himself)*, **b)** de sus padres, **c)** de él y sus amigos o **d)** del tiempo.

1. Antes de comenzar el viaje hicimos una fiesta en el Club Naval.
2. Hice planes para encontrarme con ellos al volver.
3. No hicieron las maletas hasta muy tarde.
4. Hice las maletas anteayer.
5. Hizo fresco e hizo sol.
6. Al llegar al aeropuerto, hicieron cola delante del mostrador.

20 **¿Qué hicieron ustedes?** ↓1C

Escribamos Indica si estas cosas pasaron o no la última vez que viajaste con tu familia en carro.

MODELO mi madre/hacer las maletas
Mi madre (no) hizo las maletas.

1. (yo)/hacer la maleta
2. mi hermano/hacer las camas antes de irnos
3. mis amigos/hacer una fiesta antes del viaje
4. (yo)/hacer la tarea en el carro
5. mis padres/hacer sándwiches y nosotros/comer en el carro
6. hacer buen tiempo
7. hacer frío

Comunicación

21 De vacaciones ⬇1A

Hablemos With a partner, take turns asking and answering what the weather was like and what these people did last week.

MODELO —¿Qué tiempo hizo el lunes?
—Hizo calor y mucho sol.
—¿Qué hicieron Alicia y tú?
—Jugamos al tenis.

lunes/Alicia y yo

1. lunes/yo

2. martes/mis hermanas

3. miércoles/mi madre

4. jueves/mi padre

5. viernes/María y Jorge

6. sábado/mis amigos y yo

7. sábado/mi hermano

8. domingo/mis padres

22 El fin de semana pasado ⬇1A

Hablemos In groups of three, take turns using the expressions in the word box to ask about who did these activities last weekend.

MODELO —¿Hiciste un viaje el fin de semana pasado?
—Sí, hice un viaje./No, no hice un viaje.

hacer un viaje	hacer cola en una tienda
hacer planes para salir con amigos	hacer la tarea de español
hacer el almuerzo para llevar al colegio	hacer la cama

Cultura

VideoCultura

Comparaciones

Terminal de autobuses, Lima, Perú

¿Adónde fuiste y qué hiciste la última vez que viajaste? ↓1B, 4B

En Estados Unidos, la mayoría de la gente tiene carros, y es muy común viajar en coche. Si es un viaje de larga distancia, mucha gente viaja por avión. En Perú, es más común viajar en autobús, aunque *(although)* es posible ir por avión o por tren. Estas personas hablan de su último viaje y de lo que hicieron. ¿Cómo viajaron? ¿Qué hicieron al llegar a su destino *(destination)*? ¿Hacen las mismas cosas que tú haces cuando viajas? Compara sus viajes a tus propias experiencias.

Lisette
Lima, Perú

Lisette talks about the places she visits on vacation. Do you like to travel or stay at home during vacations?

Cuando vas de vacaciones, ¿en qué medio de transporte viajas?

Bueno, cuando voy de vacaciones, a mí me encanta viajar en ómnibus porque en el camino veo los paisajes y los animales.

¿Qué haces cuando vas de vacaciones?

Cuando voy de vacaciones, voy [y] visito a los lugares turísticos que me han recomendado.

¿Adónde fuiste de vacaciones la última vez?

Bueno, fui a Cajamarca.

¿Fuiste sola o fuiste con tu familia?

Fui con mi familia.

¿Qué hicieron allí?

Más que todo fuimos a visitar a los lugares turísticos y a algunos familiares.

Paola
Lima, Perú

Paola visits her relatives during her vacation. Do you visit friends or relatives when you have a vacation?

Cuando vas de vacaciones, ¿en qué medio de transporte viajas?
Voy en bus mirando los paisajes.

¿Qué haces cuando vas de vacaciones?
Cuando voy de vacaciones, visito a mi familia, a mis amigos y los lugares turísticos.

¿Adónde fuiste de vacaciones la última vez?

Fui al departamento de Ica.

¿Fuiste sola o fuiste con tu familia?
Fui con mi familia.

¿Qué hicieron allí?
Visitamos a mi abuelita, primas, amigos y algunos lugares turísticos.

Cultura

Para comprender 1B
1. ¿Cómo le gusta viajar a Lisette?
2. ¿Qué hizo Lisette en su último viaje?
3. ¿Con quién viajó Paola a Ica?
4. ¿Qué hicieron Paola y su familia en su último viaje?
5. ¿Qué hacen Lisette y Paula cuando viajan en bus?

Para pensar y hablar 4B
Both Lisette and Paola travel their country by bus. Do people in your community normally take the bus or other ground transportation when they travel somewhere? What other forms of transportation are common? What are two advantages of ground as opposed to air travel? What are two disadvantages?

Cuaderno para hispanohablantes, pp. 77–84

Comunidad
Spanish place names in Texas 5B

When you look at a map of Texas, you'll see that many mountains, rivers, and towns have Spanish names. For example, in Central Texas there is a river called **Pedernales** (**pedernal** means *flint*). In the western tip of the state is **El Paso,** so called because it was a place to ford the *big river*, or **Río Grande.** Other cities or towns with Spanish names include **San Antonio,** named after Saint Anthony, **Llano** (*plain*), and **Refugio** (*refuge*). Spanish names for rivers in Texas include the **Colorado** (*red*), and **Nueces** (*walnuts*). On a Texas map, find ten more places or geographical features with Spanish names. Look up these words in a dictionary to find out what they mean.

San Antonio CITY LIMITS

Zaragosa Intl Bridge AUTOS LEFT LANE

BEAUMONT 23 EL PASO 857

Interstate highway signs in Texas

Vocabulario *en acción* 2

ExpresaVisión

Video/DVD

De vacaciones

Durante las vacaciones paseamos en lancha en el lago.

¡Qué divertido!

acampar

pasear en canoa

esquiar en el agua

ir de excursión

ir de pesca

pasear en bote de vela en el lago

Lugares de interés

el museo

el centro

el zoológico

el parque de diversiones

▶ **Vocabulario adicional** — Vacaciones, p. R15

Medios de transporte

Vocabulario 2

Recorrí la ciudad en autobús. Luego tomé el tren a las ruinas.

el metro

Texas | **También se puede decir...**

Mexicans and Texans call *the bus* **el camión**. In Puerto Rico and the Dominican Republic, they say **la guagua**. You'll hear **el colectivo** in Bolivia, Peru, and Ecuador.

el tren

el taxi

Más vocabulario...

Expresiones

¡Ah, tuviste suerte!	*You were lucky!*
¡Qué bien!	*How great!*
¡Qué fantástico!	*How fantastic!*
¡Qué lástima!	*What a shame!*
¡Qué mala suerte!	*What bad luck!*

Actividades

quedarse en un hotel	*to stay at a hotel*
recorrer la ciudad/ el país/la isla	*to tour the city/ the country/ the island*
tomar el sol	*to sunbathe*

el autobús

el barco

¡Exprésate!

To talk about a trip

Interactive TUTOR

¿Qué tal el viaje? *How was the trip?*	**¡Fue estupendo!/¡Fue horrible!** *It was great!/It was horrible!*
¿Adónde fueron? *Where did you go?*	**Fuimos al campo y subimos a la montaña El Misti.** *We went to the countryside and went up Misti mountain.*
¿Qué hicieron? *What did you do?*	**Conocimos las ruinas y sacamos muchas fotos.** *We visited the ruins (for the first time) and took lots of pictures.*
	Luego pasamos por la oficina de correos y por fin regresamos al hotel. *Afterwards we stopped at the post office and finally we came back to the hotel.*

Online
Vocabulario y gramática, pp. 71–73

▶ **Vocabulario adicional** — Vacaciones, p. R15

TEKS Focus

4B Demonstrate understanding of the concept of culture through comparisons

---

23 ¿Qué dices? ↘1B

Escuchemos Escucha los comentarios y escoge la mejor respuesta.

1. **a.** ¡Qué lástima!   **b.** ¡Qué bien!
2. **a.** ¡Qué mala suerte!   **b.** ¡Ah, tuviste suerte!
3. **a.** ¡Qué lástima!   **b.** ¡Qué divertido!
4. **a.** ¡Qué bien!   **b.** ¡Qué lástima!
5. **a.** ¡Qué horrible!   **b.** ¡Qué fantástico!
6. **a.** ¡Qué mala suerte!   **b.** ¡Ah, tuviste suerte!

24 En la isla ↘1B

Leamos Para las siguientes oraciones, escoge la persona del dibujo que hizo cada actividad.

1. Tomó el sol en la playa.
2. Sacó una foto de su amigo.
3. Acampó en la playa. ¡Qué bien!
4. Recorrió la isla con su mochila.
5. Subió a la montaña. ¡Qué divertido!
6. Paseó en bote de vela en el agua.
7. Paseó en canoa. ¡Qué fantástico!

25 **El viaje de Carlos** ↓1B

Leamos/Escribamos Lee la tarjeta de Carlos. Después combina los elementos. Usa las expresiones **primero, luego** y **por fin**.

> Querida Carla,
>
> Aquí estoy en Perú. Es un país estupendo. Ayer me levanté temprano y desayuné en el hotel. Salí del hotel y fui al centro en autobús. Fui a una tienda para comprar una cámara y después recorrí el centro. Luego, almorcé en un restaurante. Después del almuerzo, tomé otro autobús y fui a las ruinas. Subí a la montaña y saqué muchas fotos. Regresé al hotel, cené en el restaurante de al lado y me acosté temprano. ¡Qué día magnífico!
>
> Abrazos,
> Carlos

MODELO desayunar/salir/levantarse
Primero, se levantó, luego desayunó y por fin salió.

1. ir al centro/comprar una cámara/ir a una tienda
2. recorrer el centro/almorzar/llegar al centro
3. sacar fotos/tomar el autobús a las ruinas/subir a la montaña
4. tomar el autobús al hotel/regresar a la ciudad/salir de las ruinas
5. acostarse/cenar en un restaurante/ponerse el piyama

TEKS Focus

1B Demonstrate understanding of simple, clearly spoken, and written language when dealing with familiar topics

 Comunicación

26 **Un viaje fantástico** ↓1A

Hablemos Talk with a partner about a real vacation you have taken or make up details of an imaginary vacation. First tell where you went and how you got there (plane, train, bus, or boat). Then your partner will ask questions to find out how the trip was, and what you saw and did there.

MODELO —**Fui a Puerto Rico en barco.**
　　　　　—**¿Qué tal el viaje? ¿Qué hiciste?**
　　　　　—**El viaje fue bueno. Me gustó viajar por barco y...**

¡Exprésate!

To express hopes and wishes

Algún día me gustaría hacer un viaje a Perú.	**Quiero conocer las ruinas de Machu Picchu.**
Some day I would like to take a trip to Peru.	*I want to see the ruins at Machu Picchu.*
Si tengo suerte, voy a visitar México.	**Espero ver las pirámides.**
If I'm lucky, I'm going to visit Mexico.	*I hope to see the pyramids.*

Online
Vocabulario y gramática, pp. 71–73

Interactive TUTOR

27 Me gustaría viajar ♥1B

Leamos Paco y Ana están hablando de los viajes que quieren hacer. Completa su conversación con las palabras del cuadro.

sacar	suerte	recorrer	ir
hacer	Quiero	museo	Algún
ruinas	~~conocer~~	Qué	espero

PACO ___1___ día me gustaría ___2___ un viaje a Perú. Quiero ___3___ las montañas e ___4___ de excursión. Espero ver las ___5___ de Machu Picchu. Voy a ___6___ muchas fotos.

ANA Si tengo ___7___ voy a viajar a España. ___8___ ver el famoso ___9___ de arte en Madrid, El Prado. También ___10___ viajar por metro. Voy a ___11___ toda la ciudad en metro. ¡___12___ fantástico!

28 Espero... ♥1C

Escribamos/Hablemos Reacciona a estas actividades con una expresión de ¡Exprésate!

MODELO Me gustaría ir de excursión.
Espero ver...

1.

2.

3.

4.

Comunicación

29 El viaje de tus sueños ⬇1A

Hablemos Interview a classmate about his or her dream vacation. Ask where your partner wants to go, and what he or she wants/hopes to do and see there. Then switch roles and tell your partner about your own dream vacation.

TEKS Focus

1A Engage in oral and written exchanges of learned material to socialize and to provide and obtain information

30 Hacer planes ⬇1A, 1C

Hablemos/Escribamos Work with two or three classmates to plan a school trip. Decide where you would like to go and how you want to travel. Talk about what you want to see and do there. On a sheet of paper, summarize the main points of your trip and be prepared to present them to the class.

MODELO **Algún día, nos gustaría hacer un viaje a...**
Queremos conocer...
Si tenemos suerte, vamos a...
Esperamos ver...

Objetivos
Using informal commands, direct object pronouns, verbs followed by infinitives

GramaVisión

TUTOR

Informal commands of spelling-change and irregular verbs

1 Verbs ending in **-ger, -guir, -car, -gar,** and **-zar** have spelling changes in some command forms

	affirmative	negative
-ger	reco**g**e	*g changes to j* no reco**j**as
-guir	si**gu**e	*gu changes to g* no si**g**as
-car	bus**c**a	*c changes to qu* no bus**qu**es
-gar	lle**g**a	*g changes to gu* no lle**gu**es
-zar	empie**z**a	*z changes to c* no empie**c**es

Llega temprano al aeropuerto y **busca** a tus amigos. **No llegues** tarde.
Get to the airport early and look for your friends. Don't get there late.

¿Te acuerdas?

Do you remember how to form affirmative informal commands?

tú piensas ⟶ piensa
tú comes ⟶ come
tú escribes ⟶ escribe

Here's how to form negative informal commands.

yo pienso ⟶ no piens**es**
yo como ⟶ no com**as**
yo escribo ⟶ no escrib**as**
yo vengo ⟶ no veng**as**

2 Some verbs have irregular informal command forms.

	affirmative	negative
hacer	haz	no hagas
ir	ve	no vayas
poner	pon	no pongas
salir	sal	no salgas
ser	sé	no seas
tener	ten	no tengas
venir	ven	no vengas

Ve al aeropuerto en taxi.
Go to the airport by taxi.

No dejes nada en el taxi.
Don't leave anything in the taxi.

Online
| Vocabulario y gramática, pp. 74–76 | Actividades, pp. 67–70 |

31 **¿Es lógico?** ✈1B

 Escuchemos Decide si los consejos que Enrique les da a sus amigos son lógicos o ilógicos.

32 **Consejos para los compañeros de viajes** ✈1B

 Escribamos/Hablemos You are on vacation with some friends who don't know what to do when they travel. Read what they say and make up one affirmative command and one negative command for each comment.

MODELO —Estoy cansado. No tengo ganas de hacer nada.
—Quédate en el hotel. No recorras la ciudad hoy.

ir al zoológico	ir de excursión	visitar el museo
esquiar en el lago	quedarse en el hotel	ver las ruinas
ir al parque de diversiones	quedarse con unos amigos	recorrer la ciudad

1. No me gusta el arte. Prefiero divertirme al aire libre.
2. Tengo ganas de hacer ejercicio y ver la naturaleza *(nature)*.
3. Hace calor y quiero tomar el sol.
4. Tengo miedo de los animales y no quiero pasar el rato al aire libre.
5. No me gusta ir de compras, pero sí me encanta la arqueología.
6. No tengo mucho dinero y los hoteles del centro son caros.

Las ruinas de Machu Picchu, Perú

  # Comunicación

33 **¡Ayúdame, por favor!** ✈1A

 Hablemos Based on the photos, act out the following situation. Your partner is going on vacation and doesn't know what to do. Answer his or her questions and give some appropriate advice.

MODELO ¿Cuándo hago la maleta?
Hazla un día antes de viajar. No lleves mucha ropa.

Repaso Direct object pronouns

1 Direct object pronouns can go before the conjugated verb or be attached to the end of an infinitive.

—¿Ya conoces **la ciudad**?   *Do you already know the city?*

—No, todavía no **la** conozco.   *No, I don't know it yet.*

—¿Quieres recorrer**la** conmigo?   *Do you want to tour it with me?*

2 In affirmative commands, attach the pronoun to the end of the verb. In negative commands, place the pronoun before the conjugated verb.

Lláma**me** después de tu viaje, pero no **me** llames muy tarde.
Call me after your trip, but don't call me very late.

Online

| Vocabulario y gramática, pp. 74–76 | Actividades, pp. 67–70 |

¿Te acuerdas?

Use these pronouns in the place of direct object nouns.

me	nos
te	os
lo	los
la	las

34 Para el viaje ◆1B

Escuchemos Héctor habla de lo que va a hacer mientras está de vacaciones con su familia. Escucha las oraciones y decide de qué o de quién habla: **a)** su padre, **b)** su tarjeta de embarque, **c)** sus hermanas, **d)** sus libros de texto.

35 ¡Vamos al centro! ◆1B

Leamos/Escribamos Completa las oraciones de la conversación entre dos amigos que están viajando juntos.

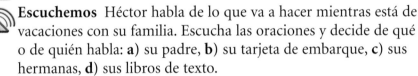

| me | te | lo | la | los | las |

—Mañana voy a visitar la ciudad. Voy a recorrer __1__ en autobús. Tengo ganas de visitar los museos del centro. ¿Quieres visitar __2__ conmigo?

—Sí, pero necesito dinero para la visita.

—Sáca __3__ del cajero automático aquí en el hotel.

—También tengo que mandar estas tarjetas. Puedo mandar __4__ mañana en el correo del centro, ¿no?

—Pues, ¿por qué no __5__ mandas desde el hotel? Oye, ¿tienes hambre? Me gustaría invitar __6__ a cenar conmigo.

—¡Con mucho gusto! ¿Quieres comer en el restaurante del hotel? No __7__ conozco.

—Es bueno, pero me gustaría probar la cocina regional. ¿Qué tal si __8__ probamos en el restaurante al lado?

TEKS Focus

1B Demonstrate understanding of simple, clearly spoken, and written language when dealing with familiar topics

36 **¿Conoces tu ciudad?** 🔻1B

Hablemos Construye oraciones y di si conoces estos lugares.

MODELO **el centro**
Lo conozco (muy) bien.

1. el zoológico
2. los museos
3. el centro comercial más cerca de tu casa
4. la piscina más cerca de tu colegio
5. el lago más cerca de tu ciudad
6. las tiendas del centro

37 **Manito, llévame contigo** 🔻1B

Hablemos Tu hermanito te hace muchas preguntas. Contesta las preguntas usando pronombres de complemento directo.

MODELO **¿Piensas visitar las ruinas de Machu Picchu? (sí)**
Sí, las voy a visitar. (Sí, voy a visitarlas.)

1. ¿Vas a visitar el Parque Nacional Manu? (sí)
2. ¿Me vas a llamar todos los días? (no)
3. ¿Vas a ver a los abuelos? (sí)
4. ¿Te puedo ayudar con las maletas? (sí)
5. ¿Vas a llevar tu cámara desechable? (sí)
6. Me vas a llevar contigo, ¿verdad? (no)

Nota cultural

Peru's Manu rainforest has more than 1,000 species of birds and 300 species of trees. Many indigenous tribes also live there. Today Manu is a Biosphere Reserve composed of three parts: the Manu National Park, protecting the natural flora and fauna; the Manu Reserve Zone, for research and tourism; and the Manu Cultural Zone, for human settlement. Research animal or plant life in the forest. 🔻2A

   Comunicación

38 **Las vacaciones de Araceli** 🔻1A

Hablemos Ask a partner about the vacation that Araceli is going to take. Your partner should answer using direct object pronouns.

MODELO **—¿Cuándo va a hacer la maleta?**
—Ya la hizo anoche.

Interactive TUTOR

Repaso Verbs followed by infinitives

1 You can use certain **verbs** followed by **infinitives** to express what someone *wants, hopes,* or *plans* to do.

me (te, le...) gustaría + **infinitive**	*. . . would like to . . .*
me (te, le...) gustaría más + **infinitive**	*. . . would prefer to . . .*
querer (ie) + **infinitive**	*to want to . . .*
esperar + **infinitive**	*to hope to . . .*
pensar (ie) + **infinitive**	*to plan (intend) to . . .*

Me gustaría ir al lago.	*I'd like to go to the lake.*
Quiero pasear en bote.	*I want to go boating.*
Espero salir con amigos.	*I hope to go out with friends.*
Pienso hacer un viaje este año.	*I plan to take a trip this year.*

2 Remember to use **tener que** to talk about what someone *has to* do.

tener que + **infinitive**　　　*to have to . . ., must . . .*

Me gustaría ir de vacaciones, pero **tengo que trabajar**.
I'd like to go on vacation, but I have to work.

Online

Vocabulario y gramática, pp. 74–76	Actividades, pp. 67–70

Vocabulario y gramática, pp. 74–76 | Actividades, pp. 67–70

Texas

Nota cultural

Within the 275,416 square miles of Texas, tourists find a variety of vacation destinations. There are five state forests, two national parks, and over 100 state parks where you can camp, hike, fish, and swim. There are also many popular amusement and water parks throughout the state. What kinds of things would you consider when planning a Texas vacation? What travel destinations in Texas have names in Spanish? ⬇ **4C**

TEKS Focus

4C Demonstrate understanding of the influence of one language and culture on another

Isla Tequile en el Lago Titicaca, Perú

---

39 **Proyectos** ⬇ **1B**

✏ **Escribamos/Hablemos** Escribe oraciones e indica qué actividades Roberto quiere hacer y qué tiene que hacer.

> **MODELO** hacer un viaje/estudiar
> **Quiere hacer un viaje. Tiene que estudiar.**

1. acampar/trabajar
2. esquiar/limpiar el baño
3. hacer la tarea/ir al lago
4. tomar el sol/hacer la maleta
5. escribir cartas/salir con amigos

40 **Lo que pensamos hacer es...** ⬇ **1B**

Leamos/Escribamos Completa el párrafo con la forma correcta del verbo más apropiado entre paréntesis.

Mi hermana mayor y su esposo ___1___ (pensar/le gustaría) ir a Alaska para las vacaciones. ___2___ (Tener ganas/Esperar) de ir de pesca y acampar. A mi padre ___3___ (querer/le gustaría) acompañarlos pero mi madre ___4___ (le gustaría/querer) viajar a Perú. El problema es que ella ___5___ (tener que/tener ganas) trabajar y no tiene tiempo para el viaje. Este año no es posible, pero algún día (yo) ___6___ (tener que/esperar) hacer un viaje a España.

41 Planes ▾1B

Escribamos Rosalinda habla de sus planes. Combina palabras de cada cuadro para hacer seis oraciones.

mis padres y yo yo mi hermana mayor mis abuelos ¿Y tú?	querer esperar pensar tener que	ver los animales pasear en bote ir de excursión esquiar mandar tarjetas visitar el museo	en el lago en el zoológico del correo en las montañas en el centro en el hotel

 Comunicación

42 Un día ▾1A

Hablemos Con un(a) compañero(a), túrnense para contestar estas preguntas.

MODELO —Un día me gustaría visitar Lima. ¿Y a ti?
—A mí me gustaría más visitar Barcelona.

1. ¿Qué ciudad te gustaría visitar un día?
2. ¿Cómo quieres ir a esa ciudad?
3. ¿Con quién quieres hacer el viaje?
4. ¿Cuántos días quieres quedarte?
5. ¿Piensas acampar, quedarte en un hotel, o quedarte en la casa de un(a) amigo(a)?
6. ¿Qué piensas hacer en esa ciudad?

43 ¿Qué quieren hacer? ¿Qué deben hacer? ▾1A

Hablemos Con un(a) compañero(a), mira los dibujos y dramatiza la conversación entre Ana y Luis.

a. ¿...para las vacaciones?

b. ¿Y tú,...?

c.

 Gramática 2

Conexiones culturales

Conexión Ciencias naturales

1 De vacaciones en Puerto Rico ↓3B

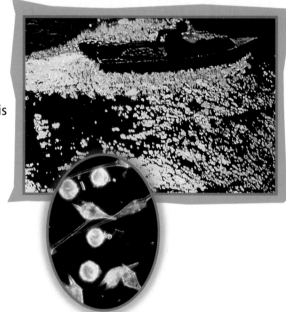

Many people in San Juan take vacations in La Parguera, a fishing village along **la Bahía Fosforescente,** or Phosphorescent Bay, on the southwest coast. Millions of tiny organisms (known as algae or dinoflagellates) glow in the water of this bay. Use Spanish resources from the Internet or the library to find out why these organisms produce light. When would a visitor be most likely to see the phosphorescent glow? Why?

a. on a moonless night with lots of big waves

b. in the middle of a stormy day

c. on a full moon night with calm water

2 La luminiscencia

These glowing sea algae are *luminescent,* which means they give off light but not heat. All of the following generate light. Which are luminescent?

a. a star **b.** a lightbulb **c.** a firefly **d.** a candle

Conexión Astronomía

Many Puerto Ricans and tourists enjoy visiting the Arecibo Observatory, the largest and most sensitive single-dish radio telescope in the world. It is located ten miles south of the city of Arecibo. Galaxies, erupting stars, clouds of gas, pulsars, and quasars give off radio waves that are invisible to the naked eye, but that can be seen using radio telescopes. The Arecibo Observatory also uses planetary radar to study planets, moons, asteroids, and comets in our solar system. This is done by sending a powerful beam of radio energy at the object and analyzing the information about the radio echo that is reflected back to the Arecibo telescope.

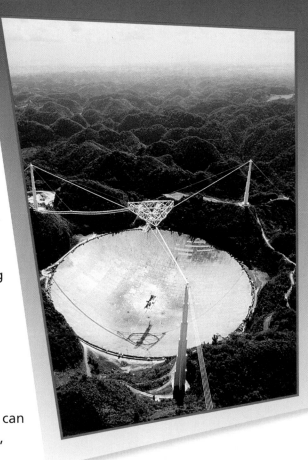

3 El radar

Radio waves are used to study distant objects in our solar system because they can be used to "see" objects through clouds, darkness, and at a great distance. Radio waves were used by the Arecibo Observatory to map Venus. This use of radio waves is also known as radar. What other uses for radar do you know about?

4 Palabras científicas ✈4A

Use a dictionary to find the Spanish words for *planet, asteroid, solar system, moon,* and *radar.* Most of these words are similar to the English words. Why do you think these words are similar?

> **TEKS Focus**
>
> **4A** Demonstrate understanding of the nature of language through comparisons

5 ¡Qué grande!

The spherical reflector of the Arecibo radio telescope is 305 meters in diameter (measurement across). Calculate the diameter in feet.
(Hint: 1 meter = 3.28 feet) .

Conexiones Culturales

¿Quién será?

Episodio 10

↪ 1B, 3A

ESTRATEGIA

Summarizing Before you read the **Novela** or watch the final episode of **¿Quién será?,** go back and summarize what has happened in the previous nine episodes. Pick only the most important moments that you think will help you understand the final episode. Write one or two sentences summarizing what happened in each episode. Do you see a pattern in your summary? Which characters appear the most often? Does summarizing in this way help you predict what might happen in the finale?

En España

La profesora está lista para tomar la decisión. ¿Quién será?

1

Profesora Castillo
Ahora sí, tenemos diez candidatos. ¿Cuáles dos deben recibir la beca para venir a estudiar en Madrid? Voy a tener que pensarlo muy bien.

Más tarde...Sofía y Nicolás reciben un e-mail.

2

Profesora Castillo Soy Aurelia Castillo Velasco. Soy la directora de la Fundación para Cultivar las Relaciones entre las Culturas de Habla Hispana. Mi asistente y yo identificamos diez candidatos para las dos becas que vamos a otorgar este año.

A CONTESTA

1. What is **La profesora** going to have to think about?
2. What kind of organization does she represent?
3. What will the candidates win?

En México

Estados Unidos

MÉXICO Golfo de México

Ciudad de México ★

Océano Pacífico

3

En Puerto Rico

Océano Atlántico San Juan ★

PUERTO RICO

Mar Caribe

Archivo Editar Ver Herramientas Ayuda

Atrás Adelante Actualizar Detener Página Inicial Buscar Favoritos Correo Imprimir

Dirección:

Es mi placer informarte que vas a recibir una beca para estudiar en Madrid por un año.

¡Enhorabuena! Me da mucho gusto ver a alguien de tu inteligencia y dedicación conseguir tus sueños. Será un placer conocerte.

4

B CONTESTA

1. What kind of scholarship has Sofía likely received?

2. What kind of scholarship has Nicolás likely received?

En México

5

Sofía ¿Lo pueden creer? Yo, ¿estudiando danza en Madrid?

Sra. Corona ¡Hija! ¡Qué bien! ¡Estoy muy orgullosa de ti!

Sofía Gracias, mamá. Van a venir a visitarme, ¿verdad? Claro que sí, hija Me encantaría conocer Madrid.

En Puerto Rico

6

Nicolás ¿Lo pueden creer? Yo, ¿estudiando dibujo en Madrid?

Sra. Ortega ¡Hijo! ¡Qué bien! ¡Estoy muy orgullosa de ti!

Nicolás Gracias, mamá. Van a venir a visitarme, ¿verdad?

Sr. Ortega Claro que sí, hijo. Me encantaría conocer Madrid.

En España

7

Profesora Castillo Marcos, ¡buen trabajo! Debes tomar unas vacaciones, viajar a una isla, tomar el sol, descansar… ¡Diviértete! Yo te llamo cuando estemos listos para empezar la investigación para el año próximo.

En Perú

8

Después de investigar al candidato peruano, Marcos recibe el mensaje de la profesora. ¿Quiere trabajar en la investigación del año próximo?

9

C CONTESTA

1. What do both sets of parents agree to do?

2. What does **La profesora** suggest that Marcos do now?

3. Do you think Marcos is interested in working on another project like this again?

Actividades

1 **¿Quién lo dijo?**

Look at the story to help you remember who said each.

1. Voy a tener que pensarlo muy bien.
2. Yo, ¿estudiando danza en Madrid?
3. ¡Hija! ¡Estoy muy orgullosa de ti!
4. ¿Lo pueden creer? Yo, ¿estudiando dibujo en Madrid?
5. Claro que sí, hijo. Me encantaría conocer Madrid.
6. Será un placer conocerte.

2 **¡Qué lío!**

Di si cada oración es cierta o falsa.

1. Marcos es el director de la fundación.
2. Sofía va a recibir una beca para estudiar baile en Madrid por dos años.
3. Nicolás va a recibir una beca para estudiar dibujo en Madrid por un año.
4. Sra. Corona no quiere visitar a Sofía en Madrid.
5. A Sr. Ortega le gustaría conocer Madrid.

3 **¿Comprendes la Novela?**

Check your understanding of the story.

1. Who is the **La profesora?**
2. What was Marcos's role in the whole process?
3. Do the two students have similar reactions to the news? What is their reaction?
4. How did the parents of the two students react? Is this the reaction you might have expected?
5. Think about the ten episodes. Was there an episode when you suspected that Sofía and Nicolás were the winners? Explain when that happened.

> **Episodio final:**
> *Now that you know what the ten candidates were for and which two of them won, can you understand the title of the video? Did the title ever help you predict what was going to happen?*

Leamos y escribamos

TEKS Focus

3A Use resources in the language and cultures being studied to gain access to information

ESTRATEGIA

para leer When you read a brochure, it is important to read with a purpose. You need to decide first what kind of information you want. If you want an overview, then a quick, general reading may be all that is necessary. If you need specific information, however, a close reading will be required.

A Antes de leer ✦3A

Read the title and subtitles of the following brochure. What kind of information does it contain? What specific facts would you expect to find under each subtitle?

¡Bienvenidos a la ciudad de Lima!
Aeropuerto Internacional Chávez

Transporte El servicio de transporte del aeropuerto a la ciudad y viceversa, se realiza por medio de**1** transporte público. Las compañías de taxis estacionan**2** sus vehículos en un área limitada, frente a la salida de los terminales nacional e internacional. La mayoría de hoteles cuentan con su propio**3** servicio de transporte.

Bancos

La moneda nacional del Perú es el nuevo sol. En los pasillos encontrará cajeros automáticos, los cuales aceptan tarjetas de crédito en moneda nacional y extranjera**4**. Las casas de cambio se encuentran en el pasillo principal**5** y en la zona de vuelos internacionales.

Información turística

En diversos lugares del aeropuerto encontrará modulos**6** con información sobre el arrendamiento**7** de coches, restaurantes, sitios turísticos de interés y una guía telefónica a los hoteles principales.

Otros servicios

En los pasillos encontrará teléfonos públicos que funcionan con monedas y tarjetas, las cuales se pueden conseguir en los diferentes quioscos**8** situados por todo el aeropuerto. Si necesita guardar**9** su equipaje por horas o por días, puede hacer uso del servicio de guardianía de equipajes, localizado en el pasillo principal.

---

1 by means of **2** park **3** have their own **4** foreign **5** main corridor **6** modules **7** rental **8** kiosk, stand **9** store

Leamos y escribamos

B **Comprensión** ◆1B

Con base en la lectura, contesta **cierto** o **falso.** Corrige las oraciones falsas.

1. Los cajeros automáticos no aceptan tarjetas de créditoes.

2. Todas las casas de cambio están en la zona internacional.

3. Los taxis se encuentran en frente de las terminales nacionales e internacionales.

4. Hay información sobre los hoteles, las atracciones turísticas y el transporte público en los módulos de información.

5. Puedes dejar tu equipaje por un fin de semana en la guardianía de equipajes.

C **Después de leer** ◆2B, 4B

Which services in the brochure might travelers arriving in Peru use? Do you think these same services are available in airports in the United States and other countries?

Interactive
TUTOR

Taller del escritor

E S T R A T E G I A

para escribir When writing about a series of events, use words such as **primero, luego, después,** and **por fin** to combine sentences.

Cartas del extranjero ◆1C
You are writing home to friends to tell them about your first few days traveling abroad. Tell where you went and include five or six events that made your trip interesting, narrating them in order. End by mentioning your plans for the next day.

1 **Antes de escribir**
Make a list of the events you will report. Then brainstorm some phrases that will link them together logically (**primero, luego, después, por fin**).

2 **Escribir y revisar**
Begin your letter with a greeting, then tell about your trip, focusing mainly on actions and events. Work in the linking phrases, being careful not to lose any clarity.

Exchange letters with a classmate. Read each other's letters checking for appropriate use of transitions and correct use of grammar, spelling, and punctuation.

3 **Publicar**
Write your letter on a large piece of paper or posterboard. On the other side illustrate one of the places you visited. Put your postcard up on the bulletin board. Which trip sounds most interesting to you?

Online
Cuaderno para hispanohablantes, pp. 77–84

Repaso capítulo 10

Vocabulario 1
- asking for and giving information
- reminding and reassuring
  pp. 224–229

1 Según las cosas o lugares dados *(given)*, di lo que tienes que hacer. ⬇1B

1.

2.

3.

4.

5.

6.

2 Gramática 1
- review of the preterite
- preterite of **-car, -gar, -zar** verbs
- preterite of **hacer**
  pp. 230–235

2 Luis escribe una carta a su prima Ana sobre su viaje. Completa la carta con los verbos correctos en el pretérito. ⬇1B

> Querida Ana,
>
> Por fin estoy en Lima. ¡El viaje fue horrible! __1__ (Pasar/Ir) en taxi hasta el aeropuerto y __2__ (salir/llegar) allí temprano, a las seis de la tarde. __3__ (Hacer/Ir) cola en el mostrador. __4__ (Ver/Comprar) el boleto y la agente __5__ (facturar/hacer) la maleta. También __6__ (sacar/salir) la tarjeta de embarque. __7__ (Ir/Pasear) a la sala de espera. Entonces __8__ (comenzar/comprar) a nevar. ¡Por eso no __9__ (abordar/salir) el avión hasta las once. ¡Qué viaje más largo!
> Escribe pronto.
>
> Tu primo, Luis

3 Vocabulario 2
- talking about a trip
- expressing hopes and wishes
  pp. 238–243

3 Escoge la respuesta que mejor completa cada oración. ⬇1B

1. Quiero ir de compras. Vamos al (correo/centro).
2. Fuimos a las ruinas pero llovió. ¡Fue (estupendo/horrible)!
3. Quiero ir al lago. ¿Qué tal si (paseamos en lancha/vamos al centro).
4. Perdí el autobús. ¡Qué (bien/mala suerte)!
5. Ana quiere ir a una isla. Va en (barco/taxi).

Repaso

4 Complete the following conversation with an informal command, a direct object pronoun, or an infinitive. ↴1B

—¿Conoces al profesor Augustino?

—No, no __1__ conozco. ¿Cómo es?

—Es interesante, pero tenemos que __2__ (estudiar) mucho. Hoy tengo que __3__ (leer) tres capítulos.

—Bueno, __4__ (empezar) a __5__ (leer) los capítulos.

—No tengo ganas de leer __6__. Tengo sueño.

—Pues, __7__ (descansar) y __8__ (leer) más tarde.

5 Contesta las siguientes preguntas en español. ↴2A, 2B

1. What material is used to build houses on the Uros Islands?

2. Name one unusual feature of trains in Peru.

3. How is the Manu rainforest in Peru preserved?

4. What makes **la Bahía Fosforescente** famous? Where is it located?

6 Escucha las siguientes oraciones. Decide si cada persona **a)** da un mandato, **b)** describe algo en el pasado o, **c)** busca información. ↴1B

7 Crea (create) una conversación entre Ana y Luis sobre lo que hicieron durante las vacaciones. ↴1A, 1C

4 Gramática 2
• informal commands of spelling-change and irregular verbs
• review of direct object pronouns
• review of verbs followed by infinitives
pp. 244–249

5 Cultura
• **Comparaciones** pp. 236–237
• **Notas culturales** pp. 226, 234, 240, 247
• **Conexiones culturales** pp. 250–251

TEKS Focus
1C Present information using familiar words, phrases, and sentences

Perú

doscientos cincuenta y nueve **259**

Repaso de Gramática 1

For the regular preterite forms of **-ar, -er,** and **-ir** verbs, see page 230. The preterite of **-car**, **-gar**, and **-zar** verbs have spelling changes.

sa**car**: yo sa**qué**   lle**gar**: yo lle**gué**   comen**zar**: yo comen**cé**

hacer			
yo	**hice**	nosotros(as)	**hicimos**
tú	**hiciste**	vosotros(as)	**hicisteis**
usted, él, ella	**hizo**	ustedes, ellos, ellas	**hicieron**

Repaso de Gramática 2

	informal commands	
	affirmative	negative
-ger	reco**g**e	no reco**j**as
-guir	si**gu**e	no si**g**as
-car	bus**c**a	no bus**qu**es
-gar	lle**g**a	no lle**gu**es
-zar	empie**z**a	no empie**c**es

For a review of informal commands of irregular verbs, see page 244.

For a review of **direct object pronoun** placement see page 246.

Use these verbs followed by infinitives to say what someone *wants, hopes, plans,* or *has* to do.

esperar + infinitive   **pensar (ie) + infinitive**

querer (ie) + infinitive   **tener que + infinitive**

me (te, le...) gustaría (más) + infinitive

Letra y sonido   c p q t

Las consonantes c, p, q, t
- The letters **c, p, q, t** are not pronounced with a puff of air as in English *cat, pen, ten, quit:*
  pa**p**a, **p**a**t**inar, **p**ar**qu**e, **c**ar**p**e**t**a, **qu**eso, **C**uz**c**o
- The letter **t** is pronounced with the tip of the tongue right behind the teeth:
  tía, **t**oalla, **t**ris**t**e, **t**raje, **t**engo, **t**arde

Trabalenguas
Pablito clavó un clavito. ¿Qué clavito clavó Pablito?

Dictado ⬇1B
Escribe las oraciones de la grabación.

Repaso de Vocabulario 1

Asking for information

abordar	*to board*
la aduana	*customs*
el aeropuerto	*airport*
el (la) agente	*agent*
allí	*there*
el avión	*airplane*
la billetera	*wallet*
el boleto de avión	*plane ticket*
la bolsa	*travel bag, purse*
el carnet de identidad	*identity card*
comenzar (ie) un viaje	*start a trip*
conseguir (i)	*to get*
el control de seguridad	*security checkpoint*
¿Dónde se puede...?	*Where can one . . . ?*
encontrarse (ue) con	*to meet up with*
esperar	*to wait*
Está(n) a la vuelta.	*It's (They're) around the corner.*
facturar el equipaje	*to check luggage*
hacer cola	*to wait in line*
hacer un viaje	*to take a trip*

irse	*to leave*
la llegada	*arrival*
Lo siento, no sé.	*I'm sorry, I don't know.*
la maleta	*suitcase*
el mapa	*map*
¿Me puede decir...?	*Can you tell me . . . ?*
el mostrador	*counter*
la oficina de cambio	*money exchange*
la pantalla	*monitor, screen*
el (la) pasajero(a)	*passenger*
el pasaporte	*passport*
perder (ie)	*to miss, to lose*
la puerta	*gate*
el reclamo de equipaje	*baggage claim*
recoger	*to pick up*
la sala de espera	*waiting room*
la salida	*departure*
sentarse (ie)	*to sit down*
los servicios	*restrooms*
la tarjeta de embarque	*boarding pass*
el vuelo	*flight*

Reminding and reassuring . . . . See page 228.

Repaso de Vocabulario 2

Talking about a trip

acampar	*to camp*
¡Ah, tuviste suerte!	*You were lucky!*
el autobús	*bus*
el barco	*boat*
la canoa	*canoe*
el centro	*downtown*
durante	*during*
esquiar en el agua	*to water ski*
¡Fue estupendo!	*It was great!*
ir de excursión	*to go hiking*
ir de pesca	*to go fishing*
la isla	*island*
el lago	*lake*
la lancha	*motorboat*
los lugares de interés	*places of interest*
los medios de transporte	*types of transportation*
el metro	*subway*
el museo	*museum*
la oficina de correos	*post office*

el país	*country*
el parque de diversiones	*amusement park*
pasar por	*to stop at/by*
pasear en bote de vela	*to go out in a sailboat*
¡Qué bien!	*How great!*
¡Qué fantástico!	*How fantastic!*
¡Qué lástima!	*What a shame!*
¡Qué mala suerte!	*What bad luck!*
quedarse en...	*to stay in . . .*
recorrer	*to tour*
las ruinas	*ruins*
sacar fotos	*to take photos*
subir a la montaña	*to climb a mountain*
el taxi	*taxi*
tomar el sol	*to sunbathe*
tomar el tren	*to take the train*
el tren	*train*
el viaje	*trip*
el zoológico	*zoo*

Expressing hopes and wishes . . . . See page 242.

Integración

capítulos 1-10

 1 Escucha las conversaciones y escoge la foto correspondiente.

↴**1B**

 **A**

 **B**

 **C**

 **D**

TEKS Focus

3A Use resources in the language and cultures being studied to gain access to information

2 Hay cinco personas que buscan información sobre vuelos. Con base en la información de la pantalla, contesta las preguntas.

↴**1B, 3A**

LLEGADAS INTERNACIONALES

HORAS	AEROLÍNEA	VUELO	ORIGEN	DESTINO	PUERTA
9:00	IBERIA	350	DALLAS	CUZCO	7
18:00	MEXICANA	119	SAN ANTONIO	LIMA	9
15:00	DELTA	230	NUEVA YORK	LIMA	11

SALIDAS INTERNACIONALES

HORAS	AEROLÍNEA	VUELO	ORIGEN	DESTINO	PUERTA
12:00	IBERIA	112	LIMA	NUEVA YORK	2
13:00	MEXICANA	256	LIMA	CIUDAD DE MÉXICO	5
8:00	DELTA	987	CUZCO	MIAMI	10

1. Nora quiere saber el número del vuelo de su amiga que llega a las 3:00 de la tarde de Nueva York.

2. Riqui tiene que recoger a su mamá que llega de Dallas. ¿A qué puerta va?

3. Susana viaja a Cuzco. ¿En qué aerolínea y vuelo viaja?

4. Tomás quiere saber a qué hora sale el vuelo para Nueva York.

5. Rosa pregunta cuántos vuelos hay entre Lima y Estados Unidos.

3 This painting shows a street vendor and townspeople in a Peruvian town, high in the Andes Mountains in South America. Imagine that this is a photo you took while on a visit there. Write a page for your travel journal about the day you took this picture.

♥ **1A, 1C**

- Tell how you traveled.
- What was the weather like?
- What did you see?
- Which foods did you eat?
- Where did you stay?

Exchange your journal entry with a classmate. After reading each other's description, ask a follow-up question of each other.

TEKS Focus

1A Engage in oral and written exchanges of learned material to socialize and to provide and obtain information

28h x 36w, oil; Columbine Galleries, Loveland CO

La Vendedora de Anticuchos por Juan de la Cruz Machicado (1943–)

4

Situación

Set up two tourist agencies in your classroom with two travel agents in each one. Make signs and posters in Spanish for different places to visit. Other students will play tourists who come in and ask about

▸ places they can visit
▸ prices
▸ necessary travel documents
▸ travel methods and schedules

The travel agents will answer with appropriate information and ask what the tourists hope to see and do on their trips. ♥ **1A, 1C**

Integración

Literatura y variedades

Leyendas
indígenas
de
América

Poesía
del
Caribe

México
lindo

Fábulas
españolas

Cuentos
juveniles

CHILE
entre
montañas
y mar

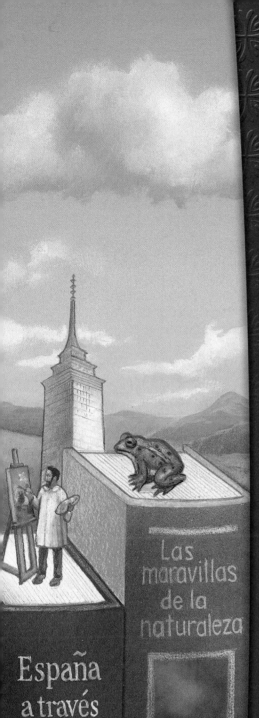

México

La comida de dos continentes

Much of the food that is consumed around the world today is made from ingredients that came originally from the Americas. Tomatoes, chocolate, corn, chile peppers, vanilla, pears, and potatoes are some of the foods that the Spanish conquistadors presented to the kings of Europe. Read the following article in order to learn more about the history of four of these foods.

ESTRATEGIA

When reading a text, look first for the main idea of each paragraph. After that, read carefully all the details that support the main idea. This wIll help you better understand the text.

El tomate: ¿fruta venenosa[1]?

El tomate es originalmente de México. Cuentan[2] que cuando los exploradores llevan el tomate a Europa en el siglo XVI, ¡nadie lo quiere comer! Por su color rojo tan fuerte, todos piensan que es una fruta venenosa. Los exploradores aseguran que lo pueden comer sin problema y la gente poco a poco empieza a probarlo[3].

En la actualidad[4], el tomate es un ingrediente básico en la preparación de platos[5] alrededor del mundo.

El chocolate: ¿para beber o comerciar?

El chocolate es original de América Central. En México, los aztecas lo usan con varios propósitos[6]. Hervido[7] con agua, miel y vainilla los hombres aztecas toman chocolate por la mañana antes del trabajo y otra vez por la tarde después de su comida. El Gran Moctezuma, último líder de los aztecas, no sólo toma su chocolate todos los días sino que le da un lugar especial en los ritos y ceremonias religiosas. También se usa el chocolate para comerciar[8].

1 poisonous   **2** they say   **3** to taste it   **4** today   **5** dishes   **6** purposes   **7** boiled   **8** to trade

El maíz: sustancia del hombre

Se dice que el maíz empieza a cultivarse[1] en América desde hace 10,000 años. Todos los miembros de la cultura maya comen maíz, desde el esclavo[2] hasta el rey. El *Popol Vuh*, libro religioso de los mayas, cuenta que el hombre mismo[3] se hace de[4] maíz. Cuando los exploradores españoles vienen a México prueban el maíz por primera vez en formas diferentes de tortillas y tamales.

Hoy en día, el maíz constituye un 20% de las calorías consumidas mundialmente[5]. En Estados Unidos se produce el 45% del maíz del mundo (mucho de éste destinado al ganado[6]) y en el continente de África el maíz es el grano que más se cultiva.

Los chiles: el picante del mundo[7]

Los chiles, sin duda, son el ingrediente más representativo de la comida mexicana en el mundo. En México hay más de cien variedades de chiles con nombres y sabores[8] diferentes. Algunos de los chiles más típicos son el serrano, el chipotle, el guajillo y el habanero, nativo del Yucatán y ¡muy picante!

Los grupos indígenas usan el chile para añadir sabor a los frijoles, las salsas, los arroces[9] y los moles.[10] Aunque el uso del chile no es tan popular entre los europeos, la llegada de éste a Asia cambia la cocina de la región para siempre. Hoy día se consumen más chiles en Tailandia que en cualquier otro país del mundo.

---

1 to grow   **2** slave   **3** man himself   **4** is made of   **5** worldwide   **6** livestock
7 world's hot spice   **8** tastes   **9** rice dishes   **10** sauces

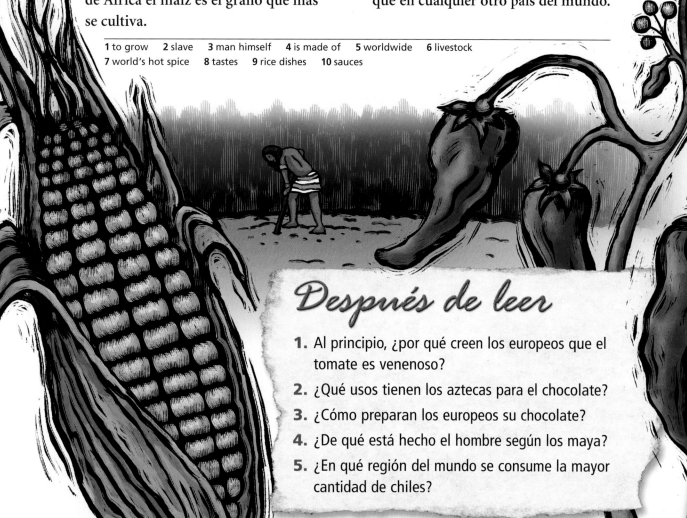

Después de leer

1. Al principio, ¿por qué creen los europeos que el tomate es venenoso?
2. ¿Qué usos tienen los aztecas para el chocolate?
3. ¿Cómo preparan los europeos su chocolate?
4. ¿De qué está hecho el hombre según los maya?
5. ¿En qué región del mundo se consume la mayor cantidad de chiles?

Argentina

Juegos de palabras 🔊

In Argentina, as in many places, word games are one of the favorite types of entertainment among children and adults. Here, two Argentinian authors present four easy riddles about common, everyday things. The first one and the last one are from the book **Adivinanzas** *(Riddles)* by Carlos Silveyna, teacher and author. The other two are riddles from the book **Los rimaqué** by Ruth Kaufman, who is also a teacher. See if you can guess the riddles.

ESTRATEGIA

Read the riddles aloud and think about the images that occur to you. Creating visual images in your mind will help you understand the text.

1 Dos buenas piernas tenemos
y no podemos andar,
pero el hombre sin nosotros
no se puede presentar.

2 Poquitos rincones[1]
encuentro en los mapas
que no haya tocado[2]
mi cuerpo de plata[3].
Bajo con las lluvias
acaricio el suelo[4]
y en pocas semanas
¡de nuevo en el cielo[5]!
A un solo lugar
jamás he llegado[6]
por más que mil veces
lo haya intentado[7].
Le ruego[8] a las nubes

le suplico[9] al viento
¿por qué nadie quiere
llevarme al desierto?

1 corners
2 has not touched
3 silver
4 I touch the ground
5 sky
6 have never arrived
7 have tried
8 I beg
9 I implore

3 Se ponen las nubes
redondas y negras
de la tierra[1] sube
olor a tormenta[2].
Un fuerte estallido[3]
y volamos los dos:
hermanos mellizos[4]
relámpago[5] y yo.
Si juntos salimos
a andar por el mundo
¿por qué llego yo
siempre segundo?

1 earth **2** storm **3** crackling
4 twins **5** lightning

¡Yo primero,
yo primero!

4 Siempre quietas[6],
siempre inquietas[7],
dormidas de día,
de noche despiertas[8].

6 still **7** restless **8** awake

Después de leer

1. En la primera adivinanza, ¿qué necesita el hombre?

2. ¿Adónde vuelven las lluvias que bajan a la tierra según la segunda adivinanza?

3. La segunda adivinanza habla de poca agua en un lugar. ¿Cuál es?

4. En la tercera, ¿cuál es el compañero del relámpago?

5. En la cuarta, ¿qué dice sobre el día y la noche?

269

El amor a la poesía

Maricel Mayor Marsán was born in Cuba but has spent most of her life living as an exile in the United States. She studied history and political science at the International University of Florida and discovered that she wanted to dedicate herself to writing. Even though she writes short stories and theatrical works, her true passion is poetry. She has published five books of poetry, including **Un corazón dividido** (1998), where she speaks of being bilingual and the difficulties of belonging to two cultures. Marsán lives in Miami.

Apuntes° de un hogar° posmoderno

Yo como a las siete,

tú comes a las ocho,

el niño come a las seis

y la niña come a las nueve.

5   Queremos ser felices a toda costa°,

todos vemos televisión separados

en nuestras respectivas
    habitaciones

siempre a la misma hora,

siempre a las diez.

Title: Notes
       home
5 no matter what

Un corazón dividido

El mío es un corazón de dudas°,
esfuerzos° que luchan entre el aquí y el allá.
Es el grito° continuo de mi ser interior.
Es "estar aquí" en sustancia°
5 pero el "estar allá" siguiéndote° a todas
     partes.
Es como una canción sin ritmo definido
que se va contigo sin terminar la tonada°.

Es ser una y otra a la vez.
Es ser una queriendo ser la otra
10 y la otra deseando ser la primera.
Es saber muy poco acerca
de aquellas cosas en las cuales crees.
Es saber menos acerca

de otras cosas que quieres expresar
15 pero tienes miedo reclamar°.
Es la transpiración de mi olor° caribeño
encima de la superficie de mi gel°
     norteamericano.

Es solamente mi corazón que late°
rápido e incesante
20 como las corrientes constantes del
     Golfo de México.

Es mi corazón dividido
secando° los finales del tiempo
como el agua de esas corrientes
sobre el Estrecho de la Florida.

---

1 doubts
2 efforts
3 scream
4 physically
5 following you
7 tune

15 to remember
16 *fig.* my soul
17 *fig.* my shell
18 beats
22 drying

Después de leer

1. En el primer poema, ¿qué es lo que más quieren los miembros de la familia?

2. En el segundo poema, ¿dónde crees que está el "allá" referido en las líneas dos y cinco?

3. ¿Quién crees que es "la una" y "la otra"?

4. ¿Por qué crees que su corazón está dividido? Explica tu respuesta.

La República Dominicana

El regalo de cumpleaños 🔊

Diógenes Valdez is a Dominican author who has written many acclaimed novels and short stories. In this story, the mother of David, a young Dominican, has spent years working in New York. In a letter to his mother, David tells her that everyone thinks that he should have more fun, that it is not good to be so sad, and that he must learn to smile. Read his mother's response and discover what the best gift is that she can give him.

ESTRATEGIA

In order to better understand a story, think about the culture that it represents. What do you know about the Dominican culture that can help you?

Querida mamá:

La abuela me ha dicho[1] que vendrás[2] pronto. Sé que dice esto para verme feliz, porque me paso mucho rato mirando tu fotografía y a veces los ojos se me llenan de lágrimas[3]. Comprendo que te fuiste a Nueva York a trabajar porque aquí cuesta mucho conseguir[4] un empleo.

En casa todos estamos bien, únicamente me preocupa[5] la abuela. Se pasa todo el día diciéndome que me divierta, que salga con los amigos, pero yo no siento deseos de hacerlo. Ha llegado a decirme que hace tiempo que no me ve sonreír[6], que parezco un niño viejo.

Sé que Nueva York es una gran ciudad y que allá se consigue de todo. Quiero que me traigas una sonrisa[7]. Estoy cansado de que me digan que no parezco feliz, sólo porque no sé sonreír.

Te quiere, tu hijo

David

Querido hijo:

Creo que tengo buenas noticias para ti. Voy a regresar pronto y aunque me pides algo que es difícil de conseguir, voy a hacer todo lo posible para complacerte[8]. Sé que costará mucho el conseguir esa sonrisa, pero puedes estar tranquilo. Espero estar contigo el mismo día de tu cumpleaños.

Tu madre que no te olvida,

Rebeca

1 has told me	4 to get	7 a smile
2 you will come	5 I worry about	8 to make you happy
3 tears	6 to smile	

Hoy es sábado 15 de agosto. Es el día del cumpleaños de David. En el aeropuerto, el niño mira los aviones[1] que despegan o aterrizan[2]. No se siente nervioso, ni emocionado. Contempla a su madre y tiene la esperanza de que en cartera[3], envuelta primorosamente[4], venga esa sonrisa. La ve salir y un nudo[5] se le forma en la garganta. Ella corre a abrazarlo[6] y por un momento David se olvida de todo.

¡Mamá!—exclama David.

¡Hijo mío! —responde la madre.

¿Has traído[7] mi sonrisa? —se atreve a preguntarle.

Ella abre la cartera y le entrega un paquetito primorosamente envuelto.

¡Aquí está!—le dice—¡Ábrelo!

David lo toma entre sus manos temblorosas[8] y con los ojos llenos de lágrimas, responde:

¡Tengo miedo de hacerlo!

David comienza a abrir el pequeño paquete. Las manos le tiemblan cuando le quita la envoltura[9]. Abre la cajita, pero dentro tan sólo hay un papelito cuidadosamente doblado. Lo abre y lee:

"Querido hijo:

Mamá ha venido a quedarse definitivamente. Ya nunca más volverá a marcharse[10]."

Entonces David abrió los ojos y abrazó a su madre nuevamente. Sin darse cuenta comenzó[11] a sonreír.

---

1 airplanes
2 take off or land
3 purse
4 carefully wrapped
5 knot
6 to hug him
7 Have you brought
8 shaking
9 takes off the wrapping
10 I'll go away again
11 he began

Después de leer

1. ¿Por qué se fue a Nueva York la madre de David?
2. Según la abuela, ¿por qué debe divertirse David más? ¿A quién se parece?
3. ¿Qué le pide David a su madre?
4. En su carta, ¿cuándo dice que va a venir la madre de David?
5. ¿Cuál es el regalo que la madre le trae? Explica.

Ollantaytambo

The Incan warrior Ollanta was made immortal thanks to the famous Peruvian writer Juan Espinoza Medrano, who wrote the drama *Ollantay* during the colonial period. Many years later, in 1780, the story was presented to the public with great success. Read about the Incan people and this famous warrior for whom the legend is named.

ESTRATEGIA

Making predictions helps prepare you to read a passage. Read the first four lines of the text and, thinking about other legends that you know, try to guess what is going to happen in this Inca legend.

Ollantay es el mejor guerrero[1] del imperio inca. Conquista regiones de la selva y lleva riquezas[2] al Inca Pachacútec.

Su casco de oro[3] le distingue como el más valiente. Todos lo admiran pero su corazón es de la princesa Cusi Coyllur.

Cuando Pachacútec se entera del amor entre el guerrero y la princesa se pone rojo de ira[4]. Castiga[5] a Ollantay y encierra a la princesa en una cueva[6].

Un día Ollantay se escapa y se convierte en jefe de los pueblos de los Andes. Gana todos los combates contra Rumiñahui, el general de Pachacútec.

Rumiñahui busca venganza[7]. Durante una fiesta emborracha[8] a los hombres de Ollantay y los hace prisioneros. El guerrero está ahora en manos del malvado Rumiñahui.

Pero en Cuzco hay un nuevo Inca, Tupac Yupanqui. Tupac es bueno y justo. Cusi Coyllur y Ollantay se casan al fin y viven en Tambo, una magnífica ciudad de piedra[9], levantada[10] al pie de la selva.

---

1 warrior   **2** riches   **3** golden helmet   **4** hatred   **5** He punishes
6 cave   **7** revenge   **8** he intoxicates   **9** rock   **10** raised

Datos geográficos

Ollantaytambo es un pueblo de la provincia de Urubamba, muy cerca de las famosas ruinas de Machu Picchu, al sur del Perú. En este pueblo todo ha permanecido[1] intacto y en sus casas siguen viviendo[2] los descendientes de sus primeros ocupantes. Allí se encuentra una antigua fortaleza inca, uno de los mejores ejemplos de la asombrosa[3] arquitectura de esta civilización. Muchas de las piedras en su construción, de más de 96 toneladas[4], fueron transportadas desde lugares lejanos, pero aún no se sabe cómo.

1 has remained   **2** continue to live   **3** astonishing   **4** tons

Después de leer

1. ¿De quién está enamorado Ollantay?
2. ¿Qué hace el Inca Pachacútec al saber de ese amor?
3. ¿Qué hace Ollantay cuando se escapa de Pachacútec?
4. ¿Cómo se salva Ollantay del malvado Rumiñahui?
5. ¿Por qué es famoso hoy en día el pueblo Ollantaytambo?
6. ¿Qué es el misterio de la construcción?

Secciones de referencia

La Península Ibérica

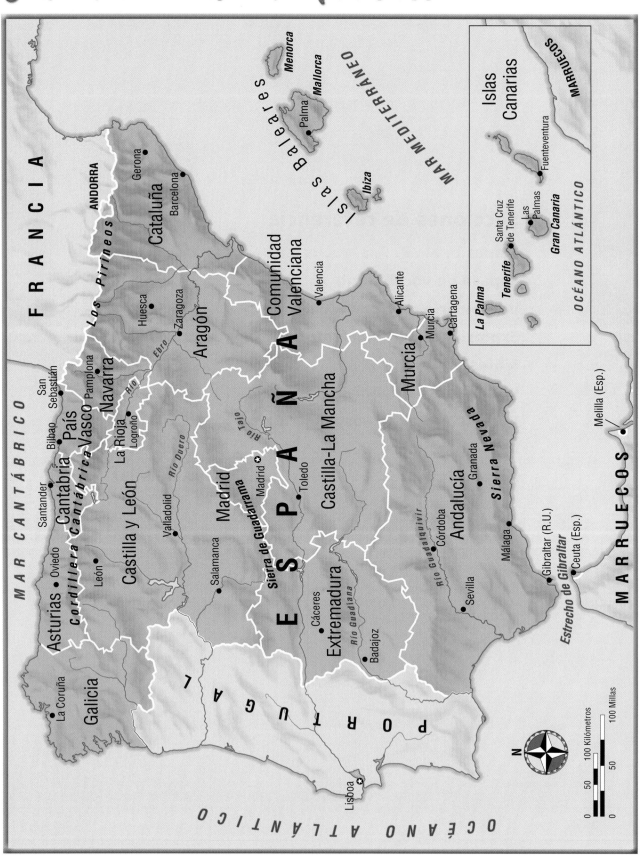

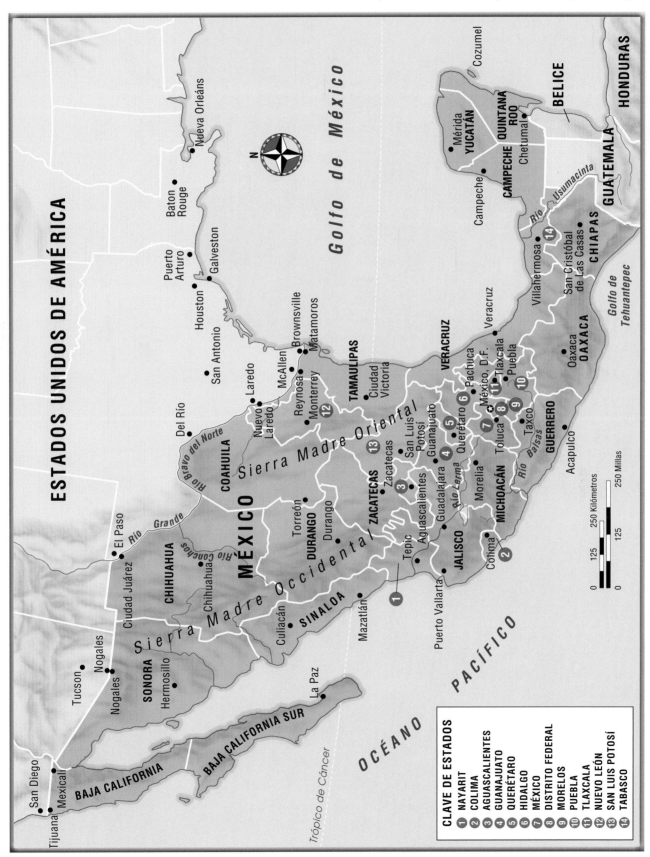

México

Golfo de México

Nueva Orleáns

Baton Rouge

Puerto Arturo

Galveston

Houston

San Antonio

Brownsville

Matamoros

McAllen

Reynosa

Laredo

Nuevo Laredo

Monterrey

Del Río

Del Rio

ESTADOS UNIDOS DE AMÉRICA

El Paso

Ciudad Juárez

Río Grande

Río Bravo del Norte

Río Conchos

CHIHUAHUA

Chihuahua

Torreón

Durango

DURANGO

COAHUILA

MÉXICO

Sierra Madre Oriental

Sierra Madre Occidental

TAMAULIPAS

Ciudad Victoria

Zacatecas

ZACATECAS

San Luis Potosí

VERACRUZ

Pachuca

México, D.F.

Querétaro

Guanajuato

Guadalajara

Río Lerma

Morelia

MICHOACÁN

Aguascalientes

Tepic

JALISCO

Colima

Toluca

Puebla

Tlaxcala

Taxco

Río Balsas

GUERRERO

Acapulco

Veracruz

Villahermosa

San Cristóbal de Las Casas

OAXACA

Oaxaca

Golfo de Tehuantepec

CHIAPAS

Puerto Vallarta

Mazatlán

Culiacán

SINALOA

Nogales

Tucson

Nogales

SONORA

Hermosillo

La Paz

BAJA CALIFORNIA SUR

BAJA CALIFORNIA

San Diego

Tijuana

Mexicali

Trópico de Cáncer

OCÉANO

PACÍFICO

Río Usumacinta

Mérida

YUCATÁN

Cozumel

QUINTANA ROO

Chetumal

BELICE

GUATEMALA

HONDURAS

Campeche

CAMPECHE

N

CLAVE DE ESTADOS
1. NAYARIT
2. COLIMA
3. AGUASCALIENTES
4. GUANAJUATO
5. QUERÉTARO
6. HIDALGO
7. MÉXICO
8. DISTRITO FEDERAL
9. MORELOS
10. PUEBLA
11. TLAXCALA
12. NUEVO LEÓN
13. SAN LUIS POTOSÍ
14. TABASCO

250 Kilómetros

250 Millas

0   125   250

0   125   250

Estados Unidos de América

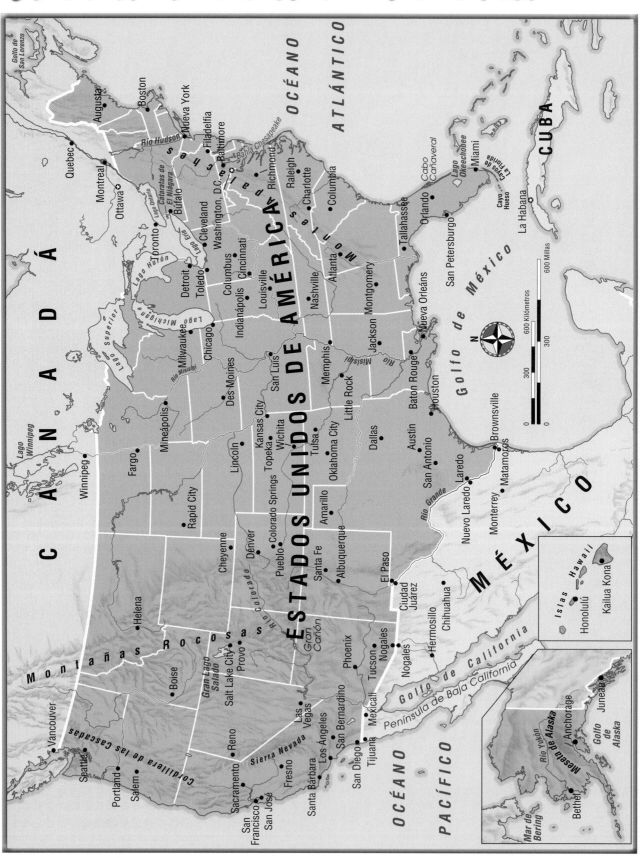

América Central y las Antillas

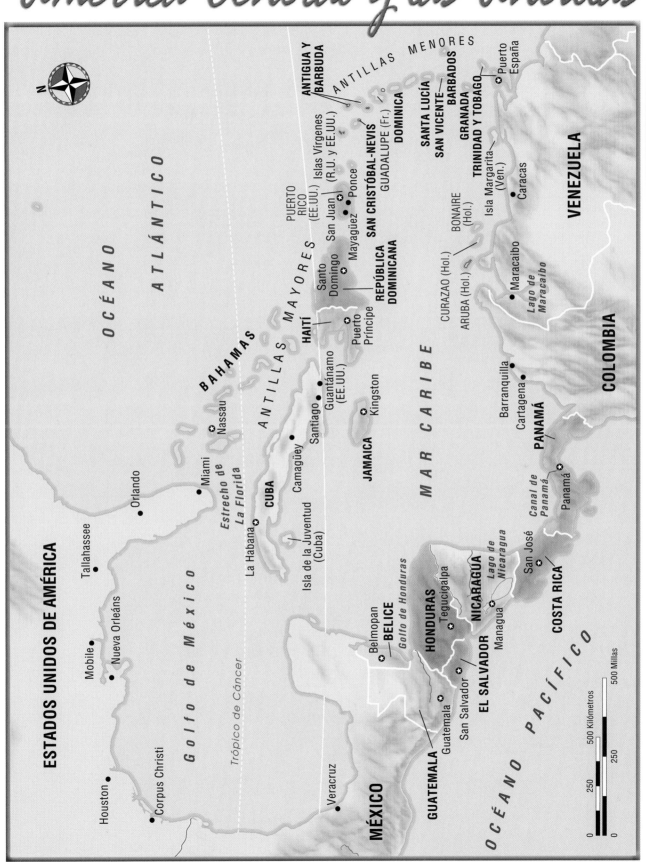

ESTADOS UNIDOS DE AMÉRICA

Houston •

Corpus Christi •

Mobile • Nueva Orleáns •

Tallahassee •

Orlando •

Miami •

OCÉANO ATLÁNTICO

Golfo de México

Trópico de Cáncer

Estrecho de La Florida

La Habana ✪

Isla de la Juventud (Cuba)

CUBA

Camagüey

Santiago

BAHAMAS

Nassau ✪

ANTILLAS

Guantánamo (EE.UU.)

JAMAICA

Kingston ✪

MAYORES

HAITÍ

Puerto Príncipe ✪

REPÚBLICA DOMINICANA

Santo Domingo ✪

PUERTO RICO (EE.UU.)

San Juan ✪ Ponce

Mayagüez

Islas Vírgenes (R.U. y EE.UU.)

SAN CRISTÓBAL-NEVIS

GUADALUPE (Fr.)

DOMINICA

ANTIGUA Y BARBUDA

ANTILLAS MENORES

SANTA LUCÍA

SAN VICENTE

BARBADOS

GRANADA

TRINIDAD Y TOBAGO

Isla Margarita (Ven.)

Puerto España ✪

Caracas •

VENEZUELA

CURAZAO (Hol.)

ARUBA (Hol.)

BONAIRE (Hol.)

Maracaibo •

Lago de Maracaibo

COLOMBIA

Barranquilla •

Cartagena •

PANAMÁ

MAR CARIBE

Canal de Panamá

Panamá ✪

San José ✪

COSTA RICA

Lago de Nicaragua

NICARAGUA

Managua ✪

Golfo de Honduras

Belmopan ✪

BELICE

HONDURAS

Tegucigalpa ✪

EL SALVADOR

San Salvador ✪

GUATEMALA

Guatemala ✪

MÉXICO

Veracruz •

OCÉANO PACÍFICO

500 Millas

500 Kilómetros

250

250

0

0

N

América del Sur

MAR DE LAS ANTILLAS

OCÉANO ATLÁNTICO

América Central

Cartagena
Maracaibo
Caracas
VENEZUELA
Orinoco
GUYANA
SURINAM
Georgetown
Cayena
Paramaribo
GUAYANA FRANCESA

Medellín
Río
Ciudad Bolívar

COLOMBIA
Bogotá

Cordillera
Río Putumayo

Islas Galápagos (Ecuador)
Quito
ECUADOR
Río
Manaus
Amazonas
Ecuador
Belén

Guayaquil
Cuenca

de los

B R A S I L

PERÚ
Recife

Andes
Lima
Cuzco
Salvador

Lago Titicaca
La Paz
Brasilia

BOLIVIA
Sucre

OCÉANO
Paraná
Río de Janeiro

PARAGUAY
San Pablo
Asunción

Trópico de Capricornio
Tucumán
CHILE
Río

PACÍFICO
ARGENTINA
Córdoba

URUGUAY
Valparaíso
Mendoza
Montevideo
Santiago
Buenos Aires
Río de la Plata

Cordillera de los

N

Andes
Bariloche
OCÉANO
ATLÁNTICO

0   500   1.000 Kilómetros
0   500   1.000 Millas

Andes
Estrecho de Magallanes
Islas Malvinas (R.U.)

Punta Arenas
Tierra del Fuego

Cabo de Hornos

Repaso de Vocabulario

This list includes words introduced in *¡Exprésate!* Level 1A, Chapters 1–5. If you can't find the words you need here, try the Spanish–English and English–Spanish vocabulary sections beginning on page R29. You will also want to reference the review of functional expressions, beginning on page R17.

¿Adónde vamos? *(Where do we go?)*

el auditorio	*auditorium*
el baile	*dance*
la biblioteca	*library*
la cafetería	*cafeteria*
la casa de...	*. . .'s house*
el centro comercial	*shopping mall*
el cine	*movie theater*
el club de...	*the . . . club*
el colegio	*school*
el concierto	*concert*
el ensayo	*rehearsal*
el entrenamiento	*practice*
la fiesta	*party*
el gimnasio	*gym*
la iglesia	*church*
el parque	*park*
el partido de...	*the . . .(sports) game*
la piscina	*swimming pool*
la playa	*beach*
la reunión	*meeting*

Pasatiempos *(Pastimes)*

alquilar videos	*to rent videos*
bailar	*to dance*
cantar	*to sing*
comer	*to eat*
correr	*to run*
descansar	*to rest*
dibujar	*to draw*
escribir cartas	*to write letters*
escuchar música	*to listen to music*
estudiar	*to study*
hablar por teléfono	*to talk on the phone*
hacer la tarea	*to do homework*
ir de compras	*to go shopping*
leer	*to read*
montar en bicicleta	*to ride a bike*
nadar	*to swim*
navegar por Internet	*to surf the Internet*
pasear	*to take a walk*
patinar	*to skate*
salir con amigos	*to go out with friends*
tocar el piano	*to play the piano*
trabajar	*to work*
ver televisión	*to watch TV*

La casa/el apartamento
(House/Apartment)

el baño	*bathroom*
el carro	*automobile*
la cocina	*kitchen*
el comedor	*dining room*
el escritorio	*desk*
el garaje	*garage*
el gato	*cat*
la habitación	*bedroom*
el jardín	*garden*
la mesa	*table*
el perro	*dog*
las plantas	*plants*
la puerta	*door*
la sala	*living room*
la silla	*chair*
el sofá	*couch*
la ventana	*window*

La comida *(Food)*

el almuerzo	*lunch*
la comida china (mexicana, italiana)	*Chinese (Mexican, Italian) food*
las frutas	*fruit*
las hamburguesas	*hamburgers*
el helado	*ice cream*
la pizza	*pizza*
las verduras	*vegetables*

Las cosas para el colegio
(Things for school)

el bolígrafo	*pen*
la calculadora	*calculator*
la carpeta	*folder*
la computadora	*computer*
el cuaderno	*notebook*
el diccionario	*dictionary*
el lápiz/los lápices	*pencil/pencils*
la mochila	*backpack*
el papel	*paper*
la regla	*ruler*
el reloj	*watch/clock*

Calendario *(Calendar)*

abril	*April*
agosto	*August*
los días de la semana	*days of the week*
diciembre	*December*
los domingos	*on Sundays*
enero	*January*
febrero	*February*
los fines de semana	*on weekends*
el invierno	*Winter*
los jueves	*on Thursdays*
junio	*June*
julio	*Julio*
los lunes	*on Mondays*
los martes	*on Tuesdays*
marzo	*March*
mayo	*May*
los meses del año	*months of the year*
los miércoles	*on Wednesdays*
noviembre	*November*
octubre	*October*
el otoño	*Fall*
la primavera	*Spring*
la próxima semana	*next week*
los sábados	*on Saturdays*
septiembre	*September*
el verano	*Summer*
los viernes	*on Fridays*

¿Cuándo y con qué frecuencia?
(When and How often?)

a tiempo	*on time*
a veces	*sometimes*
después de...	*after . . .*
luego	*then, next*
mañana	*tomorrow*
nunca	*never*
por la mañana	*in the morning*
por la noche	*at night*
por la tarde	*in the afternoon*
siempre	*always*
tarde	*late*
temprano	*early*
todos los días	*every day*

Los deportes y juegos
(Sports and Games)

el ajedrez	chess
el básquetbol	basketball
el béisbol	baseball
el fútbol	soccer
el fútbol americano	football
los juegos de mesa	table games
los videojuegos	video games
el volibol	volleyball

Descripciones (Descriptions)

alto(a)	tall
antipático(a)	mean
bajo(a)	short (height)
bonito(a)	pretty
bueno(a)	good
callado(a)	quiet
canoso(a)	grey-haired
castaño(a)	dark brown
ciego(a)	blind
cómico(a)	funny
corto(a)	short (length)
delgado(a)	thin
fácil	easy
gordo(a)	fat
grande	big
guapo(a)	handsome
inteligente	smart
interesante	interesting
joven	young
largo(a)	long
mayor	older
menor	younger
moreno(a)	dark-haired, dark-skinned
pelirrojo(a)	red-haired

pequeño(a)	small, little
perezoso(a)	lazy
pésimo(a)	awful
rubio(a)	blonde
simpático(a)	nice
sordo(a)	deaf
viejo(a)	old

La familia (Family)

la abuela	grandmother
el abuelo	grandfather
el gato	cat
la hermana	sister
el hermano	brother
la hija	daughter
el hijo	son
la madre/mamá	mother/mom
la nieta	granddaughter
el nieto	grandson
el padre/papá	father/dad
el perro	dog
la prima	female cousin
el primo	male cousin
la sobrina	niece
el sobrino	nephew
la tía	aunt
el tío	uncle

Los gustos (Things we like)

los amigos	friends
los animales	animals
los libros (de aventura, amor)	(adventure, romance) books
la música (de...)	music (by . . .)
películas	movies
las revistas	magazines

Las materias *(School subjects)*

el aleman	*German*
el arte	*art*
la biología	*biology*
las ciencias	*science*
la computación	*computer class*
la educación física	*physical education*
el español	*Spanish*
el francés	*French*
la historia	*history*
el inglés	*English*
las matemáticas	*math*
la química	*chemistry*
el salón de clase	*classroom*
el taller	*workshop*

Números 0–100 *(Numbers 0–100)*

cero	*zero*
uno	*one*
dos	*two*
tres	*three*
cuatro	*four*
cinco	*five*
seis	*six*
siete	*seven*
ocho	*eight*
nueve	*nine*
diez	*ten*
once	*eleven*
doce	*twelve*
trece	*thirteen*
catorce	*fourteen*
quince	*fifteen*
dieciséis	*sixteen*
dieciocho	*eighteen*
diecinueve	*nineteen*
veinte	*twenty*
veintiuno	*twenty-one*
veintidós	*twenty-two*
veintitrés	*twenty-three*
veinticuatro	*twenty-four*
veinticinco	*twenty-five*
veintiséis	*twenty-six*
veintisiete	*twenty-seven*
veintiocho	*twenty-eight*
veintinueve	*twenty-nine*
treinta	*thirty*
treinta y uno	*thirty-one*
treinta y dos	*thirty-two*
…	
cuarenta	*forty*
cincuenta	*fifty*
sesenta	*sixty*
setenta	*seventy*
ochenta	*eighty*
noventa	*ninety*
cien	*one hundred*

Los quehaceres *(Chores)*

arreglar el cuarto	*to clean your room*
ayudar en casa	*to help at home*
cocinar	*to cook*
cortar el césped	*to cut the grass*
cuidar a los niños	*to care for children*
hacer la cama	*to make the bed*
lavar los platos	*to wash the dishes*
limpiar	*to clean*
pasar la aspiradora	*to run the vacuum*
sacar la basura	*to take out the trash*

Vocabulario adicional

This list includes additional vocabulary that you may want to use to personalize activities. If you can't find a word you need here, try the Spanish-English and English-Spanish vocabulary sections, beginning on page R29.

Materias (School Subjects)

el álgebra	algebra
el cálculo	calculus
la contabilidad	accounting
la física	physics
la geometría	geometry
el italiano	Italian
el japonés	Japanese
el latín	Latin
la literatura	literature
el ruso	Russian

Celebraciones (Celebrations)

el bautizo	baptism
la canción	song
El Día de los Reyes	Three Kings Day
la Pascua Florida	Easter
las Pascuas	Christmas
el Ramadán	Ramadan
Rosh Hashaná	Rosh Hashanah

Comida (Food)

el ají picante (el chile)	hot pepper
el aguacate	avocado
las arvejas	peas
el azúcar	sugar
la banana (el guineo)	banana
la batida	milkshake
la cereza	cherry
la coliflor	cauliflower
el champiñón (el hongo)	mushroom
los condimentos	seasonings
los fideos	noodles
el filete de pescado	fish fillet
la lechuga	lettuce
la mayonesa	mayonnaise
el melón	cantaloupe
la mostaza	mustard
la pimienta	pepper
la piña	pineapple
el plátano	plantain

la sal	salt
el yogur	yogurt

Computadoras (Computers)

arrastrar	to drag
la búsqueda	search
buscar	to search
comenzar la sesión	to log on
la contraseña, el código	password
el disco duro	hard drive
en línea	online
grabar	to save
hacer clic	to click
la impresora	printer
imprimir	to print
el marcapáginas, el separador	bookmark
el ordenador	computer
la página Web inicial	homepage
el ratón	mouse
la Red	the Net
la tecla de aceptación	return key
la tecla de borrar, la tecla correctora	delete key
el teclado	keyboard
terminar la sesión	to log off
la unidad de CD-ROM	CD-ROM drive
el Web, la Telaraña Mundial	World Wide Web

De compras (Shopping)

cobrar	to charge
el dinero en efectivo	cash
el descuento	discount
en venta	for sale
la rebaja	sale, sale price
regatear	to bargain
la tarjeta de crédito	credit card
el (la) vendedor, -a	salesperson

Deportes y pasatiempos
(Sports and Hobbies)

el anuario	*yearbook*
las artes marciales	*martial arts*
la astronomía	*astronomy*
el ballet	*ballet*
el boxeo	*boxing*
coleccionar sellos (monedas, muñecas)	*to collect stamps (coins, dolls)*
coser	*to sew*
el drama	*drama*
la fotografía	*photography*
la gimnasia	*gymnastics*
jugar a las cartas	*to play cards*
jugar a las damas	*to play checkers*
la orquesta	*orchestra*
el patinaje en línea, (sobre hielo)	*inline (ice) skating*

En el cine o el teatro
(At the Movies or Theater)

el actor	*actor*
actuar	*to act*
la actriz	*actress*
aplaudir	*to applaud*
la butaca	*box seat*
la escena	*scene*
el escenario	*stage*
el espectáculo	*performance, show*
la estrella	*star*
la pantalla	*screen*
el telón	*curtain*

En el consultorio (At the Clinic)

la alergia	*allergy*
el antibiótico	*antibiotic*
darle a uno una inyección	*to give someone a shot*
el dolor	*pain*
los escalofríos	*chills*
estornudar	*to sneeze*
la gripe	*flu*
la medicina	*medicine*
las pastillas, las píldoras	*pills, tablets*
el síntoma	*symptom*
la tos	*cough*
toser	*to cough*

En el zoológico (At the Zoo)

el ave, las aves	*bird, birds*
el canguro	*kangaroo*
la cebra	*zebra*
el cocodrilo	*crocodile*
el delfín	*dolphin*
el elefante	*elephant*
el gorila	*gorilla*
el hipopótamo	*hippopotamus*
la jirafa	*giraffe*
el león	*lion*
la foca	*seal*
el mono, el chango	*monkey*
el oso	*bear*
el oso polar	*polar bear*
el pingüino	*penguin*
la serpiente	*snake*
el tigre	*tiger*

En la casa (Around the House)

la alfombra	*rug, carpet*
el ático	*attic*
el balcón	*balcony*
las cortinas	*curtains*
el despertador	*alarm clock*
las escaleras	*stairs*
el espejo	*mirror*
el estante	*bookcase*
el fregadero	*kitchen sink*
la galería	*porch*
la lámpara	*lamp*
el lavamanos	*bathroom sink*
la lavadora	*washing machine*
la mesita de noche	*nightstand*
los muebles	*furniture*
la secadora	*dryer*

el sillón	easy chair
el sótano	basement
el timbre	doorbell
el tocador	dresser

En las afueras y en la ciudad
(Places Around Town)

la autopista	highway
el banco	bank
la esquina	street corner
la estación de autobuses (trenes)	bus (train) station
la fábrica	factory
la ferretería	hardware store
la farmacia	drugstore
la gasolinera	gas station
el hospital	hospital
la mezquita	mosque
el mercado	market
la oficina	office
la parada de autobuses	bus stop
la peluquería	barber shop
el puente	bridge
el rascacielos	skyscraper
el salón de belleza	beauty salon
el semáforo	traffic light
el supermercado	supermarket

Instrumentos musicales
(Musical Instruments)

el acordeón	accordion
el arpa, las arpas	harp
la armónica	harmonica
el bajo	bass
la batería	drum set
el clarinete	clarinet
la flauta dulce	recorder
la flauta	flute
la guitarra	guitar
la mandolina	mandolin
las maracas	maracas
el oboe	oboe
el saxofón	saxophone
el sintetizador	synthesizer
el tambor	drum
el trombón	trombone
la trompeta	trumpet
la tuba	tuba
la tumbadora	conga drum
la viola	viola
el violín	violin

La familia (Family)

el (la) ahijado(a)	godson, goddaughter
el (la) bisabuelo(a)	great-grandfather, great-grandmother
el (la) biznieto(a)	great-grandson, great-granddaughter
el (la) cuñado(a)	brother-in-law, sister-in-law
el (la) hijastro(a)	stepson, stepdaughter
la madrina	godmother
la madrastra	stepmother
la nuera	daughter-in-law
el padrino	godfather
el padrastro	stepfather
el (la) suegro(a)	father-in-law, mother-in-law
el yerno	son-in-law

Palabras descriptivas
(Descriptive Words)

amistoso(a)	friendly
la barba	beard
bien educado(a)	well-mannered
el bigote	moustache
calvo(a)	bald
la estatura	height
flaco(a)	skinny
lindo(a)	pretty
las pecas	freckles
las patillas	sideburns
el pelo lacio	straight hair
el pelo rizado	curly hair
pesar	to weigh
tranquilo(a)	quiet

Partes del cuerpo (Parts of the Body)

la barbilla	chin
las cejas	eyebrows
la cintura	waist
el codo	elbow
la frente	forehead
los labios	lips
la muñeca	wrist
el muslo	thigh
las pestañas	eyelashes
la rodilla	knee
la sien	temple
el tobillo	ankle
la uña	nail

Profesiones (Professions)

el (la) abogado(a)	lawyer
el (la) arquitecto(a)	architect
el (la) bombero(a)	firefighter
el (la) cartero(a)	mail carrier
el (la) cocinero(a)	cook
el (la) conductor, -a	driver
el (la) constructor, -a	builder
el (la) decorador, -a	interior decorator

el (la) dentista	dentist
el (la) detective	detective
el (la) enfermero(a)	nurse
el (la) escritor, -a	writer
el hombre (la mujer) de negocios	businessman, businesswoman
el (la) ingeniero(a)	engineer
el (la) médico(a)	doctor
el (la) piloto(a)	pilot
el (la) (mujer) policía	police officer
el (la) secretario(a)	secretary

Regalos (Gifts)

la agenda	agenda, daily planner
el álbum	album
el animal de peluche	stuffed animal
los bombones	chocolates
el calendario	calendar
los claveles	carnations
la colonia	cologne
las flores	flowers
el llavero	key chain
el perfume	perfume
el rompecabezas	puzzle
las rosas	roses

Ropa (Clothes)

la bata	robe
la bufanda	scarf
el chaleco	vest
las chancletas	flip-flops
la corbata	tie
los guantes	gloves
las medias	socks, stockings, hose
las pantuflas, las zapatillas	slippers
el pañuelo	handkerchief
el paraguas	umbrella
la ropa interior	underwear
los tacones, los zapatos de tacón	high heels

Temas de actualidad (Current Issues)

el bosque tropical	rain forest
la contaminación	pollution
el crimen	crime
los derechos humanos	human rights
la economía	economy
la educación	education
la guerra	war

Vocabulario adicional

el medio ambiente	environment
el mundo	world
las noticias	news
la paz	peace
la política	politics
la tecnología	technology
la violencia	violence

Vacaciones (Vacation)

la agencia de viajes	travel agency
el andén	train platform
el asiento	seat
los cheques de viajero	traveler's checks
hacer una reservación	to make a reservation
el horario	schedule, timetable
el mar	sea

la parada	stop
el pasillo	aisle
reservado(a)	reserved
la ventanilla	window
la visa	visa
visitar los lugares de interés	to sightsee
volar	to fly

Refranes (Proverbs)

Más vale pájaro en mano que cien volando.
A bird in the hand is worth two in the bush.

Hijo no tenemos y nombre le ponemos.
Don't count your chickens before they're hatched.

Quien primero viene, primero tiene.
The early bird catches the worm.

Más vale tarde que nunca.
Better late than never.

El hábito no hace al monje.
Clothes don't make the man.

Más ven cuatro ojos que dos.
Two heads are better than one.

Querer es poder.
Where there's a will, there's a way.

Ojos que no ven, corazón que no siente.
Out of sight, out of mind.

No todo lo que brilla es oro.
All that glitters is not gold.

Caras vemos, corazones no sabemos.
You can't judge a book by its cover.

Donde una puerta se cierra, otra se abre.
Every cloud has a silver lining.

En boca cerrada no entran moscas.
Silence is golden.

Dime con quién andas y te diré quién eres.
Birds of a feather flock together.

Al mal tiempo buena cara.
When life gives you lemons, make lemonade.

Antes que te cases mira lo que haces.
Look before you leap.

Expresiones de ¡Exprésate!

Functions are the ways in which you use a language for particular purposes. In specific situations, such as in a restaurant, in a grocery store, or at school, you will want to communicate with those around you. In order to do that, you have to "function" in Spanish: you place an order, make a purchase, or talk about your class schedule.

Here is a list of the functions presented in *¡Exprésate! 1A* for Chapters 1–5 and in this book for Chapters 6–10 with the Spanish expressions you'll need to communicate in a wide range of situations. Following each function is the chapter and page number from the book where it is introduced.

Socializing

Greetings
Ch. 1, p. 8

Buenos días, señor.
Buenas noches, señora.
Buenas tardes, señorita.

Saying Goodbye
Ch. 1, p. 8

Adiós.   Hasta mañana.
Tengo que irme.   Nos vemos.
Hasta luego.   Hasta pronto.
Buenas noches.

Asking how someone is and saying how you are
Ch. 1, p. 8

Hola, ¿cómo estás?   Estoy bien/regular/mal.
¿Cómo está usted?   ¿Y usted?
¿Qué tal?   Más o menos.

Introducing people
Ch. 1, p. 10

Éste(a) es... Es un(a)   Encantado(a).
   compañero(a)   Mucho gusto.
   de clase.   Igualmente.
Ésta es... Ella es   Éste es... Él es
   mi profesora de...   mi profesor de...

Inviting others to do something
Ch. 4, p. 158

¿Qué tal si vamos a...?
No sé. ¿Sabes qué? No tengo ganas.
Vienes conmigo a..., ¿no?
¡Claro que sí! Tengo mucha hambre.
Hay una reunión del club de... el... próximo.
   Vas a ir, ¿verdad?
No, no voy a ir. Tengo que...

Talking on the phone
Ch. 8, p. 150

Aló/Bueno/Diga.   ¿De parte de quién?
Hola. ¿Está...?   Habla...
Lo siento, no está. ¿Quieres dejarle un recado?
Sí, por favor, que me llame después.
No, gracias. Llamo más tarde.
Espera un momento, ya te lo (la) paso.

Greeting, introducing others, and saying goodbye
Ch. 9, p. 196

¡Qué gusto verte!   ¡Tanto tiempo sin verte!
¿Qué hay de nuevo?   Lo de siempre.
Te presento a...   Tanto gusto.
¡Feliz...!   Chao, te llamo más tarde.
Cuídate.   Vale. Que te vaya bien.

Exchanging Information

Asking and giving names
Ch. 1, p. 6

¿Cómo te llamas?   ¿Quién es...?
¿Cómo se llama   Él (Ella) es...
   usted?   ¿Cómo se llama él (ella)?
Me llamo... ¿Y tú?   Él (Ella) se llama...
Soy...

Saying where you and others are from
Ch. 1, p. 11

¿De dónde eres?   ¿De dónde es usted?
Soy de...   ¿De dónde es...?
Es de...

Asking and giving phone numbers
Ch. 1, p. 19

¿Cuál es tu teléfono?
Es tres-dos-cinco-uno-dos-tres-uno.
¿Cuál es el teléfono de...?
Es...

Saying what time it is
Ch. 1, p. 20

¿Qué hora es?

Son las seis y cuarto de la mañana.

Es la una en punto.

Son las... y trece de la tarde.

Son las... y media de la tarde.

Son las... menos cuarto.

Son las... menos diez de la noche.

Es mediodía.

Es medianoche.

Asking and giving the date and the day
Ch. 1, p. 21

¿Qué fecha es hoy?

Es el primero (dos, tres...) de enero.

¿Qué día es hoy?

Hoy es...

Asking how words are spelled and giving e-mail addresses
Ch. 1, p. 23

¿Cómo se escribe...?

Se escribe...

¿Cuál es tu correo electrónico?

Es...

¿Cuál es el correo electrónico de...?

Es eme punto ge-o-ene-zeta-a-ele-o arroba ere-e-de punto a-ere.

Describing people
Ch. 2, p. 49

¿Cómo es...?

... es moreno(a). También es... y un poco...

¿Cómo eres? ¿Eres cómico(a)?

Sí, soy bastante cómico(a).

Asking and saying how old someone is
Ch. 2, p. 52

¿Cuántos años tienes?

Tengo ... años.

¿Cuántos años tiene...?

... tiene ... años.

¿Cuándo es tu cumpleaños?

Es el 6 de mayo.

¿Cuándo es el cumpleaños de...?

Es el...

Describing things
Ch. 2, p. 66

¿Cómo es...?   Es...

Es muy...   Es algo...

Es bastante...

Talking about what you and others want to do
Ch. 3, p. 98

¿Qué quieres hacer hoy?

Ni idea.

¿Quieres ir a... conmigo?

Está bien.

No, gracias. No quiero ir a... hoy.

Talking about everyday activities
Ch. 3, p. 109

¿Qué haces los fines de semana?

Los sábados, cuando hace buen tiempo, voy...

¿Adónde vas...?

¿Qué hace... cuando hace mal tiempo?

Le gusta...

No va a ninguna parte.

Asking and saying how often
Ch. 3, p. 112

¿Con qué frecuencia vas a...?

Casi nunca. No me gusta...

¿Te gusta...?

Sí. Después de clases, casi siempre vamos a...

A veces vamos también a...

Talking about what you and others have or need
Ch. 4, p. 141

¿Necesitas algo para el colegio?   ¿Necesitas...?

Sí, necesito muchas cosas.   Sí, necesito...

¿Tienes...?

Sí, tengo un montón.

No, no necesito nada.   No, no tengo.

Talking about classes
Ch. 4, p. 144

¿Qué clases tienes...?

Primero tengo... y después tengo...

¿Cuál es tu materia preferida?

Mi materia preferida es... Es fácil.

No me gusta la clase de... porque es difícil.

Talking about plans
Ch. 4, p. 155

¿Vas a ir a... en... el... por la...?

No, no voy a ir. El... tengo...

¿Qué vas a hacer el... próximo?

Por la tarde voy a... y después voy a ir a...
Luego voy a...

¿A qué hora vas a llegar a...?

Voy a llegar temprano (a tiempo).
No me gusta llegar tarde.

Describing people and family relationships
Ch. 5, p. 187

¿Cuántas personas hay en tu familia?

En mi familia somos... personas: mi...

¿Cómo son tus hermanos?

Todos usamos lentes. Somos... y tenemos...
   Mi... está en una silla de ruedas.

¿Cómo es tu...?

Es... Es una persona... y muy... Él (Ella) y mi...
   tienen... hijos pero no tienen...

Describing where someone lives
Ch. 5, p. 201

¿Dónde viven ustedes?

Vivimos en un apartamento. Está en un edificio
   grande de... pisos.

¿Cuál es tu dirección?

Mi dirección es calle..., número...

¿Cómo es tu casa?

Es bastante... Tiene... habitaciones, ...

Talking about your responsibilities
Ch. 5, p. 204

¿Qué haces para ayudar en casa?

A veces tengo que..., pero me parece bien.
   No es gran cosa.

¿Quién hace los quehaceres?

A menudo tengo que...

A... nunca le toca... Me parece injusto.

¿Qué te toca hacer a ti?

A mí siempre me toca... ¡Qué lata!

Commenting on food
Ch. 6, pp. 40–41

¿Qué vas a pedir?

¿Qué prefieres pedir para...?

Para tomar, puedes pedir...

En la mesa hay...

¿Qué tal si pruebas...? Son muy buenos(as) aquí.

¡Ay, no! Nunca pido... No me gusta.

Aquí preparan muy bien (mal)...

(No) estoy de acuerdo.

¡Qué ricos(as) están...!

Sí, me encantan.

¿Qué tal está(n)...?

Está(n) un poco...

Talking about meals
Ch. 6, p. 55

¿Qué desayunas?

Siempre desayuno...

¿Qué quieres hoy de almuerzo?

¿Qué tal si almorzamos...?

¿Qué hay de cena? Tengo mucha hambre.

Vamos a cenar...

Talking about your daily routine
Ch. 7, p. 86–87

Por la mañana, tengo que...

Por la tarde, después de..., voy a...

Por la noche, necesito...

¿Estás listo(a)? ¿Qué te falta hacer?

¡Ay, no! Acabo de levantarme. Tengo que... antes
   de...

¿Qué tienes que hacer?

Tengo que..., pero no encuentro...

Talking about staying fit and healthy
Ch. 7, p. 90

¿Cómo te mantienes   ¿Qué haces para
   en forma?   relajarte?

... y... Entreno...   ... También... o...

Offering and asking for help in a store
Ch. 8, p.136

¿En qué le puedo   ¿Cómo le queda(n)...?
   servir?   Me queda(n) bien/mal.

Busco...   Necesito una talla
Estoy mirando,   más grande/pequeña.
   nomás.   ¿A qué hora cierra
¿Qué número/talla   la tienda?
   usa?   Cierra a las...

Uso el/la...

Saying where you went and what you did
Ch. 8, p. 147

¿Adónde fuiste ayer/anteayer/anoche?

Fui a... a buscar... (y compré)...

¿Qué hiciste el fin de semana pasado?

Pagué una fortuna por...

Talking about your plans
Ch. 9, p. 179

¿Qué vas a hacer...?

Pienso... o...

¿Qué planes tienen para...?

Pensamos pasarlo(la) con..., como siempre.

Talking about past holidays
Ch. 9, p. 182

¿Dónde pasaron... el año pasado?

Lo (la) pasamos en casa de...

¿Qué tal estuvo?

Estuvo a todo dar. Nos reunimos a...

Preparing for a party
Ch. 9, p. 193

¿Está todo listo para la fiesta?

¿Ya terminaste con los preparativos?

Sí. Anoche compré... y preparé...

¿Qué están haciendo...?

Están colgando...

Asking for and giving information
Ch. 10, pp. 224–225

¿Dónde puedo...?

Allí, en el...

Me puede decir dónde está(n)...?

Está(n) a la vuelta.

¿Sabe Ud. a qué hora sale/llega el vuelo...?

Lo puede ver allí en esa pantalla.

Sí, sale/llega a las...

¿Dónde se puede conseguir...?

Lo siento, no sé.

Reminding and reassuring
Ch. 10, p. 228

¿Ya sacaste el dinero?

Sí, ya lo saqué.

No, todavía no. Debo pasar por el cajero automático.

¿Ya hiciste la maleta?

No, todavía tengo que hacerla.

¡Ay, dejé... en casa!

No te preocupes. Puedes comprar... en cualquier tienda.

Talking about a trip
Ch. 10, pp. 238–239

¿Qué hiciste durante las vacaciones?

¡Qué divertido!

Recorrí la ciudad en... Luego, tomé... a...

¿Qué tal el viaje?

¡Fue estupendo!

¡Fue horrible!

¿Adónde fueron?

Fuimos a...

¿Qué hicieron?

Conocimos... y sacamos muchas fotos.

Luego pasamos por... y por fin...

Expressing Attitudes and Opinions

Talking about what you and others like
Ch. 2, p. 63

¿Te gusta(n)...?   Sí, me gusta(n) mucho.

No, no me gusta(n).   ¿Te gusta(n) más... o...?

Me gusta(n) más...   Me da igual.

Talking about what you and others like to do
Ch. 3, pp. 94–95

A mis amigos y a mí   ¿A... les gusta...?

nos gusta...   A mí me gusta...

¿Qué te gusta hacer?   Sí, porque les gusta...

Asking for and giving opinions
Ch. 8, p. 133

¿Qué te parece el (la)...?

Me parece... y cuesta mucho. ¡Es un robo!

¿Cómo me queda el (la)...?

Te queda muy bien. Y está a la (última) moda.

¿Y el (la)...? Cuesta... dólares.

¡Qué caro(a)! Además, está pasado(a) de moda.

El (La)... es una ganga, ¿verdad?

Tienes razón. Es muy barato(a).

Expressing hopes and wishes
Ch. 10, p. 242

Algún día me gustaría... Espero ver...

Si tengo suerte, voy a...   Quiero conocer...

Expressing Feelings and Emotions

Talking about how you feel
Ch. 7, p. 101

Para cuidarte la salud, debes...

Te veo mal.

Es que estoy enfermo(a). Tengo catarro.

¿Qué te pasa? ¿Te duele algo?

Me siento (un poco)... y me duele(n)...

¿Qué tiene...?

Le duele(n)...

Persuading

Taking someone's order and requesting something
Ch. 6, p. 44

¿Qué desea (usted)?   ¿Desea algo de postre?

Quisiera...   Sí, ¿me trae...?

¿Y para tomar?   ¿Algo más?

Para tomar, quiero...   ¿Nos trae..., por favor?

Offering help and giving instructions
Ch. 6, p. 58

¿Necesitas ayuda?

Sí, saca... y ponlo(la) en el horno/ el microondas.

¿Puedo ayudar?

Saca... del refrigerador.

¿Por qué no preparas...?

¿Pongo la mesa?

Sí, ponla, por favor.

Giving advice
Ch. 7, p. 104

¿Sabes qué? Comes muy mal. No debes comer tanto dulce ni grasa.

Para cuidarte mejor, debes... ¿Por qué no... más temprano?

No debes...

Síntesis gramatical

NOUNS AND ARTICLES

Gender of Nouns

In Spanish, nouns (words that name a person, place, or thing) are grouped into two classes or genders: masculine and feminine. All nouns, both persons and objects, fall into one of these groups. Most nouns that end in **-o** are masculine, and most nouns that end in **-a, -ción, -tad,** and **-dad** are feminine. Some nouns, such as **estudiante** and **cliente,** can be either masculine or feminine.

Masculine Nouns	Feminine Nouns
libro	casa
chico	universidad
cuaderno	situación
bolígrafo	mesa
vestido	libertad

FORMATION OF PLURAL NOUNS

	Add **-s** to nouns that end in a vowel.		Add **-es** to nouns that end in a consonant.		With nouns that end in **-z,** the **-z** changes to a **-c.**	
SINGULAR	libro	casa	profesor	papel	vez	lápiz
PLURAL	libro**s**	casa**s**	profesor**es**	papel**es**	ve**ces**	lápi**ces**

Definite Articles

There are words that signal the gender of the noun. One of these is the *definite article.* In English, there is one definite article: *the.* In Spanish, there are four: **el, la, los, las.**

SUMMARY OF DEFINITE ARTICLES

	Masculine	Feminine
SINGULAR	**el** chico	**la** chica
PLURAL	**los** chicos	**las** chicas

CONTRACTIONS

a + el → **al**
de + el → **del**

Indefinite Articles

Another group of words that are used with nouns is the *indefinite article:* **un, una,** (*a* or *an*) and **unos, unas** (*some* or *a few*).

	Masculine	Feminine
SINGULAR	**un** chico	**una** chica
PLURAL	**unos** chicos	**unas** chicas

Pronouns

	Subject Pronouns	Direct Object Pronouns	Indirect Object Pronouns	Objects of Prepositions	Reflexive Pronouns
	yo	me	me	mí	me
	tú	te	te	ti	te
	él, ella, usted	lo, la	le	él, ella, usted	se
	nosotros, nosotras	nos	nos	nosotros, nosotras	nos
	vosotros, vosotras	os	os	vosotros, vosotras	os
	ellos, ellas, ustedes	los, las	les	ellos, ellas, ustedes	se

ADJECTIVES

Adjectives are words that describe nouns. The adjective must agree in gender (masculine or feminine) and number (singular or plural) with the noun it modifies. Adjectives that end in -**e** or a consonant only agree in number.

		Masculine	Feminine
Adjectives that end in **-o** or **-a**	SINGULAR	chico alt**o**	chica alt**a**
	PLURAL	chicos alt**os**	chicas alt**as**
Adjectives that end in **-e**	SINGULAR	chico inteligent**e**	chica inteligent**e**
	PLURAL	chicos inteligent**es**	chicas inteligent**es**
Adjectives that end in a consonant	SINGULAR	examen difícil	clase difícil
	PLURAL	exámenes difícil**es**	clases difícil**es**

Demonstrative Adjectives

	Masculine	Feminine		Masculine	Feminine
SINGULAR	**este** chico	**esta** chica	SINGULAR	**ese** chico	**esa** chica
PLURAL	**estos** chicos	**estas** chicas	PLURAL	**esos** chicos	**esas** chicas

When demonstratives are used as pronouns, they match the gender and number of the noun they replace and are written with an accent mark: **éste, éstos, ésta, éstas, ése, ésos, ésa, ésas**.

Possessive Adjectives

These words also modify nouns and tell you *whose* object or person is being referred to (*my* car, *his* book, *her* mother).

Singular		Plural	
Masculine	Feminine	Masculine	Feminine
mi libro	**mi** casa	**mis** libros	**mis** casas
tu libro	**tu** casa	**tus** libros	**tus** casas
su libro	**su** casa	**sus** libros	**sus** casas
nuestro libro	**nuestra** casa	**nuestros** libros	**nuestras** casas
vuestro libro	**vuestra** casa	**vuestros** libros	**vuestras** casas

Comparatives

Comparatives are used to compare people or things. With comparisons of inequality, the same structure is used with adjectives, adverbs, or nouns. With comparisons of equality, **tan** is used with adjectives and adverbs, and **tanto/a/os/as** with nouns.

COMPARATIVE OF INEQUALITY

$$\left.\begin{array}{l}\textbf{más}\\\textbf{menos}\end{array}\right\} + \left\{\begin{array}{l}\text{adjective}\\\text{adverb}\\\text{noun}\end{array}\right\}\ \textbf{que}\quad \left.\begin{array}{l}\textbf{más}\\\textbf{menos}\end{array}\right\} + \textbf{de} + \text{number}$$

COMPARATIVE OF EQUALITY

tan + adjective or adverb + **como**
tanto/a/os/as + noun + **como**

These adjectives have irregular comparative forms.

bueno(a) *good*	malo(a) *bad*	joven *young*	viejo(a) *old*
mejor(es) *better*	**peor(es)** *worse*	**menor(es)** *younger*	**mayor(es)** *older*

Ordinal Numbers

Ordinal numbers are used to express ordered sequences. They agree in number and gender with the noun they modify. The ordinal numbers **primero** and **tercero** drop the final **o** before a singular, masculine noun. Ordinal numbers are seldom used after 10. Cardinal numbers are used instead: **Alfonso XIII, Alfonso Trece.**

1st	**primero/a**	5th	**quinto/a**	9th	**noveno/a**
2nd	**segundo/a**	6th	**sexto/a**	10th	**décimo/a**
3rd	**tercero/a**	7th	**séptimo/a**		
4th	**cuarto/a**	8th	**octavo/a**		

Affirmative and Negative Expressions

Affirmative	Negative
algo	nada
alguien	nadie
alguno (algún), -a	ninguno (ningún), -a
o ... o	ni ... ni
siempre	nunca

Interrogative words

¿Adónde?	**¿Cuándo?**	**¿De dónde?**	**¿Qué?**
¿Cómo?	**¿Cuánto(a)?**	**¿Dónde?**	**¿Quién(es)?**
¿Cuál(es)?	**¿Cuántos(as)?**	**¿Por qué?**	

Adverbs

Adverbs make the meaning of a verb, an adjective, or another adverb more definite. These are some common adverbs of frequency.

siempre	*always*	**casi nunca**	*almost never*
nunca	*never*	**a veces**	*sometimes*
todos los días	*every day*		

Prepositions

Prepositions are words that show the relationship of a noun or pronoun to another word. These are common prepositions in Spanish.

a	*to*	**delante**	*before*	**hasta**	*until*
al lado	*next to*	**desde**	*from*	**para**	*for, in order to*
arriba	*over, above*	**detrás**	*behind*	**por**	*for, by*
con	*with*	**en**	*in, on*	**sin**	*without*
de	*of, from*	**encima**	*over, on top of*		
debajo	*under*	**hacia**	*toward*		

VERBS

Present of Regular Verbs

In Spanish, we use a formula to conjugate regular verbs. The endings change in each person, but the stem of the verb remains the same.

Infinitive	habl**ar**		com**er**		escrib**ir**	
Present	habl**o**	habl**amos**	com**o**	com**emos**	escrib**o**	escrib**imos**
	habl**as**	habl**áis**	com**es**	com**éis**	escrib**es**	escrib**ís**
	habl**a**	habl**an**	com**e**	com**en**	escrib**e**	escrib**en**

Verbs with Irregular *yo* Forms

hacer		poner		saber		salir		traer	
hago	hacemos	**pongo**	ponemos	**sé**	sabemos	**salgo**	salimos	**traigo**	traemos
haces	hacéis	pones	ponéis	sabes	sabéis	sales	salís	traes	traéis
hace	hacen	pone	ponen	sabe	saben	sale	salen	trae	traen

tener		venir		ver		conocer	
tengo	tenemos	**vengo**	venimos	**veo**	vemos	**conozco**	conocemos
tienes	tenéis	vienes	venís	ves	véis	conoces	conocéis
tiene	tienen	viene	vienen	ve	ven	conoce	conocen

Verbs with Irregular Forms

ser		estar		ir	
soy	somos	estoy	estamos	voy	vamos
eres	sois	estás	estáis	vas	vais
es	son	está	están	va	van

Present Progressive

The present progressive in English is formed by using the verb *to be* plus the *-ing* form of another verb. In Spanish, the present progressive is formed by using the verb **estar** plus the -**ndo** form of another verb.

-**ar** verbs	-**er** and -**ir** verbs
hablar → estoy habl**ando**	comer → está com**iendo**
trabajar → estás trabaj**ando**	escribir → estamos escrib**iendo**

For -**er** and -**ir** verbs with a stem that ends in a vowel, the -**iendo** changes to -**yendo:**

leer → están le**yendo**

Stem-Changing Verbs

In Spanish, some verbs have an irregular stem in the present tense. The final vowel of the stem changes from **e → ie, o → ue, u → ue,** and **e → i** in all forms except **nosotros** and **vosotros.**

e → ie		o → ue		u → ue		e → i	
preferir		**poder**		**jugar**		**pedir**	
pref**ie**ro	preferimos	p**ue**do	podemos	j**ue**go	jugamos	p**i**do	pedimos
pref**ie**res	preferís	p**ue**des	podéis	j**ue**gas	jugáis	p**i**des	pedís
pref**ie**re	pref**ie**ren	p**ue**de	p**ue**den	j**ue**ga	j**ue**gan	p**i**de	p**i**den

Some **e → ie** stem-changing verbs are:		Some **o → ue** stem-changing verbs are:		Some **e → i** stem-changing verbs are:
empezar	**venir**	**almorzar**	**dormir**	**vestirse**
pensar	**merendar**	**llover**	**probar**	**servir**
querer	**calentar**	**encontrar**	**acostarse**	
nevar	**tener**	**volver**	**costar**	

The Verbs *gustar* and *encantar*

The verb endings for **gustar** and **encantar** always agree with what is liked or loved. The indirect object pronouns always precede the verb forms.

gustar (to like)		encantar (to really like or love)	
one thing: **me** **te** **le** **nos** **os** **les** } gusta	more than one: **me** **te** **le** **nos** **os** **les** } gustan	one thing: **me** **te** **le** **nos** **os** **les** } encanta	more than one: **me** **te** **le** **nos** **os** **les** } encantan

Verbs with Reflexive Pronouns

If the subject and object of a verb are the same, include the reflexive pronoun with the verb.

lavarse		ponerse		vestirse	
me lavo	nos lavamos	me pongo	nos ponemos	me visto	nos vestimos
te lavas	os laváis	te pones	os ponéis	te vistes	os vestís
se lava	se lavan	se pone	se ponen	se viste	se visten

Here are other verbs with reflexive pronouns.

acostarse	bañarse	maquillarse	secarse
afeitarse	levantarse	peinarse	sentirse

Preterite of Regular and Irregular Verbs

The preterite is used to talk about what happened at a specific point in time.

Infinitive	Preterite of Regular Verbs	
hablar	hablé	hablamos
	hablaste	hablasteis
	habló	hablaron
comer	comí	comimos
	comiste	comisteis
	comió	comieron
escribir	escribí	escribimos
	escribiste	escribisteis
	escribió	escribieron

hacer	ir	ser	ver
hice	fui	fui	vi
hiciste	fuiste	fuiste	viste
hizo	fue	fue	vio
hicimos	fuimos	fuimos	vimos
hicisteis	fuisteis	fuisteis	visteis
hicieron	fueron	fueron	vieron

sacar	llegar	comenzar
saqué	llegué	comencé
sacaste	llegaste	comenzaste
sacó	llegó	comenzó
sacamos	llegamos	comenzamos
sacasteis	llegasteis	comenzasteis
sacaron	llegaron	comenzaron

Imperative Mood

The imperative is used to tell people to do things. Its forms are sometimes referred to as *commands*. Regular affirmative commands are formed by dropping the **s** from the end of the **tú** form of the verb. For negative commands, switch the **-as** ending to **-es** and the **-es** ending to **-as**.

(tú) hablas → habla (no hables)	you speak → speak (don't speak)
(tú) escribes → escribe (no escribas)	you write → write (don't write)
(tú) pides → pide (no pidas)	you ask for → ask for (don't ask for)

Some verbs have irregular **tú** imperative forms.

tener → ten (no tengas)	ser → sé (no seas)
venir → ven (no vengas)	hacer → haz (no hagas)
poner → pon (no pongas)	salir → sal (no salgas)
ir → ve (no vayas)	decir → di (no digas)

The Verbs *ser* and *estar*

Both **ser** and **estar** mean *to be*, but they differ in their uses.

Use **ser:**
1. with nouns to identify and define the subject
   La mejor estudiante de la clase es Katia.
2. with **de** to indicate place of origin, ownership, or material
   Carmen es de Venezuela.
   Este libro es de mi abuela.
   La blusa es de algodón.
3. to describe identifying characteristics, such as physical and personality traits, nationality, religion, and profession
   Mi tío es profesor. Es simpático e inteligente.
4. to express the time, date, season and where an event is taking place
   Hoy es sábado y la fiesta es a las ocho.

Use **estar:**
1. to indicate location or position of the subject
   Lima está en Perú.
2. to describe a condition that is subject to change
   Maricarmen está triste.
3. with the present participle (**-ndo** form) to describe an action in progress
   Mario está escribiendo un poema.
4. to convey the idea of *to look, to feel, to seem, to taste*
   Tu hermano está muy guapo hoy.
   La sopa está deliciosa.

Common Expressions

EXPRESSIONS WITH *TENER*

tener ... años	to be . . . years old	tener (mucha) prisa	to be in a (big) hurry
tener mucho calor	to be very hot	tener que	to have to
tener ganas de...	to feel like . . .	tener (la) razón	to be right
tener mucho frío	to be very cold	tener mucha sed	to be very thirsty
tener mucha hambre	to be very hungry	tener mucho sueño	to be very sleepy
tener mucho miedo	to be very afraid	tener mucha suerte	to be very lucky

EXPRESSIONS OF TIME

To ask how long someone has been doing something, use:
¿Cuánto tiempo hace que + present tense?

To say how long someone has been doing something, use:
Hace + quantity of time + **que** + present tense.
Hace **seis meses** que **vivo en Los Ángeles.**
You can also use:
present tense + **desde hace** + quantity of time
Vivo en Los Ángeles desde hace **seis meses.**

WEATHER EXPRESSIONS

Hace muy buen tiempo.	The weather is very nice.
Hace mucho calor.	It's very hot.
Hace fresco.	It's cool.
Hace mucho frío.	It's very cold.
Hace muy mal tiempo.	The weather is very bad.
Hace mucho sol.	It's very sunny.
Hace mucho viento.	It's very windy.
But:	
Está lloviendo mucho.	It's raining a lot.
Hay mucha neblina.	It's very foggy.
Está nevando.	It's snowing.
Está nublado.	It's overcast.

Vocabulario español-inglés

This vocabulary includes almost all words in the textbook, both active (for production) and passive (for recognition only). An entry in **boldface** type indicates that the word or phrase is active. Active words and phrases are practiced in the chapter and are listed on the **Repaso de gramática** and **Repaso de vocabulario** pages at the end of each chapter. You are expected to know and be able to use active vocabulary.

All other words are for recognition only. These words are found in exercises, in optional and visual material, in **Instrucciones** on pages xviii–xix, in **Geocultura,** which is referenced by chapter (1G), **Comparaciones, Leamos y escribamos, También se puede decir,** and **Literatura y variedades.** You can usually understand the meaning of these words and phrases from the context or you can look them up in this vocabulary index. Many words have more than one definition; the definitions given here correspond to the way the words are used in *¡Exprésate!.*

Nouns are listed with definite articles and plural forms when the plural forms aren't formed according to general rules. The number after each entry refers to the chapter where the word or phrase first appears or where it becomes an active vocabulary word. This vocabulary index follows the rules of the **Real Academia,** with **ch** and **ll** in the same sequence as in the English alphabet.

Stem changes are indicated in parentheses after the verb: **poder (ue).**

a *to,* 3; *on,* 4; *at,* 8; a base de *based on,* 6; a continuación *that follows,* 7; a finales *at the end,* 10G; **a la (última) moda** *in the (latest) style,* 8; a la vez *at the same time,* 8; **a la vuelta** *around the corner,* 10; **A ...les gusta...** *They like to . . . ,* 3; **a menudo** *often,* 5; **¿A qué hora vas a...?** *What time are you going to . . . ?,* 4; **a tiempo** *on time,* 4; **a todo dar** *great,* 9; **Estuvo a todo dar.** *It was great.,* 9; a través de *through,* 5G; **a veces** *sometimes,* 3
abordar *to board,* 10
abrazar *to hug,* 9
el abrazo *hug,* 9
el abrigo (over) *coat,* 8
abril *April,* 1
abrir *to open,* 4; **abrir regalos** *to open gifts,* 9
la abuela *grandmother,* 5
el abuelo *grandfather,* 5
los abuelos *grandparents,* 5
aburrido(a) *boring,* 2; **estar aburrido(a)** *to be bored,* 7
acabar de *to just (have done something),* 7
acampar *to camp,* 3
acariciar *to caress,* 7

la acción *action,* 2
el aceite de oliva *olive oil,* 1G
el acento *accent,* 1; el acento ortográfico *written accent,* 8
acerca de *about,* 8
acompañar *to go with,* 6; *to accompany,* 1G; estar a acompañar *to be accompanied,* 3
acordarse (ue) *to remember,* 9
acostarse (ue) *to go to bed,* 7
la actividad *activity,* 3
activo(a) *active,* 2
la actualidad *present time,* 6
el acuerdo *agreement;* **Estoy de acuerdo.** *I agree.,* 6; **No estoy de acuerdo.** *I disagree.,* 6
adaptado(a) *adapted,* 5G
además *besides,* 8
Adiós. *Good-bye.,* 1
adivinar *to guess,* 2
el **adjetivo** *adjective,* 5
la admiración *admiration,* 1
admirar *to admire,* 10
el adolescente *adolescent,* 3
¿adónde? *where?,* 8; **Adónde fuiste?** *Where did you go?,* 8; **¿Adónde vas...?** *Where do you go . . . ?,* 3
la aduana *customs,* 10
el adulto *adult,* 7
los aeróbicos *aerobics,* 7; hacer aeróbicos *to do aerobics,* 7
el aeropuerto *airport,* 10
afeitarse *to shave,* 7
afuera *outside,* 3

las afueras *suburbs,* 5
la agencia inmobiliaria *real estate agency,* 5
el agente, la agente *agent,* 10
agitar *to shake,* 3
agosto *August,* 1
el agua *water,* 6
el águila *eagle,* 7
ahí *there,* 4
ahora *now,* 9
ahorrar *to save money,* 8
el aire *air,* 3; el aire central *central air conditioning,* 5; el aire libre *open air,* 8
el ajedrez *chess,* 1
el ají *hot pepper,* 10G
el ajo *garlic,* 6
ajustado(a) *tight-fitting,* 8
al (a + el) *to, to the,* 3; *upon,* 6; al fin *finally,* 10; **al lado de** *next to,* 5
la alberca *swimming pool,* 3
alcanzar *to reach,* 7G
la alcoba *bedroom,* 5
alegre *happy,* 2
el alemán *German,* 4
el alfabeto *alphabet,* 1
algo *something, anything,* 4; **algo +** adjective *kind of +* adjective, 2
el algodón *cotton,* 8; **de algodón** *made of cotton,* 8
algún día *some day,* 10
algunas *some,* 2
el alimento *food,* 6
alistarse *to get ready,* 7

el allá   *there*, 8
allí   *there*, 10
el almacén   *department store*, 8
el almanaque   *almanac*, 1G
almorzar   *to have lunch*, 6
el almuerzo   *lunch*, 4
Aló   *Hello. (telephone greeting)*, 8
el alpinismo   *mountain climbing*, 7
alquilar   *to rent*, 3; **alquilar videos**
   to rent videos, 3
alrededor   *around*, 6
el altiplano   *high plateau*, 10G
alto(a)   *tall*, 2
la altura   *height*, 6G
amanecer   *to dawn*, 9
el amarillo   *yellow*, 1G
amarillo(a)   *yellow*, 8
el ambiente   *atmosphere*, 5G
amigable   *friendly*, 2
el amigo(a)   *friend*, 1; **mi mejor**
   amigo(a)   *my best friend*, 1
el amor   *love*, 8; **de amor**   *romance*, 2
amueblado(a)   *furnished*, 5
analítico(a)   *analytical*, 2
anaranjado(a)   *orange*, 8
ancho   *width*, 5G; *wide*, 8
andar   *to walk, to go*, 2; andar en
   bicicleta   *to ride a bike*, 3; dime
   con quien andas y te diré quien
   eres   *a person is known by the
   company he/she keeps*, 2
andino(a)   *of the Andes*, 7G
el anfibio   *amphibian*, 2G
la anguila   *eel*, 7
el ángulo   *angle*, 7
el anillo   *ring*, 8
el animal   *animal*, 2
el aniversario   *anniversary*, 9
el año   *year*, 2; **el Año Nuevo**   *New
   Year*, 9; **el año pasado**   *last year*, 9;
   ¿Cuántos años tiene... ?   *How old
   is . . .?*, 2; **¿Cuántos años tienes?**
   How old are you?, 2
anoche   *last night*, 9
anteayer   *day before yesterday*, 8
anterior   *previous*, 9
antes   *before*, 1; **antes de**   *before*, 7;
   de antes   *from before*, 4
antiguo(a)   *old*, 6G
antipático(a)   *unfriendly*, 2
añadir   *to add*, 6
aparecer   *to appear*, 6
el apartamento   *apartment*, 5
apasionado(a)   *passionate*, 2
apellido   *last name*, 2
apetecer   *to appeal*, 6
aplicar   *to apply*, 2
aprender   *to learn*, 1
apropiado(a)   *appropriate*, 7
aproximadamente   *approximately*, 2
los apuntes   *notes*, 8
aquella   *that*, 6
aquello   *that*, 4

aquí   *here*, 6
árabe   *Arab*, 5G
el árbol   *tree*, 1; la copa del árbol   *top
   of the tree*, 4G
los aretes   *earrings*, 8
la argamasa   *mortar*, 10G
argentino(a)   *Argentine*, 7
árido(a)   *dry*, 10G
la armonía   *harmony*, 2
armonizar   *to harmonize*, 7G
el arquitecto   *architect*, 3G
arquitectónico(a)   *architectural*,
   10G
la arquitectura   *architecture*, 2G
arreglar   *to clean up*, 5; **arreglar el**
   cuarto   *to clean the room*, 5
el arrendamiento   *rental*, 10
la arroba   *@*, 1
el arroz   *rice*, 6
el arte   *art*, 4; las artes plásticas
   sculpture, 2
la artesanía   *crafts*, 4
el artista, la artista   *artist*, 1
artístico(a)   *artistic*, 2
asegurar   *to reassure*, 6
el aseo   *restroom*, 10
así   *like this*; así que   *so*, 8; Así es,
   That's how it is., 2
asistente   *assistant*, 10
asistir a   *to attend*, 4
asomar   *to peak out*, 9
el asterisco   *asterisk*, 7
atlético(a)   *athletic*, 2
el atole   *Mexican drink made of
   cornmeal, milk or water, and
   flavoring*, 6
atraer   *to attract*, 1G
atravesar   *to cross*, 10G
atreverse   *to dare*, 9
el atún   *tuna fish*, 6
los audífonos   *earphones*, 8
el auditorio   *auditorium*, 4
aun   *even*, 2
aún   *still*, 10
aunque   *even though*, 6
el autobús   *bus*, 10
el autor   *author*, 7
el autorretrato   *self-portrait*, 6G
avanzado(a)   *advanced*, 10G
el ave (pl. las aves)   *bird*, 4G
la aventura   *adventure*, 2
averiguar   *to find out*, 10
el avión   *airplane*, 10; por avión   *by
   plane*, 10
¡Ay no!   *Oh, no!*, 6
¡ay!   *ouch*, 8
ayer   *yesterday*, 8
el aymara   *indigenous language in
   Peru*, 10G
la ayuda   *help*, 6
ayudar   *to help*, 5; **ayudar en casa**
   to help at home, 5; estamos
   ayudando   *we are helping*, 3

el azúcar   *sugar*, 6
el azul   *blue*, 1G
azul   *blue*, 5

la bahía   *bay*, 8G
bailar   *to dance*, 3; bailando
   dancing, 1; ponerse a bailar   *to
   start dancing*, 3
la bailarina   *dancer (fem.)*, 3
el baile   *dance*, 3
bajar   *to descend*, 7; **bajar de peso**
   to lose weight, 7
bajo(a)   *short*, 2
balanceado(a)   *balanced*, 6
el balcón   *balcony*, 5
balear   *to shoot*, 5
el ballet   *ballet*, 1
el baloncesto   *basketball*, 3
bañarse   *to bathe*, 7
la bandeja   *platter*, 7G
la bandera   *banner*, 9
el bandido   *bandit*, 5
el baño   *bathroom*, 5; *restroom*, 10
barato(a)   *inexpensive*, 8
la barbacoa   *barbecue*, 3G
el barco   *boat*, 10; el barquito   *little
   boat*, 5
la barranca   *cliff*, 6G
el barrio   *neighborhood*, 7G
básico(a)   *basic*, 6
el básquetbol   *basketball*, 3
basta   *it's enough*, 5
bastante + adjective   *rather* (quite)
   + adjective, 2
la basura   *trash*, 5; **sacar la basura**   *to
   take out the trash*, 5
la batalla   *battle*, 3G
el batido   *milkshake*, 8
el bebé, la bebé   *baby*, 1
beber   *to drink*, 4; **beber ponche**   *to
   drink something*, 9
la bebida   *drink*, 6
la beca   *scholarship*, 10
el béisbol   *baseball*, 3
bello(a)   *beautiful*, 2G
la biblioteca   *library*, 4
la bicicleta   *bike*, 3; **montar en**
   bicicleta   *to ride a bike*, 3
bien   *all right, fine*, 1; *really*, 2; bien
   dicho   *well said*, 6; **está bien**   *it's
   okay*, 3; **estoy bien**   *I'm fine*, 1; **me**
   parece bien   *it's all right/seems
   fine to me*, 5; **quedar bien**   *to fit
   well*, 8; **Que te vaya bien.**   *Hope
   things go well for you.*, 9
el billete   *ticket*, 10

Vocabulario español-inglés

la **billetera** *wallet*, 10
la **biología** *biology*, 4
blanco(a) *white*, 8; **en blanco** *blank*, 8
el **blanquillo** *egg*, 6
la **blusa** *blouse*, 8
la **boca** *mouth*, 7
el **bocadillo** *sandwich (Spain)*, 6, *finger food (Dom. Rep.)*, 9
el **bocadito** *small servings of food*, 7G
las **bocas** *finger food (Costa Rica)*, 9
la **boda** *wedding*, 9
la **boleta** *ticket*, 10
el **boleto de avión** *plane ticket*, 10
el **bolígrafo** *pen*, 4
la **bolsa** *purse*, 8; *bag*, 8; *travel bag*, 10
la **bomba** *music and dance style*, 2G
la **bombilla** *straw used for sipping mate*, 7
bonito(a) *pretty*, 2
el **borde** *edge*, 7G
el **borrador** *rough draft*, 1
el **bosque** *forest*, 2G; el **bosque húmedo** *rain forest*, 4G
la **botana** *finger food (Mex.)*, 9
botar *to throw out*, 5
las **botas** *boots*, 8
el **bote** *boat*, 9G; **el bote de vela** *sailboat*, 10; **pasear en bote de vela** *to go out in a sailboat*, 10
el **brazo** *arm*, 7
brillar *to shine*, 7
brindar *to offer*, 5
el **brócoli** *broccoli*, 6
bueno(a) *good*, 2; **Buenas noches.** *Good evening., Good night.*, 1; **Buenas tardes.** *Good afternoon.*, 1; **Buenos días.** *Good morning.*, 1
Bueno. *Hello. (telephone greeting)*, 8
burlarse de *to make fun of*, 8
el **burro** *donkey*, 1
buscar *to look for*, 7; **buscar un pasatiempo** *to look for a hobby*, 7; **búsquenme** *look for me*, 3

el **caballo de paso** *horse with high-stepping gait*, 10G
caber *to fit*, 10G
la **cabeza** *head*, 7
el **cacao** *cocoa*, 6G
cada *each*, xxii; **cada uno(a)** *each one*, 6; **cada vez** *each time*, 8
el **café** *coffee*, 6; **el café con leche** *coffee with milk*, 6; *brown*, 1G; **de color café** *brown*, 5

la **cafetería** *cafeteria*, 4; *coffee shop*, 6
la **caída de agua** *waterfall*, 7G
el **caimán** *caiman (reptile)*, 8G
la **caja** *box*, 9
el **cajero automático** *automatic teller machine*, 10
la **calabaza** *squash, pumpkin*, 6G; la **calabacita** *gourd used for mate tea*, 7G
los **calcetines** *socks*, 8; **un par de calcetines** *a pair of socks*, 8
la **calculadora** *calculator*, 4
la **calefacción** *heating*, 5; la **calefacción central** *central heating*, 5
el **calendario** *calendar*, 1
calentar (ie) *to heat*, 6
caliente *hot*, 6
callado(a) *quiet*, 5
la **calle** *street*, 2G
el **calor** *heat*, 3; **Hace calor.** *It's hot.*, 3; **tener calor** *to be hot*, 7
la **caloría** *calorie*, 6
la **cama** *bed*, 5; **hacer la cama** *to make the bed*, 5
la **cámara** *camera*, 10; la **cámara desechable** *disposable camera*, 10
el **camarero** *waiter*, 6
cambiar *to change*, 4
el **cambio** *change*, 9
caminar *to walk*, 7
el **camino** *path*, 10G
el **camión** *bus (Mex.)*, 10
la **camisa** *shirt*, 8
la **camiseta** *T-shirt*, 8; la **camiseta deportiva** *sport shirt*, 8
el **camote** *sweet potato*, 4G
el **campo** *countryside*, 5
la **canción** *song*, 8
candidato(a) *candidate*, 4
la **canoa** *canoe*, 10
el **cañón** *canyon*, 6G
canoso(a) *graying*, 5
cansado(a) *tired*, 7; **estar cansado(a)** *to be tired*, 7
cantar *to sing*, 3; **cantaba** *he sang*, 9
el **cantar** *singing*, 2
la **cantidad** *amount*, 2; *quantity*, 6; las **cantidades** *large numbers*, 6
el **canto** *song*, 1G
la **capilla** *chapel*, 3G
la **capital** *capital*, 1G
el **capítulo** *chapter*, 1
la **cara** *face*, 7; **cara de tortilla** *tortilla face*, 1
el **carácter** *character*, 5
la **característica** *characteristic*, 6
caracterizar *to characterize*, 5G
la **cárcel** *jail*, 8
caribeño(a) *Caribbean*, 4G
el **cariño** *affection; (addressing someone) dear*, 3; **con cariño**

affectionately, 10
la **carne** *meat, beef*, 6; la **carne de res** *beef*, 6; la **carne molida** *ground beef*, 6
el **carnet de identidad** *ID*, 10
caro(a) *expensive*, 8
la **carpeta** *folder*, 4
la **carreta** *cart*, 4G
el **carro** *car*, 2
la **carroza** *float*, 9G
la **carta** *letter*, 3
la **casa** *house*, 5; **ayudar en casa** *to help at home*, 5; **la casa de...** *...'s house*, 3; **decorar la casa** *to decorate the house*, 9
el **casabe** *flat, dry bread made from manioc*, 9G
casarse *to get married*, 10
la **cascada** *waterfall*, 2G
la **cáscara** *shell*, 2G
casi *almost*, 3, **casi nunca** *almost never*, 3, **casi siempre** *almost always*, 3
el **caso** *case*, 2
castaño(a) *brown*, 5
las **castañuelas** *castanets*, 1G
el **castellano** *Spanish*, 1G
el **castillo** *castle*, 2G
el **catalán** *language from Catalonia, Spain*, 1G
el **catálogo** *catalog*, 8
la **catarata** *cataract, waterfall*, 7G
la **catedral** *cathedral*, 1G
catorce *fourteen*, 1
el **cayo** *key*, 8G
el **cazador** *hunter*, 7G
la **cebolla** *onion*, 10G
celebérrimo(a) *most famous*, 8
la **celebración** *celebration*, 1
celebrar *to celebrate*, 9; **celebrará** *will celebrate*, 8; **se celebra** *is celebrated*, 2G
célebre *famous*, 8
celeridad *speed*, 8
celta *Celtic*, 1G
la **cena** *dinner*, 6
cenar *to eat dinner*, 6
el **centro** *downtown*, 10; *center*, 3G
el **centro comercial** *mall*, 3
el **cepillo de dientes** *toothbrush*, 7
la **cerámica** *pottery*, 4
cerca de *close to, near*, 5
cercano(a) *close*, 5
los **cereales** *cereal*, 6
el **cerebelo** *cerebellum*, 8
el **cerebro** *brain*, 8
la **ceremonia** *ceremony*, 6
cero *zero*, 1
cerrado(a) *closed*, 1
cerrar (ie) *to close*, 8
el **césped** *grass*, 5
la **cesta de paja** *straw basket*, 8G
el **ceviche** *dish made with seafood*,

lemon, and seasonings, 10G
chao *Bye,* 9
la chaqueta *jacket,* 8
charlar *to talk, to chat,* 9
el chayote *type of squash,* 4G
la chica *girl,* 8
chicano(a) *Mexican that has emigrated to the United States,* 3G
el chile *pepper,* chile en nogada *peppers in walnut and spice sauce,* 6
el chileno *Chilean,* 5
la chimenea *fireplace,* 5
el chiste *joke,* 9
el choclo *corn on the cob,* 5G
el chocolate *chocolate,* 6; *hot chocolate,* 6
el churro *sugar-coated fritter,* 6
el ciclismo *cycling,* 1
ciego(a) *blind,* 5
el cielo *heaven,* 3
cien *one hundred,* 2
la ciencia ficción *science fiction,* 2
las ciencias *science,* 4; **...de ciencias** *science . . .,*1
el científico *scientist,* 6
ciento un(o) *one hundred one,* 8
cierto(a) *true,* xxii
la cifra *number,* 8
la cima *mountain top,* 7G
cinco *five,* 1
cincuenta *fifty,* 2
el cine *movie theater,* 3
el cinturón *belt,* 8
el círculo *circle,* 3
el citrón *lemon,* 6
la ciudad *city,* 5
¡Claro que sí! *Of course.,* 4
claro(a) *clear,* 6G
la clase *class,* 3; **después de clases** *after class,* 3
clasificar *to classify,* 6
clavar *to nail,* 10
el clavo *nail,* 10
el cliente, la cliente *client,* 8
el club de... *the . . . club,* 4
el cobre *copper,* 6G
cocer *to cook,* 3
el coche *car,* 10
la cocina *kitchen,* 5; *cooking,* 3G
cocinar *to cook,* 5
el coco *coconut,* 2G
el cocodrilo *crocodile,* 8G
el código *code,* 2G
cohabitar *to live together,* 8G
la cola *line,* 10
el colectivo *bus* (Bol., Perú, Ecuador), 10
el colegio *school,* 3
colgar *to hang,* 9
la colina *hill,* 9G
la colonia *colony,* 7G
el colonizador *colonist,* 6G
el color *color,* 5

el colorido *coloring,* 7G
colorido(a) *colorful,* 4G
la columna *column,* xxii
los combates *battles,* 10
la combinación *combination,* 1
combinar *to combine,* 5G
el comedor *dining room,* 5
comenzar(ie) *to start,* 10; **comenzar un viaje** *to start a trip,* 10; comiencen *to begin,* 8
comer *to eat,* 3; se comen *are eaten,* 2G
el comercio *commerce,* 3G
el comestible *food,* 3
cómico(a) *funny,* 2
la comida *food,* 2, *lunch,* 6; **la comida china (italiana, mexicana)** *Chinese (Italian, Mexican) food,* 2; la comida típica *traditional food,* 6
como *like,* 2; *as,* 9; **como siempre** *as always,* 9
¿cómo? *how?, what?,* 1; **¿Cómo eres?** *What are you like?,* 2; **¿Cómo es...?** *What is . . . like?,* 2; **¿Cómo está(s)?** *How are you?,* 1; **¿Cómo se escribe...?** *How do you spell . . .?,* 1; **¿Cómo se llama?** *What's his (her/your) name?,* 1; **¿Cómo te llamas?** *What's your name? (fam.),* 1
la compañera de clase *classmate (female),* 1; **una compañera de clase** *a (female) classmate,* 1
el compañero de clase *classmate (male),* 1; **un compañero de clase** *a (male) classmate,* 1
la comparación *comparison,* 1
comparar *to compare,* 8
compasivo(a) *compassionate,* 6
el complemento directo *direct object,* 6
completar *to complete,* xxii
completo *complete,* 6; por completo *completely,* 6
comprar *to buy,* 8; comprarías *you would buy,* 8
las compras *shopping,* 2; estar de compras *to be on a shopping trip,* 8; **ir de compras** *to go shopping,* 3
la comprensión *comprehension,* 10
comprender *to understand,* 2; nos comprendemos *we understand each other,* 2
la computación *computer science,* 4
la computadora *computer,* 4
común *common,* 9
comunicar *to communicate,* 5
la comunidad *community,* 1
con *with,* 3; con base en *based on,* xxii; **con mis amigos** *with my friends,* 3; **con mi familia** *with my family,* 3; con motivo de *on the*

occasion of, 9; **¿Con qué frecuencia vas...?** *How often do you go . . .?,* 3; con relación a *in relation to,* 5
el concierto *concert,* 4
el concurso *competition,* 9G
el condominio *condominium,* 5
conectar *to connect,* 8G
confundido(a) *confused,* 4
confundir *to confuse,* 10
el conjunto *musical group,* 3G
conmemorar *commemorate,* 3G
conmigo *with me,* 3
conocer *to know (someone) or be familiar with a place,* 9; **conocimos...** *we visited . . .,* 10; **quiero conocer...** *I want to see . . .,* 10; se conoce *is known,* 2G
conocido(a) *known,* 2G
el conocimiento *knowledge,* 7
conquistar *to conquer,* 10
conseguir (i, i) *to get,* 10
el consejo *advice,* 7
conservar *to preserve,* 2G
considerar *to consider,* 2; *to regard,* 9
constituir *to make up,* 6
construir *to build,* 3G; construye *construct,* 10; fue construido *was built,* 3G
el consultorio médico *doctor's office,* 7
consumir *to consume,* 6; se consumen *are consumed,* 6
el consumo *consumption,* 6
contar *to count,* 1; *to tell,* 4; contando *counting,* 1; **contar chistes** *to tell jokes,* 9; contar con *to count on,* 10; cuenta *tells,* 6; cuentan *it is told,* 6
contemplar *to contemplate,* 9
contemporáneo *contemporary,* 1G
contener (ie) *to contain,* 10G; que contengan *that contain,* 10
contento(a) *happy,* 7; **estar contento(a)** *to be happy,* 7
contestar *to answer,* xxii
contigo *with you,* 3
el continente *continent,* 6
continuo *continual,* 8
contra *against,* 10
el contrario *contrary,* 6
la contribución *contribution,* 2G
contribuir *to contribute,* 8G
el control de seguridad *security checkpoint,* 10
controlar *to control,* 3G
el convento *convent,* 3G
la conversación *conversation,* xxii
convertirse *to become,* 10
el coquí *small tree frog,* 2G
el corazón *heart,* 7G
la cordillera *mountain range,* 2G
el coro *chorus,* 2
correcto(a) *right, correct,* xxii

corregir *to correct*, xxii

el correo electrónico *e-mail address*, 1; **¿Cuál es el correo electrónico de...?** *What is . . .'s e-mail address?*, 1; **¿Cuál es tu correo electrónico?** *What's your e-mail address?*, 1

correr *to run*, 3

la correspondencia *correspondence*, 1

corresponder *to correspond*, xxii; **le corresponde** *it falls to him*, 5; **que le correspondan** *that correspond to it*, 9

correspondiente *corresponding*, 8

la corriente *current*, 8

cortar *to cut*, 6; **cortar el césped** *to cut the grass*, 5

la Corte Suprema *Supreme Court*, 6

corto(a) *short*, 5

la cosa *thing*, 4; **necesito muchas cosas** *I need lots of things*, 4; **no es gran cosa** *it's not a big deal*, 5

coser *to sew*, 4

la costa *coast*, 3G

costar (ue) *to cost*, 8; **costará** *will cost*, 9

costeño(a) *coastal*, 10G

la costumbre *custom*, 5G

la creación *creation*, 3

crear *to create*, 7; **creado por** *created by*, 7G; **fue creado** *was created*, 3G

la creatividad *creativity*, 6G

creativo(a) *creative*, 2

crecer *to grow*, 9G; **crecí** *I grew up*, 3

creer *to believe*, 6; *to think*, 9

la crema *cream*, 6

la criatura *child*, 3

el cuaderno *notebook*, 4

la cuadra *block*, 5

cual: los cuales *which*, 10

el cuadro *box, chart*, xxii; *painting*, 1

¿cuál? *what?, which?*, 4; **¿Cuál es el correo electrónico de...?** *What is . . .'s e-mail address?*, 1; **¿Cuál es el teléfono de...?** *What's . . . telephone number?*, 1; **¿Cuál es tu correo electrónico?** *What's your e-mail address?*, 1; **¿Cuál es tu materia preferida?** *What's your favorite subject?*, 4; **¿Cuál es tu teléfono?** *What's your telephone number?*, 1

cualquier *any*, 10

cualquiera *whichever*, 6G

cuando *when*, 3

¿cuándo? *when?*, 2; **¿Cuándo es el cumpleaños de...?** *When is . . .'s birthday?*, 2; **¿Cuándo es tu cumpleaños?** *When is your birthday?*, 2

¿cuánto(a)? *how much?*, 4

¡cuántos! *so many!*, 4

¿cuántos(as) *How many . . .?*, 2; **¿Cuántos años tiene... ?** *How old is . . .?*, 2; **¿Cuántos años tienes?** *How old are you?*, 2

cuarenta *forty*, 2

cuarto *quarter*, 4; **menos cuarto** *a quarter to (the hour)*, 4; **y cuarto** *quarter past*, 1

el cuarto *room*, 5; **arreglar el cuarto** *to clean the room*, 5

cuatro *four*, 1

cuatrocientos *four hundred*, 8

cubierto(a) *covered*, 3

la cuchara *spoon*, 6

el cuchillo *knife*, 6

el cuello *neck*, 7

la cuenta *bill*, 6

el cuento *story*, 4

la cuerna *horn*, 2G

el cuerpo *body*, 7

el cuerpo de bomberos *fire department*, 2G

cuesta(n)... *cost(s) . . .*, 8

la cueva *cave*, 1G

el cuidado *care*, 1; **ten cuidado** *take care*, 6

cuidadosamente *carefully*, 9

cuidar *to take care of*, 5; **cuidar a mis hermanos** *take care of my brothers and sisters*, 5

cuidarse *to take care of oneself*, 7; **cuidarse la salud** *to take care of one's health*, 7; **para cuidarte la salud debes...** *to take care of your health, you should . . .*, 7; **Para cuidarte mejor, debes...** *To take better care of yourself, you should . . .*, 7; **Cuídate.** *Take care.*, 9

culinario(a) *culinary*, 6

cultivar *to cultivate*, 6

el cultivo *crop*, 4G

la cultura *culture*, 1

el cumpleaños *birthday*, 9; **¿Cuándo es el cumpleaños de...?** *When is . . .'s birthday?*, 2; **¿Cuándo es tu cumpleaños?** *When is your birthday?*, 2; **el cumpleaños de...** *birthday of . . .*, 2; **la tarjeta de cumpleaños** *birthday card*, 8

curioso(a) *odd, unusual*, 1

la curva *curve*, 3G

dado(a) *given*, 7

la danza *dance*, 1G

dar *to give*, 7; **le dan** *they give*, 7; **no des** *don't give*, 7; **se da** *is held*, 8G

darse cuenta *to realize*, 8

el dato *fact*, 10

de *of, from, in, by*, 1; *made of*, 8; **...de ciencias** *science . . .*, 1; **de color café** *brown*, 5; **¿De dónde eres?** *Where are you from? (fam.)*, 1; **¿De dónde es usted?** *Where are you from? (formal)*, 1; **¿De dónde es...?** *Where is . . . from?*, 1; **de...en...** *from . . . to . . .*, 8; **... de español** *Spanish . . .*, 1; **de la mañana** *in the morning*, 1; **de la noche** *at night*, 1; **de la tarde** *in the afternoon, evening*, 1; de nuevo *again*, 7; de nada *you're welcome*; **¿De parte de quién?** *Who's calling?*, 8; ¿de quién? *about whom?*, 1; de todo *everything*, 8; de todo tipo *all kinds*, 8; de todos modos *in any event*, 8; de veras *really*, 8

debajo *underneath*, 8; **debajo de** *underneath*, 5

deber *should*, 6; **¿Debo...?** *Should I . . .?*, 8; **No debes...** *You shouldn't . . .*, 7; se debe hacer *should be done*, 6

los deberes *chores*, 5; *responsibilities*, 5

debido a *due to*, 7G

el decibel *decibel*, 2

decidir *to decide*, xxii

decir *to say*, 3; bien dicho *well said*, 6; di *say*, 4; dice *says*, 3; diciéndome *telling me*, 9; me han dicho *they have told me*, 6; se dicen adiós *they say goodbye*, 3; si lo hubiera dicho *if I had said it*, 6; te diré *I'll tell you*, 2; yo he dicho *I have said*, 6

declarar *to declare*, 6

la decoración *decoration*, 9

decorar *to decorate*, 9; **decorar la casa** *to decorate the house*, 9

dedicado(a) a *dedicated to*, 2G

dedicar *to dedicate*, 4; es dedicada *is dedicated*, 5; dedicación *dedication*, 10; se dedica *is dedicated*, 2G

el dedo *finger*, 7; *toe*, 4G

deducir *to deduce*, 7

la definición *definition*, 10

definido(a) *defined*, 8

definitivamente *definitely*, 8; *permanently*, 9

dejar *to allow*, 3; *to leave*, 10; **dejar un recado** *to leave a message*, 8

dejar de + infinitive *to stop doing something*, 7; **dejar de fumar** *to stop smoking*, 7

del (de + el) *of the*, 2

delante de *in front of*, 5

delgado(a) *thin*, 5

delicioso(a) *delicious*, 2
demasiado(a) *too much*, 7
demostrar (ue) *to show*, 10G
dentro *inside*, 9
el departamento *apartment*, 5
el dependiente, la dependiente
   salesclerk, 8
los deportes *sports*, 2
deportivo(a) *(adj) sports*, 8
la derecha *right*, 1
el desarrollo *development*, 7G
el desastre *disaster*, 9
desayunar *to eat breakfast*, 6
el desayuno *breakfast*, 6
descansar *to rest*, 3
el descendiente *descendent*, 10
describir *to describe*, 5
descubrir *to discover*, 8; fue
   descubierto *was discovered*, 7G
desde *since*, 4; *from*, 10; ¿desde
   cuándo? *since when?*, 4; desde
   hace *since*, 6; desde joven *since*
   her youth, 8; desde luego *of*
   course, 7
desear *to want, to wish for, to desire*,
   6; deseando *wanting to*, 8
desembocar *to flow*, 10G
el deseo *desire*, 9
desesperado(a) *desperate*, 6
el desfile *parade, procession*, 4G
el desierto *desert*, 5G
la despedida *farewell*, 9; la fiesta de
   despedida *goodbye party*, 10
despertarse (ie) *to wake*, 7
despierto(a) *awake*, 7
después *after*, 3; *afterwards*, 4;
   después de *after*, 7; **después de**
   clases *after class*, 3
destinado(a) *destined*, 6
el destino *destination*, 10
el detalle *detail*, 7
determinar *to determine*, 7
detrás de *behind*, 5
di *say*, 8
el día *day*, 1; **algún día** *some day*, 10;
   el Día de Acción de Gracias
   Thanksgiving Day, 9; **el Día de la**
   Independencia *Independence*
   Day, 9; **el Día de la Madre**
   Mother's Day, 9; **el día de la**
   semana *day of the week*, 1; **el Día**
   de los Enamorados *Valentine's*
   Day, 9; **el Día del Padre** *Father's*
   Day, 9; **el día de tu santo** *your*
   saint's day, 9; **el día festivo**
   holiday, 9; **¿Qué día es hoy?**
   What day is today?, 1
diablado(a) *devilish*, 5G
el diablo *devil*, 7G
el diálogo *dialogue*, xxii
diario(a) *daily*, 3G
dibujar *to draw*, 3
el dibujo *drawing*, xxii

el diccionario *dictionary*, 4
dice (inf. decir) *(he/she) says*, 4
la dicha *happiness*, 9
diciembre *December*, 1
el dictado *dictation*, 1
diecinueve *nineteen*, 1
dieciocho *eighteen*, 1
dieciséis *sixteen*, 1
diecisiete *seventeen*, 1
los dientes *teeth*, 7
la dieta *diet*, 7; **seguir una dieta sana**
   to eat well, 7
diez *ten*, 1
diferente *different*, 2
difícil *difficult*, 4; **Es difícil.** *It's*
   difficult., 4
Diga. *Hello. (telephone greeting)*, 8
el dinero *money*, 8
el dinosaurio *dinosaur*, 1
el dios *god*, 6; gracias a Dios *thank*
   goodness, 6
la dirección *address*, 5; **Mi dirección**
   es... *My address is . . .*, 5
directamente *directly*, 4
director (-a) *director*, 10
el directorio de teléfono *phone book*, 1
disciplinado(a) *disciplined*, 2
el disco *record*, 8
el disco compacto (en blanco) *blank*
   compact disc, 8; **el disco compacto**
   en blanco *blank compact disc*, 8
diseñar *to design*, 3G; fue
   diseñado(a) *was designed*, 3G
el diseño *design*, 5G
el disfraz *costume*, 9G
disfrazar *to wear a costume*, 4G
disfrutar *to enjoy*, 2G
disponible *available*, 7
dispuesto(a) *willing*, 6G
la distancia *distance*, 10
distinguirse *to distinguish oneself*,
   10
distinto(a) *different*, 6G
la diversión *fun*, 2
diverso(a) *diverse*, 6
divertido(a) *fun*, 2; **¡Qué**
   divertido! *What fun!*, 10
divertirse *to have fun*, 1; diviértanse
   have a good time (pl.), 1; que me
   divierta *to have fun*, 9
doblado(a) *folded*, 9
doble *double*, 5
doce *twelve*, 1
el documento *document*, 1
el dólar *dollar*, 8
doler (ue) *to hurt*, 7; **Me duele(n)...**
   My . . . hurt(s)., 7; **¿Te duele algo?**
   Is something hurting you?, 7
el domingo *Sunday*, 1; **los domingos**
   on Sundays, 3
dominicano(a) *Dominican*, 9
donde *where*, 8; *to the house of*, 9
¿dónde? *where?*, 5; **¿Dónde se**

puede...? *Where can I . . .?*, 10
dorado(a) *golden*, 2
dormido(a) *asleep*, 7
dormir (ue) *to sleep*, 5; **dormir lo**
   suficiente *to get enough sleep*, 7
el dormitorio *bedroom*, 5
dos *two*, 1
dos mil *two thousand*, 8
dos millones (de) *two million*, 8
doscientos *two hundred*, 8
dramatizar *to dramatize, to role-*
   play, xxii
la duda *doubt*, 6; sin duda *without a*
   doubt, 6
dulce *sweet*, 7
el dulce *candy*, 9
la duración *duration*, 7
durante *during*, 10; *throughout*, 6G
durar *to last*, 10G
el durazno *peach*
el DVD *DVD*, 8

e *and*, 5
la economía *economy*, 3G; la
   economía doméstica *home*
   economics, 6G
la edad *age*, 2G; de más edad *the*
   oldest, 5
el edificio *building*, 5; **el edificio**
   de... pisos *. . . story building*, 5
la educación física *physical*
   education, 4
eficaz *efficient*, 10G
eficiente *efficient*, 2
el ejemplo *example*, 3G
el ejercicio *exercise*, 3; **hacer ejercicio**
   to exercise, 3
el *the* (masc.), 2
él *he*, 1; **Él es...** *He is . . .*, 1; **Él se**
   llama... *His name is . . .*, 1
el elefante *elephant*, 1
la elegancia *elegance*, 5G
elegante *elegant*, 2
el elemento *element*, 1
elevar *to raise*, 5G
la elite *elite*, 6
ella *she*, 1; A ella le gusta +
   infinitive *She likes to . . .*, 3; **Ella**
   es... *She is . . .*, 1; ella misma
   herself, 6; **Ella se llama...** *Her*
   name is . . ., 1
ellas *they (f.)*, 1
ellos *they (m.)*, 1
el elote *corn (Mexico)*, 6
emitir *to emit*, 2
emocionado(a) *excited*, 9

la **empanada** *turnover-like pastry*, 9
el **emparedado** *sandwich*, 6
empezar (ie) *to start*, 5
el **empleado, la empleada** *employee*, 7
el **empleo** *job*, 9
emplumado(a) *feathered*, 6
en *on, in, at*, 1; **en frente** *in front*, 3G; **en blanco** *blank*, 8; **en las cuales** *about which*, 8; **en negrilla** *bold*, 9; **en punto** *on the dot*, 1; **en que** *in which*, 8; **¿En que le puedo servir?** *Can I help you?*, 8
enamorado(a) *in love*, 10
Encantado(a). *Pleased to meet you., Nice to meet you.*, 1
encantar *to really like, to love*, 6
encerrar *to lock up*, 10
encima de *on top of, above*, 5
encontrar (ue) *to find*, 7; **encontrará** *will find*, 10; **se encuentra** *is/it's located* 1G; **se encuentran** *they can be found*, 6
encontrarse con alguien *to meet up with someone*, 10
energético(a) *energetic*, 2
la **energía** *energy*, 2
enero *January*, 1
la **enfermera** *nurse*, 5
enfermo(a) *sick*, 7
enfrente *in front*, 10
enhorabuena *congratulations*, 10
enrollado(a) *rolled up*, 3
la **ensalada** *salad*, 6
el **ensayo** *rehearsal*, 3
enseñar *to show, to teach*, 4; **enseñar fotos** *to show photos*, 9
entonces *then*, 4
entrar *to enter*, 4
entre *between*, 2; *in, within*, 6; *among*, 7
entregar *to hand over*, 9
la **entrenadora** *trainer*, 7
el **entrenamiento** *practice*, 3
entrenarse *to work out*, 7
la **entrevista** *interview*, 2
entrevistar *to interview*, 2
enviar *to send*, 1
la **envoltura** *wrapping*, 9
la **época** *era*, 6; la **época colonial** *Spanish colonial era*, 2G
el **equipaje** *luggage*, 10
el **equipo** *equipment*, 3G; el **equipo de transporte** *transportation equipment*, 3G
¿Eres...? *Are you . . .?*, 2
la **erupción** *eruption*, 6G
Es... *He (She, It) is . . .*, 2; **Es algo divertido.** *It's kind of fun.*, 2; **Es bastante bueno.** *It's rather good.*, 2; **Es de...** *He (She) is from . . .*, 1; **Es delicioso.** *It's delicious.*, 2; **Es el... de...** *It's the . . . of . . .*, 2; **Es el primero (dos, tres) de...** *It's the*

first (second, third) of . . ., 1; **Es la una.** *It is one o'clock.*, 1; **Es pésimo.** *It's awful.*, 2; **Es que...** *It's because; It's just that . . .*, 7; **¡Es un robo!** *It's a rip-off!*, 8
ese(a) *that*, 5
escapar *to escape*, 5
la **escena** *scene*, 3
escoger *to pick*, 9; *to choose*, 6
escolar *school (adj.)*, 4
esconder *to hide*, 4
escribir *to write*, 1; **¿Cómo se escribe...?** *How do you spell . . .?*, 1; **escribamos** *let's write*, 1; **escribir cartas** *to write letters*, 3; **se escribe...** *It's spelled . . .*, 1
el **escritor, la escritora** *writer*, 1
el **escritorio** *desk*, 5
escuchar *to listen*, 3; **escuchar música** *to listen to music*, 3; **escuchemos** *let's listen*, 1; **has escuchado** *have you heard*, 2; **he escuchado** *I have heard*, 2
la **escuela** *school*, 2; la **escuela primaria** *elementary school*, 5; la **escuela secundaria** *high school*, 9
el **escultor** *sculptor*, 4G
la **escultura** *sculpture*, 2G
ese(a) *that*, 8
eso *that*, 2
esos(as) *those*, 8
espacial *space*, 8G
la **espalda** *back*, 7
el **español** *Spanish*, 1
el **español** *Spaniard*, 6
esparcir *to spread*, 3; **está esparciendo** *is spreading*, 3
la **especia** *spice*, 8G
la **especialidad** *specialty*, 6
la **especie** *species*, 2G
específico(a) *specific*, 10
los **espejuelos** *glasses*, 5
la **esperanza** *hope*, 9
esperar *to wait*, 8; *to hope*, 10; *to expect*, 10; **Espera un momento.** *Hold on a moment.*, 8; **espero ver...** *I hope to see . . .*, 10
las **espinacas** *spinach*, 6
el **espino** *thorn*, 8
espiritual *spiritual*, 9
espontáneo(a) *spontaneous*, 2
la **esposa** *wife*, 9
el **esposo** *husband*, 5
esquiar *to ski*, 10; **esquiar en el agua** *to water ski*, 10
Está a la vuelta. *It's around the corner.*, 10
ésta, éste *this* (pron.),1; **Ésta es.../la señora...** *This is . . . /Mrs. . . .*, 1; **Éste es.../el señor...** *This is . . . /Mr. . . .*, 1
establecer *to establish*, 8G, fue **establecido** *was established*, 8G

el **establecimiento** *colony*, 8G
estacionar *to park*, 10
el **estadio** *stadium*, 4
el **estado** *state*, 2G
los **Estados Unidos** *United States*, 1
estadounidense *pertaining to the United States*, 7
estar *to be*, 1; **¿Cómo está(s)?** *How are you?*, 1; **¿Está...?** *Is . . . there?*, 8; **Está bien.** *All right.*, 3; **Está nublado.** *It's cloudy.*, 3; **estar aburrido(a)** *to be bored*, 7; **estar bien** *to be (doing) fine*, 7; **estar cansado(a)** *to be tired*, 7; **estar contento(a)** *to be happy*, 7; **estar mal** *to be (doing) badly*, 7; **estar enfermo(a)** *to be sick*, 7; **estar en una silla de ruedas** *to be in a wheelchair*, 5; **estar listo(a)** *to be ready*, 7; **estar nervioso(a)** *to be nervous*, 7; **estar triste** *to be sad*, 7; **¿Está todo listo?** *Is everything ready?*, 9; **Estoy bien, gracias.** *I'm fine, thanks.*,1; **Estoy de acuerdo.** *I agree.*, 6; **Estoy mal.** *I'm not so good.*, 1; **Estoy mirando, no más.** *I'm just looking.*, 8; **Estoy regular.** *I'm all right.*, 1; **No está.** *He/She is not here.*, 8; **Estuvo a todo dar.** *It was great.*, 9; **No estoy de acuerdo.** *I disagree.*, 6
estas, estos *these (adj.)*, 6
la **estatua** *statue*, 5G
éste *this (pron.)*, 6
este(a) *this*, 8
el **estilo** *style*, 3G
estirarse *to stretch*, 7
el **estómago** *stomach*, 7
el **Estrecho de la Florida** *Straits of Florida*, 8
la **estrella** *star*, 5
el **estrés** *stress*, 7
estricto(a) *strict*, 4
el **estudiante, la estudiante** *student*, 1; el **estudiante de intercambio** *exchange student*, 10
estudiar *to study*, 3
los **estudios** *studies*, 5; los **estudios sociales** *social studies*, 4
estupendo(a) *great*, 10; **fue estupendo** *it was great*, 10
la **etapa** *stage*, 2
el **europeo** *European*, 6G
el **evento deportivo** *sporting event*, 1
el **examen** *test*, 4; **presentar el examen de...** *to take a . . . test*, 4
exclamar *to exclaim*, 9
exclusivamente *exclusively*, 4
la **excursión** *hike*, 10; **ir de excursión** *to go on a hike*, 10
la **excursión turística** *to go on a trip*, 1
exigente *strict*, 5

existir *to exist,* 7
el éxito *success,* 10
la experiencia *experience,* 6
el explorador *explorer,* 5G
exponer *to display,* 4G
el exportador *exporter,* 8G
exportar *to export,* 1G
la exposición *exposition,* 5G, exhibition, 10G
expresar *to express,* 6G
la expresión *expression,* xxii; *saying,* 2
extender *covers,* 3G; se extiende *it extends,* 5G
la extensión *length,* 10G
extranjero(a) *foreign,* 10
el extranjero *abroad,* 10
extraño(a) *strange,* 7G
extremo(a) *far,* 7G
extrovertido(a) *outgoing,* 2

fabuloso(a) *fabulous,* 6
fácil *easy,* 4; **Es fácil.** *It's easy.,* 4
facturar *to check,* 10; **facturar el equipaje** *to check luggage,* 10
la falda *skirt,* 8
falso(a) *false,* xxii
faltar *to be missing,* 1; nos faltan *we're missing,* 3
la fama *fame,* 5G
la familia *family,* 3; **En mi familia somos...** *There are . . . people in my family.,* 5; la Familia Real *Royal Family,* 1
familiar *pertaining to the family,* 7
famoso(a) *famous,* 2
fascinar *to love, to like very much,* 2
fastidiar *to annoy,* 9
favorito(a) *favorite,* 1
febrero *February,* 1
la fecha *date,* 1
la felicidad *happiness,* 9
felicitar *to congratulate,* 9
el felino *cat,* 10G
feliz (pl. felices) *happy,* 8; **¡Feliz...!** *Happy (Merry) . . .,* 9
fenomenal *awesome,* 2
feo(a) *ugly*
festejar *to celebrate,* 9
festivo *holiday* (adj), 9
la fibra de vidrio *fiberglass,* 3G
la fiesta *party,* 2; la fiesta patria *national holiday,* 5G; la fiesta patronal *feast celebrating the patron saint,* 4G; **la fiesta sorpresa** *surprise party,* 9; **hacer una fiesta** *to have a party,* 9

la figurita *shape, figurine,* 4
el fin *end,* 9; al fin *finally,* 10
el fin de semana *weekend,* 3; **este fin de semana** *this weekend,* 4; **los fines de semana** *weekends,* 3
finales: a finales *at the end,* 10G
finalmente *finally,* 8
financiar *to finance,* 5
fino(a) *fine,* 2G
el flan *flan, custard,* 6
las flautas *rolled tortillas that are stuffed and fried,* 9
la flor *flower,* 1,
las fogatas *campfires,* 3
el folleto *pamphlet,* 7
la forma *form,* xxii
formaba *formed*
la formación geológica *geological formation,* 7G
formar *to form,* 3
formidable *formidable,* 2
la fortaleza *fortress,* 10
la fortuna *fortune,* 8
la foto *photo,* xxii; **enseñar fotos** *to show photos,* 9; **sacar fotos** *to take photos,* 10
la fotografía *photograph,* 8
el fragmento *excerpt,* 5
el francés *French,* 4
la frase *phrase,* 8; *sentence,* 9
la frecuencia *frequency,* 8; con frecuencia *often,* 8; **¿Con qué frecuencia vas...?** *How often do you go?,* 3
frecuentado(a) *visited,* 1G
frente *front;* al frente *to the front,* xxii; en frente *in front,* 3G
el fresco *cool,* 3; **Hace fresco.** *It's cool.,* 3
el frijol *bean,* 2G
frío(a) *cold,* 6; **Hace frío.** *It's cold.,* 3; **tener frío** *to be cold,* 7
la frontera *border,* 7G
la fruta *fruit,* 2; la fruta cítrica *citrus fruit,* 8G
el fuego *fire,* 3
¡Fue estupendo! *It was great!,* 10
los fuegos artificiales *fireworks,* 9; **ver los fuegos artificiales** *to see fireworks,* 9
fuera *outside,* 7G
fuera (inf. ser) *was,* 6G
fuerte *loud,* 2; *strong,* 3G
fumar *to smoke,* 7; **dejar de fumar** *to stop smoking,* 7
el funcionalismo *functional architectural style,* 6G
funcionar *to work,* 10
fundado(a) *founded,* 2G
el fútbol *soccer,* 3
el fútbol americano *football,* 3
el futuro *future,* 3
futuro(a) *future,* 5

el gabinete *cabinet,* 9
las gafas *glasses,* 5
el gallego *romance language from Galicia, Spain,* 1G
la galleta *cookie,* 9
la gana *desire;* **tener ganas de +** infinitive *to feel like doing something,* 4
la ganadería *cattle raising,* 7G
el ganado *cattle,* 3G
ganar *to win,* 5G
la ganga *bargain,* 8
el garaje *garage,* 5
la garganta *throat,* 7
la garita *sentry box,* 2G
gastar *to spend,* 8
el gato, la gata *cat,* 5
el gazpacho *cold tomato soup*
la generación *generation,* 5
generalmente *generally,* 8
el género *genre,* 8G
generoso(a) *generous,* 6
la gente *people,* 3
la geografía *geography,* 1
geográfico(a) *geographical,* 10
geometriá *geometry,* 4
gigante *giant,* 6
el gimnasio *gym,* 3
el glaciar *glacier,* 5G
la gloria *heaven,* 3
glorioso *glorious,* 9
el gobierno *government,* 1G
el Golfo de México *Gulf of Mexico,* 8
gordo(a) *fat,* 5
la gorra *cap,* 7
gótico(a) *gothic,* 3G
la grabación *recording,* 1
gracias *thank you,* 1, **Estoy bien, gracias.** *I'm fine, thanks,* 1; **no, gracias** *no thank you,* 8
gracioso(a) *witty,* 2
la graduación *graduation,* 9
gran *big,* 5; *great,* 5; *large,* 3
la granada *pomegranate,* 6
grande *big, large,* 5
el grano *grain,* 6
la grasa *fat,* 7
gratuito *free,* 1
gris *gray,* 8
gritar *to yell,* 7
la grúa *tow truck,* 9
el grupo *group,* 6
la guagua *bus (P.R., Dom. Rep.),* 10
los guandules *pigeon peas,* 6
guapo(a) *good-looking,* 2
guardar *to store,* 10
la guayabera *man's short-sleeve shirt,* 8
la guerra *war,* 7

la guía telefónica   *telephone directory,* 10

guiar   *to guide,* 10; *to drive,* 10

la güira   *percussive instrument played by scratching with a stick across a rough surface,* 9G

el guiso   *stew,* 6

la guitarra: la guitarra eléctrica   *electric guitar,* 2

gustar   *to like,* 2; **A ellos/ellas les gusta...**   *They like . . .,* 3; **le gusta...**   *he/she likes . . .,* 3; **Me gusta(n)...**   *I like . . .,* 2; **Me gusta(n)... mucho.**   *I like . . . a lot.,* 2; me gustaba   *I liked,* 4; **Me gusta(n) más...**   *I like . . . more.,* 2; **Me gustaría...**   *I would like . . .,* 8; **Me gustaría más...**   *I would prefer . . .,* 10; Me ha gustado...   *I have liked . . .,* 4; **No, no me gusta(n)...**   *No, I don't like . . .,* 2; **¿Te gusta(n)...?**   *Do you like . . .?,* 2; **¿Te gusta(n) más... o...?**   *Do you like . . . or . . . more?,* 2

el gusto   *pleasure,* 9

los gustos   *likes,* 2

haber: hubo   *there was,* 10

las habichuelas   *beans,* 2G

la habitación   *bedroom,* 5

habitar   *to inhabit,* 7G

hablar   *to talk, to speak,* 3; **Habla...**   *. . . speaking (on the telephone),* 8; **hablar por teléfono**   *to talk on the phone,* 3; hablemos   *let's talk,* 1

hacer (-go)   *to do, to make,* 4; **estamos haciendo**   *we are making/doing,* 9; están haciendo   *are making,* 3; **Hace buen (mal) tiempo.**   *The weather is nice (bad).,* 3; **Hace calor.**   *It's hot.,* 3; **Hace fresco.**   *It's cool.,* 3; **Hace frío.**   *It's cold.,* 3; Hace más de... años   *It's More than . . . years ago,* 7G; **Hace sol.**   *It's sunny.,* 3; Hace tanto... que...   *It's so . . . that . . .,* 3; Hace tiempo   *It's been a long time.,* 9; **Hace viento.**   *It's windy.,* 3; **hacer cola**   *to wait in line,* 10; **hacer ejercicio**   *to exercise,* 3; **hacer la cama**   *to make the bed,* 5; **hacer la maleta**   *to pack your suitcase,* 10; **hacer la tarea**   *to do homework,* 3; **hacer los quehaceres**   *to do chores,* 5; **hacer una fiesta**   *to have a party,* 9;

hacer un viaje   *to take a trip,* 10; **hacer yoga**   *to do yoga,* 7; hacían   *they made,* 4; **haz**   *make, do,* 6; hizo   *he/she did,* 9; **no hagas**   *don't do,* 10; **¿Qué están haciendo?**   *What are they doing?,* 9; qué hicieron   *what they did,* 9; **¿Qué hiciste?**   *What did you do?,* 8; se hace   *is made,* 6

hallar   *to find,* 7G

el **hambre**   *hunger,* 4; **tener hambre**   *to be hungry,* 4

la **hamburguesa**   *hamburger,* 2

el **Hanukah**   *Hanukkah,* 9

hasta   *until,* 5; *up to,* 5; **Hasta luego.**   *See you later.,* 1; **Hasta mañana.**   *See you tomorrow.,* 1; **Hasta pronto.**   *See you soon.,* 1

hay (inf. haber)   *there is, there are,* 4; **Hay un(a)...**   *There's a . . .,* 4

haz   *make, do,* 6; **Hazme caso.**   *Pay attention to me.,* 8

hecho(a)   *made,* 2G

la **heladería**   *ice cream shop,* 8

el **helado**   *ice cream,* 2

la hembra   *female,* 2

el hemisferio   *hemisphere,* 7G

la herencia   *inheritance;* la herencia alemana   *German cultural tradition,* 7G; la herencia española   *Spanish cultural tradition,* 10G

la **hermana**   *sister,* 5

el **hermano**   *brother,* 5

los **hermanos**   *brothers, brothers and sisters,* 5

el héroe   *hero,* 4G

la hierba   *grass,* 8G; la hierba fina   *herb,* 8G

la **hija**   *daughter,* 5

el **hijo**   *son,* 5

los **hijos**   *sons, children,* 5

el hipo   *hiccup,* 3; estar con hipo   *to have hiccups,* 3

el hipopótamo   *hippopotamus,* 1

hispano(a)   *Hispanic,* 1

hispanohablante   *Spanish-speaking,* 6

la **historia**   *history,* 4

el hogar   *home,* 3G

las hojas de maíz   *cornhusks,* 3

hola   *hi, hello* 1

el **hombre**   *man,* 8; el hombre de negocios   *businessman,* 5, los hombres   *men, humans,* 6; **para hombres**   *for men,* 8

el **hombro**   *shoulder,* 7

el homenaje   *tribute,* 1G

hondo(a)   *deep,* 8G

el honor   *honor,* 3

la hora   *hour,* 1; **¿A qué hora vas a...?**   *What time are you going to . . .?,* 4; **¿Qué hora es?**   *What time is it?,* 1

el horario   *schedule,* 3

la horchata mexicana   *sweet rice drink,* 6

la hormiga   *ant,* 6

el **horno**   *oven,* 6; el horno microondas   *microwave oven,* 6

horrible   *horrible,* 2; **¡Fue horrible!**   *It was horrible!,* 10

el **hotel**   *hotel,* 10; **quedarse en un hotel**   *to stay in a hotel,* 10

hoy   *today,* 1; hoy en día   *nowadays,* 6G; **Hoy es...**   *Today is . . .,* 1; **¿Qué día es hoy?**   *What day is today?,* 1

el **huevo**   *egg,* 6

húmedo(a)   *damp;* el bosque húmedo   *rainforest,* 4G

el huracán   *hurricane,* 3

la idea   *idea,* 6; la idea principal   *main idea,* 6

el idioma   *language,* 1G; idioma oficial   *official language,* 1G

identificar   *to identify,* 10

la iglesia   *church,* 3

igual que   *same as,* 2

igualmente   *equally,* 8

Igualmente.   *Likewise.,* 1

la iguana   *iguana,* 1

ilustrar   *to illustrate,* 5

imaginar   *to imagine,* 2

el imperativo   *imperative,* 9

el imperio   *empire,* 10G

imponente   *imposing,* 6

importado(a)   *imported,* 5G

la importancia   *importance,* 6

impresionante   *impressive,* 7G

incaico(a)   *Incan,* 7G

incesante   *without stopping,* 8

inclusive   *including,* 8

incluso   *including,* 8G

incomparable   *incomparable,* 5

la independencia   *independence,* 6G

independiente   *independent,* 2

indicar   *to indicate,* xxii

indígena   *indigenous,* 6G

la influencia   *influence,* 1G

Inglaterra   *England,* 7G

el **inglés**   *English,* 4

injusto   *unfair,* 5; **Me parece injusto.**   *I don't think that's fair. It seems unfair to me.,* 5

inmediato(a)   *immediate,* 10G

inmenso(a)   *immense,* 6

el inmigrante   *immigrant,* 7G

inmigrar *to immigrate,* 7G

el insecto *insect,* 2

inseparable *inseparable,* 3

inspirar *to inspire,* 1G

el instrumento *instrument,* 8G

intacto(a) *intact,* 10

intelectual *intellectual,* 2

inteligente *intelligent,* 2

la intensidad *intensity,* 7

el interés *of interest,* 10

interesante *interesting,* 2

internacional *international,* 6

interrumpir *to interrupt,* 4

el invasor *invader,* 4G

inventar *to invent,* 4

el inventario *inventory,* 8

inventivo(a) *inventive,* 2

la investigación *research,* 4G

el invierno *winter,* 3

inviolable *inviolable,* 5

la invitación *invitation,* 9; **mandar invitaciones** *to send invitations,* 9

el invitado *guest,* 9; el invitado de honor *guest of honor,* 9

invitar *to invite,* 9

ir *to go,* 2; **¿Adónde fuiste?** *Where did you go?,* 8; fue *went,* 8; fuimos *we went,* 8; **ir a** + infinitive *to be going to (do something),* 4; **ir de compras** *to go shopping,* 3; **ir de excursión** *to go hiking,* 10; **ir de pesca,** *to go fishing,* 10; **no vayas** *don't go,* 7; **quiero ir...** *I want to go . . .,* 2; se va *leaves,* 6; **¿Vas a...?** *Are you going to the . . .?,* 4; **Vas a ir, ¿verdad?** *You're going to go, aren't you?,* 4; **ve** *go,* 6

irse *to leave,* 10

la isla *island,* 10

italiano(a) *Italian,* 6

la izquierda *left*

el jabón *soap,* 7

el jamón *ham,* 6

el jardín *garden,* 5

el jefe *chief,* 10

el jersey *sweater,* 8

la jirafa *giraffe,* 1

joven *young,* 5

el joven, la joven *young person,* 9; **los jóvenes** *young people,* 9

la joyería *jewelry store,* 8

el juego *game,* 3; **el juego de mesa** *board game,* 3; el juego de palabras *word game,* 7

el jueves *Thursday,* 1; **los jueves** *on Thursdays,* 3

el jugador *player,* 2G

jugar (ue) *to play,* 3

el jugo *juice,* 6; **el jugo de** *. . . juice,* 6

el juguete *toy,* 8

la juguetería *toy store,* 8

el juicio *judgment,* 6

julio *July,* 1

junio *June,* 1

juntos(as) *together,* 1

justo(a) *fair, just,* 10

el karate *karate,* 1

el kilómetro *kilometer,* 3

el kiosko *stand or stall,* 9G

la *the* (fem. article), 2

la *you, it,* (pronoun), 6; *you,* 9

las labores *chores,* 5

el lado: por todos lados *everywhere,* 8G

el lago *lake,* 10

la lágrima *tear,* 9

la lana *wool,* 8; **de lana** *made of wool,* 8

la lancha *motorboat,* 10; **pasear en lancha** *to go out in a motorboat,* 10

el lápiz (pl. los lápices) *pencil,* 4

largo(a) *long,* 5

las *the* (pl. fem. article), 2

las *you, them* (pronoun), 6

la lástima *pity,* 8; ¡Qué lástima! *What a shame!,* 8

la lata *can,* 9

latinoamericano(a) *Latin American,* 1

lavar *to wash,* 5; **lavar los platos** *to wash the dishes,* 5

lavarse *to wash,* 7

le *to/for him, her, you,* 2

la leche *milk,* 6

leer *to read,* 3; al leer *upon reading,* 6; antes de leer *before reading,* 1; leamos *let's read,* 1; leer en voz alta *to read aloud,* 6; se leen *are read,* 5

el legado *legacy,* 8G

lejano(a) *distant,* 10

lejos *far,* 9; **lejos de** *far from,* 5

la lengua *language,* 9

los lentes *glasses,* 5; **usar lentes** *to wear glasses,* 5

lento(a) *slow,* 4G

el león *lion,* 1

les *to/for you* (pl.), *them,* 2

levantar *to lift,* 7; **levantar pesas** *to lift weights,* 7

levantarse *to get up,* 7

la leyenda *legend,* 10

libre *free,* 6G

la librería *bookstore,* 8

el libro *book,* 2; **el libro de amor** *romance book,* 2; **el libro de aventura** *adventure book,* 2

el líder, la líder *leader,* 2

el limón *lemon,* 6

limpiar *to clean,* 5; limpio(a) *clean,* 5

lindo(a) *beautiful, pretty,* 6

listo(a) *ready,* 7; **estar listo(a)** *to be ready,* 7; **¿Está todo listo?** *Is everything ready?,* 9

llamado(a) *called,* 9G

llamar *to call,* 9; **llamar por teléfono** *to make a phone call,* 8; **Llamo más tarde.** *I'll call back later.,* 8; **Te llamo más tarde.** *I'll call you later.,* 9

la llegada *arrival,* 10

llegar *to arrive, to get there,* 4; al llegar *upon arriving,* 6; ha llegado *she has come,* 9

llenar *to fill up,* 3

lleno(a) *full,* 9

llevar *to wear,* 8; *to take,* 6; lo llevó *took it,* 6G; lleva años trabajando *he has been working for years,* 9

llevarse *to get along,* 2

llover (ue) *to rain,* 3; **llueve (mucho)** *it rains (a lot),* 3

lo *him, it,* 6; *you,* 9; **lo siento** *I'm sorry,* 8

lo: lo de siempre *same as usual,* 9; lo que *what,* 6; lo que pasa *what is happening,* xxii

loco *crazy,* 5

lógico(a) *logical,* 2

el lonche *lunch (Southwest U.S.),* 6

los *the* (pl. masc.), 2

los *you, them* (pronoun), 6

luchar *to struggle,* 8; *to fight,* 4G

luego *then, later,* 4

el lugar *place,* 1G

los lugares de interés *places of interest,* 10

la luna *moon,* 9

lunes *Monday,* 3; **los lunes** *on Mondays,* 3

la luz *light,* 7G

el macho *male,* 2
la madera *wood,* 5G
la madre *mother,* 5
madrina *godmother,* 1
el maestro *master,* 7G
magnífico(a) *magnificent,* 4
el maíz *corn,* 6
majestuoso(a) *majestic,* 9G
mal *bad;* **Estoy mal.** *I'm not so good.,* 1; **Te veo mal.** *You don't look so well.,* 7
la maleta *suitcase,* 10
malo(a) *bad,* 2
malvado(a) *evil,* 10
la mamá *mom,* 5
el mamífero *mammal,* 4G
la mañana *morning,* 4; **por la mañana** *in the morning,* 4
mañana *tomorrow,* 4; **Hasta mañana.** *See you tomorrow.,* 1
mandar *to send,* 9; **mandar invitaciones** *to send invitations,* 9; **mandar tarjetas** *to send cards,* 9
el mandato *command,* 6
manejar *to manage,* 7
la manera *way,* 9
la mano *hand,* 7
el manojo *bunch,* 8
mantener *to preserve, to keep,* 6
mantenerse (ie) *to maintain,* 7; **mantenerse (ie) en forma** *to stay in shape,* 7
la manzana *apple,* 6
el mapa *map,* 10
el maquillaje *makeup,* 7
maquillarse *to put on makeup,* 7
marcado(a) *marked,* 7
marcar *to set, to dial,* 1
marcharse *to leave,* 9
el marisco *shellfish,* 5G
marítimo(a) *maritime,* 3G
marrón *brown,* 2; **los ojos marrones** *brown eyes,* 5
el martes *Tuesday,* 1; **los martes** *on Tuesdays,* 3
marzo *March,* 1
más *more,* 2; **Más o menos.** *So-so.,* 1; **más que** *more than,* 8; **más... que** *more ... than,* 8
la masa *dough,* 3
la máscara *mask,* 2G
la mascarada *masquerade,* 4G
el mate *Argentine and Paraguayan tea,* 7
las matemáticas *mathematics,* 3
la materia *subject,* 4; **las materias obligatorias** *required subjects,* 4; **las materias opcionales** *elective,* 4
matutino(a) *(in the) morning,* 4

mayo *May,* 1
mayor(es) *older,* 5; *greater,* 3G
la mayoría *majority,* 4G
la mazorca *corn on the cob,* 6
me *to/for me,* 2; **Me da igual.** *It's all the same to me.,* 2; **Me duele(n)...** *My ... hurt(s),* 7; **Me gusta(n)...** *I like ...,* 2; **Me gusta(n) más...** *I like ... more.,* 2; **Me gusta(n)... mucho.** *I like ... a lot.,* 2; **Me llamo...** *My name is ...,* 1; **No, no me gusta(n)...** *No, I don't like ...,* 2; **Me parece bien.** *It seems fine to me.,* 5; **Me parece injusto.** *It's not fair.,* 5
me, 9
mecánico *mechanic,* 5
la medalla *medal,* 5G
mediano(a) *medium,* 4
la medianoche *midnight,* 1
médico(a) *medical,* 7
medio(a) *half,* 4; **y media** *half past,* 1
los medios de transporte *means of transportation,* 10
el mediodía *midday, noon,* 1
medir (i) *to measure,* 5G
mejor(es) *better, best,* 7
el melocotón *peach,* 6
menor(es) *younger,* 5
menos *less,* 8; **menos cuarto** *quarter to ...,* 1; **menos que** *less than,* 8; **menos... que** *less ...than,* 8
el mensaje *message,* 7G
la mente *mind,* 4
el mercado *market,* 6; **el mercado al aire libre** *open-air market,* 8
merendar (ie) *to have a snack,* 5
el merengue *music and dance style,* 9G
la merienda *snack,* 6
la mesa *table,* 5; **poner la mesa** *to set the table,* 6
los meses del año *months of the year,* 1
meter *to put in,* 8
meterse *to set,* 9
metódico(a) *methodical,* 2
el metro *meter,* 1G
el metro *subway,* 10
mezclar *to mix,* 6; mezcla *mixture,* 6
la mezquita *mosque,* 1G
mí *me,* 5; **A mí me gusta +** infinitive *I like to ...,* 3; **a mí me toca...** *I have to ...,* 5
mi(s) *my,* 1; **mi mejor amigo(a)** *my best friend,* 1, **mi profesor(-a)** *my teacher,* 1
la miel *honey,* 6
el miembro *member,* 3
mientras *while,* 6
el miércoles *Wednesday,* 1; **los miércoles** *on Wednesdays,* 3
mil *one thousand,* 8; *miles*

thousands, 2
la milla cuadrada *square mile,* 3
un millón (de) *one million,* 8; **dos millones (de)** *two million,* 8
mío *mine,* 8
mirar *to look,* 9; **Estoy mirando, no más.** *I'm just looking.,* 8; **mirar las vitrinas** *to window shop,* 8
la misa *Mass,* 9
la misión *mission,* 3G
mismo(a) *same,* 6
el misterio *mystery,* 2
misterioso(a) *mysterious,* 2
la mitad *half,* 6G
la mochila *backpack,* 4
la moda *style, fashion,* 8; **a la última moda** *in the latest fashion,* 8; **muy de moda** *very fashionable,* 8; **pasado(a) de moda** *out of style,* 8
modelar *to shape,* 4
moderno(a) *modern,* 7
el módulo *module,* 10
el mogote *knoll,* 9G
el mole *sauce made with chiles and flavored with chocolate,* 6
el molino *windmill,* 1G
el momento *moment,* 6; **Espera un momento.** *Hold on a moment.,* 8
la monarquía parlamentaria *constitutional monarchy,* 1G
la moneda *currency,* 2; *coin,* 8
el mono *monkey,* 4G
la montaña *mountain,* 10; **subir a la montaña** *to go up a mountain,* 10
montañoso(a) *mountainous,* 7G
montar *to ride,* montar a caballo *to ride a horse,* 3G; **montar en bicicleta** *to ride a bike,* 3
un montón *a ton,* 4
el monumento *monument,* 1G
el morado *purple,* 1G
morado(a) *purple,* 8
moreno(a) *dark-skinned; dark-haired,* 2
morir (ue) *to die,* 5; murió *died,* 5
el moro *rice and beans,* 9G
el mosaico *mosaic,* 6G
el mosquito *mosquito,* 2
el mostrador *counter,* 10
mostrar (ue) *to show,* 1G
el movimiento *movement,* 4G
la muchacha *girl,* 1
el muchacho *boy,* 1
mucho *a lot (of),* 2; *much,* 4; **Mucho gusto.** *Pleased/Nice to meet you.,* 1
muchos(as) *a lot of, many,* 4
mudarse *to move,* 8G
mudéjar *Moslem,* 5G
la muerte *death,* 4G
la mujer *woman,* 8; **la mujer de negocios** *business woman,* 5; **para mujeres** *for women,* 8

mundialmente *worldwide*, 6

el mundo *world*, 1G; todo el mundo *everybody*, 9

el mural *mural painting*, 6G

la muralla *wall, rampart*, 1G

el museo *museum*, 10

la música *music*, 2; **la música de...** *music of/by . . .*, 2; la música clásica *classical music*, 2G

el músico *musician*, 2

muy + adjective *very*, 2

nacer *to be born*, 7G; había nacido *had been born*, 7G; nacido(a) *born*, 8G

nacional *national*, 1

nada *nothing*, 4; *not anything*, 5

nadar *to swim*, 3

nadie *nobody, not anybody*, 5

la naranja *orange*, 6

el naranjo *orange tree*, 8G

la nariz *nose*, 7

la natación *swimming*, 7

nativo(a) *native*, 6

la naturaleza *nature*, 2

la navaja *razor*, 7

navegar *to sail*, 5; *to navigate*, 10; **navegar por Internet** *to surf the Internet*, 3

la Navidad *Christmas*, 9

la necesidad *necessity*, 7

necesitar *to need*, 4; **¿Necesitas algo?** *Do you need anything?*, 4; **Necesito muchas cosas.** *I need a lot of things.*, 4; **No, no necesito nada.** *No, I do not need anything.*, 4

negarse *to refuse*, 5

negociable *negotiable*, 5

el negocio *business*, 9

negro(a) *black*, 5

nervioso(a) *nervous*, 7

nevar (ie) *to snow*, 3

ni *neither, nor*, 7; **Ni idea.** *I have no idea.*, 3

el nido *nest*, 1

la nieta *granddaughter*, 5

el nieto *grandson*, 5

los nietos *grandsons, grandchildren*, 5

nieva *it snows*, 3

la niña *girl*, 1

ninguno(a) *no, none*, 10G; **ninguna parte** *nowhere*, 3; **no va a ninguna parte** *he/she doesn't go anywhere*, 3

el niño *male child*, 8

los niños *children*, 8

el nivel del mar *sea level*, 9G

no no, 3; *not, do not*, 5; **No debes...** *You shouldn't . . .*, 7; **No es gran cosa.** *It's not a big deal.*, 5; **No está.** *He/She is not here.*, 8; **No estoy de acuerdo.** *I disagree.*, 6; **no, gracias** *no thank you*, 8; **no más** *just, only*, 8; **No sé.** *I don't know.*, 4; **No, no me gusta(n)...** *No, I don't like . . .*, 2; **No, no necesito nada.** *No, I do not need anything.*, 4; **No, no voy a ir.** *No, I'm not going to go.*, 4; **No seas...** *Don't be . . .*, 7; **no va a ninguna parte** *he/she doesn't go anywhere*, 3; **No vayas.** *Don't go.*, 7

¿no? *right?*, 4

la Nochebuena *Christmas Eve*, 9

la Nochevieja *New Year's Eve*, 9

nocturno(a) *(in the) evening*, 4

nombrado(a) *named*, 9G

el nombre *name*, 10

el noreste *northeast*, 2G

normalmente *normally*, 4

el noroeste *northwest*, 7G

el norte *north*, 5G

norteamericano(a) *North American*, 8

norteño(a) *northern*, 5G

Noruega *Norway*, 7G

nos *(to/for) us*, 2; **Nos vemos.** *See you.*, 1

nosotros(as) *we*, 1

la nota *grade*, 6

la noticia *news*, 9

novecientos *nine hundred*, 8

la novela *novel*, 3

noventa *ninety*, 2

noviembre *November*, 1

la nube *cloud*, 7

nuestro(a) *our*, 5

nuestros(as) *our*, 5

nuevamente *again*, 9

nueve *nine*, 1

nuevo(a) *new*, 2

la nuez (pl. las nueces) *nuts*, 6

el número *number*, 1; *shoe size*, 8

numeroso(a) *numerous*, 2G

nunca *never*, 5; **casi nunca** *almost never*, 3; nunca más *never again*, 6

la nutricionista *nutritionist*, 7

o *or*, 2

oaxaqueño *from the Mexican state of Oaxaca*, 6

el objetivo *objective*, 1

el objeto *object*, 1

la obra *work*, 7G; la obra de teatro *play*, 6G; la obra maestra *masterpiece*, 6G

observar *to observe*, 1

la ocasión *occasion*, 9

occidental *western*, 7G

ochenta *eighty*, 2

ocho *eight*, 1

ochocientos *eight hundred*, 8

el ocio *leisure time*, 8

octubre *October*, 1

el ocupante *occupant*, 10

ocupar *to occupy*, 7G

ocurrir *to occur*; ¿se te ocurren? *do they occur to you?*, 4

la oficina *office*, 5

la oficina de cambio *money exchange*, 10

la oficina de correos *post office*, 10

ofrecer *to offer*, 6

el oído *ear*, 7

oír *to hear*, 2; oyes *(you) hear*, 2; se oye *is heard*, 2

los ojos *eyes*, 5; los ojos borrados *hazel eyes*, 5; los ojos cafés *brown eyes*, 5; **tener los ojos azules** *to have blue eyes*, 5

la ola *wave*, 2G

la olla *pot*, 4G

olor *smell*, 7

olvidar *to forget*, 9; no te olvides *don't forget*, 8

once *eleven*, 1

la oportunidad *opportunity*, 5

la oración *sentence*, xxii

el orden *order*, 1; el orden cronológico *chronological order*, 8

ordenar *to organize*, 3; está ordenando *is organizing*, 3

organizado(a) *organized*, 2

organizar *to organize*, 10

orgulloso(a) *proud*, 6

el origen *origin*, 6G

originalmente *originally*, 3G

os *(to/for) you* (pl.), 2

el oso *bear*, 1

el otoño *fall*, 3

otro(a) *other*, 4; *another*, 6

otros(as) *other, others*, 6

el paciente *patient*, 7

el padre *father*, 5

los padres *parents*, 5; los padres peregrinos *pilgrims*, 8G

pagar *to pay*, 8; **pagar una fortuna** *to pay a fortune*, 8

la **página** *page*, xxii; la página Web *Web page*, 1

el **país** *country*, 6; el país de origen *native country*, 6

el paisaje *landscape*, 4G

el pájaro *bird*, 9

la palabra *word*, xxii; la palabra clave *key word*, 1

el palacio *palace*, 1

el **pan** *bread*, 6; **el pan dulce** *pastries*, 6; **el pan tostado** *toast*, 6

la **pantalla** *monitor, screen*, 10

los **pantalones (vaqueros)** *pants (jeans)*, 8

los **pantalones cortos** *shorts*, 8

la pantomima *pantomime*, 9

la **pantorrilla** *calf*, 7

el **papá** *dad*, 5

el Papá Noel *Santa Claus*, 9

la **papa** *potato*, 6; **las papas fritas** *french fries*, 6

el **papel** *paper*, 4

las **papitas** *potato chips*, 9

el paquete *package*, 9

el **par** *pair*, 8

para *for*, 4; *to, in order to*, 7

el paraíso *paradise*, 8G

parecer *to seem*, 5; *to think*, 8; me parece *it seems to me*, 9; **Me parece bien.** *it's all right/seems fine to me*, 5; **Me parece injusto.** *I don't think that's fair; It seems unfair to me.*, 5; no parezco *I don't seem to be.*, 9; **¿Qué te parece...?** *What do you think of . . .?*, 8

parecido(a) *similar*, 2

la pared *wall*, 10G

la pareja *pair*; en parejas *in pairs*, xxii, *couple*, 3

el paréntesis *parenthesis*, 8

el pareo *matching*, 1

el pariente *relative*, 5

el **parque** *park*, 3; **el parque de diversiones** *amusement park*, 10

el párrafo *paragraph*, xxii

la parrilla *barbecue*, 7

la parrillada *Argentine barbecue*, 7G

la parte *part*, 6

participar *to participate*, 1

particular *particular*, 6

el **partido de...** *the . . . game*, 4

la pasa *raisin*, 6

el pasado *past*, 8

pasado mañana *day after tomorrow*, 4

pasado(a) *last*, 8; **el año pasado** *last year*, 9

pasado(a) de moda *out of style*, 8

el pasaje *ticket*, 10

el **pasajero, la pasajera** *passenger*, 10

el pasapalo *finger food (Ven.)*, 9

el **pasaporte** *passport*, 10

pasar *to spend (time, occasion)*, 9; con quien tú te pasas *who you spend time with*, 2; **la pasamos en casa de...** *we spent it at . . .'s house*, 9; lo que pasa *what is happening*, 9; **pasar el rato solo(a)** *to spend time alone*, 3; **pasar la aspiradora** *to vacuum*, 5; **pasar por** *to go by*, 10; *to go through*, 2; qué pasa *what's happening*, 6

pasártelo(la) *to get someone (for a telephone call)*, 8

el **pasatiempo** *hobby*, 7; **buscar un pasatiempo** *to look for a hobby*, 7

pasear *to go for a walk*, 3; *to go out in*, 10; **pasear en bote de vela** *to go out in a sailboat*, 10; **pasear en lancha** *to go out in a motorboat*, 10

el pasillo *corridor*, 10

la **pasta de dientes** *toothpaste*, 7

el **pastel** *cake*, 6

el pastel en hojas *mashed plantain dough filled with meat and wrapped in plantain leaves*, 9

la patata *potato*, 1G; *sweet potato*, 6

el patinaje en hielo *ice skating*, 7

patinar *to skate*, 3

el **patio** *patio, yard*, 5

la patrona *patron*, 9G

la pava *kettle used to make mate*, 7

el pavo *turkey*, 6G

el payaso *clown*, 4G

el **pecho** *chest*, 7

pedir (ie) *to order*, 6

peinarse *to comb your hair*, 7

el peine *comb*, 7

la **película** *film, movie*, 2; (de ciencia ficción, de terror, de misterio) *(science fiction, horror, mystery)*, 2

el peligro de extinción *danger of extinction*, 8G

pelirrojo(a) *red-headed*, 2

el **pelo** *hair*, 5

la pelota *ball*, 9G

pensar (ie) *to think*, 8; **pensar + inf.** *to plan*, 9; **Pensamos...** *We plan to . . .*, 9

peor(es) *worse*, 8

pequeño(a) *small*, 5; **bastante pequeño(a)** *pretty small*, 5

la pera *pear*, 1

perder (ie) *to lose*, 10; *to miss*, 10; **perder el vuelo** *miss the flight*, 10; si me pierden *if you lose me*

perdido(a) *lost*, 10G

perdone *I'm sorry*, 1

el perezoso *sloth*, 4G

perezoso(a) *lazy*, 2

perfecto *perfect*, 8

el periódico *newspaper*, 8G

la perla *pearl*, 2G

permiso *excuse me*, 9

permitir *to allow*, 6

pero *but*, 5

el **perro, la perra** *dog*, 5

la **persona** *person*, 2

el personaje *character*, 1G; el personaje ficticio *fictional character*, 1G

la personalidad *personality*, 2

las **pesas** *weights*, 7; **levantar pesas** *to lift weights*, 7

la **pesca** *fishing*, 10; **ir de pesca** *to go fishing*, 10; la pesca comercial *commercial fishing*, 8G

el **pescado** *fish*, 6

pescar *to fish*, 10

pésimo(a) *very bad*, 2

el **peso** *weight*, 7

el **pez** *fish*, 1

la picadera *finger food (Dom. Rep.)*, 9

el **picante** *spice*, 6

picante *spicy*, 6

el **picnic** *picnic*, 9; **tener un picnic** *to have a picnic*, 9

el pico *peak*, 1G

el pico de gallo *spicy relish made with tomatoes, hot peppers, and onions*, 3

el **pie** *foot*, 7

la piedra *stone*, 5G

la **pierna** *leg*, 7

la pieza *bedroom*, 5; *piece*, 4

la pileta *swimming pool*, 3

la **piñata** *piñata*, 9

el pingüino *penguin*, 7G

pintado(a) *painted*, 2G

pintar *to paint*; fue pintado *was painted*, 1

el pintor *painter*, 2G

pintoresco(a) *picturesque*, 7G

la pintura *painting*, 1; la pintura al óleo *oil painting*, 3G

la **pirámide** *pyramid*, 10; la pirámide alimenticia *food pyramid*, 7

la **piscina** *pool*, 3

el **piso** *floor*, 5; **de... pisos** *. . .-story*, 5

el **piyama** *pajamas*, 7

la **pizza** *pizza*, 2

el placer *pleasure*, 9

planes *plan*, 9; **¿Qué planes tienen para...?** *What plans do you have for . . .?*, 9

plano(a) *flat*, 7G

las **plantas** *plants*, 5

el plátano *plantain*, 8G

platicar *to chat*, 3

el **plato** *dish, plate*, 6; **lavar los platos** *to wash the dishes*, 5; **el plato hondo** *bowl*, 6; el plato típico *traditional dish*, 2

la **playa** *beach*, 3

la playera *T-shirt*, 8

la **plaza de comida** *food court in a mall*, 8

la **plena** *music and dance style,* 2

la **población** *population,* 1G

poblado(a) *populated,* 4G

pobre *poor,* 8

poco(a) *few, little, not much,* 4; poco a poco *little by little,* 4; **un poco** *a little,* 2

pocos(as) *few, not many,* 4

poder (ue) *to be able to, can,* 6

el **poema** *poem,* 8

la **poesía** *poetry,* 8

el **poeta, la poeta** *poet,* 5G

el **policía** *police officer,* 5

el **pollo** *chicken,* 6; el pollo frito *fried chicken,* 2G

el **ponche** *punch,* 9

poner (-go) *to put,* 4; **no pongas** *don't put,* 10; **pon** *put,* 6; poner en orden *to put in order,* xxii; poner huevos *to lay eggs,* 2; poner la comida *to set out the food,* 9; **poner la mesa** *to set the table,* 6; tener puesto(a) *to have on,* 8

ponerse *to put on,* 7, *to get,* 6; ponerse *to start,* 7; ponerse a bailar *to start dancing,* 3; ponerse en contacto *to get in contact,* 5; ponerse rojo *to flush, to turn red,* 10

por *in, by,* 4; por ejemplo *for example,* 6G; por eso *that's why,* 6; **por favor** *please,* 6; por fin *at last,* 8; **por la mañana** *in the morning,* 4; por la noche *at night,* 2; **por la tarde** *in the afternoon,* 4; por lo general *generally,* 8; por lo menos *at least,* 9; por más que *no matter how much,* 7; por medio de *by means of,* 10

¿por qué? *why?,* 2

la **porción** *portion, serving,* 7

porque *because,* 2

posible *possible,* 4

el **postre** *dessert,* 6

el **pozole** *soup made with hominy, meat, and chile,* 6

practicando *practicing,* 7

practicar deportes *to play sports,* 3

el **precio** *price,* 1; el precio de entrada *entry fee,* 1

precolombino(a) *of the New World era before the arrival of Europeans,* 2G

precoz *precocious,* 4

la **preferencia** *preference,* 3

preferido(a) *favorite,* 4

preferir (ie) *to prefer,* 6

la **pregunta** *question,* xxii

preguntar *to ask,* xxii

prehistórico(a) *prehistoric,* 7

preocuparse *to worry,* 10; **No te preocupes.** *Don't worry.,* 10

preparar *to prepare,* 6

prepararse *to get ready,* 7

los **preparativos** *preparations,* 9

la **preposición** *preposition,* 2

la **presentación** *introduction,* 9

presentar *to present,* 6; *to introduce,* 9; **presentar el examen** *to take an exam,* 4; se presentó *was performed,* 10; **te presento a...** *I'd like you to meet . . .,* 9

presentarse *to present oneself,* 6

el **presente** *present,* 9

prestar: prestar atención *to pay attention,* 7

el **pretérito** *preterite,* 8

la **primavera** *spring,* 3

el **primero** *first,* 1

primero(a) *first,* 4

el **primo, la prima** *cousin,* 5; el primo hermano, la prima hermana *first cousin,* 5

los **primos** *cousins,* 5

la **princesa** *princess,* 10

principal *main,* 4G; *primary,* 9G

la **prisa** *hurry;* **tener prisa** *to be in a hurry,* 4

el **prisionero** *prisoner,* 10

probar (ue) *to try, to taste,* 6

producir *to produce,* 1

el **producto** *product,* 3G; los productos petroleros *petroleum products,* 3G; los productos químicos *chemicals,* 3G

el **profesor** *teacher (male),* 1; **mi profesor** *my teacher,* 1

la **profesora** *teacher (female),* 1; **mi profesora** *my teacher,* 1

prometer *to promise,* 8

el **pronombre** *pronoun,* 6; el pronombre de complemento directo *direct object pronoun,* 9; el pronombre reflexivo *reflexive pronoun,* 7

pronto *soon,* 1; **Hasta pronto.** *See you soon.,* 1; tan pronto *as soon,* 9

la **propiedad** *property,* 5

propio(a) *own,* 4

el **propósito** *purpose,* 6

el **provecho** *benefit;* Buen provecho. *Enjoy your meal.,* 6

la **provincia** *province,* 10

próximo(a) *next,* 4; **la próxima semana** *next week,* 4; **el** *(day of the week)* **próximo** *next (day of the week),* 4

el **proyecto** *project,* 1

publicar *to publish,* 1

el **pueblo** *town, village,* 4; el pueblo natal *birth place,* 3

¿Puedo...? *Can I . . .?,* 6

el **puente** *bridge,* 8G

la **puerta** *door,* 5; *gate,* 10

el **puerto** *port,* 3G

el **puesto** *stall,* 9G

la **pulsera** *bracelet,* 8

el **punto** *dot,* 1

el **punto de vista** *point of view,* 9

puntual *punctual, on time,* 2

el **puré de papas** *mashed potatoes,* 6

que *that;* que me llame después *tell him/her to call me later,* 8; **Que te vaya bien.** *Hope things go well for you.,* 9

¡Qué...! *How . . .!,* 6; ¡Qué bien! *How great!,* 10; ¡Qué fantástico! *How fantastic!,* 10; ¡Qué gusto verte! *It's great to see you!,* 9; **¡Qué lástima!** *What a shame!,* 10; ¡Qué lata! *What a pain!,* 5; **¡Qué mala suerte!** *What bad luck!,* 10

¿qué? *what?,* 1; **¿Qué clases tienes ...?** *What classes do you have . . .?,* 4; ¿Qué día es hoy? *What day is today?,* 1; **¿Qué están haciendo?** *What are they doing?,* 9; **¿Qué fecha es hoy?** *What's today's date?,* 1; **¿Qué hace...?** *What does . . . do?,* 3; **¿Qué haces para ayudar en casa?** *What do you do to help out at home?,* 5; **¿Qué haces...?** *What do you do . . .?,* 3; **¿Qué haces para relajarte?** *What do you do to relax?,* 7; ¿Qué hay de nuevo? *What's new?,* 9; **¿Qué hiciste?** *What did you do?,* 8; ¿Qué hora es? *What time is it?,* 1; **¿Qué planes tienen para...?** *What plans do you have for . . .?,* 9; **¿Qué quieres hacer?** *What do you want to do?,* 3; **¿Qué tal?** *How's it going?,* 1; **¿Qué tal...?** *How is . . .?,* 6; **¿Qué tal estuvo?** *How was it?,* 9; **¿Qué tal si...?** *How about if. . .?,* 6; **¿Qué tal si vamos a...?** *How about if we go to . . .?,* 4; **¿Qué te falta hacer?** *What do you still have to do?,* 7; **¿Qué te gusta hacer?** *What do you like to do?,* 3; **¿Qué te pasa?** *What's wrong with you?,* 7; **¿Qué te toca hacer a ti?** *What do you have to do?,* 5; **¿Qué tiempo hace?** *What's the weather like?,* 3; **¿Qué tiene...?** *What's the matter with . . .?,* 7; **¿Qué tienes que hacer?** *What do you have to do?,* 7; **¿Qué vas a hacer?** *What are you going to do?,* 4

el **quechua** indigenous *language in Peru*, 10G

quedar *to fit, to look*, 8; *to remain*, 3G; **¿Cómo me queda...?** *How does it fit?*, 8; **quedar bien/mal** *to fit well/badly*, 8

quedarse *to stay*, 9; **quedarse en...** *to stay in . . .*, 10

los **quehaceres** *household chores*, 5; **hacer los quehaceres** *to do chores*, 5

querer (ie) *to want to*, 3; *to love*, 9; **quiero conocer...** *I want to see . . .*, 10; **queriendo** *wanting to*, 8; **Quiero ir...** *I want to go . . .*, 3

querido(a) *dear*, 9

la **quesadilla** *tortillas with melted cheese*, 3G

el **queso** *cheese*, 6

¿quién? *who?*, 1; **¿De parte de quién?** *Who's calling?*, 8; **Quién es...?** *Who's. . .?*, 1; **¿de quién?** *about whom?*, 1

¿quiénes? *who?* (pl.), 2

la **química** *chemistry*, 4

quince *fifteen*, 1

la **quinceañera** *girl's fifteenth birthday*, 9

quinientos *five hundred*, 8

el **quiosco** *stand*, 10

Quisiera... *I would like . . .*, 6

quitarse *to take off*, 7

la **raíz** (pl. las **raíces**) *root*, 1G

la **rana** *frog*, 2

los **rancheros** *overalls*, 3

rápidamente *quickly*, 6

rápido(a) *fast*, 8

raro *odd, strange*, 3

rato: pasar el rato... *to spend time . . .* el **rato libre** *free time*, 4

reaccionar *to react*, 10

el **realismo** *realism*, 1

realizar *to carry out*, 10, ha realizado *has carried out*, 10G

el **recado** *message*, 8

la **recámara** *bedroom*, 5

recibir *to receive*, 9; **recibir regalos** *to receive gifts*, 9

reclamar *to reclaim*, 6G

el **reclamo de equipaje** *baggage claim*, 10

recoger *to pick up*, 10

la **recomendación** *recommendation*, 7

reconocido(a) *well-known*, 1G

recordar *to remember*, 6

recorrer *to tour*, 10

el **recorrido** *tour*, 4

el **recreo** *recreation time*, 4

la **red** *network*, 10G

redondo(a) *round*, 7

reducir *to reduce*, 7

referir *to refer*, 3; se refiere *refers*, 3G

reflejar *to reflect*, 1G

el **refrán** *proverb, saying*, 6

el **refresco** *soft drink*, 6

el **refrigerador** *refrigerator*, 6

el **refugio de fauna** *wildlife refuge*, 8G

el **regalo** *gift*, 9; **abrir regalos** *to open gifts*, 9; **recibir regalos** *to receive gifts*, 9

regatear *to bargain*, 8

la **región** *region*, 3

regional *regional*, 6

la **regla** *ruler*, 4

regresar *to return, to go back*, 4

regular *all right*, 1; **estoy regular** *I'm all right*, 1

regularidad: con regularidad *regularly*, 6

reírse *to laugh*, 8; ríe *he/she laughs*, 9; se ríen *they laugh*, 8

relajarse *to relax*, 7

religioso(a) *religious*, 1

el **reloj** *watch, clock*, 4

remodelado(a) *remodeled*, 5

remojar *to soak*, 3

remoto(a) *distant*, 5

el **renacuajo** *tadpole*, 2

el **repaso** *review*, 1

representar *to represent*, 3

representativo(a) *representative*, 6

la **respuesta** *answer*, xxii

la **república** *republic*, 5G

el **res** *beast, livestock*; la **carne de res** *beef*, 6

la **reservación** *reservation*, 6

requerir (ie) *to require*, 7

la **resolución de Año Nuevo** *New Year's resolution*, 9

resolver (ue) *to solve*, 7

respectivo(a) *respective*, 8

responder *to answer*, 9

la **respuesta** *answer*, 3

el **restaurante familiar** *family restaurant*, 3

el **retrato** *portrait*, 1G

la **reunión** *meeting*, 3; *reunion*, 9

reunir *to bring together*, 1G

reunirse *to get together*, 9; **reunirse con (toda) la familia** *to get together with the (whole) family*, 9

revisar *to check, to revise, to correct*, 1

la **revista** *magazine*, 3; **la revista de tiras cómicas** *comic book*, 8

el **revolucionario** *revolutionary*, 9G

el **rey** *king*, 1

rico(a) *magnificent*, 9

ridículo(a) *ridiculous*, 8

riguroso(a) *harsh*, 5G

el **río** *river*, 3G

las **riquezas** *riches*, 10

riquísimo(a) *delicious*, 6

el **ritmo** *rhythm*, 5G; el ritmo del momento *the latest rhythm*, 1

el **rito** *ritual*, 6

el **robo: ¡Es un robo!** *It's a rip-off!*, 8

rodeado(a) *surrounded*, 1G

rodear *to surround*, 7G

el **rodeo** *rodeo*, 3G

rojo(a) *red*, 8

romántico(a) *romantic*, 2

el **rompecabezas** *puzzle*, 4

la **ropa** *clothes*, 4

rubio(a) *blond*, 2

las **ruinas** *ruins*, 10

la **rutina** *routine*, 2

el **sábado** *Saturday*, 1; **los sábados** *on Saturdays*, 3

saber *to know*, 4; **saber de** *to know about*, 4; no sabe cómo *doesn't know how*, 9; **No sé.** *I don't know.*, 4; **¿Sabes qué?** *You know what?*, 4; Sé. *I know.*, 9

el **sabor** *flavor*, 9

sacar *to take out*, 6; **sacar el dinero** *to get money*, 10; **sacar fotos** *to take photos*, 10; **sacar la basura** *to take out the trash*, 5; sacar una idea *to get an idea*, 4

el **saco** *jacket*, 8

sal *go out, leave*, 6

la **sal** *salt*, 6

la **sala** *living room*, 5; **la sala de espera** *waiting room*, 10; la sala de juegos *game room*, 5

salado(a) *salty*, 6

la **salida** *departure*, 10; *exit*, 10

salir (-go, ie) *to go out*, 3; *to leave*, 4; **no salgas** *don't leave*, 10; que salga *to go out*, 9; **sal** *go out, leave*, 6; salir bien *to work out well*, 7; **salir con amigos** *to go out with friends*, 3

el **salón** *room*, 1; **el salón de clase** *classroom*, 4

la **salsa** *sauce, gravy*, 6; **la salsa picante** *hot sauce*, 6

el **salto** *waterfall*, 2G

el **salto en el tiempo** *time warp*, 7

la **salud** *health*, 7

saludable *healthy*, 6

saludar   *to greet,* 1
el saludo   *greeting,* 9
salvarse   *to save oneself,* 10
el salvavidas   *lifeguard,* 1
el sancocho   *stew made with meat, root vegetables and plantains,* 9G
las sandalias   *sandals,* 8
el sándwich de...   *. . . sandwich,* 6
los sanitarios   *restrooms,* 10
sano(a)   *healthy,* 7; **seguir una dieta sana**   *to eat a balanced diet,* 7
el santo, la santa   *saint,* 2G
sé   *be,* 6
la secadora de pelo   *hair dryer,* 7
secarse   *to dry,* 7
la sección rítmica   *rhythm section,* 8G
seco(a)   *dry,* 2G
secreto(a)   *secret,* 1
la sed   *thirst,* 4; **tener sed**   *to be thirsty,* 4
la seda   *silk,* 8; **de seda**   *made of silk,* 8
seguir (i)   *to follow,* 10; **seguir (i) una dieta sana**   *to eat a balanced diet,* 7; sigue el modelo   *follow the model,* xxii; siguiéndote   *following you,* 8
según   *according to,* 2
el segundo   *second,* 4
segundo(a)   *second,* 6
seis   *six,* 1
seiscientos   *six hundred,* 8
la selección   *selection,* 6
la selva   *jungle,* 10
la semana   *week,* 4; **el día de la semana**   *day of the week,* 1; **esta semana**   *this week,* 4; **la próxima semana**   *next week,* 4
la Semana Santa   *Holy Week,* 9
el señor   *sir, Mr.,* 1; *gentleman,* 8
el Señor   *the Lord,* 9
la señora   *ma'am; Mrs.,* 1
la señorita   *miss,* 1
la sensación   *feeling,* 1
sentarse (ie)   *to sit down,* 10
sentir (ie)   *to feel,* 9
sentirse (ie)   *to feel,* 7
separados   *separately,* 8
separar   *to separate,* 1G
septiembre   *September,* 1
ser   *to be,* 1; **¿Cómo eres?**   *What are you like?,* 2; **¿Cómo es...?**   *What is . . . like?,* 2; No puede ser. *It can't be true.,* 9; **no seas**   *don't be,* 7; **sé**   *be,* 6; **será**   *will be,* 10; **Soy...**   *I'm . . .,* 2; **Soy de...**   *I'm from . . .,* 1
el ser   *being,* 8
la serenata   *serenade,* 9
la serenidad   *serenity,* 1
la serie   *series,* 6G
serio(a)   *serious,* 2
la serpiente   *serpent,* 6

el servicio   *restroom,* 10
la servilleta   *napkin,* 6
servir (i)   *to serve,* 6; **¿En qué le puedo servir?**   *Can I help you?,* 8
sesenta   *sixty,* 2
el seso   *brain,* 4
setecientos   *seven hundred,* 8
setenta   *seventy,* 2
si   *if,* 3; si no   *otherwise,* 3
sí   *yes,* 4
siempre   *always,* 5; **casi siempre**   *almost always,* 3; **como siempre**   *as always,* 9
la sierra   *mountain range,* 10G
siete   *seven,* 1
el siglo   *century,* 3G
el significado   *meaning,* 7
significar   *to mean,* 2
siguiente   *following,* 5; **lo siguiente**   *the following,* 6
la sílaba   *syllable,* 2
la silla   *chair,* 5; **la silla de ruedas**   *wheelchair,* 5
el símbolo   *symbol,* 2
simpático(a)   *friendly,* 2
simplemente   *simply,* 6
sin   *without,* 6; sin embargo   *however,* 6
la sinagoga   *synagogue,* 9
sincero(a)   *sincere,* 2
sino   *but also,* 6
los sirvientes   *servants,* 8
el sistema   *system,* 10G
el sitio   *place,* 3; *site,* 7
la situación   *situation,* 5
sobre   *over,* 3; *on,* 4; *about,* 2
la sobrina   *niece,* 5
el sobrino   *nephew,* 5
los sobrinos   *nephews, nieces and nephews,* 5
sociable   *social,* 2
el sofá   *sofa,* 5
el sol   *sun,* 3; **Hace sol.**   *It's sunny.,* 3
solamente   *only,* 3G
el soldado   *soldier,* 6G
soler   *to usually do,* 5; suele   *usually,* 5
sólido(a)   *solid,* 6
solo(a)   *alone,* 3; **pasar el rato solo(a)**   *to spend time alone,* 3;
sólo   *only,* 7
el sombrero   *hat,* 8
somos (inf. ser)   *we are,* 5; **somos... personas**   *there are . . . people,* 5
Son las...   *It's . . . o'clock.,* 1
el sonido   *sound,* 2G
la sopa   *soup,* 6; **la sopa de verduras**   *vegetable soup,* 6
sordo(a)   *deaf,* 5
sorprendido(a)   *surprised,* 8
Soy...   (inf. ser)   *I'm . . .,* 2; **Soy de...**   *I'm from . . .,* 1
su(s)   *his, her, its, their,* 5

suave   *soft,* 7
subir   *to rise,* 7
subir a la montaña   *to go up a mountain,* 10; **subir de peso**   *to gain weight,* 7
el subtítulo   *subtitle,* 10
sucio(a)   *dirty,* 6
el sudeste   *south east,* 10G
el sueño   *dream,* 1G
la suerte   *luck,* 10; **si tengo suerte...**   *if I'm lucky . . .,* 10; **tuviste suerte**   *you were lucky,* 10
el suéter   *sweater,* 8
suficiente   *enough,* 7; **dormir lo suficiente**   *to get enough sleep,* 7
la sugerencia   *suggestion,* 7
sugerir   *to suggest,* 6
Suiza   *Switzerland,* 7G
la superficie   *surface,* 8
el sur   *south,* 2G
sureño(a)   *southern,* 7G
el surf a vela   *windsurfing,* 9G
sus   *his/her,* 4; *their, your,* 5
la sustancia   *substance,* 6
suyo(a)   *his,* 4G

Tailandia   *Thailand,* 6
taíno(a)   *belonging to the Tainos, Native Americans dominant in early Puerto Rico,* 2G
tal   *such,* 7; tal vez   *perhaps,* 4
la talla   *(clothing) size,* 8
tallado(a)   *carved, cut,* 10G
los tallarines   *noodles,* 7
el taller   *workshop,* 4
la tamalada   *gathering to make tamales,* 3G
los tamales   *tamales,* 9
el tamaño   *size*
también   *also,* 2
la tambora   *drum,* 9G
tampoco   *neither, not either,* 5
tan   *so,* 10G
tan sólo   *only,* 9
tan... como   *as . . . as,* 8
tanto   *so much,* 7; *as much,* 1G; tanto... como...   *both . . . and . . .,* 3G; **Tanto gusto.**   *So nice to meet you.,* 9; **Tanto tiempo.**   *It's been a long time.,* 1; **¡Tanto tiempo sin verte!**   *Long time, no see.,* 9
la tapa   *small servings of food,* 7G
tardar   *to take;* ¿Cuánto tardas? *How long do you take?,* 4
la tarde   *afternoon,* 4; **esta tarde**   *this afternoon,* 4; **por la tarde**   *in the*

afternoon, 4

tarde *late*, 4; **más tarde** *later*, 8

la **tarea** *homework*, 1; **hacer la tarea** *to do homework*, 3

la **tarjeta** *greeting card*, 8; *card*, 9; **mandar tarjetas** *to send cards*, 9; **la tarjeta de cumpleaños** *birthday card*, 8; la tarjeta de crédito *credit card*, 10; **la tarjeta de embarque** *boarding pass*, 10; la tarjeta postal *postcard*, 10

el **tataranieto** *great-great-grandson*, 10

el **taxi** *taxi*, 10

te *(to/for) you*, 2; **¿Te duele algo?** *Is something hurting you?*, 7; **¿Te gusta(n)...?** *Do you like ...?*, 2; **¿Te gusta(n) más... o...?** *Do you like ... or ... more?*, 2; **Te llamo más tarde.** *I'll call you later.*, 9; **Te presento a...** *I'd like you to meet ...*, 9; **Te veo mal.** *You don't look well.*, 7

el **teatro** *theater*, 8

el **techo de zinc** *sheet-metal roof*, 9G

la **tecnología** *technology*, 4

tejano(a) *Texan*, 3G

el **tejido** *weaving*, 10G

la **tele** *TV*, 4

el **teléfono** *telephone number*, 1; *telephone*, 8; **¿Cuál es el teléfono de...?** *What's ...'s telephone number?*, 1; **¿Cuál es tu teléfono?** *What's your telephone number?*, 1; **hablar por teléfono** *to talk on the phone*, 3; llamar por teléfono *to make a phone call*, 8; el teléfono público *pay phone*, 10

la **televisión** *television (TV)*, 3; **ver televisión** *to watch TV*, 3

el **tema** *theme*, 6

temblar *to shake*, 9

tembloroso(a) *trembling*, 9

la **temperatura** *temperature*, 2G

templado(a) *temperate*, 2G

el **templo** *temple*, 9

temprano *early*, 4

ten *have*, 6

el **tenedor** *fork*, 6

tener (-go, ie) *to have*, 4; **Cuántos años tiene...?** *How old is ...?*, 2; **¿Cuántos años tienes?** *How old are you?*, 2; **Él (Ella) tiene... años.** *He's (She's) ... years old.*, 2; **no tengas** *don't have*, 10; **ten** *have*, 6; tendrán que separarse *will have to separate*, 3; **tener calor** *to be hot*, 7; **tener catarro** *to have a cold*, 7; **tener frío** *to be cold*, 7; **tener ganas** *to feel like (doing something)*, 4; **tener ganas de +** infinitive *to feel like doing something*, 4; **tener hambre** *to be*

hungry, 4; **tener los ojos azules** *to have blue eyes*, 5; **tener miedo** *to be scared*, 7; **tener prisa** *to be in a hurry*, 4; tener puesto *to have on*, 3; **tener que +** infinitive *to have to (do something)*, 4; **tener razón** *to be right*, 8; **tener sed** *to be thirsty*, 4; **tener sueño** *to be sleepy*, 7; **tener suerte** *to be lucky*, 10; **tener un picnic** *to have a picnic*, 9; **Tengo que irme.** *I've got to go.*, 1; **Tengo... años.** *I am ... years old.*, 2; **Tiene... años.** *He's (She's) ... years old.*, 2; tuvo *had*, 7G

el **tenis** *tennis*, 3

el **tentempié** *snack*, 3G

el **tercero** *third*, 4

terminar *to finish*, 9

la **terraza de comidas** *food court in a mall*, 8

el **territorio** *territory*, 6G

el **terror** *horror*, 2

el **testimonio** *testimony*, 6G

el **texto** *text*, 6

ti *you (emphatic)*, 3; a ti *to you*, 6; A ti te gusta + infinitive *You like ...*, 3; para ti *for you*, 2

la **tía** *aunt*, 5

el **tico** *nickname for Costa Rican*, 4G

el **tiempo** *weather*, 3; *time*, 1G; **a tiempo** *on time*, 4; **cuando hace buen/mal tiempo** *when the weather's good/bad*, 3

la **tienda de...** *... store*, 8

tiene *he/she/it has*, 2; **¿Cuántos años tiene...?** *How old is ...?*, 2; **Él (Ella) tiene... años.** *He's (She's) ... years old.*, 2; **Tiene... años.** *He's (She's) ... years old.*, 2

tienes *you have*, 4; **¿Cuántos años tienes?** *How old are you?*, 2; **¿Tienes...?** *Do you have ...?*, 4

la **tierra** *earth*, 6; *land*, 6G

el **tigre** *tiger*, 2

la **tilde** *wavy line above the ñ*, 1

tímido(a) *shy*, 2

la **tinta** *ink*, 10

el **tío** *uncle*, 5

los **tíos** *uncles, uncles and aunts*, 5

típico(a) *typical*, 2G

el **tipo** *type; de todo tipo all kinds*, 8; el **título** *title*, 5

la **toalla** *towel*, 7

tocar *to play*, 3; *to touch*, 8; **A mí siempre me toca...** *I always have to ...*, 5; **A... nunca le toca...** *It's never ...'s turn; ... never has to ...*, 5; Le toca a él. *It's his turn.*, 9; **¿Qué te toca hacer a ti?** *What do you have to do?*, 5, Te toca a ti. *It's your turn.*, 6; **tocar el piano** *to play the piano*, 3; tocar la puerta

to knock on the door, 3

el **tocino** *bacon*, 6

todavía *yet*, 10; *still*, 1G; **todavía no** *not yet*, 10

todo(a) *all, every*, 2; *whole*, 9; todo el mundo *everybody*, 9; de todo *everything*, 8; de todo tipo *all kinds*, 8; **todos(as)** *everyone*, 5; **todos los días** *every day*, 3

tomar *to drink*, 6; *to eat*, 8; *to take*, 9; siguen tomándolo *keep drinking it*, 6; *to take*, 7; **tomar el sol** *to sunbathe*, 10; tomar las cosas con calma *to take things calmly*, 7; tomar una decisión *to make a decision*, 9; **tomar un batido** *to have a milkshake*, 8

el **tomate** *tomato*, 6

la **tonelada** *ton*, 10

tonto(a) *dumb*, 2

el **tornado** *tornado*, 3

la **toronja** *grapefruit*, 3G

la **torta** *sandwich (Mexico)*, 6

la **tortilla** *Spanish omelet*, 1G; *pancake-like bread made from corn*, 6

la **tortuga** *turtle*, 1

el **tostón** *fried green plantain*, 2G

trabajador(a) *hard-working*, 2

trabajar *to work*, 3

el **trabajo** *job*, 3; *work*, 4

el **trabalenguas** *tongue twister*, 1

la **tradición** *tradition*, 2

tradicional *traditional*, 1G

traer (-igo) *to bring*, 4; me trajo *he/she brought me*, 4; quiero que me traigas *I want you to bring me*, 9

el **tráfico** *traffic*, 3G

tragar *to swallow*, 2

el **traje** *suit*, 3; *dress*, 1G

el **traje de baño** *swimsuit*, 8

tranquilo(a) *quiet*, 5; *calm*, 9

la **transpiración** *perspiration*, 8

transportar *to transport*, 10; fueron transportadas *were transported*, 10

el **transporte** *transportation*, 10

el **trasto** *utensil, piece of junk*, 2

tratar *to try*, 10

travieso(a) *mischievous*, 5

trece *thirteen*, 1

treinta *thirty*, 1

treinta y cinco *thirty-five*, 2

treinta y dos *thirty-two*, 2

treinta y uno *thirty-one*, 1

el **tren** *train*, 10

tres *three*, 1

trescientos *three hundred*, 8

el **trigal** *wheat field*, 2

el **trigo** *wheat*, 2

triste *sad*, 7; **estar triste** *to be sad*, 7

el **trozo** *piece*, 6

tú *you*, 1
tu(s) *your*, 5
el **turismo** *tourism*, 8G
el **turista** *tourist*, 1G
turnarse *to take turns*, xxii
el **turno** *shift*, 4
tutear *to speak to someone informally*, 10
los **tuyos, las tuyas** *yours*, 9

último(a) *latest*, 8; **la última vez** *last time*, 8
el **último, la última** *last one*, 3
un(a) *a, an*, 4; **un poco** *a little*, 2; **un montón** *a ton*, 4
únicamente *only*, 9
único(a) *only*, 4G
la **unidad** *unity*, 3G
la **universidad** *university*, 5
uno *one*, 1
unos(as) *some*, 4
urgente *urgent*, 1
usar *to use, to wear*, 8; **usar el/la...** *to wear size . . . in shoes/clothes*, 8; **usar lentes** *to wear glasses*, 5; **usando** *using*, xxii
el **uso** *use*, 6
usted *you* (formal), 1
ustedes *you* (pl.), 1
los **útiles escolares** *school supplies*, 4
utilizar *to use*, 7
la **uva** *grape*, 1
¡Uy! *Oh!*, 1

Vale. *Okay.*, 9
valeroso(a) *brave*, 4G
valiente *brave*, 5
la **valija** *suitcase*, 10
el **valle** *valley*, 3G
vamos *let's go, we go*, 3
el **vaquero** *cowboy*, 3G
vaquero(a) *referring to cowboys*, 3G
los **vaqueros** *jeans*, 8
varias *various*, 6G
la **variedad** *variety*, 6
vas *you are going*, 4; **¿Vas a (a la)...?** *Are you going to the. . .?*, 4; **Vas a ir, ¿verdad?** *You're going to go, aren't you?*, 4

el **vasco** *language from Basque Province, Spain*, 1G
la **vasija** *pot*, 4
el **vaso** *glass*, 6
ve *go*, 6
veces *times*, 7; **a veces** *sometimes*, 3; **hay veces** *there are times*, 4
veinte *twenty*, 1
veintiún *twenty-one*, 1
ven *come*, 6
vencido(a) *defeated*, 6; **no se da por vencido** *doesn't give up*, 6
el **vendedor** *vendor*, 8
vender *to sell*, 8; **se vende** *for sale*, 5; **se venden** *are sold*, 8; **vender de todo** *to sell everything*, 8
venir *to come*, 4; **ha venido** *has come*, 9; **no vengas** *don't come*, 10; **ven** *come*, 6; **venga** *will come*, 9; **vienes conmigo a...** *you're coming with me . . .*, 4
la **ventana** *window*, 5
el **ventanal** *large window*, 6G
la **ventura** *happiness*, 5
ver *to watch, to see*, 4; **nunca ha visto** *never has seen*, 6; **Te veo mal.** *You don't look so well.*, 7; **ver televisión** *to watch television*, 3; **vi** *I saw*, 8
el **verano** *summer*, 3
el **verbo** *verb*, xxii
la **verdad** *truth*, 2
¿verdad? *right?*, 4
verde *green*, 5; **verde mar** *sea green*, 5G
las **verduras** *vegetables*, 2
vespertino(a) *(in the) afternoon*, 4
el **vestido** *dress*, 8
vestirse (i) *to get dressed*, 7
vete *go*, 7
vez *time*, 4; **cada vez** *each time*, 8; **hay veces** *there are times*, 4; **la última vez** *last time*, 8
el **viaje** *trip*, 10
el **viajero** *traveler*, 10
la **vida** *life*, 3G
el **video** *video*, 3; **alquilar videos** *to rent videos*, 3
los **videojuegos** *video games*, 2
los **viejitos** *older folks*, 3
viejo(a) *old*, 5
el **viento** *wind*, 3; **Hace viento.** *It's windy.*, 3
el **viernes** *Friday*, 1; **los viernes** *on Fridays*, 3
el **Viernes Santo** *Good Friday*, 1
el **violín** *violin*, 1
visitar *to visit*, 6
la **vista** *view*, 5
la **vitrina** *shop window*, 8; **mirar las vitrinas** *to window shop*, 8
vivir *to live*, 5
vivo(a) *bright*, 5G

el **vocabulario** *vocabulary*, xxii
volar *to fly*, 7
el **volcán** *volcano*, 4G
el **volibol** *volleyball*, 3
volver (ue) *to go (come) back*, 5; **nunca más volverá** *never will do it again*, 9; **se vuelve** *it becomes*, 6
vosotros(as) *you* (plural; informal), 1
el **vuelo** *flight*, 10
vuestra(s) *your*, 5
vuestro(s) *your*, 5

el **wáter** *restroom*, 10
el **windsurf** *windsurfing*, 7

y *and*, 1; **y cuarto** *fifteen after*, 1; **y media** *half past*, 1
ya *already*, 10
Ya te lo (la) paso. *I'll get him (her).*, 8
la **yerba mate** *herb used to make mate*, 7
yo *I*, 1
el **yogur** *yogurt*, 7
la **yuca** *yucca*, 8G

la **zanahoria** *carrot*, 6
la **zapatería** *shoe store*, 8
las **zapatillas de tenis** *tennis shoes*, 8
los **zapatos** *shoes*, 4; **los zapatos de tenis** *tennis shoes*, 8
la **zona** *area*, 4; **la zona residencial** *residential area*, 5
el **zoológico** *zoo*, 10
el **zumo** *juice (Spain)*, 6

Vocabulario inglés-español

This vocabulary includes all of the words presented in the **Vocabulario** sections of the chapters. These words are considered active—you are expected to know them and be able to use them. Expressions are listed under the English word you would be most likely to look up.

Spanish nouns are listed with the definite article and plural forms, when applicable. If a Spanish verb is stem-changing, the change is indicated in parentheses after the verb: **dormir (ue)**. The number after each entry refers to the chapter in which the word or phrase is introduced.

To be sure you are using Spanish words and phrases in their correct context, refer to the chapters listed. You may also want to look up Spanish phrases in **Expresiones de ¡Exprésate!**, pp. R17–R20.

a little   *un poco*, 2
a lot   *mucho*, 2
a lot of, many   *muchos(as)*, 4
a ton   *un montón*, 4
a, an   *un(a)*, 4
active   *activo(a)*, 2
to **add**   *añadir*, 6
address   *la dirección*, 5; **My address is...** *Mi dirección es...*, 5; e-mail address *correo electrónico*, 1
adventure *la aventura*, 2; **adventure book** *el libro de aventura*, 2
after   *después*, 3; *después de*, 7; **after class** *después de clases*, 3
afternoon   *la tarde*, 4; **this afternoon** *esta tarde*, 4; **in the afternoon** *por la tarde*, 4
afterwards   *después*, 4
agent   *el agente, la agente*, 10
agree: I don't agree.   *No estoy de acuerdo.*, 6; *Estoy de acuerdo*, 6; **I don't agree.**, 6
airplane   *el avión*, 10; **by plane** *por avión*, 10
airport   *el aeropuerto*, 10
all   *todas*, 1; *todo(a)*, 2
all right   *regular*, 1
to **allow**   *dejar*, 3
almost   *casi*, 3; **almost never** *casi nunca*, 3; **almost always** *casi siempre*, 3
alone   *solo(a)*, 3
alphabet   *el alfabeto*, 1
already   *ya*, 10
also   *también*, 2
always   *siempre*, 5; **almost always** *casi siempre*, 3; **as always** *como siempre*, 9
amusement park   *el parque de diversiones*, 10
an   *un, una*, 4
and   *y*, 1
animal   *el animal*, 2
anniversary   *el aniversario*, 9
any   *cualquier*, 10
anything   *algo*, 4; *nada*, 4
apartment   *el apartamento*, 5
apple   *la manzana*, 6
April   *abril*, 1
Are you...?   *¿Eres...?*, 2
arm   *el brazo*, 7
around the corner   *a la vuelta*, 10
arrival   *la llegada*, 10
to **arrive**   *llegar*, 4
art   *el arte*, 4
as...as   *tan...como*, 8
as always   *como siempre*, 9
at   *a(l)*, 8; **@** *la arroba*, 1
athletic   *atlético(a)*, 2
to **attend**   *asistir a*, 4
auditorium   *el auditorio*, 4
August   *agosto*, 1
aunt   *la tía*, 5
automatic teller machine   *el cajero automático*, 10
awesome   *fenomenal*, 2

back   *la espalda*, 7, **I'll call back later** *Llamo más tarde*, 8; **to go (come) back** *volver (ue)*, 5
backpack   *la mochila*, 4
bacon   *el tocino*, 6
bad   *malo(a)*, 2
bag   *bolsa*, 8
baggage   *el equipaje*, 10; **baggage claim** *el reclamo de equipaje*, 10
bargain   *la ganga*, 8
baseball   *el béisbol*, 3

basketball   *el básquetbol*, 3
to **bathe**   *bañarse*, 7
bathroom   *el baño*, 5
be   *sé*, 6
to **be able to**   *poder*, 6
to **be**   *estar*, 1; **How are you?** *¿Cómo está(s)?*, 1; **to be alright** *estar regular*, 1; **to be bored** *estar aburrido(a)* 7; **to be familiar with (a place)** *conocer*, 9; **to be fine** *estar bien*, 1; **to be hungry** *tener hambre*, 4; **to be tired** *estar cansado(a)*, 7; **to be happy** *estar contento(a)* 7; **to be sick** *estar enfermo(a)* 7; **to be in a hurry** *tener prisa*, 7; **to be in a wheelchair** *estar en una silla de ruedas*, 5; **to be ready** *estar listo(a)*, 7; **to be nervous** *estar nervioso(a)* 7; **to be right** *tener razón*, 7; **to be sad** *estar triste*, 7; **to be scared** *tener miedo*, 7; **to be sleepy** *tener sueno*, 7; **to be lucky** *tener suerte*, 7; **to be thirsty** *tener sed*, 7; **don't be** *no estés*, 7
to **be**   *ser*, 1; **don't be** *no seas*, 7
beach   *la playa*, 3
because   *porque*, 2
bed   *la cama*, 5; **to make the bed** *hacer la cama*, 5; **to go to bed** *acostarse (ue)*, 7
bedroom   *la habitación*, 5
beef   *la carne*, 6
before   *antes de*, 7
behind   *detrás de*, 5
besides   *además*, 8
best   *el/la/los/las mejor(es)*, 1
better   *mejor(es)*, 7
big   *grande*, 5
bike   *la bicicleta*, 3; **to ride a bike** *montar en bicicleta*, 3
bill   *la cuenta*, 6

biology *la biología*, 4
birthday *el cumpleaños*, 9; **When is …'s birthday?** *¿Cuándo es el cumpleaños de…?*, 2; **When is your birthday?** *¿Cuándo es tu cumpleaños?*, 2; **…birthday's** *el cumpleaños de…*, 2; **birthday card** *la tarjeta de cumpleaños*, 8; **girl's fifteenth birthday** *quinceañera*, 9
black *negro(a)*, 5
blank *en blanco*, 8
blind *ciego(a)*, 5
blond *rubio(a)*, 2
blouse *la blusa*, 8
blue *azul*, 5; **to have blue eyes** *tener los ojos azules*, 5
board game *el juego de mesa*, 3
to **board** *abordar*, 10
boarding pass *la tarjeta de embarque*, 10
boat *el barco*, 10
book *el libro*, 2; **adventure book** *el libro de aventura*, 2; **comic book** *la revista de tiras cómicas*, 8; **romance book** *el libro de amor*, 2
bookstore *la librería*, 8
boots *las botas*, 8
boring *aburrido(a)*, 2; **to be bored** *estar aburrido*, 7
bowl *el plato hondo*, 6
boy *el muchacho*, 1
bracelet *la pulsera*, 8
bread *el pan*, 6
breakfast *el desayuno*, 6
to **bring** *traer (igo)*, 4
broccoli *el brócoli*, 6
brother *el hermano*, 5
brothers, brothers and sisters *los hermanos*, 5
brown *castaño(a)*, 5; *de color café*, 5
building *el edificio*, 5; **…story building** *el edificio de… pisos*, 5
bus *el autobús*, 10
but *pero*, 5
to **buy** *comprar*, 8; **you would buy** *comprarías*, 8
by plane *por avion*, 10
Bye *chao*, 9

cafeteria *la cafetería*, 4
cake *el pastel*, 6
calculator *la calculadora*, 4
calf *la pantorrilla*, 7
to **call** *llamar*, 9; **I'll call back later.** *Llamo más tarde.*, 8
camera *la cámara*, 10; **disposable camera** *la cámara desechable*, 10
to **camp** *acampar*, 10

can *poder*, 6
Can I…? *¿Puedo…?*, 6
Can I help you? *¿En que le puedo servir?*, 8
candy *el dulce*, 9
canoe *la canoa*, 10
car *el carro*, 2
card *la tarjeta*, 8
carrot *la zanahoria*, 5
cat *el gato, la gata*, 5
to **celebrate** *festejar*, 9; *celebrar*, 9
cereal *los cereales*, 6
chair *la silla*, 5; **wheelchair** *la silla de ruedas*, 5
to **chat** *charlar*, 9
to **check** *facturar*, 10; **to check luggage** *facturar el equipaje*, 10
checkpoint: security checkpoint *control de seguridad*, 10
cheese *el queso*, 6
chemistry *la química*, 4
chess *el ajedrez*, 2
chest *el pecho*, 7
chicken *el pollo*, 6
chocolate *el chocolate*, 6
chores *los quehaceres*, 5
Christmas *la Navidad*, 9; **Christmas Eve** *la Nochebuena*, 9
church *la iglesia*, 3
city *la ciudad*, 5
class *la clase*, 3; **after class** *después de clases*, 3
classmate (female) *la (una) compañera de clase*, 1
classmate (male) *el (un) compañero de clase*, 1
to **clean** *limpiar*, 5
to **clean the room** *arreglar el cuarto*, 5
client *el cliente, la cliente*, 8
climb *subir*, 10
clock *el reloj*, 4
close to, *cerca de*, 5
to **close** *cerrar (ie)*, 8
clothes *la ropa*, 4
cloudy *nublado*, 7
club *el club de…*, 4
coat *el abrigo*, 8
coffee *el café*, 6; **coffee with milk** *el café con leche*, 6, **coffee shop** *la cafetería*, 6
cold *frío(a)*, 6; **It's cold.** *Hace frío.*, 3; **to be cold** *tener frío*, 7;
to **have a cold** *tener catarro*, 7
comb *el peine*, 7
to **comb your hair** *peinarse*, 7
to **come** *venir*, 4; **come** *ven*, 6; **don't come** *no vengas*, 10; **to come back** *volver*, 5; **you're coming with me to …** *vienes conmigo a…*, 4
comic book *la revista de tiras cómicas*, 8

compact disc *el disco compacto*, 8; **blank compact disc** *el disco compacto en blanco*, 8
computer *la computadora*, 4, **computer science** *la computación*, 4
concert *el concierto*, 4
to **cook** *cocinar*, 5
cookie *la galleta*, 9
cool *fresco*, 3 **It's cool.** *Hace fresco.*, 3
corn *el maíz*, 6
to **cost** *costar (ue)*, 8; **costs … cuesta(n)…**, 8; **it will cost** *costará*, 9
cotton *el algodón*, 8; **made of cotton** *de algodón*, 8
counter *el mostrador*, 10
country *el país*, 10
countryside *el campo*, 5
court: food court in a mall *la terraza de comidas*, 8
cousin *el primo, la prima*, 5
custard *el flan*, 6
customs *la aduana*, 10
to **cut** *cortar*, 6; **to cut the grass** *cortar el césped*, 5

dad *el papá*, 5
dance *el baile*, 3
to **dance** *bailar*, 3; **dancing** *bailando*, 1; **to start dancing** *ponerse a bailar*, 3
dark: dark-skinned; dark-haired *moreno(a)*, 2
date *la fecha*, 1
daughter *la hija*, 5
day *el día*, 1; **day after tomorrow** *pasado mañana*, 4; **day before yesterday** *anteayer*, 8; **day of the week** *el día de la semana*, 1; **Father's Day** *el Día del Padre*, 9; **holiday** *el día festivo*, 9; **Independence Day** *el Día de la Independencia*, 9; **Mother's Day** *el Día de la Madre*, 9; **Thanksgiving Day** *el Día de Acción de Gracias*, 9; **some day** *algún día*, 10; **Valentine's Day** *el Día de los Enamorados*, 9; **What day is today?** *¿Qué día es hoy?*, 1; **your saint's day** *el día de tu santo*, 9
deaf *sordo(a)*, 5
December *diciembre*, 1
to **decorate** *decorar*, 9; **to decorate the house** *decorar la casa*, 9
decoration *la decoración*, 9

delicious *delicioso(a)*, 2; *riquísimo(a)*, 6
to delight *encantar*, 6
department store *el almacén*, 8
departure *la salida*, 10
to desire *desear*, 6
desk *el escritorio*, 5
dessert *el postre*, 6
destination *el destino*, 10
destined *destinado(a)*, 6
detail *el detalle*, 7
to determine *determinar*, 7
dictionary *el diccionario*, 4
diet *la dieta*, 7; to eat well *seguir una dieta sana*, 7
difficult *difícil*, 4; It's difficult. *Es difícil.*, 4
dining room *el comedor*, 5
dinner *la cena*, 6
disc: compact disc *disco compacto*, 8; blank compact disc *el disco compacto en blanco*, 8
dish, *el plato*, 6
disposable *desechable*, 10; disposable camera *la cámara desechable*, 10
Do you like...? *¿Te gusta(n)...?*, 2
to do *hacer*, 4; we are doing *estamos haciendo*, 9; to do homework *hacer la tarea*, 3; to do chores *hacer los quehaceres*, 5; to do yoga *hacer yoga*, 7; do *haz*, 6; don't do *no hagas*, 10; What are they doing? *¿Qué están haciendo?*, 9; What did you do? *¿Qué hiciste?* 8
dog *el perro, la perra*, 5
door *la puerta*, 5
dot: on the dot *en punto*, 1
downtown *el centro*, 10
to draw *dibujar*, 3
dress *el vestido*, 8
dressed: to get dressed, *vestirse (i)*, 7
to drink *beber*, 4; to drink punch *beber ponche*, 9; *tomar*, 6
to dry *secarse*, 7
during *durante*, 10
DVD *el DVD*, 8

ear *el oído*, 7
early *temprano*, 4
earphones *los audífonos*, 8
earrings *los aretes*, 8
easy *fácil*, 4; It's easy. *Es fácil.*, 4
to eat a balanced diet *seguir una dieta sana*, 7; to eat breakfast *desayunar*, 6; to eat dinner *cenar*, 6; to eat lunch *almorzar (ue)*, 6;

4 to eat well *seguir una dieta sana*, 7
to eat *comer*, 3; *tomar*, 8
egg *el huevo*, 6
eight *ocho*, 1
eight hundred *ochocientos*, 8
eighteen *dieciocho*, 1
eighty *ochenta*, 2
eleven *once*, 1
e-mail address *el correo electrónico*, 1; What is...'s e-mail address? *¿Cuál es el correo electrónico de...?* 1; What's your e-mail address? *¿Cuál es tu correo electrónico?*, 1
English *el inglés*, 4
enough *suficiente*, 7; to get enough sleep *dormir lo suficiente*, 7
evening *la tarde*, 1
everybody *todos (as)*, 5
everything *todo*, 8
to exercise *hacer ejercicios*, 3
to expect *esperar*, 9
expensive *caro(a)*, 8
eyes *los ojos*, 5; to have blue eyes *tener los ojos azules*, 5

face *la cara*, 7
fall *el otoño*, 3
family *la familia*, 3; There are... people in my family. *En mi familia somos...*, 5
familiar: to be familiar *conocer*, 9
fantastic: How fantastic! *¡Qué fantástico!*, 10
fat (in food) *la grasa*, 7
fat (overweight) *gordo(a)*, 5
father *el padre*, 5; Father's Day *el Día del Padre*, 9
favorite *preferido(a)*, 4
flan *el flan*, 6
February *febrero*, 1
to feel *sentirse (ie)*, 7; to feel like doing something *tener ganas de + infinitive*, 4
few *pocos(as)*, 4
fifteen *quince*, 1
fifteenth: girl's fifteenth birthday *quinceañera*, 9
fifty *cincuenta*, 2
film *la película*, 2
to find *encontrar (ue)*, 7
fine *bien*, 1; I'm fine *Estoy bien*, 1
finger *el dedo*, 7
finish *terminar*, 9
fireworks *los fuegos artificiales*, 9
first *el primero*, 1
first (adj) *primero(a)*, 4
fish *el pescado*, 6

to fish *pescar*, 10
fishing *la pesca*, 10; to go fishing *ir de pesca*, 10
to fit *quedar*, 8; How does it fit? *¿Cómo me queda?*, 8
five *cinco*, 1
five hundred *quinientos*, 8
flight *el vuelo*, 10
floor *el piso*, 5
folder *la carpeta*, 4
to follow *seguir (i)*, 10
food *la comida*, 2; Chinese (Italian, Mexican) food *la comida china (italiana, mexicana)*, 2, food court in a mall *la plaza (terraza) de comida*, 8
foot *el pie*, 7
football *el fútbol americano*, 3
for *para*, 4
for example *por ejemplo*, 6G
fork *el tenedor*, 7
formidable *formidable*, 2
fortune *la fortuna*, 8
forty *cuarenta*, 2
four *cuatro*, 1
four hundred *cuatrocientos*, 8
fourteen *catorce*, 1
French *el francés*, 4
French fries *las papas fritas*, 6
frequency *la frecuencia*, 8
Friday *el viernes*, 1; on Fridays *los viernes*, 3
friend *el amigo* (male), *la amiga* (female), 1
from *de*, 1
fruit *la fruta*, 2
fun *divertido(a)*, 2; What fun! *¡Qué divertido!*, 10

to gain weight *subir de peso*, 7
game: board game *el juego de mesa*, 3; the...game *el partido de...*, 4
garage *el garaje*, 5
garden *el jardín*, 5
German *el alemán*, 4
to get dressed *vestirse (i)*, 7
to get someone (for a telephone call), *pasartelo(la)*, 8
to get together *reunirse*, 9
to get up *levantarse*, 7
to get *conseguir (i, i)*, 10
gift *el regalo*, 9
girl *la muchacha*, 1
girl's fifteenth birthday *la quinceañera*, 9
to give *dar*, 7; don't give *no des*, 7
glass *el vaso*, 6

glasses *los lentes*, 5; **to wear glasses** *usar lentes*, 5
go *ve*, 6
to go *ir*, 2; **Where did you go?** *¿Adónde fuiste?* 8; **to go shopping** *ir de compras*, 2; **to go hiking** *ir de excursión*, 10; **don't go** *no vayas*, 7; **I want to go…** *quiero ir…* 2; **Are you going to the…?** *¿Vas a…?*, 4; **You're going to go, aren't you?** *Vas a ir, ¿verdad?*, 4; **to go back** *regresar*, 4; *volver (ue)*, 5
to go for a walk *pasear*, 3
go out *sal*, 6
to go out *salir*, 3; **to go out with friends** *salir con amigos*, 3; **to go out in a sailboat (motorboat)** *pasear en bote de vela (lancha)*, 10
to go to bed *acostarse (ue)*, 7
good *bueno(a)*, 2; **Good evening., Good night.** *Buenas noches.* 1; **Good afternoon.** *Buenas tardes.*, 1; **Good morning.** *Buenos días.*, 1
good-looking *guapo(a)*, 2
Goodbye. *Adiós.*, 1
graduation *la graduación*, 9
grandchildren *los nietos*, 5
granddaughter *la nieta*, 5
grandfather *el abuelo*, 5
grandmother *la abuela*, 5
grandparents *los abuelos*, 5
grandson *el nieto*, 5
grandsons, grandchildren *los nietos*, 5
grass *el césped*, 5; **to cut the grass** *cortar el césped*, 5
gravy *salsa*, 6
gray *gris*, 8
graying *canoso(a)*, 5
great *estupendo(a)*, 10; *a todo dar*, 10; **it was great** *fue estupendo*, 10
green *verde*, 5
greeting card *la tarjeta*, 8
guest *el (la) invitado(a)*, 9
guitar *la guitarra*, 9
gym *el gimnasio*, 3

hair *el pelo*, 5; **to comb your hair** *peinarse*, 7; **hair dryer** *la secadora de pelo*, 7
half *medio*, 1; **half past** *y media*, 1
ham *el jamón*, 6
hamburger *la hamburguesa*, 2
hand *la mano*, 7
hang *colgar (ue)*, 9
Hanukkah *el Hanukah*, 9
happy *contento(a)*, 7; **to be happy** *estar contento(a)*, 7

Happy (Merry)… *¡Feliz…!*, 9
hard *difícil*, 4
hard-working *trabajador(a)*, 2
hat *el sombrero*, 8
to have *tener (-go, ie)*, 4; **have** *ten*, 6; **don't have** *no tengas*, 10; **to have a cold** *tener catarro*, 7; **to have a milkshake** *tomar un batido*, 8; **to have a picnic** *tener un picnic*, 9; **to have blue eyes** *tener los ojos azules*, 5; **to have to do something** *tener que + infinitive*, 4; **I have to…** *A mí me toca…*, 5
to have a party *hacer una fiesta*, 9; **to have a snack** *merendar*, 5; **to have lunch** *almorzar*, 5
he *él*, 1; **He is…** *Él es…*, 1
head *la cabeza*, 7
health *la salud*, 7
heat *el calor*, 3
to heat *calentar (ie)*, 6
Hello. *Aló.,; Bueno.,; Diga.*, 8
help *la ayuda*, 6; **to help at home** *ayudar en casa*, 5
hi, hello *hola*, 1
hike *la excursión*, 10; **to go on a hike** *ir de excursión*, 10
his *su(s)*, 5
history *la historia*, 4
hobby *el pasatiempo*, 7; **to look for a hobby** *buscar un pasatiempo*, 7
holiday *el día festivo*, 9
Holy Week *la Semana Santa*, 9
homework *la tarea*, 3
Hope things go well for you. *Que te vaya bien.*, 9
horrible *horrible*, 2; **It was horrible!** *¡Fue horrible!*, 10
horror *el terror*, 2
hot *caliente*, 6; **hot sauce**, 6
hot chocolate *el chocolate*, 6
hotel *el hotel*, 10; **to stay in a hotel** *quedarse en un hotel*, 10
hour *la hora*, 1
house *casa*, 5; **…'s house** *la casa de…*, 3; **to decorate the house** *decorar la casa*, 9
household chores *los quehaceres*, 5
how *¿cómo?*, 1; **How are you?** *¿Cómo está(s)?*, 1; **How do you spell…** *¿Cómo se escribe…?*, 1; **How does it fit?** *¿Cómo me queda?*, 8; **How fantastic!** *¡Qué fantástico!*, 10; **How great!** *¡Qué bien!*, 10; **How many…** *¿cuántos(as)?*, 2; **how much?** *¿cuánto(a)?*, 4; **How often do you go…?** *¿Con qué frecuencia vas…?*, 3; **How old are you?** *¿Cuántos años tienes?*, 2
hunger *el hambre*, 4
hungry, to be *tener hambre*, 4

to hurt *doler (ue)*, 7; **My…hurt(s)** *Me duele(n)…* 7; **Is something hurting you?** *¿Te duele algo?* 7

ID *carnet de identidad*, 10
I *yo*, 1
I agree. *Estoy de acuerdo*, 6; **I don't agree.** *No estoy de acuerdo.*, 6
I have no idea. *Ni idea.*, 3
I want to see… *quiero conocer…*, 10
I would like… *Quisiera…*, 6
I'd like you to meet… *Te presento a…*, 9
I'll get him (her). *Ya te lo (la) paso.*, 8
I'm fine. *Estoy bien.*, 1
I'm sorry *lo siento*, 8
I'm… *Soy…*, 2; **I'm from** *Soy de…*, 1
I'm not so good. *Estoy mal.*, 1
ice cream *el helado*, 2
ice cream shop *la heladería*, 8
ID *el carnet de identidad*, 10
Independence Day *El Día de la Independencia*, 9
in front of *delante de*, 5
in the (latest) fashion *a la (última) moda*, 8
in, by *por*, 4
inexpensive *barato(a)*, 8
intellectual *intelectual*, 2
intelligent *inteligente*, 2
interest *el interés*, 10
interesting *interesante*, 2
to interrupt *interrumpir*, 4
to introduce *presentar*, 9
invitation *la invitación*, 9
to invite *invitar*, 9
island *la isla*, 10
it *lo, la*, 6
It seems all right/fine to me. *Me parece bien.*, 5
it snows *nieva*, 3
It's a rip-off! *¡Es un robo!*, 8
It's all the same to me. *Me da igual.*, 2
It's awful. *Es pésimo.*, 2
It's cold. *Hace frío.*, 3
It's cool. *Hace fresco.*, 3
It's delicious. *Es delicioso.*, 2
It's hot. *Hace calor.*, 3
It's kind of fun. *Es algo divertido.*, 2
It's not a big deal. *No es gran cosa*, 5
It's okay. *Está bien.*, 3
It's rather good. *Es bastante bueno.*,
It's sunny. *Hace sol.*, 3
It's windy. *Hace viento.*, 3

jacket *la chaqueta*, 8; *el saco*, 8
January *enero*, 1
jeans *los vaqueros*, 8
jewelry store *la joyería*, 8
job *el trabajo*, 3
joke *el chiste*, 9; **to tell jokes** *contar chistes*, 9
juice *el jugo*, 6
July *julio*, 1
June *junio*, 1
to just(**have done something**) *acabar de*, 7

kitchen *la cocina*, 5
knife *el cuchillo*, 6
to know (facts) *saber*, 4; **I don't know** *no sé*, 4; **to know people** *conocer*, 9

lake *el lago*, 10
large *grande*, 6
last *pasado(a)*, 8; **last night** *anoche*, 9
late *tarde*, 4; **later** *más tarde*, 8; **latest** *último(a)*, 8
lazy *perezoso(a)*, 2
to leave *irse*, 10; *dejar*, 10; **leave** *salir*, 3; *sal*, 6; **to leave a message** *dejar un recado*, 8; **don't leave** *no salgas*, 10
leg *la pierna*, 7
letter *la carta*, 3
library *la biblioteca*, 4
lift *levantar*, 7; **to lift weights** *levantar pesas*, 7
to like: **I (you . . .) like** *me (te, ...gusta(n))*, 2; *me gustaría* 10
Likewise. *Igualmente.*, 1
line *la cola*, 10; **to wait in line** *hacer cola*, 10
to listen *escuchar*, 3; **to listen to music** *escuchar música*, 3
little (adv.) *poco*, 2; **a little** *un poco*, 2
live *vivir*, 5
living room *la sala*, 5
long *largo(a)*, 5; **Long time no see.** *¡Tanto tiempo sin verte!*, 9
to look *mirar*, 8
to look for *buscar*, 7; **to look for a hobby** *buscar un pasatiempo*, 7

to lose weight *bajar de peso*, 7
to lose *perder*, 10
luck *la suerte*, 10
luggage *el equipaje*, 10
lunch *el almuerzo*, 4; *la comida*, 6; **to have lunch** *almorzar*, 5

ma'am; Mrs. *la señora*, 1
made,
magazine *la revista*, 3
mail *el correo*, 7
to maintain *mantenerse(ie)*, 7; **to stay in shape** *mantenerse en forma*, 7
to make *hacer*; 4; **make** *haz*, 6; **to make the bed**, 5
makeup *el maquillaje*, 7
mall *el centro comercial*, 3
man *el hombre*, 6; **for men** *para hombres*, 8
many *muchos (as)*, 4
map *el mapa*, 10
March *marzo*, 1
Mass *la misa*, 9
mathematics *las matemáticas*, 4
May *mayo*, 1
me *mí*, 5; *me*, 9
meat *la carne*, 6
to meet *encontrarse(ue)*, 10
meeting *la reunión*, 3
Merry . . . *¡Feliz...!*, 9
message *el recado*, 8
midday, noon *el mediodía*, 1
midnight *la medianoche*, 1
milk *la leche*, 6
milkshake *el batido*, 8
million *un millón de*, 8
mischievous *travieso(a)*, 5
miss *la señorita*, 1
to miss *perder(ie)*, 10
mix *mezclar*, 6
mom *la mamá*, 5
moment *un momento*, 8
Monday *lunes*, 3; **on Mondays** *los lunes*, 3
money *el dinero*, 8
money exchange *la oficina de cambio*, 10
monitor, screen *la pantalla*, 10
months of the year *los meses del año*, 1
month *mes*, 1
more *más*, 2; **more than** *más que*, 8; **more . . . than** *más... que*, 8
morning *la mañana*, 1
mother *la madre*, 5; **Mother's Day** *El Día de la Madre*, 9
motorboat *la lancha*, 10; **to go out in a motorboat** *pasear en lancha*, 10

mountain *la montaña*, 10
mouth *la boca*, 7
movie *la película*, 2
movie theater *el cine*, 3
museum *el museo*, 10
music *la música*, 2; **music by . . .** *la música de*, 2
my *mi(s)*, 1
mystery *el misterio*, 2

napkin *la servilleta*, 6
neck *el cuello*, 7
need *necesitar*, 4
neither, not either *tampoco*, 5; *ni*, 7
nephew *el sobrino*, 5
nervous *nervioso(a)*, 7; **to be nervous** *estar nervioso(a)*, 7
never *nunca*, 5; **almost never** *casi nunca*, 3
New Year's Eve *la Nochevieja*, 9
next *próximo(a)*, 4; **next to** *al lado de*, 5
nice *simpático(a)*, 2; **Nice to meet you.** *Encantado(a)*, 1; *Mucho gusto.*, 1
niece *la sobrina*, 5
nine *nueve*, 1
nine hundred *novecientos*, 8
nineteen *diecinueve*, 1
ninety *noventa*, 2
no *no*, 3
nobody, not anybody *nadie*, 5
noon *mediodía*, 1
nor *ni*, 7
nose *la nariz*, 7
not yet *todavía no*, 10
notebook *el cuaderno*, 4
nothing *nada*, 4
novel *la novela*, 2
November *noviembre*, 1
now *ahora*, 9
nowhere *ninguna parte*, 3
number *el número*, 1

October *octubre*, 1
Of course! *¡Claro que sí!*, 4
of the *del, de la*, 2
of *de*, 1
office: post office, 10
officer: *post officer*, 5
often *a menudo*, 5
Oh, no! *¡Ay, no!*, 6
Okay. *Vale.*, 9
old *viejo(a)*, 5
older *mayor(es)*, 5

on the dot *en punto,* 1
on time *a tiempo,* 4
on top of, above *encima de,* 5
one *uno,* 1
one hundred *cien,* 2
one hundred one *ciento uno,* 8
one million *millón (de),* 8
one thousand *mil,* 8
only *sólo,* 7; *no más,* 8
to **open** *abrir,* 4; **to open gifts** *abrir regalos,* 9
or *o,* 2
orange *la naranja,* 6; *anaranjado(a),* 8
order *pedir (ie),* 6
to **organize** *organizar,* 10
our *nuestro(a)(s),* 5
out of style *pasado(a) de moda,* 8
outgoing *extrovertido(a),* 2
oven *el horno,* 6
overcoat *el abrigo,* 8

to **pack your suitcase** *hacer la maleta,* 10
pain: What a pain! *¡Que lata!,* 5
pair *el par,* 8
pajamas *el piyama,* 7
pants (jeans) *los pantalones (vaqueros),* 7
paper *el papel,* 4
parents *los padres,* 5
park *el parque,* 3; **amusement park** *el parque de diversiones,* 10
party, to have a *hacer una fiesta,* 9; **surprise party** *la fiesta de sorpresa,* 9
pass: *boarding pass,* 10
passenger *el pasajero, la pasajera,* 10
passport *el pasaporte,* 10
pastry *el pan dulce,* 6
patio *el patio,* 5
to **pay** *pagar,* 8
peach *el durazno,* 6
pen *el bolígrafo,* 4
pencil *el lápiz (pl. los lápices),* 4
person *la persona,* 2
photo *la foto,* 9; **to show photos** *enseñar fotos,* 9; **to take photos** *sacar fotos* 10
physical education *la educación física,* 4
to **pick up** *recoger,* 10
picnic *el picnic,* 9
piñata *la piñata,* 9
pizza *la pizza,* 2
place *el lugar,* 10
plane ticket *el boleto de avión,* 10
plans *planes,* 9
plants *las plantas,* 5

plate *el plato,* 6
to **play sports** *practicar deportes,* 3
to **play an instrument** *tocar,* 3; **to play the piano** *tocar el piano,* 3; **a game or sport** *jugar (ue),* 3; **to play sports** *practicar deportes,* 3
to **play a game or sport** *jugar (ue),* 3
please *por favor,* 6
Pleased to meet you. *Encantado(a).,* 1; *Mucho gusto.,* 1
police officer *el (la) policía,* 5
pool *la piscina,* 3
porch *el patio,* 5
post office *la oficina de correos,* 10
potato *la papa,* 6; **potato chips** *las papitas,* 9
practice *el entrenamiento,* 3
to **prefer** *preferir (ie),* 6
preparations *los preparativos,* 9
to **prepare** *preparar,* 6
pretty *bonito(a),* 2
punch *el ponche,* 9
purple *morado(a),* 8
purse *la bolsa,* 8
to **put** *poner,* 4; **put** *pon,* 6; **don't put** *no pongas,* 10; **to put on makeup** *maquillarse,* 7; **to put on** *ponerse,* 7
pyramid *la pirámide,* 10

quarter past (the hour) *y cuarto,* 1
quarter to (the hour) *menos cuarto,* 4
quiet *callado(a),* 5

to **rain** *llover (ue),* 3; **it rains a lot** *llueve mucho,* 3
rather *bastante* + adjective, 2
razor *la navaja,* 7
to **read** *leer,* 3
ready *listo(a),* 7; **to be ready** *estar listo(a),* 7
to **receive** *recibir,* 9; **to receive gifts** *recibir regalos,* 9
red *rojo(a),* 8
red-headed *pelirrojo(a),* 2
refrigerator *el refrigerador,* 6
rehearsal *el ensayo,* 3
relax *relajarse,* 7
to **rent** *alquilar,* 3; **to rent videos** *alquilar videos,* 3
to **rest** *descansar,* 3
restroom *el baño,* 5; *el servicio,* 10
to **return, to go back** *regresar,* 4; *volver,* 5

rice *el arroz,* 6
to **ride a bike** *montar en bicicleta,* 3
right? *¿no?,* 4; *¿verdad?,* 4; **to be right** *tener razón*
ring *el anillo,* 8
rip off: It's a rip-off! *¡Es un robo!,* 8
romance book *el libro de amor,* 2
romantic *romántico(a),* 2
room *el cuarto,* 5
ruins *las ruinas,* 10
rule *la regla,* 4
to **run** *correr,* 3

sad *triste,* 7; **to be sad** *estar triste,* 7
sailboat *el bote de vela,* 10; **to go out in a sailboat** *pasear en bote de vela,* 10
salad *la ensalada,* 6
salesclerk *el dependiente, la dependiente,* 8
salty *salado(a),* 6
same as usual *lo de siempre,* 9
sandals *las sandalias.* 8
sandwich *el sándwich,* 6
Saturday *el sábado,* 1; **on Saturdays** *los sábados,* 3
sauce, gravy *la salsa.* 6; **hot sause** *la salsa picante,* 6
to **save: to save money** *ahorrar dinero,* 8
school *el colegio,* 3
school supplies *los útiles escolares,* 4
science *las ciencias,* 4; **science fiction** *la ciencia ficción,* 2; **computer science** *la computación,* 4
security checkpoint *el control de seguridad,* 10
to **see** *ver,* 4; **See you tomorrow.** *Hasta mañana.,* 1; **See you.** *Nos vemos.,* 1
to **seem** *parecer,* 5
to **sell** *vender,* 8
to **send** *mandar,* 9
September *septiembre,* 1
serious *serio(a),* 2
to **serve** *servir (i),* 6
to **set** *poner (-go),* 6; **to set the table** *poner la mesa,* 6
seven *siete,* 1
seven hundred *setecientos,* 8
seventeen *diecisiete,* 1
seventy *setenta,* 2
to **shave** *afeitarse,* 7
shirt *la camisa,* 8
shoe store *la zapatería,* 8
shoes *los zapatos,* 4; **tennis shoes**

los zapatos de tenis, 8
shop (class) *el taller,* 4
shop window *la vitrina,* 8; **to window shop** *mirar las vitrinas,* 8; **to go shopping** *ir de compras,* 2
short (height) *bajo(a),* 2; (length) *corto(a),* 5
shorts *los pantalones cortos,* 8
should *deber,* 6
shoulder *el hombro,* 7
to show *enseñar,* 4; **to show photos** *enseñar fotos,* 9
shy *tímido(a),* 2
sick: to be *estar enfermo(a),* 7
silk *la seda,* 8
silly *tonto(a),* 3
to sing *cantar,* 3
sir, Mr. *el señor,* 1
sister *la hermana,* 5
to sit down *sentarse,* 10
six *seis,* 1
six hundred *seiscientos,* 8
sixteen *dieciséis,* 1
sixty *sesenta,* 2
size, *la talla,* 8; **shoe size** *el número,* 8
to skate *patinar,* 3
to ski *esquiar,* 10; **to water ski** *esquiar en el agua,* 10
skirt *la falda,* 8
to sleep *dormir,* 5; **to get enough sleep** *dormir lo suficiente,* 7
small *pequeño(a).* 5; **pretty small** *bastante pequeño,* 5
to smoke *fumar,* 7; **to stop smoking** *dejar de fumar,* 7
to snack *merendar (ie),* 5
to snow *nevar (ie),* 3
so-so *más o menos,* 1
so much *tanto,* 7
soap *el jabón,* 7
soccer *el fútbol,* 3
socks *los calcetines,* 8; **a pair of socks** *un par de calcetines,* 8
sofa *el sofá,* 5
soft drink *el refresco,* 6
some *unos(as),* 4
some day *algún día,* 10
something *algo,* 4
sometimes *a veces,* 3
son *el hijo,* 5
soup *la sopa,* 6; **vegetable soup** *la sopa de verduras,* 6
Spanish *el español,* 1
to speak *hablar,* 3
to spend time alone *pasar el rato solo(a),* 3
to spend (money) *gastar,* 8; (time) *pasar,* 9
spicy *picante,* 6
spinach *las espinacas,* 6
spoon *la cuchara,* 6

sports *los deportes,* 2
spring *la primavera,* 3
stadium *el estadio,* 4
to start *empezar (ie),* 5; *comenzar (ie),* 10; **to start a trip** *comenzar un viaje,* 10
to stay *quedarse,* 10; **to stay in shape** *mantenerse (ie) en forma,* 7
stomach *el estómago,* 7
to stop doing something *dejar de +* infinitive, 7
store *la tienda de...,* 8
story *el piso,* 5; **...story building** *el edificio de . . .pisos,* 5
to stretch *estirarse,* 7
student *el estudiante, la estudiante,* 1
to study *estudiar,* 3
style *la moda,* 8; **in the latest style** *a la última moda* 8; **out of style** *pasado de moda,* 8
subject *la materia,* 4
suburbs *las afueras,* 5
subway *el metro,* 10
suitcase *la maleta,* 10
summer *el verano,* 3
Sunday *el domingo,* 1; **on Sundays** *los domingos,* 3
supplies: school supplies *los materiales escolares,* 4
to surf the Internet *navegar por internet,* 7
surprise party *la fiesta de sorpresa,* 9
sweater *el suéter,* 8
sweet *dulce,* 7
to swim *nadar,* 3
swimsuit *el traje de baño,* 8
synagogue *la sinagoga,* 9

table *la mesa,* 5
to take care of *cuidar,* 5; **to take care of oneself** *cuidarse,* 7; **Take care.** *Cuídate.,* 9
to take off *quitarse,* 7
to take out *sacar,* 6; **to take out the trash** *sacar la basura,* 5
to take *tomar,* 9; **to take photos** *sacar photos,* 10; **to take a test** *presentar el examen,* 4
to talk *hablar,* 3; *charlar,* 10
tall *alto(a),* 2
tamales *los tamales,* 9
to taste *probar (ue),* 6
taxi *el taxi,* 10
teacher *la profesora* (**female**), *el profesor* (**male**), 1
teeth *los dientes,* 7
telephone number *el teléfono,* 1

television *la televisión,* 3; **to watch TV** *mirar la televisión,* 3
to tell jokes *contar chistes,* 9
temple *el templo,* 9
ten *diez,* 1
tennis *el tenis,* 3; **tennis shoes** *los zapatos de tenis,* 8
test *el examen,* 4; **to take a ... test** *presentar el examen de...,* 4
Thanksgiving Day *el Día de Acción de Gracias,* 9
thank you *gracias,* 1
that *ese(a),* 8
the *el, la, los, las,* 2
their *su(s),* 5
them *los, las,* 6
then *luego,* 4
there *allí,* 10
there is, there are *hay,* 4
these *estos, estas,* 8
they *ellas, ellos,* 1
They like to ... *A ...les gusta...,* 3
thin *delgado(a),* 5
thing *la cosa,* 4
to think *pensar(ie),* 8
thirst *la sed,* 4
thirteen *trece,* 1
thirty *treinta,* 1
this *ésta, éste,* 1; **this** *este(a),* 8
those *esos, esas,* 8
three *tres,* 1
three hundred *trescientos,* 8
throat *la garganta,* 7
Thursday *el jueves,* 1; **on Thursdays** *los jueves,* 3
ticket *el boleto,* 10; **plane ticket** *el boleto de avión,* 10
time *el rato,* 3
tired *cansado(a),* 7; **to be tired** *estar cansado,* 7
to/for me *me,* 2; **you** *te,* 2; **us** *nos,* 2; **him, her, you, them** *le(s),* 2
toast *el pan tostado,* 6
today *hoy,* 1
tomato *el tomate,* 6
tomorrow *mañana,* 4
ton: a ton of *un montón,* 4
too much *demasiado(a),* 7
toothbrush *el cepillo de dientes,* 7
toothpaste *la pasta de dientes,* 7
to tour *recorrer,* 10
towel *la toalla,* 7
toy *el juguete,* 8
toy store *la juguetería,* 8
train *el tren,* 10
trash *la basura,* 5
trip *el viaje,* 10
to try, taste *probar (ue),* 6
T-shirt *la camiseta,* 8
Tuesday *el martes,* 1; **on Tuesdays** *los martes,* 3

tuna fish *el atún*, 6
turnover-like pastry *la empanada*, 9
twelve *doce*, 1
twenty *veinte*, 1
two *dos*, 1
two hundred *doscientos*, 8
two thousand *dos mil*, 8

ugly *feo(a)*, 2
uncle *el tío*, 5
under, underneath *debajo (de)*, 5
unfair *injusto*, 5
unfriendly *antipático(a)*, 2
until *hasta*, 5; **See you later.** *Hasta luego.*, 1; **See you tomorrow.** *Hasta mañana.*, 1; **See you soon.** *Hasta pronto.*, 1
up to *hasta*, 5
us *nos*, 2; *nosotros(as)*, 3
usual: the usual *lo de siempre*, 9

to vacuum *pasar la aspiradora*, 5
vacuum cleaner *aspiradora*, 4
Valentine's Day *el Día de los Enamorados*, 9
vegetables *las verduras*, 2
very *muy + adjective*, 2
very bad *pésimo(a)*, 2
video *el video*, 3
video games *los videojuegos*, 2
volleyball *el volibol*, 3

to wait *esperar*, 8
waiting room *la sala de espera*, 10
to wake *despertarse (ie)*, 7
to walk *caminar*, 7; **to go for a walk** *pasear*, 3
wallet *la billetera*, 10
to want *querer (ie)*, 3
to wash *lavar*, 5 **to wash the dishes** *lavar los platos*, 5; *lavarse*, 7
watch (clock) *el reloj*, 4
to watch *ver*, 4; **to watch television** *ver televisión*, 3
water *el agua (f.)*, 6; **to water ski** *esquiar en el agua*, 10
we *nosotros(as)*, 1
to wear *llevar*, 8; **to wear glasses** *usar lentes*, 5

weather *el tiempo*, 3; **The weather is nice (bad).** *Hace buen (mal) tiempo.*, 3
wedding *la boda*, 9
Wednesday *el miércoles*, 1; **on Wednesdays** *los miércoles*, 3
week *la semana*, 4
weekend *el fin de semana*, 3; **weekends** *los fines de semana*, 3
weight *el peso*, 7; **to gain weight** *subir de peso*, 7; **to lose weight** *bajar de peso*, 7
weights *las pesas*, 7; **to lift weights** *levantar pesas*, 7
What? *¿Cómo?*, *¿Qué?*, 1; **What a pain!** *¡Qué lata!*, 5; **What a shame!** *¡Qué lástima!*, 10; **What bad luck!** *¡Qué mala suerte!*, 10; **What are you going to do?** *¿Qué vas a hacer?*, 7; **What fun!** *¡Qué divertido!*, 10; **What are you like?** *¿Cómo eres?*, 2; **What day is today?** *¿Qué día es hoy?*, 1; **What did you do?** *¿Qué hiciste?*, 8; **What do you do to help at home?** *¿Qué haces para ayudar en casa?*, 5; **What do you do to relax?** *¿Qué haces para relajarte?*, 7; **What do you have to do?** *¿Qué tienes que hacer?*, 7; **What do you like to do?** *¿Qué te gusta hacer?*, 3; **What do you still have to do?** *¿Qué te falta hacer?*, 7; **What do you want to do?** *¿Qué quieres hacer?*, 3; **What does …do?** *¿Qué hace...?*, 3; **What is …like?** *¿Cómo es...?*, 2; **What plans do you have for …?** *¿Qué planes tienen para...?*, 9; **What time are you going to…?** *¿A qué hora vas a...?*, 4; **What time is it?** *¿Qué hora es?*, 3; **What is …'s e-mail address?** *¿Cuál es el correo electrónico de...?*, 1; **What's … telephone number?** *¿Cuál es el teléfono de...?*, 1; **what?, which?** *¿cuál?*, 4; **What's his (her, your) name?** *¿Cómo se llama?*, 1; **What's new?** *¿Qué hay de nuevo?*, 9; **What's the matter with …?** *¿Qué tiene...?*, 7; **What's the weather like?** *¿Qué tiempo hace?*, 3; **What's today's date?** *¿Qué fecha es hoy?*, 1; **What's wrong with you?** *¿Qué te pasa?*, 7; **What's your name?** *¿Cómo te llamas?*, 1
wheelchair *la silla de ruedas*, 5; **to be in a wheelchair** *estar en una silla de ruedas*, 5
when *cuando*, 3
when? *¿cuándo?*, 2
where? *¿dónde?*, 5; **Where can I …?**

¿Dónde se puede...? 10; **Where did you go?** *¿Adónde fuiste?*, 8; **from where** *de dónde*, 1
white *blanco(a)*, 8
whole *todo(a)*, 9
Who's calling? *¿De parte de quién?*, 8
Who's…? *¿Quién es...?*, 1
why *¿por qué?*, 2
window *la ventana*, 5; **to window shop** *mirar las vitrinas*, 8
winter *el invierno*, 3
to wish for *desear*, 6
with *con*, 3
with me *conmigo*, 3
with you *contigo*, 3
witty *gracioso(a)*, 2
woman *la mujer*, 5
wool *la lana*, 8; **made of wool** *de lana*, 8
work *trabajar*, 3; *el trabajo*, 4
to work out *entrenarse*, 7
workshop *el taller*, 4
to worry *preocuparse*, 10; **Don't worry.** *No te preocupes.*, 10
worse *peor(es)*, 8
to write *escribir*, 1; **How do you spell …?** *¿Cómo se escribe...?* 1; **It's spelled …** *se escribe*, 1

yard *el patio*, 5
year *el año*, 2; **New Year** *el Año Nuevo* 9; **last year** *el año pasado*, 9
yellow *amarillo(a)*, 8
yes *sí*, 4
yesterday *ayer*, 8
yoga: to do yoga *hacer yoga*, 7
you *usted, ustedes,* (formal)1; *tú, vosotros(as),* (informal) 1; **You were lucky!** *Ah, ¡tuviste suerte!*, 10
young *joven*, 5
young people *los jóvenes*, 9
younger *menor(es)*, 5
your *tu(s), su(s), vuestro(a)(s)*, 5

zero *cero*, 1
zoo *el zoológico*, 10

Índice gramatical

Page numbers in boldface type refer to the first presentation of the topic. Other page numbers refer to grammar structures presented in the **¡Exprésate!** features, subsequent references to the topic, or reviewed in **Repaso de Gramática.** Page numbers beginning with R refer to the **Síntesis gramatical** in this Reference Section (pages R20–R27). The designations (IA) and (IB) following the page numbers refer to **¡Exprésate!** IA and **¡Exprésate!** IB.

a: for clarification **70 (IA);** with pronouns **102 (IA);** after **ir** or **jugar 116 (IA);** combined with **el** to form **al 116 (IA);** with time **150 (IA),** 176 (IA); with **empezar: 196 (IA);** with infinitives **160 (IB),** 176 (IA), 196 (IA); personal **200 (IB)**

abrir: 162 (IA); all preterite tense forms **230 (IB)**

acabar de: 94 (IB), 122 (IB)

acostarse: all present tense forms **92 (IB),** 96 (IB)

accent marks: **26,** 38 (IA), 84 (IA), 110 (IB), 168 (IB), 202 (IB), 214 (IB)

adjectives: function of **54 (IA),** 84 (IA); agreement with nouns–masculine and feminine **56 (IA),** 84 (IA), R17; singular and plural **56 (IA),** 84 (IA), R17; placement **146 (IA);** demonstrative adjectives all forms **140 (IB),** 168 (IB), R14; possessive adjectives all forms **192 (IA),** 222 (IA), R17; with **sentirse 106 (IB);** with **ser** 82 (IA), 84 (IA); irregular comparative forms **140 (IB),** 168 (IB), R18; with **quedar 142 (IB),** 168 (IB)

adónde: 116 (IA), 154 (IB), R18; see also question words

adverbs: adverbs of frequency **111 (IA),** R19; adverbs of sequence **142 (IA);** adverbs of time **20 (IA);** with **quedar 142 (IB),** 168 (IB)

agreement: nouns and adjectives: **68 (IA),** 84 (IA), 192 (IA), R17; see also adjectives; nouns and definite articles **68 (IA),** 84 (IA), R16; nouns and indefinite articles **146 (IA),** R16; nouns and possessive adjectives **192 (IA),** R17; verbs and reflexive pronouns **102 (IA) (IB)**

al: 116 (IA), 200 (IB)

almorzar: 194 (IA), R24; all present tense froms **222 (IA)**

-ando: 202 (IB), 214 (IB), R20

antes de: 94 (IB), 122 (IB), R19 see also prepositions

-ar verbs: regular present tense **114 (IA),** 130 (IA), 194 (IA), R19; regular preterite tense **152 (IB),** R21; affirmative commands **62 (IB),** 64 (IB), 76 (IB), **108 (IB),** 110 (IB), R22; negative command forms **108 (IB),** 110 (IB), 122 (IB); see also verbs

articles: definite **el, la, los, las 68 (IA),** 70 (IA), 160 (IA), 92 (IB); indefinite **un, una, unos, unas 146 (IA),** 176 (IA)

asistir: 162 (IA)

beber: 162 (IA)

buscar: commands **244 (IB)**

calendar expressions: dates, days of the week, months **21 (IA)**

cantar: all present tense forms **114 (IA)**

cien(to) 138 (IB); see also numbers

comenzar: all preterite tense forms **232 (IB),** 260 (IB)

comer: 100 (IA), 114 (IA); all present tense forms **162 (IA),** 176 (IA), 194 (IA); all preterite tense forms **186 (IB),** 186 (IB), 214 (IB)

commands (imperatives): **62 (IB),** 64 (IB), 76 (IB), 108 (IB), 110 (IB), 122 (IB), 198 (IB), 244 (IB), 246 (IB), R22; affirmative informal commands **62 (IB),** 64 (IB), 76 (IB), 108 (IB), 110 (IB), 122 (IB), 198 (IB), 244 (IB), 246 (IB), R22; negative informal commands **108 (IB),** 110 (IB), 122 (IB), 198 (IB), 246 (IB), R22; irregular verbs **62 (IB),** 76 (IB), 108 (IB), 244 (IB), R22; spelling-change verbs **-ger, -car, -gar, -zar, -guir 244 (IB),** R22; with pronouns **64 (IB),** 76 (IB), 110 (IB), 122 (IB), 246 (IB)

cómo: 6 (IA), 23 (IA), 49 (IA), **58 (IA),** 66 (IA), 84 (IA), 187 (IA), 201 (IA), R18; see also question words

comparative adjective **mayor, mejor, menor, peor 140 (IB),** 168 (IB)

comparisons: with adjectives using **más... que, menos... que, tan... como 140 (IB),** 168 (IB), R18; **tanto (a)... como, tantos(as)... como 140 (IB),** 168 (IB), R18

comprar: all preterite tense forms 152 (IB)

con: with pronouns 102 (IA), 130 (IA); see also prepositions

conjunctions: **porque 70 (IA)**

conmigo: 102 (IA)

conocer: all present tense forms **200 (IB);** with personal **a 200 (IB),** 214 (IB)

contigo: 102 (IA)

contractions: **al 116 (IA),** 200 (IB), R16; **del 72 (IA),** 116 (IA), R16

correr: 162 (IA)

costar: 138 (IB), 168 (IB)

cuál: 19 (IA), 23 (IA), **58 (IA),** R18; see also question words

cuándo: 58 (IA), 84 (IA), R18; see also question words

cuánto: agreement with nouns **146 (IA),** 176 (IA), R18; see also question words

dates (calendar): **21 (IA)**

days of the week: **21 (IA),** 160 (IA)

de: used in showing possession or ownership **72 (IA),** 84 (IA), 192 (IA); to indicate a type of thing **72 (IA),** 142

u→ue stem-changing verbs: **jugar 116 (IA),** 194 (IA), R20
un(o): 138 (IB); see also numbers
una, uno, unos, unas: 146 (IA), 176 (IA), R16; see also indefinite articles
ustedes and **vosotros** contrasted **14 (IA),** 38 (IB); see also subject pronouns

venir: all present tense forms **150 (IA),** 176 (IA), R19; commands 62 (IB), 76 (IB), 108 (IB), 244 (IB); present tense instead of present progressive tense 202 (IB); see also verbs
ver: all present tense forms **164 (IA),** R19; all preterite tense forms **184 (IB),** R21; see also verbs
verbs: in sentences **12 (IA),** 38 (IA); irregular verb **ser** 6 (IA), 10 (IA), 11 (IA), 12 (IA), **24 (IA),** 38 (IA), 54 (IA), 58 (IA), 84 (IA), 46 (IB), 62 (IB), 256 (IA), 106 (IB), 108 (IB), 244 (IB), R24; regular **-ar** all present tense forms **114 (IA),** 130 (1A), R19; irregular verb **ir** all present tense forms **116 (IA),** 130 (1A), R20; **ir a** + infinitive **160 (IA),** 176 (IA), 188 (IB); all preterite tense forms **154 (1B),** 168 (IB), 186 (IB), 230 (IB), R21; present instead of present progressive **202 (IB);** regular **-er** and **-ir** all present tense forms **162 (IA),** 176 (IA), 194 (IA), R19; irregular verb **ver** all present tense forms **164 (IA),** R19, all preterite tense forms **184 (IB),** R21; e→ie stem-changing verbs: **196 (IA),** 96 (IB); **querer 104 (1A),** 130 (1A), 196 (IA), 48 (IB), 96 (IB); **nevar 118 (IA); tener 148 (IA),** 196 (IA), 50 (IB), 248 (IB); **venir 150 (IA),** 202 (IB), 248 (IB); **empezar 196 (IA); merendar 196 (IA),** 184 (IB); **preferir 50 (IB),** 76 (IB); **calentar 62 (IB); pensar 188 (IB); servir 48 (IB);** all present tense forms 76 (IB), R19; present participle **202 (IB),** R20; u→ue stem-changing verbs: R20; **jugar 116 (IA),** 130 (1A), 194 (IA), 76 (IB); o→ue stem-changing verbs: R20; **llover 118 (IA),** 194 (IA); **almorzar, volver 194 (IA); dormir 194 (IA),** 48 (IB), 50 (IB), 96 (IB); present participle **202 (IB),** R20; **probar 50 (IB),** 76 (IB), 168 (IB); **poder 50 (IB),** 76 (IB), 96 (IB); **acostarse 92 (IB),** 96 (IB); **encontrar 96 (IB); costar 138 (IB),** 168 (IB); verbs with irregular **yo** forms 176 (IA), R20; **tener 148 (IA),** 176 (IA), 196 (IA); **venir 150 (IA),** 176 (IA); **hacer 164 (IA),** 176 (IA); **poner 164 (IA),** 176 (IA); **salir 164 (IA),** 176 (IA); **traer 164 (IA),** 176 (IA); **ver 164 (IA),** 176 (IA); **saber 164 (IA),** 176 (IA); **conocer 200 (IB),** 214 (IB); irregular verb **estar** 8 (IA), 58 (IA), **206 (IA),** 46 (IB), 51 (IB), 106 (IB), 202 (IB), 214 (IB), R22; e→ie stem-changing verbs: R20; **pedir 48 (IB),** 76 (IB), 96 (IB); **servir 48 (IB),** 50 (IB); **vestirse 92 (IB),** 96 (IB); commands 62 (IB), 64 (IB), 76 (IB), 108 (IB), 110 (IB), 198 (IB), 244 (IB), 246 (IB), 260 (IB), R22; command forms of irregular verbs **62 (IB),** 76 (IB), 108 (IB), 122 (IB), 244 (IB), 260 (IB), R22; verbs with reflexive pronouns **afeitarse, bañarse, despertarse, entrenarse, estirarse, lavarse, levantarse, maquillarse, peinarse, ponerse, prepararse, quitarse, relajarse, secarse 92 (IB); acostarse, vestirse 92 (IB),** 94 (IB), 96 (IB); all preterite tense forms of regular verbs **152 (IB),** 184 (IB), 186 (IB), 214 (IB), 230 (IB), 260 (IB), R21; regular **-ar** verbs all preterite tense forms **152 (IB),** 156 (IB), 168 (IB), 184 (IB), 186 (IB), 214 (IB), 230 (IB), 260 (IB), R21; preterite tense forms of spelling-change verbs **232 (IB),** 260 (IB); regular **-er** and **-ir** verbs all preterite tense forms **184 (IB),** 186 (IB), 214 (IB), 230 (IB), 260 (IB), R21;

present progressive tense **202 (IB),** 214 (IB), R20; preterite tense forms of **-car, -gar, -zar 232 (IB);** command forms of spelling-change verbs **-ger, -car, -gar, -zar, -guir 244 (IB),** R22; verbs followed by infinitives **196 (IA),** 210 (IA), 94 (IB), 248 (IB)
vestirse: all present tense forms 96 (IB)

weather: with **hacer 118 (IA),** 234 (IB), R23; see also **hacer**

Agradecimientos

STAFF CREDITS

Editorial
Barbara Kristof, Douglas Ward, Priscilla Blanton, Amber P. Martin

Editorial Development Team
Beatriz Malo Pojman, Jaishree Venkatesan, Janet Welsh Crossley, Jean Miller, Konstanze Alex Brown, Lynda Cortez, Marion Bermondy, Paul Provence

Editorial Staff
Glenna Scott, Geraldine Touzeau-Patrick, Hubert W. Bays, J. Elisabeth Wright, Milagros Escamilla, Rita Ricardo, Sara Anbari, Virginia Dosher, Yamilé Dewailly, Zahydée G. Minnick

Editorial Permissions
Ann B. Farrar, Yuri Muñoz

Book Design
Kay Selke, Marta Kimball, Marc Cooper, Robin Bouvette, José Garza, Sally Bess, Bruce Albrecht, Ed Diaz, Liann Lech

Image Acquisitions
Curtis Riker, Jeannie Taylor, Cindy Verheyden, Stephanie Friedman, Sam Dudgeon, Victoria Smith, Michelle Rumpf

Media Design
Richard Metzger, Chris Smith

Design New Media
Edwin Blake, Kimberly Cammerata

Production, Manufacturing, and Inventory
Beth Prevelige, Diana Rodriguez, Rose Degollado, Jevara Jackson, Rhonda Fariss, Jennifer Craycraft

New Media
Kenneth Whiteside, Lydia Doty, Jamie Lane, Chris Pittman, Cathy Kuhles, Nina Degollado

eLearning Systems
Beau Clark, Jim Bruno, Annette Saunders

ACKNOWLEDGMENTS

For permission to reprint copyrighted material, grateful acknowledgment is made to the following sources:

Children's Book Press, San Francisco, CA: "Baile en El Jardín" from *In My Family/En mi familia* by Carmen Lomas Garza, translated into Spanish by Francisco X. Alarcón. Text copyright © 1996 by Carmen Lomas Garza. "La Tamalada" from *Family Pictures/Cuadros de famila* by Carmen Lomas Garza, translated into Spanish by Rosalma Zubizarreta. Text copyright © 1990 by Carmen Lomas Garza. "La Montaña del Alimento" from *The Legend of Food Mountain/La Montaña del Alimento,* adapted by Harriet Rohmer, translated into Spanish by Alma Flor Ada and Rosalma Zubizarreta. Copyright © 1982 by Children's Book Press.

Dover Publications, Inc.: From "El Fracaso Matemático de Pepito" from *First Spanish Reader: A Beginner's Dual-Language Book,* edited by Angel Flores. Copyright © 1988 by Angel Flores.

Ediciones de la Fundación Corripio, Inc.: From "Regalo de Cumpleaños" by Diógenes Valdez from *Cuentos Dominicanos Para Niños,* vol. V. Copyright © 2000 by Ediciones de la Fundación Corripio, Inc.

Editorial Fundacion Ross: "Dos buenas piernas tenemos..." and "Siempre quietas,..." from *Adivinanzas para mirar en el espejo* by Carlos Silveyra. Copyright © 1985 by Editorial Fundacion Ross.

Editorial Sudamericana S.A.: "2" and "16" from *Los Rimaqué* by Ruth Kaufman. Copyright © 2002 by Editorial Sudamericana S.A.

HarperCollins Publishers: From "Una antigua casa encantada" from *Mi país inventado* by Isabel Allende. Copyright © 2003 by Isabel Allende.

Francisco J. Briz Hidalgo, www.elhuevodechocolate.com: "Una moneda de ¡Ay!" by Juan de Timoneda from *El huevo de chocolate* web site, accessed on September 10, 2003 at http://www.elhuevodechocolate.com. Copyright © by Francisco J. Briz Hidalgo.

Maricel Mayor Marsán: From "Un corazón dividido" from *Un corázon dividido/ A Split Heart* by Maricel Mayor Marsán. Copyright © 1998 by Maricel Mayor Marsán. From "Apuntes de un hogar postmoderno" from Impronta de los Rincones by Maricel Mayor Marsán. Copyright © by Maricel Mayor Marsán.

Museum of New Mexico Press: "Los Cuatro Elementos" from Cuentos: *Tales from the Hispanic Southwest,* selected and adapted in Spanish by José Griego y Maestas. Copyright © 1980 by Museum of New Mexico Press.

Scholastic Inc.: From "Ollantay Tambo" from *Ahora,* vol. 3, no. 2, September/October 1996. Copyright © 1996 by Scholastic Inc. From "Gustavo" from *Ahora,* vol. 4, no. 2, November/December 1997. Copyright © 1997 by Scholastic Inc.

PHOTOGRAPHY CREDITS

Abreviations used: c-center, b-bottom, t-top, l-left, r-right, bkgd-background.

AUTHORS: Page iii (Smith) Courtney Baker, courtesy Stuart Smith; (McMinn) courtesy John McMinn; (Madrigal Velasco) courtesy Sylvia Madrigal; (Humbach) courtesy Nancy Humbach.

TABLE OF CONTENTS: Page v (br) Don Couch/HRW; vi (b, c) Victoria Smith/HRW; (t) family photo in frame: ©Image100; photo by: Victoria Smith/HRW; vii (cr) Don Couch/HRW; (tr)

©Robert Frerck/Odyssey/Chicago; viii (cr) Don Couch/HRW; (tr) Michael Everett/D. Donne Bryant Photography; ix (cr, tr) Sam Dudgeon/HRW; x (cr, tr) John Langford/HRW; xi (cr) Don Couch/HRW; (tr) Digital Image copyright ©2006 PhotoDisc.

WHY STUDY SPANISH: Page xii (Argentina) ©Jeremy Woodhouse, digitalvision; (Chile Don) Couch/HRW; (Costa Rica) ©Buddy Mays/CORBIS; (Dominican) Republic John Langford/HRW; (Mexico) Corbis Images; (Peru) Don Couch/HRW; (Spain) Corbis Images; xiii (bl, tr) Alvaro Ortiz/HRW; (br, cart) Don Couch/HRW; (mural) John

Langford/HRW; xiv (b) Sam Dudgeon/HRW; (cl) ©Royalty-Free/CORBIS; (cr) Edward M. Pio Roda. (tm) & ©2003 CNN. An AOL Time Warner Co. All Rights Reserved; xv (br) ©Image 100 Ltd; (t) Alvaro Ortiz/HRW.

IN SPANISH CLASS: Page xvi (bl) HRW; (tr) ©Brand X Pictures. COMMON NAMES: Page xvii (bkgd) Alvaro Ortiz/HRW. DIRECTIONS: Page xviii (b) Digital Image copyright ©2006 PhotoDisc; xix (bl) Digital Image copyright ©2006 EyeWire; (br) Digital Image copyright ©2006 Artville; (tl) Randall Hyman/HRW; (tr) Sam Dudgeon/HRW. TIPS FOR LEARNING SPANISH: Page xx (b) Alvaro Ortiz/HRW; (cl, tr) ©Brand X Pictures; xxi (b, cr) Digital Image copyright ©2006 PhotoDisc; (cl) ©Royalty-Free/CORBIS; (tl) Don Couch/HRW; (tr) John Langford/HRW.

BRIDGE CHAPTER: Page xxii (all) Victoria Smith/HRW; 1 (b, t) John Langford/HRW; 2 (b) Alvaro Ortiz/HRW; (tl, tr) Don Couch/HRW; 3 (c, t) Alvaro Ortiz/HRW; 4 (1,2, 4) Martha Granger/Edge Video Productions/HRW; (3) Christine Galida/HRW; 5 (1, 2, 3, 5, Juan) Martha Granger/Edge Video Productions/HRW; (4) M. L. Miller/Edge Video Productions/HRW; 10 (all) Victoria Smith/HRW; 11 (b) John Langford/HRW; (t) Don Couch/HRW; 12 (all) Dennis Fagan/HRW; 13 (bailar) Martha Granger/Edge Video Productions/HRW; (básquetbol) Peter Van Steen/HRW; (béisbol) Michelle Bridwell/Frontera Fotos; (fútbol) David Young-Wolff/PhotoEdit; (hablar) ©Telegraph Colour Library/FPG International; (juegos) Victoria Smith/HRW; 16 (a, b) Corbis Images; (c, cl) Victoria Smith/HRW; (d) photographer/Painet Inc; (e) ©Nik Wheeler/CORBIS; 20 (all) family photo in frame: ©Image100; photo by: Victoria Smith/HRW; 21 (b) Don Couch/HRW; (t) John Langford/HRW; 22 (all insets) Victoria Smith/HRW; (bkgd) Don Couch/HRW; 23 (tl) Don Couch/HRW; 27 (1) Robert Fried Photography; (2) Sam Dudgeon/HRW; (3, 4) Michelle Bridwell/HRW; (5, 7) Michelle Bridwell/Frontera Fotos; (6, 8, cocinar) Christine Galida/HRW; 28 (bl) ©Comstock, Inc; (br) Peter Van Steen/HRW; (cl) Dennis Fagan/HRW; (cr) Digital Image copyright ©2006 EyeWire; (tl) Don Couch/HRW; 29 (1, 2) David Phillips/Words & Images; (3) Martha Granger/Edge Video Productions/HRW; (4) John Langford/HRW; (papá) Sam Dudgeon/HRW; 30 (br) ©Jan Butchofsky-Houser/CORBIS; (tl) Don Couch/HRW; 31 (c) ©Gabe Palmer/CORBIS; (tl) Don Couch/HRW; 32 (bl) Digital Image copyright ©2006 PhotoDisc; (br) David Young-Wolff/PhotoEdit; (cr) Alvaro Ortiz/HRW; 33 (br) Victoria Smith/HRW; (cr) David Phillips/Words & Images; (tl) ©Image100.

CHAPTER 6 All photos by Don Couch/HRW except: Page 34 (c) ©Danny Lehman/CORBIS; (tc) ©Getty Images/The Image Bank; 35 (bl, cr, tl) ©Robert Frerck/Odyssey/Chicago; (tr) Mark Newman/Bruce Coleman, Inc; 36 (b) ©Royalty-Free/CORBIS; (tl) ©Charles & Josette Lenars/CORBIS; (tr) ©Archivo Iconografico, S.A./CORBIS; 37 (cr) George H. H. Huey; (tl) Charlene E. Friesen/D. Donne Bryant Photography; 41 (cola) Victoria Smith/HRW; 43 (1) Sam Dudgeon/HRW; (tr , 5) Victoria Smith/HRW; 45 (3) Michelle Bridwell/HRW; (4) Victoria Smith/HRW; (5) Sam Dudgeon/HRW; 46 (bl) Victoria Smith/HRW; 47 (4, soup) Michelle Bridwell/HRW; 48 (bl) Victoria Smith/HRW; 49 (all) Victoria Smith/HRW; 50 (bl) Victoria Smith/HRW; 51 (tr) ©Robert Frerck/Odyssey/Chicago; 52 (tl) Victoria Smith/HRW; 53 (br) Gary Russ/HRW; (tl) John Langford/HRW; 55 (cl) Corbis Images; 60 (bl) John Langford/HRW; 61 (2) Digital Image copyright ©2006 PhotoDisc; (3) Victoria Smith/HRW; (t) Michelle Bridwell/HRW; 64 (br) ©

Scott Tevan/photohouston.com; 74 (br) Victoria Smith/HRW.

CHAPTER 7 All photos by Don Couch/HRW except: Page 80 (c) Peter Lang/D. Donne Bryant Photography; (cr) Jean Lee/AP/Wide World Photos; (tr) ©Tony West/PICIMPACT/CORBIS; 81 (bc) Luis Martin/D. Donne Bryant Photography; (br) ©Alissa Crandall/CORBIS; (cr) ©Hubert Stadler/CORBIS; (tr) Michael Everett/D. Donne Bryant Photography; 82 (bl) ©Hubert Stadler/CORBIS; (br) Museo Xul Solar; (tl) Peter Lang/D. Donne Bryant Photography; 83 (tl) ©Russell Gordon/Odyssey/Chicago; (tr) Victoria Smith/HRW; 89 (comb, makeup, shirt/jeans, soap, toothbrush, towels) Sam Dudgeon/HRW; (hairdryer) Digital Image copyright ©2006 PhotoDisc; (pajamas) Victoria Smith/HRW; (tr) Digital Image copyright ©2006 PhotoDisc; 90 (bl) Jean Lee/AP/Wide World Photos; 91 (1) Martha Cooper/Viesti Collection, Inc; (2, 6) Christine Galida/HRW; (3) Bob Daemmrich/Stock Boston; (4, 5) John Langford/HRW; 92 (bl) Elizabeth Grivs/TxDOT; 93 (1) John Langford/HRW; (2) ©John Foxx/Alamy Photos; (3) Bob Daemmrich/The Image Works; (4) Image Source/elektraVision/PictureQuest; (tr) Stockbyte/PictureQuest; 95 (cl, r) Dennis Fagan/HRW; (cr) ©Jose Luis Pelaez, Inc./CORBIS; (l, t) Peter Van Steen/HRW; 96 (bl) Victoria Smith/HRW; 99 (br) Isaac Menashe/Icon SMI/NewsCom; 107 (cl) ©Image Source; (cr, l) Peter Van Steen/HRW; (r) ©RubberBall Productions; 108 (bl) John Langford/HRW; 110 (all) ©2006 Radlund & Associates for Artville/HRW; 111 (all) http://www.latinosportslegends.com; 118 (bl) Peter Van Steen/HRW; 120 (tc, tl) Dennis Fagan/HRW; (tr) Peter Van Steen/HRW.

CHAPTER 8 All photos by Sam Dudgeon/HRW except: Page 126 (tr) ©Owaki - Kulla/CORBIS; 127 (bl) Werner Bertsch/Bruce Coleman, Inc; (br) ©Richard Bickel/CORBIS; (tc) Masa Ushioda/Bruce Coleman, Inc; (tr) Kennedy Space Center/NASA; 128 (br) ©Mildrey Guillot; (tl) ©Tony Arruza/CORBIS; 129 (cr) ©Latin Focus; (t) ©Robert Frerck/Odyssey/Chicago; 136 (bl) Michelle Bridwell/Frontera Fotos; 142 (bl) Alvaro Ortiz/HRW; 145 (br) Corbis Images; (t) Don Couch/HRW; 146 (anillo, aretes, pulsera) Victoria Smith/HRW; (audífonos, CD) Digital Image copyright ©2006 PhotoDisc; (tarjetas) Don Couch/HRW; 148 (2) Corbis Images; (4) Digital Image copyright ©2006 PhotoDisc; (5) Don Couch/HRW; (7 CDs,) Victoria Smith/HRW; 150 (cl) ©Arthur Tilley/Getty Images/Taxi; 151 (tl) Digital Image copyright ©2006 PhotoDisc; (tr) Martha Granger/Edge Video Productions/HRW; 153 (2, 3) Victoria Smith/HRW; (4) Image Source Ltd/Alamy; (5) Digital Image copyright ©2006 EyeWire; (6) Dennis Fagan/HRW; (t) Bob Daemmrich/The Image Works; 154 (l) ©Latin Focus; 155 (1, 2, tr) Victoria Smith/HRW; (5) Digital Image copyright ©2006 PhotoDisc; 158 (all) HRW file photo; 170 (all) Victoria Smith/HRW.

CHAPTER 9 All photos by John Langford/HRW except: Page 172 (c) ©Jeremy Horner/CORBIS; (tr) Martha Cooper/Viesti Collection, Inc; 173 (br) ©Giraud Philippe/Corbis Sygma; (cr, tl) Suzanne Murphy-Larronde; (tl) David Pou; (tr) Tom Bean; 174 (cl, tr) David Pou; 175 (br, tc) David Pou; (cl) age fotostock/Suzanne Murphy-Larronde, 2006; 178 (Acción de Gracias) ©Bob Daemmrich/Getty Images/Stone; (bkgd, t) Victoria Smith/HRW; (Enamorados) Christine Galida/HRW; (Hanukkah) Pam Ostrow/Index Stock Imagery/PictureQuest; (Navidad) Michael Matisse/Photodisc/PictureQuest; (Nochevieja) Christine Galida/HRW; (Semana Santa) Andres Leighton/AP/Wide World Photos; 179 (abrir, mandar, recibir)

Sam Dudgeon/HRW; (fuegos) Corbis Images; (mandar) Victoria Smith/HRW; 181 (1, 4) Peter Van Steen/HRW; (2) ©Tom and Dee Ann McCarthy/Index Stock Imagery/PictureQuest; (3) ©Creatas/PictureQuest; 185 (c, l) Peter Van Steen/HRW; (r) Victoria Smith/HRW; 186 (bl) Victoria Smith/HRW; 187 (tl) Victoria Smith/HRW; (tr) Sam Dudgeon/HRW; 188 (bl) David Pou; 190 (br) Sam Dudgeon/HRW; 191 (br) Ric Vasquez/AP/Wide World Photos; (tl) Gary Russ/HRW; 192 (bkgd) Corbis Images; (galletas, papitas, ponche) Victoria Smith/HRW; (mailbox) Marta Kimball/HRW; 194 (l) Jose Carrillo/PhotoEdit Inc; 197 (all) Martha Granger/Edge Video Productions/HRW; 200 (1) The Kobal Collection; (2) Eric Risberg/AP/Wide World Photos; (3) The Kobal Collection; (4) ©Bettmann/CORBIS; (l) Courtesy of the Texas Folklife Festival ; (Segovia) ©Hulton-Deutsch Collection/CORBIS; 204–205 (various) Richard Hutchings/HRW; 204 (tl) Bob Daemmrich/Stock Boston; 212 (1) ©Brand X Pictures; (2, 5) Digital Image copyright ©2006 PhotoDisc; (3-clock) ©Comstock; (3-hats, 4, 6) Corbis Images.

CHAPTER 10 All photos by Don Couch/HRW except: Page 218 (tr) ©Jack Fields/CORBIS; 219 (bl) Todd Wolf; (br) Erwin and Peggy Bauer/Animals Animals/Earth Scenes; (tc) ©Wolfgang Kaehler/CORBIS; 220 (bl) ©Diego Lezama Orezzoli/CORBIS; (tl) Digital Image copyright ©2006 PhotoDisc; 221 (cr) Ricardo Choy Kifox/AP/Wide World Photos; (tc) ©William Albert Allard/National Geographic Image Collection; 225 (t) Victoria Smith/HRW; 226 (tl) Robert·Frerck/Woodfin Camp & Associates; 228 (l) Martha Granger/Edge Video Productions/HRW; 229 (tl) Martha Granger/Edge Video Productions/HRW; 233 (1) Peter Van Steen/HRW; (2) Digital Image copyright ©2006 PhotoDisc; (4) Dean Berry/Index Stock Imagery, Inc; 248 (cl) Courtesy of Texas Highways Magazine; ©2006 PhotoDisc; 242 (1) ©Rick Doyle/CORBIS; (2, 4) ©Index Stock; (3) ©William Sallaz/CORBIS; (cr) Digital Image copyright ©2006 PhotoDisc; 243 (cl, cr) Martha Granger/Edge Video Productions/HRW; (tl) Ron Chapple/Thinkstock/PictureQuest; 244 (bl) Victoria Smith/HRW; 245 (br) Digital Image copyright ©2006 PhotoDisc; (cr) ©COMSTOCK, Inc; 247 (cr) ©Michael & Patricia Fogden/CORBIS; 249 (tr) Stephanie Maze/Woodfin Camp & Associates; 250 (c) Dr. Paul A. Zahl/Photo Researchers, Inc; (tr) Richard Rowan/Photo Researchers, Inc; 258 (tl) Digital Image copyright ©2006 PhotoDisc.

LITERATURA Y VARIEDADES: Page 271 (tl) Courtesy of Maricel Mayor Marsan; 272 (cr) Victoria Smith/HRW; 273 (cr) Victoria Smith/HRW; (tr) ©William James Warren/CORBIS; 274 (r) ©Bettmann/CORBIS; 275 (all) ©Wolfgang Kaehler/CORBIS.

REVIEW VOCABULARY: Page R7 (bl) Digital Image copyright ©2006 PhotoDisc; (r) ©BananaStock; (tl) Sam Dudgeon/HRW; R8 (cl) Alvaro Ortiz/HRW; (cr) Don Couch/HRW; (t) Digital Image copyright ©2006 PhotoDisc; R9 (bl) Don Couch/HRW; (br) Alvaro Ortiz/HRW; (cr, tr) Gary Russ/HRW; (tl) Sam Dudgeon/HRW; R10 (bl) Corbis Images; (cl) ©RubberBall/Alamy Photos; (cr) Digital Image copyright ©2006 PhotoDisc; (tl) ©Digital Vision; R11 (bl) Don Couch/HRW; (br) ©Dennis Degnan/CORBIS; (tl) ©Buddy Mays/CORBIS.

NOVELA STILL PHOTOS: Spain - Don Couch/HRW; Puerto Rico - John Langford/HRW; Mexico, Peru - Don Couch/HRW.

ICONS: (CULTURA) Don Couch/HRW; (VOCABULARIO 1) John Langford/HRW; (VOCABULARIO 2) Don Couch/HRW.

Texas Essential Knowledge and Skills for Languages Other Than English

Levels I and II—Novice Progress Checkpoint

Knowledge and skills

1. Communication The student communicates in a language other than English using the skills of listening, speaking, reading, and writing.

The student is expected to:

A. engage in oral and written exchanges of learned material to socialize and to provide and obtain information;

B. demonstrate understanding of simple, clearly spoken, and written language such as simple stories, high-frequency commands, and brief instructions when dealing with familiar topics; and

C. present information using familiar words, phrases, and sentences to listeners and readers.

2. Cultures The student gains knowledge and understanding of other cultures.

The student is expected to:

A. demonstrate an understanding of the practices (what people do) and how they are related to the perspectives (how people perceive things) of the cultures studied; and

B. demonstrate an understanding of the products (what people create) and how they are related to the perspectives (how people perceive things) of the cultures studied.

3. Connections The student uses the language to make connections with other subject areas and to acquire information.

The student is expected to:

A. use resources (that may include technology) in the language and cultures being studied to gain access to information; and

B. use the language to obtain, reinforce, or expand knowledge of other subject areas.

4. Comparisons The student develops insight into the nature of language and culture bycomparing the student's own language and culture to another.

The student is expected to:

A. demonstrate an understanding of the nature of language through comparisons of the student's own language and the language studied;

B. demonstrate an understanding of the concept of culture through comparisons of the student's own culture and the cultures studied; and

C. demonstrate an understanding of the influence of one language and culture on another.

5. Communities The student participates in communities at home and around the world by using languages other than English.

The student is expected to:

A. use the language both within and beyond the school setting through activities such as participating in cultural events and using technology to communicate; and

B. show evidence of becoming a lifelong learner by using the language for personal enrichment and career development.